DEATH AND DYING
END-OF-LIFE CONTROVERSIES

ISSN 1532-2726

DEATH AND DYING
END-OF-LIFE CONTROVERSIES

Sandra Alters

INFORMATION PLUS® REFERENCE SERIES
Formerly Published by Information Plus, Wylie, Texas

Detroit • New York • San Francisco • New Haven, Conn. • Waterville, Maine • London

THOMSON

™

GALE

Death and Dying: End-of-Life Controversies

Sandra Alters
Paula Kepos, Series Editor

Project Editor
John McCoy

Permissions
Shalice Caldwell-Shah, Emma Hull,
Jacqueline Key

Composition and Electronic Prepress
Evi Seoud

Manufacturing
Cynthia Bishop, Drew Kalasky

ISBN-13: 978-0-7876-5103-9 (set)
ISBN-10: 0-7876-5103-6 (set)
ISBN-13: 978-1-4144-0410-3
ISBN-10: 1-4144-0410-7
ISSN 1532-2726

This title is also available as an e-book.
ISBN-13: 978-1-4144-1045-6 (set)
ISBN-10: 1-4144-1045-X (set)
Contact your Thomson Gale sales representative for ordering information.

Printed in the United States of America
10 9 8 7 6 5 4 3 2 1

TABLE OF CONTENTS

PREFACE

Death and Dying: End-of-Life Controversies is part of the *Information Plus Reference Series*. The purpose of each volume of the series is to present the latest facts on a topic of pressing concern in modern American life. These topics include today's most controversial and most studied social issues: abortion, capital punishment, care for the elderly, crime, health care, the environment, immigration, minorities, social welfare, women, youth, and many more. Although written especially for the high school and undergraduate student, this series is an excellent resource for anyone in need of factual information on current affairs.

By presenting the facts, it is Thomson Gale's intention to provide its readers with everything they need to reach an informed opinion on current issues. To that end, there is a particular emphasis in this series on the presentation of scientific studies, surveys, and statistics. These data are generally presented in the form of tables, charts, and other graphics placed within the text of each book. Every graphic is directly referred to and carefully explained in the text. The source of each graphic is presented within the graphic itself. The data used in these graphics are drawn from the most reputable and reliable sources, in particular from the various branches of the U.S. government and from major independent polling organizations. Every effort has been made to secure the most recent information available. The reader should bear in mind that many major studies take years to conduct, and that additional years often pass before the data from these studies are made available to the public. Therefore, in many cases the most recent information available in 2006 dated from 2003 or 2004. Older statistics are sometimes presented as well, if they are of particular interest and no more recent information exists.

Although statistics are a major focus of the *Information Plus Reference Series*, they are by no means its only content. Each book also presents the widely held positions and important ideas that shape how the book's subject is discussed in the United States. These positions are explained in detail and, where possible, in the words of their proponents. Some of the other material to be found in these books includes: historical background; descriptions of major events related to the subject; relevant laws and court cases; and examples of how these issues play out in American life. Some books also feature primary documents, or have pro and con debate sections giving the words and opinions of prominent Americans on both sides of a controversial topic. All material is presented in an even-handed and unbiased manner; the reader will never be encouraged to accept one view of an issue over another.

HOW TO USE THIS BOOK

Death is one of the universal human experiences. This and its ultimately unknowable nature combine to make it a topic of great interest to most Americans. How we die and how we deal with the deaths of others evokes profound religious and/or ethical issues about which many people hold very strong beliefs. When these beliefs are in conflict with those of others, they can result in some of the most serious and divisive controversies in the modern United States. This book examines how Americans deal with death, with a particular focus on the highly charged political and moral issues of living wills, life-sustaining treatments, end-of-life care funding, and physician-assisted suicide.

Death and Dying: End-of-Life Controversies consists of eleven chapters and three appendices. Each of the chapters is devoted to a particular aspect of death and dying in the United States. For a summary of the information covered in each chapter, please see the synopses provided in the Table of Contents at the front of the book.

Chapters generally begin with an overview of the basic facts and background information on the chapter's topic, then proceed to examine subtopics of particular interest. For example, Chapter 6: Suicide, Euthanasia, and Physician-Assisted Suicide begins with background information on how suicide and euthanasia have been regarded by different cultures throughout history. The chapter then moves on to deal with suicide and euthanasia in the United States more specifically, including how many Americans commit suicide. The controversies in the United States surrounding physician-assisted suicide and euthanasia are then discussed in depth. This includes reports on studies of who requests physician assistance in committing suicide and why; an examination of organizations and individuals who support and oppose euthanasia and assisted suicide; and a history of Oregon's Death with Dignity Act and its consequences. Finally, legal physician-assisted suicide as practiced in Europe, and its impact on the United States, is scrutinized. Readers can find their way through a chapter by looking for the section and subsection headings, which are clearly set off from the text. Or, they can refer to the book's extensive Index if they already know what they are looking for.

Statistical Information

The tables and figures featured throughout *Death and Dying: End-of-Life Controversies* will be of particular use to the reader in learning about this issue. These tables and figures represent an extensive collection of the most recent and important statistics on death, as well as related issues—for example, graphics in the book cover death rates for suicide; reasons for choosing hospice care; Medicare coverage of various end-of-life needs; the rise in life expectancy over the last century; and public opinion about the most fearful aspects of death. Thomson Gale believes that making this information available to the reader is the most important way in which we fulfill the goal of this book: to help readers understand the issues and controversies surrounding death and dying in the United States and reach their own conclusions.

Each table or figure has a unique identifier appearing above it for ease of identification and reference. Titles for the tables and figures explain their purpose. At the end of each table or figure, the original source of the data is provided.

In order to help readers understand these often complicated statistics, all tables and figures are explained in the text. References in the text direct the reader to the relevant statistics. Furthermore, the contents of all tables and figures are fully indexed. Please see the opening section of the Index at the back of this volume for a description of how to find tables and figures within it.

Appendices

In addition to the main body text and images, *Death and Dying: End-of-Life Controversies* has three appendices. The first is the Important Names and Addresses directory. Here the reader will find contact information for a number of government and private organizations that can provide further information on aspects of death and dying. The second appendix is the Resources section, which can also assist the reader in conducting his or her own research. In this section the author and editors of *Death and Dying: End-of-Life Controversies* describe some of the sources that were most useful during the compilation of this book. The final appendix is the Index.

ADVISORY BOARD CONTRIBUTIONS

The staff of Information Plus would like to extend its heartfelt appreciation to the Information Plus Advisory Board. This dedicated group of media professionals provides feedback on the series on an ongoing basis. Their comments allow the editorial staff who work on the project to continually make the series better and more user-friendly. Our top priorities are to produce the highest-quality and most useful books possible, and the Advisory Board's contributions to this process are invaluable.

The members of the Information Plus Advisory Board are:

- Kathleen R. Bonn, Librarian, Newbury Park High School, Newbury Park, California

- Madelyn Garner, Librarian, San Jacinto College—North Campus, Houston, Texas

- Anne Oxenrider, Media Specialist, Dundee High School, Dundee, Michigan

- Charles R. Rodgers, Director of Libraries, Pasco-Hernando Community College, Dade City, Florida

- James N. Zitzelsberger, Library Media Department Chairman, Oshkosh West High School, Oshkosh, Wisconsin

COMMENTS AND SUGGESTIONS

The editors of the *Information Plus Reference Series* welcome your feedback on *Death and Dying: End-of-Life Controversies*. Please direct all correspondence to:

Editors
Information Plus Reference Series
27500 Drake Rd.
Farmington Hills, MI 48331-3535

CHAPTER 1
DEATH THROUGH THE AGES: A BRIEF OVERVIEW

Strange, is it not? That of the myriads who Before us passed the door of Darkness through, Not one returns to tell us of the road, Which to discover we must travel too.

Omar Khayyám

Death is the inevitable conclusion of life, a universal destiny that all living creatures share. Although all societies throughout history have realized that death is the certain fate of human beings, different cultures have responded to it in different ways. Through the ages, attitudes toward death and dying have changed and continue to change, shaped by religious, intellectual, and philosophical beliefs and conceptions. In modern times, advances in medical science and technology continue to influence ideas about death and dying.

ANCIENT TIMES

Archaeologists have found that as early as the Paleolithic period (about 2.5 to 3 million years ago), humans held metaphysical beliefs about death and dying. Tools and ornaments excavated at burial sites suggest that our earliest ancestors believed that some element of a person survived the dying experience.

Ancient Hebrews (circa 1020–586 BCE), while acknowledging the existence of the soul, were not preoccupied with the afterlife. They lived according to the commandments of their God, to whom they entrusted their eternal destiny. Early Egyptians (circa 2900–950 BCE), on the other hand, thought that preservation of the dead body (mummification) guaranteed a happy afterlife. They believed that a person had a dual soul—the *ka* and the *ba*. The *ka* was the spirit that dwelled near the body, while the *ba* was the vitalizing soul that lived on in the netherworld. Similarly, the ancient Chinese (circa 2500–1000 BCE) also believed in a dual soul, one part of which continued to exist after the death of the body. It was this spirit that the living venerated during ancestor worship.

Among the ancient Greeks (circa 2600–1200 BCE), death was greatly feared. Greek mythology—full of tales of gods and goddesses who exacted punishment on disobedient humans—caused the living to follow rituals meticulously when burying their dead so as not to displease the gods. Although reincarnation is usually associated with Asian religions, some Greeks were followers of Orphism, a religion that taught that the soul underwent numerous reincarnations until purification was achieved.

THE CLASSICAL AGE

Mythological beliefs among the ancient Greeks persisted into the classical age. The Greeks believed that after death the psyche—a person's vital essence—lived on in the underworld. The Greek writer Homer (circa 800–700 BCE) greatly influenced classical Greek attitudes about death through his epic poems the *Iliad* and the *Odyssey*. Greek mythology was freely interpreted by writers after Homer, and belief in eternal judgment and retribution continued to evolve throughout this period.

Certain Greek philosophers also influenced conceptions of death. Pythagoras (circa 580–500 BCE), for example, opposed euthanasia ("good death," or mercy killing) because it might disturb the soul's journey toward final purification as planned by the gods. On the other hand, Socrates (circa 470–399 BCE) and Plato (circa 428–347 BCE) believed that people could choose to end their lives if they were no longer useful to themselves or the state.

Like Socrates and Plato, the classical Romans (circa 509–264 BCE) believed that a person suffering from intolerable pain or an incurable illness should have the right to choose a "good death." They considered euthanasia a "mode of dying" that allowed a person's right to take control of an intolerable situation and distinguished it from suicide, an act considered to be a shirking of responsibilities to one's family and to humankind.

THE MIDDLE AGES

During the European Middle Ages (circa 500–1485), death—with its accompanying agonies—was accepted as a destiny everyone shared, but it was still feared. As a defense against this phenomenon that could not be explained, medieval people confronted death together, as a community. Because medical practices in this era were crude and imprecise, the ill and dying person often endured prolonged suffering. A lengthy period of dying, however, gave the dying individual an opportunity to feel forewarned about impending death, to put his or her affairs in order, and to confess sins. The medieval Church, with its emphasis on the eternal life of the soul in Heaven or Hell, held great power over people's notions of death.

By the late Middle Ages the fear of death had intensified due to the Black Death—the great plague of 1347–51. The Black Death killed more than twenty-five million people in Europe alone. Commoners watched not only their neighbors stricken but also saw church officials and royalty struck down: Queen Eleanor of Aragon and King Alfonso XI of Castile met with untimely deaths, and so did many at the papal court at Avignon, France. With their perceived "proper order" of existence shaken, the common people became increasingly preoccupied with their own deaths and with the Last Judgment, God's final and certain determination of the character of each individual. Because the Last Judgment was closely linked to an individual's disposition to Heaven or Hell, the event of the plague and such widespread death was frightening.

THE RENAISSANCE

From the fourteenth through the sixteenth centuries, Europe experienced new directions in economics, the arts, and social, scientific, and political thought. Nonetheless, obsession with death did not diminish with this "rebirth" of Western culture. A new self-awareness and emphasis on humans as the center of the universe further fueled the fear of dying.

By the sixteenth century many European Christians were rebelling against religion and had stopped relying on church, family, and friends to help ease their passage to the next life. The religious upheaval of the Protestant Reformation of 1520, which emphasized the individual nature of salvation, caused further uncertainties about death and dying.

The seventeenth century marked a shift from a religious to a more scientific exploration of death and dying. Lay people drifted away from the now disunited Christian Church toward the medical profession, seeking answers in particular to the question of "apparent death," a condition in which people appeared to be dead but were not. In many cases unconscious patients mistakenly believed to be dead were hurriedly prepared for burial by the clergy, only to "come back to life" during burial or while being transported to the cemetery.

An understanding of death and its aftermath was clearly still elusive, even to physicians who disagreed about what happened after death. Some physicians believed that the body retained some kind of "sensibility," after death. Thus, many people preserved cadavers so that the bodies could "live on." Alternatively, some physicians applied the teachings of the Catholic Church to their medical practice and believed that once the body was dead, the soul proceeded to its eternal fate and the body could no longer survive. These physicians did not preserve cadavers and pronounced them permanently dead.

THE EIGHTEENTH CENTURY

The fear of apparent death that took root in the seventeenth century resurfaced with great intensity during the eighteenth century. Coffins were built with contraptions to enable any prematurely buried person to survive and communicate from the grave. (See Figure 1.1.)

For the first time the Christian Church was blamed for hastily burying its "living dead," particularly because it had encouraged the abandonment of "pagan" burial traditions such as protracted mourning rituals. In the wake of apparent death incidents, more lengthy burial traditions were revived.

THE NINETEENTH CENTURY

In the nineteenth century premature and lingering deaths remained commonplace. Death typically took place in the home following a lengthy deathbed watch. Family members prepared the corpse for viewing in the home, not in a funeral parlor. However, this practice changed during the late nineteenth century, when professional undertakers took over the job of preparing and burying the dead. They provided services such as readying the corpse for viewing and burial, building the coffin, digging the grave, and directing the funeral procession. Professional embalming and cosmetic restoration of bodies became widely available, all carried out in a funeral parlor where bodies were then viewed instead of in the home.

Cemeteries changed as well. Prior to the early nineteenth century, American cemeteries were unsanitary, overcrowded, weed-filled places bearing an odor of decay. That began to change in 1831 when the Massachusetts Horticultural Society purchased seventy-two acres of fields, ponds, trees, and gardens in Cambridge and built

FIGURE 1.1

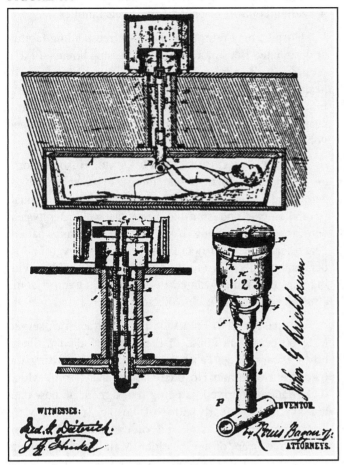

Device for indicating life in buried persons, 1882

Mount Auburn cemetery. This cemetery was to become a model for the landscaped garden cemetery in the United States. These cemeteries were tranquil places where those grieving could visit the graves of loved ones and find comfort in the beautiful surroundings.

Literature of the time often focused on and romanticized death. Death poetry, consoling essays, and mourning manuals became available after 1830, which comforted the grieving with the concept that the deceased were released from worldly cares in Heaven and that they would be reunited there with other deceased loved ones. The deadly lung disease tuberculosis—called consumption at the time—was pervasive during the nineteenth century in Europe and the United States. The disease caused sufferers to develop a certain appearance—an extreme pallor and thinness, with a look often described as haunted—that actually became a kind of fashion statement. The fixation on the subject by writers such as Edgar Allan Poe and the English Romantic poets helped fuel the public's fascination with death and dying. In the late twentieth and early twenty-first centuries the popularization of the "Goth look" is sometimes associated with the tubercular appearance.

Spiritualism

By the mid-nineteenth century the romanticizing of death took on a new twist in America. Spiritualism, in which the living communicated directly with the dead, began in 1848 in the United States with Maggie and Katie Fox of Hydesville, New York. The sisters claimed to have communicated with the spirit of a man murdered by a former tenant in their house. The practice of conducting "sittings" to contact the dead gained instant popularity. Mediums, such as the Fox sisters, were supposedly sensitive to "vibrations" from the disembodied souls that temporarily lived in that part of the spirit world just outside the earth's limits.

This was not the first time people had tried to communicate with the dead. Spiritualism has been practiced in cultures all over the world. For example, many Native Americans believe shamans (priests or medicine men) have the power to communicate with the spirits of the dead. The Old Testament (I Samuel 28:7–19) recounts the visit of King Saul to a medium at Endor who summoned the spirit of the prophet Samuel, which predicted the death of Saul and his sons.

The mood in the United States in the 1860s and 1870s was ripe for Spiritualist séances. Virtually everyone had lost a son, husband, or other loved one during the Civil War (1861–65). Some survivors wanted assurances that their loved ones were all right; others were simply curious about life after death. Those who had drifted away from traditional Christianity embraced this new Spiritualism, which claimed scientific proof of survival after physical death.

THE MODERN AGE

Modern medicine has played a vital role in the way people die and, consequently, the manner in which the dying process of a loved one affects relatives and friends. With advancements in medical technology, the dying process has become depersonalized, as it has moved away from the familiar surroundings of home and family to the sterile world of hospitals and strangers. Certainly, the institutionalization of death has not diminished the fear of dying. Now the fear of death also involves the fear of separation: for the living, the fear of not being present when a loved one dies, and for the dying, the prospect of facing death without the comforting presence of a loved one.

Changing Attitudes

In the last decades of the twentieth century, attitudes about death and dying slowly began to change. Aging baby boomers (people born between 1946 and 1964), facing the deaths of their parents, began to confront their own mortality. While medical advances continue to increase life expectancy, they have raised an entirely new set of issues associated with death and dying. For example, how long should advanced medical technology be used to keep comatose people alive? How should the elderly or incapacitated be cared for? Is it reasonable for people to stop medical treatment, or even actively end their lives, if that is what they wish?

The works of psychiatrist Elisabeth Kubler-Ross, including the pioneering book *On Death and Dying* (New York: Macmillan Publishing Company, 1969), have helped individuals from all walks of life confront the reality of death and restore dignity to those who are dying. One of the most respected authorities on death, grief, and bereavement, Kubler-Ross and her theories have influenced medical practices undertaken at the end of life, as well as the attitudes of physicians, nurses, clergy, and others who care for the dying.

During the late 1960s, medical education was revealed to be seriously deficient in areas related to death and dying. But initiatives underway in the late twentieth and early twenty-first centuries have offered more comprehensive training about end-of-life care. With the introduction of in-home hospice care, more terminally ill people have the option of spending their final days at home with their loved ones. With the veil of secrecy lifted and open public discussions about issues related to the end of life, Americans appear more ready to learn about death and to learn from the dying.

Hospice Care

In the Middle Ages hospices were refuges for the sick, the needy, and travelers. The modern hospice movement developed in response to the need to provide humane care to terminally ill patients, while at the same time lending support to their families. The English physician Dame Cicely Saunders is considered the founder of the modern hospice movement—first in England in 1967 and later in Canada and the United States. The soothing, calming care provided by hospice workers is called palliative care, and it aims to relieve patients' pain and the accompanying symptoms of terminal illness, while providing comfort to patients and their families.

Hospice may refer to a place—a freestanding facility or designated floor in a hospital or nursing home—or to a program such as hospice home care, in which a team of health care professionals helps the dying patient and family at home. Hospice teams may involve physicians, nurses, social workers, pastoral counselors, and trained volunteers.

WHY PEOPLE CHOOSE HOSPICE CARE. Hospice workers consider the patient and family to be the "unit of care" and focus their efforts on attending to emotional, psychological, and spiritual needs as well as physical comfort and well-being. With hospice care, as a patient nears death, medical details move to the background as personal details move to the foreground to avoid providing care that is not wanted by the patient, even if some clinical benefit might be expected.

THE POPULATION SERVED. Hospice facilities served 621,100 people in 2000; of these, 85.5% died while in hospice care. (See Table 1.1. Note: at this writing the National Home and Hospice Care Survey, from which these data are derived, is being redesigned; no new data are available.) Nearly 80% of hospice patients were sixty-five years of age and older, and 26.5% were eighty-five years of age or older. Male hospice patients numbered 309,300, while 311,800 were female. The vast majority was white (84.1%). Approximately half of the patients served were unmarried, but most of these unmarried patients were widowed. Nearly 79% of patients used Medicare as their primary source of payment for hospice services.

Although more than half (57.5%) of those admitted to hospice care in 2000 had cancer (malignant neoplasms) as a primary diagnosis, patients with other primary diagnoses, such as Alzheimer's disease and heart, respiratory, and kidney diseases, were also served by hospice. (See Table 1.2. No new home and hospice care data are available at this writing.)

TABLE 1.1

Hospice care discharges by length of service, according to selected patient characteristics, 2000

Discharge characteristic	Discharges Number	Discharges Percent distribution	Length of service in days — Percent distribution Total	Less than 30 days	30 days or more	Average length of service	Median length of service
Total	**621,100**	**100.0**	**100.0**	**62.8**	**37.2**	**46.9**	**15.6**
Sex							
Male	309,300	49.8	100.0	66.7	33.3	42.8	14.5
Female	311,800	50.2	100.0	58.9	41.1	50.9	18.1
Age at discharge							
Under 65 years	126,900	20.4	100.0	64.1	35.9	43.9	15.0
65 years and over	494,300	79.6	100.0	62.4	37.6	47.7	16.3
65–74 years	153,100	24.7	100.0	65.0	35.0	41.2	16.4
75–84 years	176,400	28.4	100.0	62.3	37.7	50.6	16.5
85 years and over	164,800	26.5	100.0	60.2	39.8	50.5	15.9*
Race[a]							
White	522,500	84.1	100.0	62.6	37.4	46.7	14.8
Black or African American and other races	64,300	10.3	100.0	68.5	31.5	53.6*	15.8
Black or African American	50,100	8.1	100.0	66.8	33.2	61.1*	14.9*
Unknown	34,400	5.5	100.0	55.5	44.5*	36.7	26.8*
Marital status at discharge							
Married	293,400	47.2	100.0	67.5	32.5	40.0	11.7
Not married	289,500	46.6	100.0	58.8	41.2	54.1	18.5
Widowed	206,400	33.2	100.0	58.7	41.3	53.5	18.4*
Divorced or separated	35,200	5.7	100.0	63.1	36.9	74.8*	14.3*
Single or never married	47,900	7.7	100.0	56.3	43.7	41.5	19.5*
Unknown	38,300	6.2	100.0	56.4*	43.6*	45.3	24.2*
Primary source of payment							
Medicare	488,000	78.6	100.0	61.5	38.5	48.1	16.7
All other sources	133,200	21.4	100.0	67.6	32.4	42.4	10.3*
Medicaid	31,400	5.1	100.0	73.7	26.3*	24.3	5.4*
Private[b]	80,600	13.0	100.0	64.4	35.6	49.4*	11.0*
Other[c]	21,100	3.4	100.0	70.9	29.1*	42.5	7.0*
Reason for discharge							
Died	531,000	85.5	100.0	66.7	33.3	42.4	13.6
Did not die	90,200	14.5	100.0	39.5	60.5	73.1	43.6*
Services no longer needed from agency[d]	49,000	7.9	100.0	29.2*	70.8	86.2	64.7
Transferred to inpatient care[e]	14,500	2.3	100.0	*	63.9*	81.7	71.0
Other and unknown	26,700	4.3	100.0	60.2*	39.8*	44.4	10.0*

*Data do not meet standard of reliability or precision (sample size is less than 30) and are, therefore, not reported. If shown with a number, data should not be assumed reliable because the sample size is 30–59.
[a]Prior to 1998, only one race was recorded. Since 1998, more than one race may be recorded. The categories "White" and "Black or African American" include only those discharges for whom that one race was reported. Discharges for whom more than one race was reported are included in "Black or African American and other races."
[b]Includes private insurance, own income, family support, Social Security benefits, retirement funds, and welfare.
[c]Includes unknown source and no charge for care.
[d]Includes recovered, stabilized, treatment plan completed, no longer eligible for hospice care, and insurance coverage no longer available.
[e]Includes transferred to hospital, nursing home, or other inpatient or residental care.
Notes: Numbers may not add to totals because of rounding. Percents and average and median lengths of service are based on the unrounded figures.

SOURCE: Barbara J. Haupt, "Table 1. Number and Percent Distribution of Hospice Care Discharges by Length of Service, according to Selected Patient Characteristics: United States, 2000," in "Characteristics of Hospice Care Discharges and Their Length of Service: United States, 2000," *Vital and Health Statistics*, series 13, no. 154, August 2003, http://www.cdc.gov/nchs/data/series/sr_13/sr13_154.pdf (accessed November 8, 2005)

TABLE 1.2

Hospice care discharges, by primary and all-listed diagnoses at admission, 2000

Diagnosis	Primary diagnosis[a]		All-listed diagnoses[b]	
	Number of discharges	Percent	Number of diagnoses	Percent
Total	621,100	100.0	1,437,500	100.0
Infectious and parasitic diseases	11,400*	1.8*	18,900*	1.3*
Human immunodeficiency virus (HIV) disease	9,400*	1.5*	9,700*	0.8*
Neoplasms	363,000	58.4	599,300	41.7
Malignant neoplasms	357,000	57.5	592,000	46.8
Malignant neoplasms of large intestine and rectum	51,500	8.3	60,000	4.7
Malignant neoplasm of trachea, bronchus and lung	120,500	19.4	146,100	11.5
Malignant neoplasm of bone, connective tissue and skin	10,500*	1.7*	46,000	3.6
Malignant neoplasm of breast	16,400	2.6	18,000	1.4
Malignant neoplasm of female genital organs	15,200*	2.5*	15,700*	1.2*
Malignant neoplasm of prostate	20,600	3.3	33,700	2.7
Malignant neoplasm of urinary organs	15,500	2.5	26,900	2.1
Malignant neoplasm of hemotopoietic tissue	22,500	3.6	30,600	2.4
Malignant neoplasm of other and unspecified sites	84,200	13.6	214,900	17.0
Endocrine, nutritional, and metabolic diseases and immunity disorders	*	*	60,100	4.2
Diabetes mellitus	*	*	47,100	3.7
Mental disorders	23,800	3.8	58,600	4.1
Diseases of the nervous system and sense organs	32,100	5.2	64,700	4.5
Alzheimer's disease	16,900*	2.7*	27,600*	2.2*
Diseases of the circulatory system	72,900	11.7	243,100	16.9
Heart disease	42,500	6.8	109,200	8.6
Ischemic heart disease	*	*	21,600*	1.7*
Congestive heart failure	23,500	3.8	49,600	3.9
Cerebro vascular disease	16,900	2.7	37,800	3.0
Other diseases of the circulatory system	29,600	4.8	83,900	6.6
Diseases of the respiratory system	42,800	6.9	124,200	8.6
Chronic obstructive pulmonary disease and allied conditions	27,600	4.4	65,800	5.2
Diseases of the digestive system	12,000*	1.9*	36,100	2.5
Diseases of the genito urinary system	7,600*	1.2*	32,200	2.2
Diseases of the musculoskeletal system and connective tissue	*	*	22,800*	1.6*
Symptoms, signs and ill-defined conditions	34,800	5.6	92,900	6.5
Supplementary classification	*	*	23,700*	1.6*
Posthospital aftercare	*	*	16,600*	1.3*
Unknown or no diagnosis	*	*	. . .	. . .

*Figure does not meet standard of reliability or precision because the sample size is less than 30 if shown without an estimate. If shown with an estimate, the sample size is between 0 and 59.
. . . Category not applicable.
[a]Primary diagnosis is the diagnosis that is chiefly responsible for the discharges's admission to hospice care.
[b]Up to six diagnoses are recorded for each patient at admission.
Notes: Numbers may not add to totals because of rounding. Percentages are based on the unrounded numbers.

SOURCE: "Table 13. Number and Percentage of Hospice Care Discharges, by Primary and All-Listed Diagnoses at Admission: United States, 2000," *National Home and Hospice Care Data*, Centers for Disease Control and Prevention, National Center for Health Statistics, 2003, http://www.cdc.gov/nchs/data/nhhcsd/hospicecaredischarges00.pdf (accessed November 8, 2005)

CHAPTER 2
REDEFINING DEATH

TRADITIONAL DEFINITION OF DEATH

The processes of human life are sustained by many factors, but oxygen is the key to life. Respiration and blood circulation provide the body's cells with the oxygen needed to perform their life functions. When an injury or a disease compromises respiration or circulation, a breakdown in the oxygen supply can occur. As a result, the cells, deprived of essential life-sustaining oxygen, deteriorate. Using the criteria of a working heart and lungs, defining death was once quite simple—a person was considered dead once he or she stopped breathing or was without a detectable heartbeat.

A NEW CRITERION FOR DEATH

Advances in medical science have complicated the definition of death. Life-saving measures such as cardiopulmonary resuscitation (CPR) or defibrillation (electrical shock) can restart cardiac activity. The development of the mechanical respirator in the 1950s also prompted a change in the concept of death. An unconscious patient, unable to breathe without assistance, could be kept alive with a respirator and, based on the heart and lung criteria, the patient could not be declared dead.

Further complicating the issue was the transplantation of the first human heart. Experimental organ transplantation has been performed since the early 1900s. In the 1960s transplantation of organs such as kidneys became routine practice. Kidneys could be harvested from a patient whose heart had stopped and who therefore could be declared legally dead. A successful heart transplant, on the other hand, required a beating heart from a "dead" donor. On December 3, 1967, South African surgeon Christiaan Barnard transplanted a heart from a fatally injured accident victim into a man named Louis Washkansky.

Physicians who had been debating how best to handle patients whose life functions were supported mechanically now faced a new dilemma. With the first successful heart transplant, such patients now became potential heart donors, and it became necessary to ensure that a patient was truly dead before the heart was actually removed. Thus physicians proposed a new criterion for death—irreversible cessation of brain activity, or what many termed "brain death."

The Harvard Criteria

In 1968 the Ad Hoc Committee of the Harvard Medical School to Examine the Definition of Brain Death was organized. The goal of the Harvard Brain Death Committee, as it was also known, was to redefine death. On August 5, 1968, the committee published its report, "A Definition of Irreversible Coma," in the *Journal of the American Medical Association.* This landmark report, known as the Harvard Criteria, listed the following guidelines for identifying irreversible coma:

- Unreceptivity and unresponsivity—the patient is completely unaware of externally applied stimuli and inner need. He/she does not respond even to intensely painful stimuli.

- No movements or breathing—the patient shows no sign of spontaneous movements and spontaneous respiration and does not respond to pain, touch, sound, or light.

- No reflexes—the pupils of the eyes are fixed and dilated. The patient shows no eye movements even when the ear is flushed with ice water or the head is turned. He/she does not react to harmful stimuli and exhibits no tendon reflexes.

- Flat electroencephalogram (EEG)—this shows lack of electrical activity in the cerebral cortex.

The Harvard Criteria could not be used unless reversible causes of brain dysfunction, such as drug intoxication and hypothermia (abnormally low body temperature—below 32.2 degrees centigrade or 89.96 degrees Fahrenheit core temperature), had been ruled out. The committee further recommended that the four tests be repeated twenty-four hours after the initial test.

The Harvard committee stated, "Our primary purpose is to define irreversible coma as a new criterion for death." Despite this, the committee in effect reinforced brain death—a lack of all neurological activity in the brain and brain stem—as the legal criterion for the death of a patient. A patient who met all four guidelines could be declared dead, and his or her respirator could be withdrawn. The committee added, however, "We are concerned here only with those comatose individuals who have no discernible central nervous system activity." Brain death differs somewhat from irreversible coma; patients in deep coma may show brain activity on an EEG, even though they may not be able to breathe on their own. People in a persistent vegetative state are also in an irreversible coma; however, they show more brain activity on an EEG than patients in deep coma and are able to breathe without the help of a respirator. Such patients were not considered dead by the committee's definition because they still had brain activity.

Criticisms of the Harvard Criteria

In 1978 Public Law 95–622 established the ethical advisory body called the President's Commission for the Study of Ethical Problems in Medicine and Biomedical and Behavioral Research. Later, President Ronald Reagan assigned the President's Commission the task of defining death. The President's Commission reported that "the 'Harvard Criteria' have been found to be quite reliable. Indeed, no case has yet been found that met these criteria and regained any brain functions despite continuation of respirator support."

The President's Commission, however, noted the following deficiencies in the Harvard Criteria:

• The phrase "irreversible coma" is misleading. Coma is a condition of a living person. A person lacking in brain functions is dead and, therefore, beyond the condition called coma.

• The Harvard Brain Death Committee failed to note that spinal cord reflexes can continue or resume activity even after the brain stops functioning.

• "Unreceptivity" cannot be tested in an unresponsive person who has lost consciousness.

• The committee had not been "sufficiently explicit and precise" in expressing the need for adequate testing of brain stem reflexes, especially apnea (absence of the impulse to breathe, leading to an inability to breathe spontaneously). Adequate testing to eliminate drug and metabolic intoxication as possible causes of the coma had also not been spelled out explicitly.

Metabolic intoxication refers to the accumulation of toxins (poisons) in the blood resulting from kidney or liver failure. Though these toxins can severely impair brain functioning and cause coma, the condition is potentially reversible.

• Although all persons who satisfy the Harvard Criteria are dead (with irreversible cessation of whole-brain functions), many dead individuals cannot maintain circulation long enough for re-testing after a twenty-four-hour interval.

THE GOVERNMENT REDEFINES DEATH

In 1981 the President's Commission published *Defining Death: Medical, Legal and Ethical Issues in the Determination of Death* (http://www.bioethics.gov/reports/past_commissions/defining_death.pdf). In its report to President Ronald Reagan and the Congress, the Commission proposed a model statute, the Uniform Determination of Death Act, the guidelines of which would be used to define death:

• [Determination of Death.] An individual who has sustained either (1) irreversible cessation of circulation and respiratory functions, or (2) irreversible cessation of all functions of the entire brain, including the brain stem, is dead. A determination of death must be made in accordance with accepted medical standards.

• [Uniformity of Construction and Application.] This Act shall be applied and construed to effectuate its general purpose to make uniform the law with respect to the subject of this Act among states enacting it.

Brain Death

The President's Commission incorporated two formulations or concepts of the "whole-brain definition" of death. The Commission stated that these two concepts were "actually mirror images of each other. The Commission has found them to be complementary; together they enrich one's understanding of the 'definition' [of death]."

The first whole-brain formulation states that death occurs when the three major organs—the heart, lungs, and brain—suffer an irreversible functional breakdown. These organs are closely interrelated, so that if one stops functioning permanently, the other two will also stop working. While traditionally the absence of the "vital signs" of respiration and circulation have signified death, this is simply a sign that the brain, the core organ, has permanently ceased to function. Even if individual cells or organs continue to live, the body as a whole cannot survive for long. Therefore, death can be declared even before the whole system shuts down.

The second whole-brain formulation "identifies the functioning of the whole brain as the hallmark of life because the brain is the regulator of the body's integration." Because the brain is the seat of consciousness and the director of all bodily functions, when the brain dies, the person is considered dead.

Reason for Two Definitions of Death

The President's Commission claimed that its aim was to "supplement rather than supplant [take the place of] the existing legal concept." The brain-death criteria were not being introduced to define death in a new way. In most cases the cardiopulmonary definition of death would be sufficient. Only comatose patients on respirators would be diagnosed using the brain-death criteria.

Criteria for Determination of Death

The Commission did not include in the proposed Uniform Determination of Death Act any specific medical criteria for diagnosing brain death. Instead it had a group of medical consultants develop a summary of currently accepted medical practices. The Commission stated that "such criteria—particularly as they relate to diagnosing death on neurological grounds—will be continually revised by the biomedical community in light of clinical experience and new scientific knowledge." These Criteria for Determination of Death read as follows (with medical details omitted here):

1. An individual with irreversible cessation of circulatory and respiratory functions is dead. A) Cessation is recognized by an appropriate clinical examination. B) Irreversibility is recognized by persistent cessation of functions during an appropriate period of observation and/or trial of therapy.

2. An individual with irreversible cessation of all functions of the entire brain, including the brainstem, is dead. A) Cessation is recognized when evaluation discloses that cerebral cortical and brainstem functions are absent. B) Irreversibility is recognized when evaluation discloses that: the cause of coma is established and is sufficient to account for the loss of brain functions; the possibility of recovery of any brain functions is excluded; and the cessation of all brain functions persists for an appropriate period of observation and/or trial of therapy.

The Criteria for Determination of Death further warn that conditions such as drug intoxication, metabolic intoxication, and hypothermia may be confused with brain death. Physicians should practice caution when dealing with young children and persons in shock. Infants and young children, who have more resistance to neurological damage, have been known to recover brain functions. Shock victims, on the other hand, might not test well due to a reduction in blood circulation to the brain.

The Brain-Death Concept and Brain-Death Criteria around the World

Since the development of brain-death criteria in the United States, most countries have adopted the brain-death concept. Nevertheless, determining brain death varies worldwide. One reason has to do with cultural or religious beliefs. For example, in Japan it is believed that the soul lingers in the body for some time after death. Such a belief may influence the length of time the patient is observed before making the determination of death.

Eelco F. M. Wijdicks of the Mayo Medical Center in Rochester, Minnesota, surveyed brain-death criteria throughout the world and reported his results in "Brain Death Worldwide: Accepted Fact but No Global Consensus in Diagnostic Criteria" (*Neurology*, vol. 58, no. 1, January 8, 2002). Wijdicks obtained brain-death guidelines for adults in eighty countries and determined that seventy of the eighty countries had guidelines for clinical practice in determining brain death. In examining these guidelines Wijdicks found major differences in the procedures used for diagnosing brain death in adults. For example, in some countries brain-death criteria are left up to the physician to determine, while in other countries written guidelines are extremely complicated. In some countries confirmatory laboratory tests are mandatory, while in others they are not. Due to these and many other differences in brain-death diagnostic criteria across countries, Wijdicks suggests that countries worldwide consider standardizing procedures to determine brain death.

What are the diagnostic criteria for determining brain death in the United States? In "Variability among Hospital Policies for Determining Brain Death in Adults" (*Critical Care Medicine*, vol. 32, no. 6, June 2004), David Powner, Michael Hernandez, and Terry Rives explain that there is no federally mandated definition for brain death or method for certifying brain death. Thus, states have adopted the Uniform Determination of Death Act as described in the prior section. Within each hospital, however, actual clinical practice is determined by the medical staff and administrative committees. The researchers studied six hundred randomly selected hospitals to determine whether differences exist among hospital policies for certification of brain death. They determined that differences exist and suggested that policies be standardized. Wijdicks and Ronald E. Cranford list clinical criteria for brain death in "Clinical Diagnosis of Prolonged States of Impaired Consciousness in Adults" (*Mayo Clinic Proceedings*, vol. 80, no. 8, August 2005). (See Table 2.1.)

Brain Death and Persistent Vegetative State

In the past people who suffered severe head injuries usually died from apnea. Today rapid emergency medical

TABLE 2.1

Criteria for brain death

Coma
Absence of motor responses
Absence of pupillary responses to light and pupils at midposition with respect to dilatation (4–6 mm)
Absence of corneal reflexes
Absence of caloric responses
Absence of gag reflex
Absence of coughing in response to tracheal suctioning
Absence of respiratory drive at PaCO$_2$ that is 60 mm Hg or 20 mm Hg above normal baseline values

SOURCE: Eelco F.M. Wijdicks and Ronald E. Cranford, "Table 3. Clinical Criteria for Brain Death," in "Clinical Diagnosis of Prolonged States of Impaired Consciousness in Adults," *Mayo Clinic Proceedings*, vol. 80, no. 8, August 2005

TABLE 2.2

Criteria for a persistent vegetative state (PVS)

1. No evidence of awareness of themselves or their environment; they are incapable of interacting with others
2. No evidence of sustained, reproducible, purposeful, or voluntary behavioral responses to visual, auditory, tactile, or noxious stimuli
3. No evidence of language comprehension or expression
4. Intermittent wakefulness manifested by the presence of sleep-wake cycles
5. Sufficiently preserved hypothalamic and brainstem autonomic functions to survive if given medical and nursing care
6. Bowel and bladder incontinence
7. Variably preserved cranial nerve (pupillary, oculocephalic, corneal, vestibulo-ocular, and gag) and spinal reflexes

SOURCE: Eelco F.M. Wijdicks and Ronald E. Cranford, "Table 1. Criteria for the Diagnosis of a Persistent Vegetative State," in "Clinical Diagnosis of Prolonged States of Impaired Consciousness in Adults," *Mayo Clinic Proceedings*, vol. 80, no. 8, August 2005

FIGURE 2.1

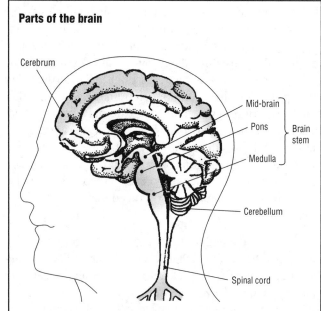

Parts of the brain

Cerebrum
Mid-brain
Pons
Brain stem
Medulla
Cerebellum
Spinal cord

SOURCE: "Figure 2. Anatomic Interrelationships of Heart, Lungs, and Brain," in *Defining Death: A Report on the Medical, Legal and Ethical Issues in the Determination of Death*, President's Commission for the Study of Ethical Problems in Medicine and Biomedical and Behavioral Research, July 1981, http://www.bioethics.gov/reports/past_commissions/defining_death.pdf (accessed November 1, 2005)

intervention allows them to be placed on respirators before breathing stops. In some cases the primary brain damage may be reversible, and unassisted breathing eventually resumes. In many cases, however, brain damage is irreversible, and, if the respirator is not disconnected, it will continue to pump blood to the dead brain.

The brain stem, traditionally called the lower brain, is usually more resistant to damage from oxygen deprivation, or anoxia. Less serious brain injury may cause irreversible damage to the cerebrum, or higher brain, but may spare the brain stem. (See Figure 2.1.) When

the cerebrum is irreversibly damaged yet the brain stem still functions, the patient goes into a persistent vegetative state (PVS), also called persistent noncognitive state. PVS patients, lacking in the higher-brain functions, are awake but unaware. They swallow, grimace when in pain, yawn, open their eyes, and may even breathe without a respirator. Table 2.2 lists the criteria for the diagnosis of a persistent vegetative state.

The case of Karen Ann Quinlan called attention to the ramifications of the persistent vegetative state. In 1975 Quinlan suffered a cardiopulmonary arrest after ingesting a combination of alcohol and drugs. In 1976 Joseph Quinlan was granted court permission to discontinue artificial respiration for his comatose daughter. Even after life support was removed, Karen remained in a persistent vegetative state until she died of multiple infections in 1985.

A more recent case that has refocused national attention on the persistent vegetative state is that of Terri Schiavo, who entered a PVS in 1990, when her brain was deprived of oxygen during a heart attack brought on by an eating disorder. Her husband argued that she would never recover and that his wife would not want to be kept alive by artificial means. He petitioned a Florida court to remove her feeding tube. In October 2003 a Florida judge ruled that the tube should be removed. But Schiavo's parents believed that their daughter would recover and requested that Florida Governor Jeb Bush intervene. The Florida legislature subsequently gave Governor Bush the authority to override the courts, and the feeding tube was reinserted six days after its removal.

In May 2004 the law that allowed Governor Bush to intervene in the case was ruled unconstitutional by a Florida appeals court. The case was then appealed to the U.S. Supreme Court, which in January 2005 refused to hear the appeal and reinstate the Florida law. In March 2005 doctors removed Terri Schiavo's feeding tube. She died thirteen days later. An autopsy showed extensive damage throughout the cerebrum. Damage was so severe that the autopsy report noted that Schiavo must have been blind.

Patients in a persistent vegetative state are not dead, and so the brain-death criteria do not apply to them. They can survive for years with artificial feeding and antibiotics for possible infections. The President's Commission reported on a patient who remained in a persistent vegetative state for thirty-seven years: Elaine Esposito, who lapsed into a coma after surgery in 1941 and died in 1978.

THE NEAR-DEATH EXPERIENCE

The term "near-death experience" was first used by Dr. Raymond Moody in *Life after Life* (Harrisburg, PA: Stackpole Books, 1976), a compilation of interviews with people who claimed to have come back from the dead. A decade earlier, Dr. Elisabeth Kubler-Ross investigated out-of-body episodes recounted by her patients.

The near-death experience is not a phenomenon limited to modern times. It has been recounted in various forms of mysticism, as well as by well-known historical figures such as the Greek philosopher Plato (circa 428–347 BCE) and Benedictine historian and theologian St. Bede (circa 672–735). It appears, however, that the development and administration of emergency resuscitation has contributed to widespread reports of near-death experiences.

Some people who were revived after having been declared clinically dead have recounted remarkably similar patterns of experiences. They reported leaving their body and watching, in a detached manner, while others tried to save that body. They felt no pain, but rather experienced complete serenity. After traveling through a tunnel, they encountered a radiant light. Some claimed they had met friends and relatives who had died; many attested to seeing their whole lives replayed and of ultimately being given either a choice or a command to return to their bodies.

Many people who have had a near-death experience believe that they have experienced a spiritual event of great importance. For example, they may believe that they saw, or even entered, the afterlife. Studies conducted during the 1990s indicated that the near-death experience might be related to one or more physical changes in the brain. These changes include the gradual onset of anoxia (oxygen deprivation) in the brain; residual electrical activity in the brain; the release of endorphins in response to stress; or drug-induced hallucinations produced by drug therapies used during resuscitation attempts or resulting from prior drug abuse.

Not everyone who has been close to death has had a near-death experience. These experiences are atypical reactions to trauma, and the involvement of the temporal lobes of the brain in these experiences has been explored by researchers for decades. Most recently, Willoughby Britton and Richard Bootzin investigated temporal lobe functioning in forty-three individuals who had experienced life-threatening events. Of these forty-three participants, twenty-three reported having had near-death experiences during those events ("Near-Death Experiences and the Temporal Lobe," *Psychological Science*, vol. 15, no. 4, April 2004). The researchers found that people who reported near-death experiences had more of certain types of temporal lobe activity than those who did not have such experiences. The researchers concluded that "altered temporal lobe functioning may be involved in the near-death experience and that individuals who have had such experiences are physiologically distinct from the general population."

CHAPTER 3
THE END OF LIFE: ETHICAL CONSIDERATIONS

Defining death has become a complex matter. Innovative medical technology, while saving many lives, has also blurred the lines between life and death. The controversy about the definition of death is but one of the ethical issues, or principles of moral conduct, related to end-of-life care and decision making. For example, should a son or daughter request the withdrawal of nutrition and hydration from a parent in a persistent vegetative state, knowing that parent's respect for the sanctity of life? Does a physician honor a patient's do-not-resuscitate request when it goes against the physician's ethical convictions? Who should determine when medical care is futile and no longer benefits the dying patient?

The answers to questions about care at the end of life, as well as decisions made by persons who are dying and by their loved ones, vary in response to cultural influences, family issues, and spiritual beliefs. Historical, social, cultural, political, and religious convictions shape ethical beliefs about death and guide the actions of health care professionals and persons who are terminally ill. For people of faith, religious convictions are vitally important when making end-of-life decisions.

RELIGIOUS TEACHINGS

All major religions consider life sacred. When it comes to death and dying, they take seriously the fate of the soul, be it eternal salvation (as in Christian belief) or reincarnation (as in Buddhist philosophy).

Roman Catholicism

According to Catholic teachings, death is contrary to God's plan for humankind. In the Old Testament story of Genesis, when God created human beings, he did not intend for them to die. But when Adam and Eve—the first humans—disobeyed God in the Garden of Eden, physical death was the consequence of their sin. In the New Testament section of the Bible, Jesus Christ was the Son of God who, out of love for humankind, was born into the world and died as a man. God raised Jesus from the dead after his crucifixion to live eternally with him in Heaven, and Jesus promised humankind the same opportunity. According to Christian doctrine, Jesus thus "transformed the curse of death into a blessing" (*Catechism of the Catholic Church, Second Edition, English Translation*, Doubleday, 1997).

HISTORY. Early Christians believed that God was the giver of life, and therefore he alone could take life away. They viewed euthanasia as usurping that divine right. The early Christian philosopher St. Augustine (circa 354–430) taught that people must accept suffering because it comes from God. According to Augustine, suffering not only helps one grow spiritually but also prepares Christians for the eternal joy that God has in store for them. Moreover, the healthy were exhorted to minister to the sick not for the purpose of helping to permanently end their suffering, but in order to ease their pain.

St. Thomas Aquinas (circa 1225–74), considered one of the greatest Catholic theologians, taught that ending one's suffering by ending one's life was sinful. To help another take his or her life was just as sinful. However, in 1516 Sir Thomas More (circa 1477–1535), an English statesman, humanist, and loyal defender of the Catholic Church, published *Utopia*, which described an ideal country governed by reason. More argued that if a disease is not only incurable but also causes pain that is hard to control, it is permissible to free the sufferer from his or her painful existence. This was a major departure from the medieval acceptance of suffering and death as the earthly price to be paid for eternal life.

PRINCIPLE OF DOUBLE EFFECT. Catholic moral theologians were said to have developed the ethical principle known as the "Rule of Double Effect." According to this principle, "Effects that would be morally wrong if caused intentionally are permissible if foreseen but unintended."

For example, a physician prescribes an increased dosage of the painkiller morphine to ease a patient's pain, not to bring about his or her death. However, it is foreseen that a potent dosage may depress the patient's respiration and hasten death. The *Catechism of the Catholic Church* states:

> The use of painkillers to alleviate the sufferings of the dying, even at the risk of shortening their days, can be morally in conformity with human dignity if death is not willed as either an end or a means, but only foreseen and tolerated as inevitable.

ON EUTHANASIA. Over the years, Catholic theologians have debated balancing the preservation of God-given life with the moral issue of continuing medical treatments that are of no apparent value to patients. In 1957 Pope Pius XII stated that if a patient is hopelessly ill, physicians may discontinue heroic measures "to permit the patient, already virtually dead, to pass on in peace" ("The Prolongation of Life"). He added that if the patient is unconscious, relatives may request withdrawal of life support under certain conditions.

In *Nutrition and Hydration: Moral and Pastoral Reflections* the Committee for Pro-Life Activities of the National Conference of Catholic Bishops (Washington, DC: NCCB, 1992) stated:

> In the final stage of dying, one is not obligated to prolong the life of a patient by every possible means: "When inevitable death is imminent in spite of the means used, it is permitted in conscience to make the decision to refuse forms of treatment that would only secure a precarious and burdensome prolongation of life, so long as the normal care due the sick person in similar cases is not interrupted."

The Eastern Orthodox Church

The Eastern Orthodox Church resulted from the division between Eastern and Western Christianity during the eleventh century. Differences in doctrines and politics, among other things, caused the separation. The Eastern Orthodox Church does not have a single worldwide leader like the Roman Catholic pope. Instead, national jurisdictions called "Sees" are each governed by a bishop.

Eastern Orthodoxy relies on the Scriptures, tradition, and the decrees of the first seven ecumenical councils to regulate its daily conduct. In matters of present-day morality, such as the debates on end-of-life issues, contemporary Orthodox ethicists explore possible courses of action that are in line with the "sense of the Church." The sense of the Church is deduced from Church laws and dissertations of the Fathers of the Church, as well as previous council decisions. Their recommendations are subject to further review.

"The Stand of the Orthodox Church on Controversial Issues," by the Reverend Stanley Harakas, Th.D. (http://www.goarch.org/en/ourfaith/articles/article7101.asp), states,

"The Orthodox Church has a very strong pro-life stand which in part expresses itself in opposition to doctrinaire advocacy of euthanasia." However, the article quotes current Orthodox theology to clarify that "the Church distinguishes between euthanasia and the withholding of extraordinary means to prolong life. It affirms the sanctity of human life and man's God-given responsibility to preserve life. But it rejects an attitude which disregards the inevitability of physical death."

Protestantism

The different denominations of Protestantism have varying positions about euthanasia. While many hold that active euthanasia is morally wrong, they believe that prolonging life by extraordinary measures is not necessary. In other words, though few would condone active euthanasia, many accept passive euthanasia. (Active euthanasia involves the hastening of death through the administration of lethal drugs. Passive euthanasia refers to withdrawing life support or medical interventions necessary to sustain life, such as removing a patient from a ventilator.) Among the Protestant denominations that support the latter view are the Jehovah's Witnesses, the Church of Jesus Christ of Latter-Day Saints (Mormons), the Lutheran Churches, the Reformed Presbyterians, the Presbyterian Church in America, the Christian Life Commission of the Southern Baptist Convention, and the General Association of the General Baptists.

Some denominations have no official policy on active or passive euthanasia. However, many individual ethicists and representatives within these churches agree with other denominations that active euthanasia is morally wrong but that futile life supports serve no purpose. Among these churches are the Seventh Day Adventists, the Episcopal Church, and the United Methodist Church.

Christian Scientists believe that prayer heals all diseases. They claim that illnesses are mental in origin and therefore cannot be cured by outside intervention, such as medical help. Some also believe that seeking medical help while praying diminishes or even cancels the effectiveness of the prayers. Because God can heal even those diseases others see as incurable, euthanasia has no practical significance among Christian Scientists.

The Unitarian Universalist Association, a union of the Unitarian and Universalist Churches, is perhaps the most liberal when it comes to the right to die. The Association believes that "human life has inherent dignity, which may be compromised when life is extended beyond the will or ability of a person to sustain that dignity." Furthermore, "Unitarian Universalists advocate the right to self-determination in dying, and the release from civil or criminal penalties of those who, under proper safeguards, act to honor the right of terminally ill patients to select the time of their own deaths" (http://www.uua.org/actions/health/88die-dignity.html).

Judaism

In the United States there are three main branches of Judaism. The Orthodox tradition adheres strictly to Jewish laws. Conservative Judaism advocates adapting Jewish precepts to a changing world, but all changes must be consistent with Jewish laws and tradition. Reform Judaism, while accepting the ethical laws as coming from God, generally considers the other laws of Judaism as "instructional but not binding."

Like the Roman Catholics, Jews believe that life is precious because it is a gift from God. No one has the right to extinguish life, because one's life is not his or hers in the first place. Generally, rabbis from all branches of Judaism agree that active euthanasia is not morally justified. It is tantamount to murder, which is forbidden by the Torah (the Five Books of Moses). Moreover, Jewish teaching holds that men and women are stewards entrusted with the preservation of God's gift of life and therefore are obliged to hold on to that life as long as possible.

PROLONGING LIFE VERSUS HASTENING DEATH. While Jewish tradition maintains that a devout believer must do everything possible to prolong life, this admonition is subject to interpretation even among Orthodox Jews.

The Torah and the Talmud provide the principles and laws that guide Jews. The Talmud—the definitive rabbinical compilation of Jewish laws, lore, and commentary—has provided continuity to Jewish culture by interpreting the Torah and adapting it to the constantly changing situations of Jewish people.

On the subject of prolonging life versus hastening death, when that life is clearly nearing death, the Talmud narrates a number of situations involving people who are considered "goses" (literally, the death rattle is in the patient's throat, or one whose death is imminent). Scholars often refer to the story of Rabbi Haninah ben Teradyon, who, during the second century, was condemned to be burned to death by the Romans. To prolong his agonizing death, the Romans wrapped him in some wet material. At first the rabbi refused to hasten his own death; however, he later agreed to have the wet material removed, thus bringing about a quicker death.

Some Jews interpret this Talmudic narration to mean that in the final stage of a person's life, it is permissible to remove any hindrance to the dying process. In this modern age of medicine, this may mean implementing a patient's wish, such as the do-not-resuscitate directive or the withdrawal of artificial life support.

Islam

Islam was founded by the prophet Muhammad in the seventh century. The Qur'an (also transliterated as Koran), which is composed of God's revelations to Muhammad, and the Sunnah, Muhammad's teachings and deeds, are the sources of Islamic beliefs and practice. Although there are numerous sects and cultural diversities within the religion, all Muslims (followers of Islam) are bound by a total submission to the will of Allah, or God. The basic doctrines of Allah's revelations were systematized into definitive rules and regulations that now comprise the Shari'ah, or the religious law that governs the life of Muslims.

Muslims look to the Shari'ah for ethical guidance in all aspects of life, including medicine. Sickness and pain are part of life and must be accepted as Allah's will. They should be viewed as a means to atone for one's sins. Death, on the other hand, is simply a passage to another existence in the afterlife. Those who die after leading a righteous life will merit the true life on Judgment Day. The Qur'an (chapter 2, verse 28) states, "How do you disbelieve in God seeing you were dead and He gave you life and then He shall cause you to die, then He shall give you life, then unto Him you shall be returned?"

Islam teaches that life is a gift from Allah; therefore, no one can end it except Allah. The prophet Muhammad said, "Whosoever takes poison and thus kills himself, his poison will be in his hand; he will be tasting it in Hell, always abiding therein, and being accommodated therein forever." While an ailing person does not have the right to choose death, even if he or she is suffering, Muslims heed the following admonition (*Islamic Code of Medical Ethics*, Kuwait Document, Kuwait Rabi 1, 1401, First International Conference on Islamic Medicine, 1981):

> [The] doctor is well advised to realize his limit and not transgress it. If it is scientifically certain that life cannot be restored, then it is futile to diligently [maintain] the vegetative state of the patient by heroic means.... It is the process of life that the doctor aims to maintain and not the process of dying. In any case, the doctor shall not take a positive measure to terminate the patient's life.

Hinduism

The Eastern religious tradition of Hinduism is founded on the principle of reincarnation—the cycle of life, death, and physical rebirth. Hindus believe that death and dying are intricately interwoven with life, and that the individual soul undergoes a series of physical life cycles before uniting with Brahman, or God. "Karma" refers to the ethical consequences of a person's actions during a previous life, which determine the quality of his or her present life. A person can neither change nor escape his or her karma. By conforming to "dharma," the religious and moral law, an individual is able to fulfill obligations from the past life. Life is sacred because it offers one the chance to perform good acts toward the goal of ending the cycle of rebirths.

A believer in Hinduism, therefore, views pain and suffering as personal karma, and serious illness as a consequence of past misdeeds. Death is simply a passage to another rebirth, which brings one closer to God. Artificial medical treatments to sustain life are not recommended, and medical intervention to end life is discouraged. Active euthanasia simply interrupts one's karma and the soul's evolution toward final liberation from reincarnations.

Buddhism

Buddhism, like Hinduism, is based on a cycle of reincarnation. To Buddhists, the goals of every life are emancipation from "samsara," the compulsory cycle of rebirths, and attainment of "nirvana," enlightenment or bliss. Like the Hindus, Buddhists believe that sickness, death, and karma are interrelated. Followers of Siddhartha Gautama, also called Buddha (circa 563–483 BCE), the founder of Buddhism, claim that Buddha advised against taking too strict a position when it comes to issues such as the right to die.

The fourteenth Dalai Lama, Tenzin Gyatso, spiritual leader of Tibetan Buddhism, has commented on the use of mechanical life support when the patient has no chance to recover. Rather than advocating or condemning passive euthanasia, he advised that each case be considered individually (Sogyal Rinpoche, *The Tibetan Book of Living and Dying*, San Francisco, CA: Harper, 1992):

> If there is no such chance for positive thoughts [Buddhists believe that a dying person's final thoughts determine the circumstances of his next life], and in addition a lot of money is being spent by relatives simply in order to keep someone alive, then there seems to be no point. But each case must be dealt with individually; it is very difficult to generalize.

BIOETHICS AND MEDICAL PRACTICE

Since ancient times, medical practice has been concerned with ethical issues. But only since the last half of the twentieth century have rapid advances in medicine given rise to so many ethical dilemmas. In matters of death and dying the debate continues on such issues as physicians' honoring a patient's do-not-resuscitate order, withholding food and fluids, and withdrawing artificial respiration.

There are four basic tenets of bioethics: autonomy, beneficence, nonmaleficence, and justice. Autonomy refers to self-rule and self-determination. Beneficence is action that is in the best interest of the patient. Nonmaleficence means to do no harm. Justice is the practice of treating patients in comparable circumstances the same way, and also refers to equitable distribution of resources, risks, and costs. Although bioethics is subject to change and reinterpretation, medical practice continues to rely on these principles to guide the actions of physicians and other health care providers.

The Hippocratic Oath

The earliest written document to deal with medical ethics is generally attributed to Hippocrates (circa 460–370 BCE), known as the father of medicine. For more than two thousand years the Hippocratic Oath has been adopted by Western physicians as a code of ethics, defining their conduct in the discharge of their duties. In part, the oath states:

> I will follow that method of treatment, which, according to my ability and judgment, I consider for the benefit of my patients, and abstain from whatever is deleterious [harmful] and mischievous. I will give no deadly medicine to anyone if asked, nor suggest any such counsel.

Nonetheless, some scholars claim that the giving of "deadly medicine" did not refer to euthanasia. During the time of Hippocrates, helping a suffering person end his or her life was common practice. The oath might therefore have been more an admonition to the medical profession to avoid acting as an accomplice to murder, rather than to refrain from the practice of euthanasia.

Some physicians believe that literal interpretation of the oath is not necessary. It simply offers guidelines that allow for adaptation to modern-day situations. In fact, in 1948 the World Medical Association modified the Hippocratic Oath to call attention to the atrocities committed by Nazi physicians. Known as the Declaration of Geneva, the document reads in part:

> I will practice medicine with conscience and dignity. The health and life of my patient will be my first consideration.... I will not permit consideration of race, religion, nationality, party politics, or social standing to intervene between my duty and my patient. I will maintain the utmost respect for human life from the time of its conception. Even under threat, I will not use my knowledge contrary to the laws of humanity.

The Physician's Role

Even in ancient times, as can be gleaned from the Hippocratic Oath, physicians believed they knew what was best for their patients. Patients relied on their doctors' ability and judgment, and usually did not question the treatments prescribed. Doctors were not even required to tell their patients the details of their illness, even if they were terminally ill.

Beginning in the 1960s many patients assumed a more active role in their medical care. The emphasis on preventive medicine encouraged people to take responsibility for their own health. Physicians were faced with a new breed of patients who wanted to be active participants in their health care. Patients also wanted to know more about modern technologies and procedures that were evolving in medicine. With this new health consciousness, physicians and hospitals assumed the responsibility for informing and educating patients, and increasingly were legally liable for failing to inform patients of the consequences of medical treatments and procedures.

To compound the complexity of the changing patient-physician relationship, modern technology, which could sometimes prolong life, was also prolonging death. Historically, physicians had been trained to prevent and combat death, rather than to deal with dying patients, communicate with the patient and the family about a terminal illness, prepare them for an imminent death, or respond to a patient requesting assisted suicide.

Until the late 1990s, medical education programs offered very little in the area of end-of-life care. Drs. J. Andrew Billings and Susan Block reported that a 1991 survey of medical school deans revealed that only 11% of schools offered a full-term course on death and dying ("Palliative Care in Undergraduate Medical Education," *Journal of the American Medical Association*, vol. 278, no. 9, September 3, 1997). About 52% offered death education as part of other required courses, while another 30% offered only one or two lectures as part of another course. In 1997, while some medical schools offered information on dealing with death as part of other required courses, only 5 of 126 medical schools in the United States offered a separate required course on death and dying.

This situation began to improve in the late 1990s. The Education for Physicians on End-of-Life Care (EPEC) Project, developed in 1998 by the American Medical Association (AMA), is an ambitious training program that aims to provide physicians with the knowledge they need to care for dying patients. The curriculum emphasizes development of skills and competence in the areas of communication, ethical decision making, palliative care, psychosocial issues, and pain and symptom management. The program became fully operational in 1999 and provides curricula to all leaders of medical societies, medical school deans, and major medical organizations. The EPEC Project was supported from 1996 to 2003 with funding from the Robert Wood Johnson Foundation. After 2003 it was sponsored by and housed at Northwestern University Medical School in Chicago with a mission to educate all health care professionals on the essential clinical competencies in end-of-life care.

In 2002 Amy M. Sullivan and her colleagues surveyed associate deans at sixty-two accredited U.S. medical schools to determine attitudes and practices of end-of-life care teaching in the undergraduate medical curriculum ("End-of-Life Care in the Curriculum: A National Study of Medical Education Deans," *Academic Medicine*, vol. 79, no. 8, August 2004). Research results revealed that 29% of the deans surveyed reported that their medical schools offered courses or clerkships primarily focused on end-of-life care. However, two-thirds of the medical school deans admitted that not enough time was devoted

TABLE 3.1

Perceptions of associate deans of barriers to teaching end-of-life care at U.S. medical schools, 2002

Barrier	A lot	A moderate amount	Only a little/ not at all
Lack of time	54%	29%	17%
Lack of faculty expertise	21%	32%	47%
Lack of funding	17%	27%	56%
Faculty perception that current teaching is adequate	4%	38%	58%
End-of-life care is a low priority	9%	24%	67%
Lack of faculty leader	15%	17%	69%
Lack of clinical services	2%	19%	79%
Lack of faculty interest	2%	19%	79%
Lack of teaching materials	2%	15%	83%

SOURCE: Amy M. Sullivan, et al., "Table 3. Perceptions of 51 Associate Deans of Barriers to Teaching End-of-Life Care at U.S. Medical Schools, 2002," in "End-of-Life Care in the Curriculum: A National Study of Medical Education Deans," *Academic Medicine*, vol. 79, no. 8, August 2004

in the curriculum to this topic. Table 3.1 shows the perceptions of these deans as to the barriers to teaching end-of-life care at U.S. medical schools. The most significant barrier is lack of time in the curriculum, followed by lack of faculty expertise and lack of funding.

Contemporary Ethical Guidelines for Physicians

Physicians are trained to save lives, not to let people die. Advanced medical technology, with respirators and parenteral nutrition (artificial feeding devices that provide nutrition to an otherwise unconscious patient), can prolong the process of dying. Dr. Ira Byock, in *Dying Well: The Prospect for Growth at the End of Life* (New York: G. P. Putnam's Sons, 1997), admitted:

> A strong presumption throughout my medical education was that all seriously ill people required vigorous life-prolonging treatments, including those who were expected to die, even patients with advanced, chronic illness such as widespread cancer, end-stage congestive heart failure, and kidney or liver failure. It even extended to patients who saw death as a relief from the suffering caused by their illness.

The Council on Ethical and Judicial Affairs of the AMA published guidelines for physicians dealing with patients in nonemergency situations ("Decisions Near the End of Life," http://www.ama-assn.org/apps/pf_new/pf_online?f_n=browse&doc=policyfiles/HnE/H-140.966.HTM). They were originally written in 1991, reaffirmed in 1996 and 1997, and appended in 2000. The following guidelines are the most recent as of this writing:

> Our AMA believes that:
>
> 1. The principle of patient autonomy requires that physicians must respect the decision to forgo life-sustaining treatment of a patient who possesses decision-making capacity. Life-sustaining treatment is any medical treatment that serves to prolong life without reversing the underlying medical condition. Life-sustaining treatment

includes, but is not limited to, mechanical ventilation, renal dialysis, chemotherapy, antibiotics, and artificial nutrition and hydration.

2. There is no ethical distinction between withdrawing and withholding life-sustaining treatment.

3. Physicians have an obligation to relieve pain and suffering and to promote the dignity and autonomy of dying patients in their care. This includes providing effective palliative treatment even though it may foreseeably hasten death. More research must be pursued, examining the degree to which palliative care reduces the requests for euthanasia or assisted suicide.

4. Physicians must not perform euthanasia or participate in assisted suicide. A more careful examination of the issue is necessary. Support, comfort, respect for patient autonomy, good communication, and adequate pain control may decrease dramatically the public demand for euthanasia and assisted suicide. In certain carefully defined circumstances, it would be humane to recognize that death is certain and suffering is great. However, the societal risks of involving physicians in medical interventions to cause patients' deaths is too great to condone euthanasia or physician-assisted suicide at this time.

5. Our AMA supports continued research into and education concerning pain management. (CEJA Rep. B, A-91; Reaffirmed by BOT Rep. 59, A-96; Reaffirmation A-97; Appended: Sub. Res. 514, I-00)

Another prominent professional medical organization, the American College of Physicians (ACP), revised its recommendations about end-of-life care in the fourth edition of its code of ethics, *The American College of Physicians Ethics Manual* (Philadelphia, PA: ACP, 1998, http://www.annals.org/cgi/content/full/128/7/576). It is the most recent edition of the manual as of this writing. Its guidelines for decision-making near the end of life emphasize that capable and informed adults nearly always have the legal and ethical right to refuse treatment. They advise physicians to practice empathy, to compromise, and to negotiate with patients who wish to forego recommended treatment. The guidelines offer an approach to clinical ethical decision making that not only involves defining the problems and reviewing facts and uncertainties, but also considers the patient's emotional state, ethnicity, culture, and religious traditions.

PATIENT AUTONOMY

According to the principle of patient autonomy, competent patients have the right to self-rule—to choose among medically recommended treatments and refuse any treatment they do not want. To be truly autonomous, they have to be told about the nature of their illness, prospects for recovery, the course of the illness, alternative treatments, and treatment consequences. After thoughtful consideration, a patient makes an informed choice and grants "informed consent" to treatment.

Decisions about medical treatment may be influenced by the patient's psychological state, family history, culture, values, and religious beliefs.

Once informed by their physicians about their illnesses and medical options, patients also have the right to forego treatment. Former first lady Jacqueline Kennedy Onassis, after a difficult battle to arrest her non-Hodgkin's lymphoma, refused further treatment. When doctors told Ms. Onassis that the cancer had spread to her brain and liver and that there was nothing else they could do, she asked to go home. She signed a living will that forbade any heroic measures should the doctor diagnose her condition as hopeless. Once home, she received only palliative care (care to relieve symptoms rather than cure), lapsed into a coma, and died soon after, on May 19, 1994.

Not All Patients Want to Know

While patient autonomy is a fundamental aspect of medical ethics, not all patients want to know about their illnesses or to be involved in decisions about their terminal care. H. Russell Searight and Jennifer Gafford in "Cultural Diversity at the End of Life: Issues and Guidelines for Family Physicians" (*American Family Physician*, vol. 71, no. 3, February, 2005, http://www.aafp.org/afp/20050201.515.pdf) note that the concept of patient autonomy is not easily applied to members of some racial or ethnic groups. Searight and Gafford explained the three basic dimensions in end-of-life treatment that vary culturally: communication of bad news, locus of decision making, and attitudes toward advance directives and end-of-life care.

Members of some ethnic groups, such as many Africans and Japanese, soften bad news by using terms that do not overtly state that a person has a potentially terminal condition. For example, the term "growth" or "blood disease" may be used rather than telling a person they have a cancerous tumor or leukemia. That idea is taken one step further in many Hispanic, Chinese, and Pakistani communities in which the terminally ill are generally protected from knowledge of their condition. Many reasons exist for this type of behavior, such as viewing the discussion of serious illness and death as disrespectful or impolite, not wanting to cause anxiety or eliminate hope in the patient, or believing that speaking about a condition makes it real. Many people of Asian and European cultures believe that it is cruel to inform a patient of a terminal diagnosis.

The phrase "locus of decision making" refers to those making the end-of-life decisions: the physician, the family, and/or the patient. The locus of decision-making varies among cultures. The North American cultural norm is individual decision for one's own medical care. Koreans and Mexican Americans often approach end-of-life decision making differently, abiding by a collective decision process in which relatives make treatment choices for a family member without that person's input. Eastern Europeans and Russians often look to the physician as the expert in end-of-life decision-making. In Asian, Indian, and Pakistani cultures, physicians and family members may share decision making.

An advance directive (often called a living will) is a written statement that explains a person's wishes about end-of-life medical care. Completion of advance directives varies among cultures. For example, Searight and Gafford noted that approximately 40% of elderly Caucasians have completed advance directives, while only 16% of elderly African-Americans have done the same.

Polly Mazanec and Mary Kay Tyler note in "Cultural Considerations in End-of-Life Care: How Ethnicity, Age, and Spirituality Affect Decisions When Death Is Imminent" (*Home Healthcare Nurse*, vol. 22, no. 5, May 2004) that there are many differences among African-Americans, Chinese Americans, Filipino Americans, and Hispanic or Latino Americans regarding the role of the family at the end of life, preferences for the environment of the dying person, and preparation of the body after death. Mazanec and Tyler suggest that often a lack of attention to such cultural needs in end-of-life care can be a predominant factor in a person's experience of dying.

Due to differences among cultures regarding various facets of end-of-life decision making and preparedness, it appears important for physicians to realize patient autonomy is far from a universally held ideal. There are differences of opinion not only among ethnic groups but also within each ethnic group, such as differences with age. People bring their cultural values to bear on decisions about terminal care.

Health Care Proxies and Surrogate Decision Makers

When a patient is incompetent to make informed decisions about his or her medical treatment, a proxy or a surrogate must make the decision for that patient. Some patients, in anticipation of being in a position of incompetence, will execute a durable power of attorney for health care, designating a proxy. Most people choose family members or close friends who will make all medical decisions, including the withholding or withdrawal of life-sustaining treatments.

When a proxy has not been named in advance, health care providers usually involve family members in medical decisions. Most states have laws that govern surrogate decision making. Some states designate family members, by order of kinship, to assume the role of surrogates.

THE DESIRE TO DIE

AIDS (acquired immunodeficiency syndrome) has directed societal attention to end-of-life decision making because patients infected with HIV (human immunodeficiency virus), which weakens the immune system and leads to AIDS, are faced with decisions about life-prolonging therapies for a disease that as yet has no cure. They know that a number of disorders await them as their immune system is progressively destroyed, including severe wasting, infections, intense pain, blindness, and dementia. Some AIDS patients who do not wish to undergo this protracted dying process or deplete family resources in prolonged care may ask for a physician's aid to hasten death. Likewise, many patients with incurable cancer who are suffering as they die would like their death to be hastened.

Diane E. Meier et al surveyed 3,021 physicians younger than sixty-five years from the 1996 American Medical Association Physician Master File in August 1996 ("Characteristics of Patients Requesting and Receiving Physician-Assisted Death," *Archives of Internal Medicine*, vol. 163, no. 13, July 14, 2003). The researchers wanted to determine patient characteristics associated with acts of physician-assisted suicide. Physician-assisted suicide was defined as "writing a prescription or administering a lethal injection with the primary intention of ending the patient's life." Of the 3,021 physicians surveyed, 1,902 (63%) responded.

More than half the patients requesting and receiving physician-assisted death were male (61%) and most of the patients were white (89%). Nearly half (47%) of those in the sample were college graduates, and nearly half (47%) had cancer as a primary diagnosis. Infection with HIV was the primary diagnosis for 13%. Thirty-eight percent were experiencing severe pain and 42% were experiencing severe discomfort other than pain. About half (49%) were depressed (as diagnosed by their physicians) at the time of their request; 53% were dependent for most or all of their personal care; and 42% were bedridden. Nearly three-quarters of those in the sample (72%) were expected to live one month or more, while the remaining 28% were expected to live less than a month. About half of those in the sample requested a lethal prescription (52%) to hasten their death.

Meier and her colleagues analyzed their survey data to identify factors associated with a physician honoring a request for aid in dying. The factor most likely to predict that a physician would honor such a request was the specificity of the request. That is, specific requests for assistance, such as requests for lethal prescriptions or lethal injections, were predictors of requests being honored, while nonspecific requests were not predictors of requests being honored. Other predictors of physicians' decisions to honor patients' requests for assistance in dying included severe pain, severe discomfort other than pain, and a life expectancy of less than one month. Some patients were believed to be depressed at the time of their request, and although physicians did honor some of these requests, they were less likely to honor a request if they knew the patient was depressed.

Further analysis of the survey data identified factors associated with a physician honoring a request for aid in dying for patients requesting a lethal injection and those requesting a prescription for a lethal dose of medication. For patients requesting a lethal injection, those with severe physical discomfort other than pain and patients with a life expectancy of less than one month were significantly more likely to have their request honored than patients without these characteristics. For patients requesting a prescription for a lethal dose of medication, those with severe pain and severe physical discomfort other than pain were significantly more likely to have their request honored than patients without these characteristics. In both groups patients who were depressed at the time of their requests were less likely to have their requests honored than those who were not depressed.

Marijke C. Jansen-van der Weide, Bregje D. Onwuteaka-Philipsen, and Gerrit van der Wal published a study in 2005 that revealed characteristics of patients in the Netherlands who explicitly requested euthanasia or physician-assisted suicide between April 2000 and December 2002. Table 3.2 shows that, as in the Meier study, more than half the patients requesting euthanasia and assisted suicide (EAS) were male (54%). Most of the patients were diagnosed with cancer (90%), a greater percentage than in the Meier study. Although only 9% were diagnosed with depression, 92% were "feeling bad." The three most often cited reasons for requesting EAS were pointless suffering (75%), deterioration or loss of dignity (69%), and weakness or tiredness (60%).

Results of the Jansen-van der Weide et al study shed some light on reasons why physicians were reluctant to grant requests for EAS (see Table 3.3.) Of the 570 patients who had initially requested EAS, sixty-five died before EAS was administered, seventy-two died before a final decision was rendered, sixty-eight changed their mind and no longer wanted EAS, 101 were refused, and 253 had their requests carried out. Physicians caring for patients in all five categories were reluctant to grant the EAS request in some cases. Physicians caring for 52% of the "refused" patients cited doubts about their patients' hopeless and unbearable suffering. This doubt was prevalent across groups. Other common doubts expressed by physicians were those about the availability of alternative treatment, personal doubts in particular cases, doubts about the patient being depressed, and doubts about a well-considered and persistent request. Not usually significant in a physician's reluctance to grant EAS were concerns that the patient was too close to death, that the request for EAS was voluntary, and that the family was against EAS.

Table 3.4 shows the odds ratio (OR) for factors associated with refusing a request for EAS. A factor shown in the table with a high OR was more likely than a factor with a lower OR to influence a physician to refuse a request for EAS. The table shows that the factor most likely to have influenced a physician to refuse an EAS request was the patient not being competent or fully competent (did not have all of his or her mental faculties). Two other factors associated with refusal were the physician's perception that the patient's unbearable or hopeless suffering was experienced to a lesser extent than would be necessary to consider EAS. The lower portion of the table shows that depression was the reason most likely to have influenced a patient to request EAS, while not wanting to burden their family was the second most influential factor.

TABLE 3.2

Characteristics of patients who explicitly request euthanasia and physician-assisted suicide (EAS), Netherlands, 2000–02

Characteristic	Patients, percent[a]					
	EAS (Sample size = 940)	Died before performance (Sample size = 217)	Died before final decision (Sample size = 164)	No longer wanted EAS (Sample size = 144)	Request refused (Sample size = 150)	Total (Population = 1681)[b]
Sex						
Male	54	57	61	53	46	54
Female	46	43	40	47	54	45
Age, years						
<40	3	5	1	4	3	3
40–64	43	43	46	38	26	41
65–79	41	41	37	39	41	41
≥80	13	11	16	19	30	15
Diagnosis						
Cancer	90	90	87	84	57	86
MS or ALS	2	3	0	3	3	2
Old age or general deterioration	0[c]	1	2	4	11	2
COPD	2	3	1	1	2	2
Heart failure	1	1	3	2	3	2
Other	5	2	7	6	25	7
Symptoms						
Feeling bad	92	85	88	76	77	87
Tiredness	89	87	83	72	70	84
Not active	78	73	75	69	71	75
Lack of appetite	81	75	79	62	53	75
Pain	50	46	42	36	21	45
Nausea	42	38	29	27	15	36
Difficulty breathing	31	34	29	23	11	29
Coughing	22	22	22	13	10	20
Vomiting	25	16	17	14	6	20
Anxiousness	13	24	28	30	25	19
Depression	9	16	22	22	32	15
No clear consciousness	5	9	10	6	8	7
Confusion	4	5	13	7	10	6
Bedsores	6	3	4	4	4	5
Reasons for requesting EAS						
Pointless suffering	75	71	61	52	38	67
Deterioration or loss of dignity	69	64	66	55	51	65
Weakness or tiredness	60	60	51	54	39	56
Pain	31	34	31	31	18	30
Fear of suffocating	21	24	22	17	9	20
Disability or immobility	20	18	13	13	20	19
Not wanting to be a burden on family	13	18	23	27	33	18
Tired of living	15	14	15	22	37	17
Vomiting	17	14	7	10	2	14
Depressed	4	7	8	10	18	7
Other	6	4	2	6	11	5
Reasons pertained mainly to						
Current situation	62	46	46	35	54	54
Future situation	4	18	20	31	11	12
Both	34	36	34	34	34	34

Notes: Abbreviations: ALS, amyotrophic lateral sclerosis; COPD, chronic obstructive pulmonary disease; EAS, euthanasia and physician-assisted suicide; MS, multiple sclerosis.
[a]Percentages have been rounded. Percentage of missing observations per group: EAS, between 0.4% and 4.5%; patient died before performance, between 0.5% and 3.2%; patient died before final decision, between 0.6% and 4.3%; patient no longer wanted EAS, between 0% and 6.7%; and request refused, between 0.7% and 4.0%.
[b]Including 34 cases in which the patient was still alive when the questionnaire was filled out and 32 cases in which it was unknown what had happened.
[c]Percentage of less than 0.5%.

SOURCE: Marijke C. Jansen-van der Weide, et al., "Table 1. Characteristics of Patients Who Explicitly Request EAS," in "Granted, Undecided, Withdrawn, and Refused Requests for Euthanasia and Physician-Assisted Suicide," *Archives of Internal Medicine*, vol. 165, no. 15, August 8/22, 2005

TABLE 3.3

Reasons for reluctance to grant the EAS request, Netherlands, 2000–02

Variable	EAS[b]	Died before performance	Died before final decision	No longer wanted EAS[b]	Request refused	Total[c]
			Patients, percent[a]			
Reasons for reluctance in granting the request[d]						
Sample size (n)	253	65	72	68	101	570
Doubts about hopeless and unbearable suffering	28	30	27	24	52	34
Doubts about availability of alternative treatment	19	23	29	37	38	27
Personal doubts of the physician in this particular case	23	30	25	12	23	23
Doubts about patient being depressed	12	14	12	22	29	17
Doubts about well-considered and persistent request	6	7	17	25	18	13
Pressure of next-of-kin on request	8	9	21	10	7	10
Fear of judicial consequences	15	2	8	3	6	9
Doubts about patient's competence	5	7	12	5	8	7
Never perform EAS[b]	4	2	12	3	13	7
Dependent on consultant's judgment	15	5	2	2	1	7
Doubts about patient's insight into his/her illness	5	2	10	7	9	6
Patient is too close to death	3	2	6	7	1	3
Doubts about voluntary request	3	0	0	0	3	2
Family is against EAS[b]	2	0	8	2	1	2
Other	3	5	4	3	1	3

[a]Percentages have been rounded. Percentage of missing observations per group: EAS, between 0.8% and 1.8%; patient died before performance, between 3.4% and 3.7%; patient died before final decision, between 2.0% and 6.1%; patient no longer wanted EAS, between 1.4% and 4.2%; and request refused, between 1.3% and 2.8%.
[b]EAS=Euthanasia and physician-assisted suicide.
[c]Including 34 cases in which the patient was still alive when the questionnaire was filled out and 32 cases in which it was unknown what had happened.
[d]Percentage of missing observations was high and differed per group: EAS, 37%; patient died before performance, 31%; patient died before final decision, 26%; patient no longer wanted EAS, 13%; and request refused, 2%.

SOURCE: Adapted from Marijke C. Jansen-van der Weide, et al., "Table 3. Consultation and Discussion with Colleagues and Reasons for Reluctance to Grant the Explicit Request in the Decision-Making Process," in "Granted, Undecided, Withdrawn, and Refused Requests for Euthanasia and Physician-Assisted Suicide," *Archives of Internal Medicine*, vol. 165, no. 15, August 8/22, 2005

TABLE 3.4

Factors associated with refusing a request for EAS, Netherlands, 2000–02

Factor	Odds ratio (sample size = 1090)
Patient not (fully) competent	21.0
Unbearable suffering "to a lesser extent"	15.0
Hopeless suffering "to a lesser extent"	11.0
Explicit request	
Completely	1.0
To a high degree	3.3
To a lesser degree	4.7
Alternative treatments available	4.4
Physician's age, years	
<40	3.1
40–50	1.1
≥50	1.0
Reasons for requesting EAS	
Depression	5.3
Not wanting to be a burden on family	2.4
Deterioration or loss of dignity	0.32
Pointless suffering	0.30
Fear of suffocation	0.24
Vomiting	0.18

Note: EAS=Euthanasia and physician-assisted suicide. The most important reason for requesting EAS concerns future situation, patient's age, and patient's sex.

SOURCE: Marijke C. Jansen-van der Weide, et al., "Table 4. Factors Associated with Refusing a Request for EAS," in "Granted, Undecided, Withdrawn, and Refused Requests for Euthanasia and Physician-Assisted Suicide," *Archives of Internal Medicine*, vol. 165, no. 15, August 8/22, 2005

CHAPTER 4

THE END OF LIFE: MEDICAL CONSIDERATIONS

CAUSES OF DEATH

During the twentieth century the primary causes of death in the United States changed. In the 1800s and early 1900s infectious (communicable) diseases such as influenza, tuberculosis, and diphtheria were the leading causes of death. These have been replaced by chronic diseases; heart disease, cancer (malignant neoplasms), and stroke (cerebrovascular diseases) were the three leading causes of death in 2003. (See Table 4.1.)

In 2003 the age-adjusted death rate (which accounts for changes in the age distribution of the population across time) for heart disease was 232.3 deaths per one hundred thousand people, while that for cancer was 190.1 per one hundred thousand persons. (See Table 4.1.) Together, these two diseases accounted for 50.7% of all deaths in the United States in 2003. Deaths from heart disease have been decreasing since 1950, while cancer mortality has been dropping only since 1990.

Not surprisingly, the leading causes of death vary by age. For those ages one to forty-four, accidents and their adverse effects were the leading causes of death in 2002 and 2003, as well as the leading cause of death for those ages one to thirty-four in 1999, 2000, and 2001. For those ages thirty-five to forty-four, cancer was the leading cause of death in 1999, 2000, and 2001, with accidents and their adverse effects second, and heart disease third. Cancer and heart disease caused most deaths among those forty-five years and older from 1999 to 2003. (See Table 4.2.) The Institute of Medicine of the National Academies reports that heart disease, cancer, and stroke "disproportionately affect older people"—those sixty-five years of age and over, which is supported by the figures in Table 4.2.

According to an HIV/AIDS Surveillance Report begun in 1993, 1996 marked the first year a decline occurred in U.S. deaths due to AIDS. This downward trend in annual numbers of deaths due to AIDS continued

from 1998 through 2000. From 2001 to 2003 the number of cases increased and plateaued with slightly higher numbers of total deaths. (See Table 4.3.) In 2004 the number of deaths from AIDS decreased. From 2000 through 2004 most males with AIDS contracted HIV via male-to-male sexual contact or injection drug use. Most females contracted the virus by heterosexual contact or injection drug use. Children most often contracted the virus perinatally (immediately before and after birth) from infected mothers. The South and the Northeast, respectively, experienced more AIDS deaths during these years than other parts of the United States.

AIDS, the final stage of HIV infection, has had a tremendous effect on society. This epidemic has brought a painful, drawn-out process of dying to many, including young adults—an age group previously relatively untouched by death, particularly from infectious disease.

THE STUDY TO UNDERSTAND PROGNOSES AND PREFERENCES FOR OUTCOMES AND RISKS OF TREATMENTS (SUPPORT)

During the twentieth century in the United States, the process of dying shifted from the familiar surroundings of home to the hospital. While hospitalization ensures that the benefits of modern medicine are readily available, many patients dread leaving the comfort of their homes and losing, to some extent, control over their end-of-life decisions.

Between 1989 and 1994, in an effort to "improve end-of-life decision making and reduce the frequency of a mechanically supported, painful, and prolonged process of dying," a group of investigators from various disciplines undertook the largest study of death and dying ever conducted in the United States. The project, known as the Study to Understand Prognoses and Preferences for Outcomes and Risks of Treatments (SUPPORT), included more than nine thousand patients who suffered

TABLE 4.1

Death rates for the 15 leading causes of death, 2003, and percent change, 2002–03

[Death rates on an annual basis per 100,000 population: age-adjusted rates per 100,000 U.S. standard population]

					Age-adjusted death rate				
							Ratio		
			Percent	2003	Percent change				Hispanic to
Rank*	Cause of death	Number	of total deaths	crude death rate	2003	2002 to 2003	Male to female	Black to white	Non-Hispanic white
...	All causes	2,448,288	100.0	841.9	832.7	−1.5	1.4	1.3	0.8
1	Diseases of heart	685,089	28.0	235.6	232.3	−3.5	1.5	1.3	0.8
2	Malignant neoplasms	556,902	22.7	191.5	190.1	−1.8	1.5	1.2	0.7
3	Cerebrovascular diseases	157,689	6.4	54.2	53.5	−4.8	1.0	1.5	0.8
4	Chronic lower respiratory diseases	126,382	5.2	43.5	43.3	−0.5	1.4	0.7	0.4
5	Accidents (unintentional injuries)	109,277	4.5	37.6	37.3	1.1	2.2	1.0	0.8
6	Diabetes mellitus	74,219	3.0	25.5	25.3	−0.4	1.3	2.1	1.6
7	Influenza and pneumonia	65,163	2.7	22.4	22.0	−2.7	1.4	1.1	0.8
8	Alzheimer's disease	63,457	2.6	21.8	21.4	5.9	0.8	0.8	0.6
9	Nephritis, nephrotic syndrome and nephrosis	42,453	1.7	14.6	14.4	1.4	1.4	2.3	1.0
10	Septicemia	34,069	1.4	11.7	11.6	−0.9	1.2	2.3	0.8
11	Intentional self-harm (suicide)	31,484	1.3	10.8	10.8	−0.9	4.3	0.4	0.4
12	Chronic liver disease and cirrhosis	27,503	1.1	9.5	9.3	−1.1	2.2	0.9	1.6
13	Essential (primary) hypertension and hypertensive renal disease	21,940	0.9	7.5	7.4	5.7	1.0	2.8	1.0
14	Parkinson's disease	17,997	0.7	6.2	6.2	5.1	2.2	0.4	0.5
15	Assault (homicide)	17,732	0.7	6.1	6.0	−1.6	3.6	5.7	2.9
...	All other causes (residual)	416,932	17.0	143.4	...	...	...	...	...

... Category not applicable.
*Rank based on number of deaths.

SOURCE: Donna L. Hoyert, et al., "Table 2. Percentage of Total Deaths, Death Rates, Age-Adjusted Death Rates for 2003, Percentage Change in Age-Adjusted Death Rates from 2002 to 2003 and Ratio of Age-Adjusted Death Rates by Race and Sex for the 15 Leading Causes of Death for the Total Population in 2003: United States," in *Deaths: Final Data for 2003, Health E-Stats*, Centers for Disease Control and Prevention, National Center for Health Statistics, January 19, 2006, http://www.cdc.gov/nchs/data/hestat/finaldeaths03_tables.pdf#2 (accessed February 27, 2006)

from life-threatening illnesses. Patients enrolled in the study had about a 50% chance of dying within six months.

The researchers published the results of their study in "A Controlled Trial to Improve Care for Seriously Ill Hospitalized Patients" (*Journal of the American Medical Association*, vol. 274, no. 20, November 22/29, 1995). The SUPPORT investigators hypothesized that increased communication between patients and physicians, better understanding of patients' wishes, and the use of computer-based projections of patient survival would result in "earlier treatment decisions, reductions in time spent in undesirable states before death, and reduced resource use."

Phase I of the study was observational. The researchers reviewed patients' medical records and interviewed patients, surrogates (people who make decisions if patients became incompetent), and physicians. Discussions and decisions about life-sustaining measures were observed.

The researchers interviewed patients, families, and surrogates about the patients' thoughts on cardiopulmonary resuscitation (CPR), their perceptions of their quality of life, the frequency and severity of their pain, and their satisfaction with the care provided. The physicians who acknowledged responsibility for the patients' medical decisions were also interviewed to determine their understanding of patients' views on CPR and how patients' wishes influenced their medical care. The surrogates were again interviewed after the patients' deaths.

Problems with End-of-Life Care

Phase I of SUPPORT found a lack of communication between physicians and patients, showed aggressive treatment of dying patients, and revealed a disturbing picture of hospital death. Of the 4,301 patients, 31% expressed a desire that CPR be withheld. But only 47% of physicians reported knowledge of their patients' wishes. About half (49%) of patients who requested not to be resuscitated did not have a do-not-resuscitate (DNR) order in their medical charts. Of the 79% who died with a DNR order, 46% of the orders were written within only two days of death.

The patients' final days in the hospital included an average of eight days in "generally undesirable states"— in an intensive care unit (ICU), receiving artificial respiration, or in a coma. More than a third (38%) stayed ten days in the ICU, while almost half (46%) were mechanically ventilated within three days prior to death. Surrogates reported that 50% of conscious patients complained of moderate or severe pain at least half the time in their last three days.

TABLE 4.2

Death rates, by age, for the 15 leading causes of death, 1999–2003

[Rates on an annual basis per 100,000 population in specified group; age-adjusted rates per 100,000 U.S. standard population. Rates are based on populations enumerated as of April 1 for 2000 and estimated as of July 1 for all other years.]

Cause of death and year	All ages[a]	Under 1 year[b]	1–4 years	5–14 years	15–24 years	25–34 years	35–44 years	45–54 years	55–64 years	65–74 years	75–84 years	85 years and over	Age-adjusted rate
All causes													
2003	841.9	700.0	31.5	17.0	81.5	103.6	201.6	433.2	940.9	2,255.0	5,463.1	14,593.3	832.7
2002	847.3	695.0	31.2	17.4	81.4	103.6	202.9	430.1	952.4	2,314.7	5,556.9	14,828.3	845.3
2001	848.5	683.4	33.3	17.3	80.7	105.2	203.6	428.9	964.6	2,353.3	5,582.4	15,112.8	854.5
2000	854.0	736.7	32.4	18.0	79.9	101.4	198.9	425.6	992.2	2,399.1	5,666.5	15,524.4	869.0
1999	857.0	736.0	34.2	18.6	79.3	102.2	198.0	418.2	1,005.0	2,457.3	5,714.5	15,554.6	875.6
Diseases of heart													
2003	235.6	11.0	1.2	0.6	2.7	8.2	30.7	92.5	233.2	585.0	1,611.1	5,278.4	232.3
2002	241.7	12.4	1.1	0.6	2.5	7.9	30.5	93.7	241.5	615.9	1,677.2	5,466.8	240.8
2001	245.8	11.9	1.5	0.7	2.5	8.0	29.6	92.9	246.2	635.1	1,725.7	5,664.2	247.8
2000	252.6	13.0	1.2	0.7	2.6	7.4	29.2	94.2	261.2	665.6	1,780.3	5,926.1	257.6
1999	259.9	13.8	1.2	0.7	2.8	7.6	30.2	95.7	269.9	701.7	1,849.9	6,063.0	266.5
Malignant neoplasms													
2003	191.5	1.9	2.5	2.6	4.0	9.4	35.0	122.2	343.0	770.3	1,302.5	1,698.2	190.1
2002	193.2	1.8	2.6	2.6	4.3	9.7	35.8	123.8	351.1	792.1	1,311.9	1,723.9	193.5
2001	194.4	1.6	2.7	2.5	4.3	10.1	36.8	126.5	356.5	802.8	1,315.8	1,765.6	196.0
2000	196.5	2.4	2.7	2.5	4.4	9.8	36.6	127.5	366.7	816.3	1,335.6	1,819.4	199.6
1999	197.0	1.8	2.7	2.5	4.5	10.0	37.1	127.6	374.6	827.1	1,331.5	1,805.8	200.8
Cerebrovascular diseases													
2003	54.2	2.5	0.3	0.2	0.5	1.5	5.5	15.0	35.6	112.9	410.7	1,370.1	53.5
2002	56.4	2.9	0.3	0.2	0.4	1.4	5.4	15.1	37.2	120.3	431.0	1,445.9	56.2
2001	57.4	2.7	0.4	0.2	0.5	1.5	5.5	15.1	38.0	123.4	443.9	1,500.2	57.9
2000	59.6	3.3	0.3	0.2	0.5	1.5	5.8	16.0	41.0	128.6	461.3	1,589.2	60.9
1999	60.0	2.7	0.3	0.2	0.5	1.4	5.7	15.2	40.6	130.8	469.8	1,614.8	61.6
Chronic lower respiratory diseases													
2003	43.5	0.8	0.3	0.3	0.5	0.7	2.1	8.7	43.3	163.2	383.0	635.1	43.3
2002	43.3	1.0	0.4	0.3	0.5	0.8	2.2	8.7	42.4	163.0	386.7	637.6	43.5
2001	43.2	1.0	0.3	0.3	0.4	0.7	2.2	8.5	44.1	167.9	379.8	644.7	43.7
2000	43.4	0.9	0.3	0.3	0.5	0.7	2.1	8.6	44.2	169.4	386.1	648.6	44.2
1999	44.5	0.9	0.4	0.3	0.5	0.8	2.0	8.5	47.5	177.2	397.8	646.0	45.4
Accidents (unintentional injuries)													
2003	37.6	23.6	10.9	6.4	37.1	31.5	37.8	38.8	32.9	44.1	101.9	278.9	37.3
2002	37.0	23.5	10.5	6.6	38.0	31.5	37.2	36.6	31.4	44.2	101.3	275.4	36.9
2001	35.7	24.2	11.2	6.9	36.1	29.9	35.4	34.1	30.3	42.8	100.9	276.4	35.7
2000	34.8	23.1	11.9	7.3	36.0	29.5	34.1	32.6	30.9	41.9	95.1	273.5	34.9
1999	35.1	22.3	12.4	7.6	35.3	29.6	33.8	31.8	30.6	44.6	100.5	282.4	35.3

TABLE 4.2

Death rates, by age, for the 15 leading causes of death, 1999–2003 [CONTINUED]

[Rates on an annual basis per 100,000 population in specified group; age-adjusted rates per 100,000 U.S. standard population. Rates are based on populations enumerated as of April 1 for 2000 and estimated as of July 1 for all other years.]

Cause of death and year	All ages[a]	Under 1 year[b]	1–4 years	5–14 years	15–24 years	25–34 years	35–44 years	45–54 years	55–64 years	65–74 years	75–84 years	85 years and over	Age-adjusted rate
Diabetes mellitus													
2003	25.5	d	d	0.1	0.4	1.6	4.6	13.9	38.5	90.8	181.1	317.5	25.3
2002	25.4	d	d	0.1	0.4	1.6	4.8	13.7	37.7	91.4	182.8	320.6	25.4
2001	25.1	d	d	0.1	0.4	1.5	4.3	13.6	37.8	91.4	181.4	321.8	25.3
2000	24.6	d	d	0.1	0.4	1.6	4.3	13.1	37.8	90.7	179.5	319.7	25.0
1999	24.5	d	d	0.1	0.4	1.4	4.3	12.9	38.3	91.8	178.0	317.2	25.0
Influenza and pneumonia													
2003	22.4	8.0	1.0	0.4	0.5	0.9	2.2	5.2	11.2	37.3	151.1	666.1	22.0
2002	22.8	6.5	0.7	0.2	0.4	0.9	2.2	4.8	11.2	37.5	156.9	696.6	22.6
2001	21.8	7.4	0.7	0.2	0.5	0.9	2.2	4.6	10.7	36.3	148.5	685.6	22.0
2000	23.2	7.6	0.7	0.2	0.5	0.9	2.4	4.7	11.9	39.1	160.3	744.1	23.7
1999	22.8	8.4	0.8	0.2	0.5	0.8	2.4	4.6	11.0	37.2	157.0	751.8	23.5
Alzheimer's disease													
2003	21.8	d	d	d	d	d	d	0.2	2.0	20.9	164.4	802.4	21.4
2002	20.4	d	d	d	d	d	d	0.1	1.9	19.7	158.1	752.3	20.2
2001	18.9	d	d	d	d	d	d	0.2	2.1	18.7	147.5	710.3	19.1
2000	17.6	d	d	d	d	d	d	0.2	2.0	18.7	139.6	667.7	18.1
1999	16.0	d	d	d	d	d	d	0.2	1.9	17.4	129.5	601.3	16.5
Nephritis, nephrotic syndrome and nephrosis													
2003	14.6	4.5	d	0.1	0.2	0.7	1.8	4.9	13.6	40.1	109.5	293.1	14.4
2002	14.2	4.3	d	0.1	0.2	0.7	1.7	4.7	13.0	39.2	109.1	288.6	14.2
2001	13.9	3.3	d	0.0	0.2	0.6	1.7	4.6	13.0	40.2	104.2	287.7	14.0
2000	13.2	4.3	d	0.1	0.2	0.6	1.6	4.4	12.8	38.0	100.8	277.8	13.5
1999	12.7	4.4	d	0.1	0.2	0.6	1.6	4.0	12.0	37.1	97.6	268.9	13.0
Septicemia													
2003	11.7	6.9	0.5	0.2	0.4	0.8	2.1	5.3	13.1	32.6	85.0	202.5	11.6
2002	11.7	7.3	0.5	0.2	0.3	0.8	1.9	5.2	12.6	34.7	86.5	203.0	11.7
2001	11.3	7.7	0.7	0.2	0.3	0.7	1.8	5.0	12.3	32.8	82.3	205.9	11.4
2000	11.1	7.2	0.6	0.2	0.3	0.7	1.9	4.9	11.9	31.0	80.4	215.7	11.3
1999	11.0	7.5	0.6	0.2	0.3	0.7	1.8	4.6	11.4	31.2	79.4	220.7	11.3
Intentional self-harm (suicide)													
2003	10.8	…	…	0.6	9.7	12.7	14.9	15.9	13.8	12.7	16.4	16.9	10.8
2002	11.0	…	…	0.6	9.9	12.6	15.3	15.7	13.6	13.5	17.7	18.0	10.9
2001[c]	10.8	…	…	0.7	9.9	12.8	14.7	15.2	13.1	13.3	17.4	17.5	10.7
2000	10.4	…	…	0.7	10.2	12.0	14.5	14.4	12.1	12.5	17.6	19.6	10.4
1999	10.5	…	…	0.6	10.1	12.7	14.3	13.9	12.2	13.4	18.1	19.3	10.5

TABLE 4.2

Death rates, by age, for the 15 leading causes of death, 1999–2003 [CONTINUED]

[Rates on an annual basis per 100,000 population in specified group; age-adjusted rates per 100,000 U.S. standard population. Rates are based on populations enumerated as of April 1 for 2000 and estimated as of July 1 for all other years.]

Cause of death and year	All ages[a]	Under 1 year[b]	1–4 years	5–14 years	15–24 years	25–34 years	35–44 years	45–54 years	55–64 years	65–74 years	75–84 years	85 years and over	Age-adjusted rate
Chronic liver disease and cirrhosis													
2003	9.5	[d]	[d]	[d]	[d]	0.9	6.8	18.3	23.0	29.5	30.0	20.1	9.3
2002	9.5	[d]	[d]	[d]	0.1	0.9	7.0	18.0	22.9	29.4	31.4	21.4	9.4
2001	9.5	[d]	[d]	[d]	0.1	1.0	7.4	18.5	22.7	30.0	30.2	22.2	9.5
2000	9.4	[d]	[d]	[d]	0.1	1.0	7.5	17.7	23.8	29.8	31.0	23.1	9.5
1999	9.4	[d]	[d]	[d]	0.1	1.0	7.3	17.4	23.7	30.6	31.9	23.2	9.6
Essential (primary) hypertension and hypertensive renal disease													
2003	7.5	[d]	[d]	[d]	0.1	0.2	0.8	2.5	6.3	16.9	51.7	188.9	7.4
2002	7.0	[d]	[d]	[d]	0.1	0.2	0.8	2.3	5.7	16.0	48.2	180.4	7.0
2001	6.8	[d]	[d]	[d]	0.1	0.3	0.7	2.4	5.8	15.5	47.7	171.9	6.8
2000	6.4	[d]	[d]	[d]	[d]	0.2	0.8	2.3	5.9	15.1	45.5	162.9	6.5
1999	6.1	[d]	[d]	[d]	[d]	0.2	0.7	2.2	5.5	15.2	43.6	152.1	6.2
Parkinson's disease													
2003	6.2	[d]	[d]	[d]	[d]	[d]	[d]	0.2	1.3	12.7	67.8	138.2	6.2
2002	5.9	[d]	[d]	[d]	[d]	[d]	[d]	0.1	1.2	12.2	63.9	135.2	5.9
2001	5.8	[d]	[d]	[d]	[d]	[d]	[d]	0.1	1.2	11.7	64.6	134.2	5.9
2000	5.6	[d]	[d]	[d]	[d]	[d]	[d]	0.1	1.1	11.5	61.9	131.9	5.7
1999	5.2	[d]	[d]	[d]	[d]	[d]	[d]	0.1	1.0	11.0	58.2	124.4	5.4
Assault (homicide)													
2003	6.1	8.5	2.4	0.8	13.0	11.3	7.0	4.9	2.8	2.4	2.5	2.2	6.0
2002	6.1	7.5	2.7	0.9	12.9	11.2	7.2	4.8	3.2	2.3	2.3	2.1	6.1
2001[c]	7.1	8.2	2.7	0.8	13.3	13.1	9.5	6.3	4.0	2.9	2.5	2.4	7.1
2000	6.0	9.2	2.3	0.9	12.6	10.4	7.1	4.7	3.0	2.4	2.4	2.4	5.9
1999	6.1	8.7	2.5	1.1	12.9	10.5	7.1	4.6	3.0	2.6	2.5	2.4	6.0

Note: ". . ." = Category not applicable.

[a]Figures for age not stated included in "all ages" but not distributed among age groups.

[b]Death rates for "under 1 year" (based on population estimates) differ from infant mortality rates (based on live births).

[c]Figures include September 11, 2001 related deaths for which death certificates were filed as of October 24, 2002.

[d]Figure does not meet standards of reliability or precision.

SOURCE: "Table 9. Death Rates by Age and Age-Adjusted Death Rates for the 15 Leading Causes of Death in 2003: United States, 1999–2003," unpublished table from Centers for Disease Control and Prevention, National Center for Health Statistics, February 27, 2006

TABLE 4.3

Estimated numbers of deaths of persons with AIDS, by year of death and selected characteristics, 2000–04

	Year of death					Cumulative through 2004[a]
	2000	2001	2002	2003	2004	
Age at death (years)						
<13	52	46	32	28	18	5,094
13–14	8	4	11	7	16	266
15–19	41	44	39	43	32	1,055
20–24	167	215	167	175	184	8,808
25–29	710	635	595	569	505	44,516
30–34	1,993	1,744	1,555	1,373	1,157	96,357
35–39	3,346	3,292	3,108	2,969	2,404	116,206
40–44	3,523	3,835	3,726	3,800	3,378	100,633
45–49	3,081	3,121	3,364	3,432	3,016	67,842
50–54	1,966	2,152	2,396	2,524	2,314	39,936
55–59	1,007	1,141	1,228	1,403	1,343	22,452
60–64	593	655	621	726	701	12,946
≥65	652	728	702	801	730	13,004
Race/ethnicity						
White, not Hispanic	5,325	5,194	5,210	5,091	4,316	229,220
Black, not Hispanic	8,605	9,011	8,974	8,950	7,978	201,045
Hispanic	3,025	3,195	3,117	3,537	3,228	93,163
Asian/Pacific Islander	95	100	91	81	82	3,272
American Indian/Alaska Native	66	81	84	73	91	1,578
Transmission category						
Male adult or adolescent						
Male-to-male sexual contact	5,955	6,068	6,016	5,990	5,450	256,053
Injection drug use	4,070	4,074	4,062	4,116	3,308	109,070
Male-to-male sexual contact and injection drug use	1,324	1,366	1,323	1,322	1,180	39,467
Heterosexual contact	1,389	1,528	1,513	1,634	1,548	24,268
Other[b]	195	166	167	160	113	9,843
Subtotal	12,933	13,202	13,080	13,222	11,599	438,701
Female adult or adolescent						
Injection drug use	1,892	1,907	1,977	1,989	1,744	41,178
Heterosexual contact	2,150	2,342	2,331	2,470	2,327	39,576
Other[b]	87	91	91	101	67	4,142
Subtotal	4,129	4,340	4,400	4,560	4,138	84,897
Child (<13 years at diagnosis)						
Perinatal	72	66	59	61	57	4,982
Other[c]	5	3	6	6	4	533
Subtotal	77	69	65	67	61	5,515
Region of residence						
Northeast	5,200	5,130	5,213	5,654	4,019	169,693
Midwest	1,622	1,646	1,623	1,199	1,234	50,333
South	7,078	7,386	7,361	7,839	7,192	181,690
West	2,567	2,683	2,585	2,428	2,540	108,183
U.S. dependencies, possessions, and associated nations	672	766	763	730	814	19,214
Total[d]	**17,139**	**17,611**	**17,544**	**17,849**	**15,798**	**529,113**

Note: These numbers do not represent reported case counts. Rather, these numbers are point estimates, which result from adjustments of reported case counts. The reported case counts are adjusted for reporting delays and for redistribution of cases in persons initially reported without an identified risk factor. The estimates do not include adjustment for incomplete reporting.

[a]Includes persons who died with AIDS, from the beginning of the epidemic through 2004.

[b]Includes hemophilia, blood transfusion, perinatal, and risk factor not reported or not identified.

[c]Includes hemophilia, blood transfusion, and risk factor not reported or not identified.

[d]Includes persons of unknown race or multiple races and persons of unknown sex. Cumulative total includes 836 persons of unknown race or multiple races. Because column totals were calculated independently of the values for the subpopulations, the values in each column may not sum to the column total.

SOURCE: "Table 7. Estimated Numbers of Deaths of Persons with AIDS, by Year of Death and Selected Characteristics, 2000–2004—United States," in *HIV/AIDS Surveillance Report: Cases of HIV Infection and AIDS in the United States, 2004*, vol. 16, November 2005, http://www.cdc.gov/hiv/stats/2004SurveillanceReport.pdf (accessed November 17, 2005)

Phase II: Intervention to Improve Care

Phase II of SUPPORT was implemented to address the shortcomings documented in Phase I. It tested an intervention delivered by experienced nurses and lasted another two years, involving patient participants with characteristics similar to those in Phase I. This time, however, the doctors were given printed reports about the patients and their wishes regarding life-sustaining treatments. SUPPORT nurses facilitated the flow of information among patients, families, and health care personnel, and helped manage patients' pain. To determine if the intervention worked in addressing problems in the care of seriously ill hospitalized patients at medical centers, researchers measured outcomes on five quantitative outcomes: incidence and timing of DNR orders; patient-physician agreement on CPR preferences; days in an intensive care unit in a comatose condition or receiving mechanical ventilation; pain; and hospital resource use.

RESULTS OF PHASE II. The SUPPORT intervention failed to produce changes in the outcomes that were measured (Patricia A. Murphy et al, "Under the Radar: Contributions of the SUPPORT Nurses," *Nursing Outlook*, vol. 49, no. 5, September/October 2001). Bernard Lo ("Improving Care Near the End of Life: Why Is It So Hard?," *Journal of the American Medical Association*, vol. 274, no. 20, November 22/29, 1995) believes that the results reported in the SUPPORT study raise more questions than answers. Among other issues, Lo claims that while Phase I showed poor doctor-patient communication, Phase II, instead of directly addressing this shortcoming, added a third party, the SUPPORT nurses, to do the physicians' job.

Patricia Murphy and her colleagues note that their analysis of SUPPORT nurses' narratives suggests, however, that the nurses made a difference during the intervention in ways that were not acknowledged by the measurement of the five quantitative outcomes. The nurses supported patients and their families, brought them information, and helped them interpret it. They note that many of the nurses' narratives suggest that effective communication is a precondition of patient or family readiness "to hear a grave prognosis, engage in serious decision making, or 'let go' of a loved one."

B. A. Ditillo in "The Emergence of Palliative Care: A New Specialized Field of Medicine Requiring an Interdisciplinary Approach" (*Critical Care Nursing Clinics of North America*, vol. 14, no. 2, June 2002) suggests that the movement in the United States to improve end-of-life care (the palliative care movement) is a result of the SUPPORT study. Ditillo notes that "the delivery of effective palliative care requires an interdisciplinary team approach in order to meet the complex needs of patients and families." These complex needs include help in understanding various life-sustaining treatments and support to decide whether to accept or refuse such treatments at the end of life.

LIFE-SUSTAINING TREATMENTS

Life-sustaining treatments, also called life support, can take over many functions of an ailing body. Under normal conditions, when a patient suffers from a treatable illness, life support is a temporary measure used only until the body can function on its own. The ongoing debate about prolonging life-sustaining treatments concerns the incurably ill and permanently unconscious.

Cardiopulmonary Resuscitation

Cardiopulmonary resuscitation (CPR) is composed of two basic life-support skills administered in the event of cardiac or respiratory arrest: artificial circulation and artificial respiration. Cardiac arrest may be caused by a heart attack, which is an interruption of blood flow to the heart muscle. A coronary artery clogged with an accumulation of fatty deposits is a common cause of interrupted blood flow to the heart. Respiratory arrest, on the other hand, may be the result of an accident such as drowning, or the final stages of a pulmonary disease such as emphysema.

In CPR artificial circulation is accomplished by compressing the chest rhythmically to cause blood to flow sufficiently to give a person a chance for survival. Artificial respiration is accomplished by breathing into the victim's nose and mouth. It is important that CPR be done properly, or it may not be effective and may harm the victim. Heath care professionals may go beyond typical CPR procedures and deliver oxygen directly into the lungs through a tube inserted down the trachea (windpipe). Rarely, a tracheotomy is performed. In this procedure an opening is made in the windpipe through which a breathing tube is inserted. Electrical shock and medication may also be used to "jump start" the heart.

CPR, initially intended for healthy individuals who unexpectedly suffered heart stoppage, is now widely used in a variety of circumstances. While CPR does not always work (it has a 20–50% success rate in healthy people), it does help save lives. Generally, following CPR, healthy people eventually resume normal lives. The outcome is quite different, however, for patients in the final stages of a terminal illness. Nancy Dubler and David Nimmons (*Ethics on Call*, New York: Harmony Books, 1992) observe that for people with a terminal disease, dying after being "successfully" resuscitated virtually ensures a slower, harder, more painful death.

REFUSAL OF CPR WITH A DO-NOT-RESUSCITATE ORDER. A person not wishing to be resuscitated in case of cardiac or respiratory arrest may ask a physician to write a DNR order on his or her chart. This written order instructs health care personnel not to initiate CPR, which can be very important because CPR is usually performed in an emergency. Even if a patient's living will includes refusal of CPR, emergency personnel rushing to a patient have no time to check the living will. A DNR order on a patient's chart is more accessible.

NONHOSPITAL DNR ORDERS. Most hospitals have policies governing DNR orders in the event a patient has no advance directives refusing CPR. (An advance directive is a written document stating how you want medical decisions to be made if you lose the ability to

FIGURE 4.1

State laws governing nonhospital do-not-resuscitate (DNR) orders, 2004

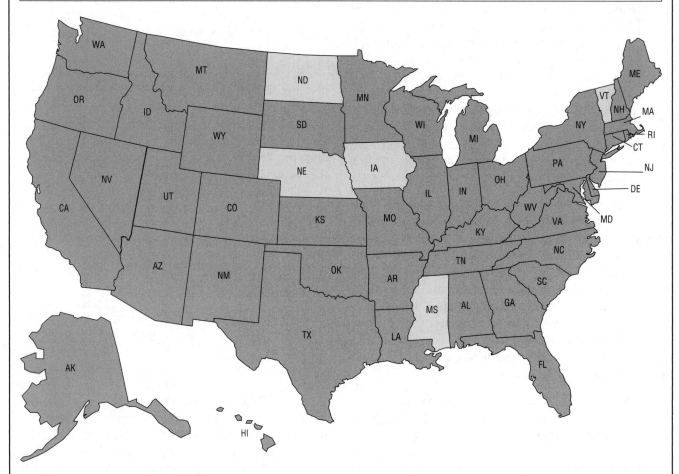

☐ States with statutes or protocols authorizing nonhospital DNR orders (the District of Columbia and 45 states: Alabama*, Alaska, Arizona, Arkansas, California, Colorado, Connecticut, Delaware, Florida, Georgia, Hawaii, Idaho, Illinois, Indiana, Kansas, Kentucky, Louisiana, Maine*, Maryland, Massachusetts*, Minnesota*, Michigan, Missouri*, Montana, Nevada, New Hampshire, New Jersey*, New Mexico, New York, North Carolina, Ohio, Oklahoma, Oregon*, Pennsylvania, Rhode Island, South Carolina, South Dakota*, Tennessee, Texas, Utah, Virginia, Washington, West Virginia, Wisconsin and Wyoming).

☐ Jurisdictions without statutes or protocols authorizing nonhospital DNR orders (5 states: Iowa, Mississippi, Nebraska, North Dakota, and Vermont).

*States that have not enacted nonhospital DNR statutes but have regulations; or local or state-wide protocols adopted by government agencies or by private, professional organizations that regulate nonhospital DNR orders.

Note: This map refers to statutes that address DNR orders in the nonhospital setting only. Some of these statutes explicitly apply also to inpatient situations. However, most hospitals already have institutional policies regarding DNR orders, in compliance with the accreditation standards of the Joint Commission on Accreditation of Health Care Organizations.

SOURCE: "State Laws and Protocols Governing Nonhospital Do-Not-Resuscitate (DNR) Orders," in *End-of-Life Law Digest*, The National Hospice and Palliative Care Organization, 2004

make those decisions for yourself.) Outside the hospital setting, such as at home, people who do not want CPR performed in case of an emergency can request a nonhospital DNR order from their physicians. (See Figure 4.1 for a map of the United States showing states that had laws authorizing nonhospital DNR orders as of January 2004.) Also called a pre-hospital DNR order, it instructs emergency medical personnel to withhold CPR. The DNR order may be on a bracelet, necklace, or a wallet card. However, laypersons performing CPR on an individual with a nonhospital DNR order cannot be prosecuted by the law.

Mechanical Ventilation

When a patient's lungs are not functioning properly, a ventilator, or respirator, breathes for the patient. Oxygen is supplied to the lungs through a tube inserted through the mouth or nose into the windpipe. Mechanical ventilation is generally used to temporarily maintain normal breathing in those who have been in serious accidents or who suffer from a serious illness, such as pneumonia.

Today, a person who suffers cardiac or respiratory arrest is attached to a respirator after CPR has restarted the heart. In some cases, if the patient needs ventilation indefinitely, the physician might perform a tracheotomy to open a hole in the neck for placement of the breathing tube in the windpipe. Even if a patient has irreversible brain damage, as long as the brain stem is functioning, the person is considered alive and the mechanical respirator cannot be withdrawn.

Ventilators are also used on terminally ill patients. In these cases the machine keeps the patient breathing but does nothing to cure the disease. Those preparing a living will are advised to give clear instructions about their desires regarding continued use of an artificial respirator that could prolong the process of dying.

Artificial Nutrition and Hydration

Artificial nutrition and hydration (ANH) is another modern-day technology that has further complicated the dying process. Today, nutrients and fluids supplied intravenously or through a stomach or intestinal tube can indefinitely sustain the nutritional and hydration needs of comatose and terminally ill patients. ANH has a strong emotional impact because it relates to basic sustenance. In addition, the symbolism of feeding can be so powerful that families who know that their loved one would not want to be kept alive may still feel that not feeding is wrong. However, appetite loss is common in dying patients and is not a significant contributor to their suffering. As discussed in "Artificial Nutrition and Hydration and End-of-Life Decision Making" (National Hospice and Palliative Care Organization, 2005, http://www.caringinfo.org/files/public/QA_artificial_Nutrition_booklet.pdf), the withdrawal of ANH from a dying patient does not lead to a long and painful death. Moreover, evidence exists that avoiding ANH contributes to a more comfortable death.

ANH has traditionally been used in end-of-life care when patients experience a loss of appetite and difficulty swallowing. Health care practitioners use ANH to prolong life, prevent aspiration pneumonia (inflammation of the lungs due to inhaling food particles or fluid), maintain independence and physical function, and decrease suffering and discomfort. However, artificial nutrition and hydration do not always accomplish these goals, as noted in the Hospice and Palliative Nurses Association (HPNA) position paper "Artificial Nutrition and Hydration in End-of-Life Care" (*Home Healthcare Nurse*, vol. 22, no. 5, May 2004). The position paper points out that results of studies "show that tube feeding does not appear to prolong life in most patients with life-limiting, progressive diseases; moreover, complications from tube placement may increase mortality. Furthermore, artificially delivered nutrition does not protect against aspiration and in some patient populations may actually increase the risk of aspiration and its complications."

The American Dietetic Association (ADA) has taken the formal position that "the development of clinical and ethical criteria for the nutrition and hydration of persons through the life span should be established by members of the health care team. Registered dietitians should work collaboratively to make nutrition, hydration, and feeding recommendations in individual cases" ("Position of the American Dietetic Association: Ethical and Legal Issues in Nutrition, Hydration, and Feeding," *Journal of the American Dietetic Association*, vol. 102, no. 5, May 2002). The ADA suggests that the patient should determine the extent of his or her nutrition and hydration, and that shared decision making should occur between health care professionals and the family when the patient cannot make such decisions.

Kidney Dialysis

Kidney dialysis is a medical procedure by which a machine takes over the function of the kidneys in removing waste products from the blood. Dialysis can be used when an illness or injury temporarily impairs kidney function. It may also be used by patients with irreversibly damaged kidneys awaiting organ transplantation.

Kidney failure may also occur as an end-stage of a terminal illness. While dialysis may cleanse the body of waste products, it cannot cure the disease. People who wish to let their illness take its course may refuse dialysis. They will eventually lapse into a coma and die.

DISORDERS OF CONSCIOUSNESS

A coma is a deep state of unconsciousness caused by damage to the brain, often from illness or trauma. Most people in a coma recover within a few days, but some do not. Figure 4.2 shows the possible outcomes for those who do not recover from a coma quickly. For some, their brain dies. That is, they irreversibly lose all cerebral and brainstem function. Table 2.1 in Chapter 2 lists the clinical criteria for brain death.

More typically, patients who do not recover quickly from a coma progress to a vegetative state. Those in a vegetative state for one month are then referred to as being in a persistent vegetative state (PVS), and after a longer period (see Figure 4.2) are referred to as being in a permanent vegetative state. "Permanent" implies no chance of recovery.

Table 2.2 in Chapter 2 lists the criteria for the diagnosis of a persistent vegetative state. As Table 2.2 shows, patients in a PVS are unaware of themselves or their environment. They do not respond to stimuli, understand language, or have control of bowel and bladder functions. They are intermittently awake but are not conscious—a condition often referred to as "eyes open unconsciousness."

FIGURE 4.2

Flow chart of cerebral insult and coma

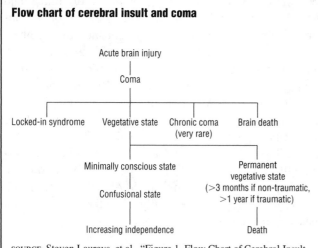

SOURCE: Steven Laureys, et al., "Figure 1. Flow Chart of Cerebral Insult and Coma," in "Brain Function in Coma, Vegetative State, and Related Disorders," *The Lancet Neurology*, vol. 3, no. 9, September 2004, pp. 537–46, © 2004 with permission from Elsevier

TABLE 4.4

Criteria for a minimally conscious state (MCS)

To diagnose a minimally conscious state, limited but clearly discernible evidence of self- or environmental awareness must be demonstrated on a reproducible or sustained basis by one or more of the following behaviors

1. Follows simple commands
2. Gestural or verbal yes/no responses (regardless of accuracy)
3. Intelligible verbalization
4. Purposeful behavior, including movements or affective behaviors that occur in contingent relationship to relevant environmental stimuli and are not due to reflexive activity. Some examples of qualifying purposeful behavior are
    Appropriate smiling or crying in response to the linguistic or visual content of emotional but not to neutral topics or stimuli
    Vocalizations or gestures that occur in direct response to the linguistic content of questions
    Reaching for objects that demonstrates a clear relationship between object location and direction of reach
    Touching or holding objects in a manner that accommodates the size and shape of the object
    Pursuit eye movement of sustained fixation that occurs in direct response to moving or salient stimuli

SOURCE: Eelco F.M. Wijdicks and Ronald E. Cranford, "Table 2. Criteria for a Minimally Conscious State," in "Clinical Diagnosis of Prolonged States of Impaired Consciousness in Adults," *Mayo Clinic Proceedings*, vol. 80, no. 8, August 2005

Some patients in a PVS may recover further to regain partial consciousness. This condition is called a minimally conscious state (MCS). Table 4.4 lists the criteria for a minimally conscious state. Partial consciousness (MCS) means that perception is severely altered, but the patient shows an awareness of self or the environment and exhibits behaviors such as following simple commands and smiling or crying at appropriate times. Some patients emerge from a MCS and some remain in a minimally conscious state permanently.

Another disorder of consciousness that rarely occurs after a coma is locked-in syndrome. The patient with locked-in syndrome has full consciousness, but all the voluntary muscles of the body are paralyzed except (usually) for those that control vertical eye movement and blinking. Persons with locked-in syndrome communicate primarily with eye or eyelid movements.

Treatment of PVS Patients

In "The Vegetative and Minimally Conscious States: Consensus-Based Criteria for Establishing Diagnosis and Prognosis" (*Neurorehabilitation*, vol. 19, no. 4, 2004), Joseph T. Giacino discusses implications for treatment of patients in both a vegetative and a minimally conscious state. He notes that early interventions should focus on maintaining the patient's physical health and preventing complications. Standard interventions include stretching exercises, skin care, nutritional supplementation, and pain management. In minimally conscious patients, functional communication systems and interaction should be established. If the patient does not improve and the criteria for permanence of the condition are met, decisions must be made concerning changes in the level of care and whether life-sustaining treatment should be withdrawn.

At this time professionals having expertise in the evaluation and management of patients with disorders of consciousness should be consulted to determine an appropriate course of action.

Chances of Recovery

Giacino summarizes the consensus opinion of the major professional organizations in neurorehabilitation and neurology concerning, among other things, the prognosis of patients in a vegetative state (VS). The article notes that the probability of recovery of consciousness from a vegetative state depends on the length of time a patient has been in this condition and whether it was brought on by traumatic injuries or by non-traumatic causes.

After three months in a vegetative state, the probability of recovering from a trauma-induced VS is approximately 35% and from a non-trauma-induced VS is 10%. Of the 35% who will recover from a trauma-induced VS, about 20% will still have severe disabilities at one year post-injury while the remaining 15% will have moderate to good outcomes.

Of those persons with trauma-induced VS who do not begin recovery by three months, 35% will die and the other 30% will remain in a VS at one year post-injury. Of those alive at six months, approximately 30% will die, 50% will remain in a VS, and 15% will recover consciousness by twelve months.

Of those people with non-trauma-induced VS who do not begin recovery by three months, approximately half will die during the next nine months and the other half will remain in a VS. No cases of recovery after six months in a non-trauma-induced VS have been documented.

ORGAN TRANSPLANTATION

Most organ and tissue donations are from people who have died as a result of brain injury and subsequent brain death. Once death is pronounced, the body is kept on mechanical support (if possible) to maintain the organs until it is determined whether the person will be a donor.

There are some organ and tissue donations that can come from living people. For example, it is possible to lead a healthy life with only one of the two kidneys that humans are born with, so people with two health kidneys will sometimes donate one to someone in need. Portions of the liver, lungs, and pancreas have also been transplanted out of a living donor, but this is less common. In most cases, living donors make their donations to help a family member or close friend.

Organ transplantation has come a long way since the first kidney was transplanted from one identical twin to another in 1954. The introduction in 1983 of cyclosporine, an immunosuppressant drug that helps prevent the body's immune system from rejecting a donated organ, made it possible to successfully transplant a variety of organs and tissues.

Figure 4.3 and Figure 4.4 show the organs and tissues transplantable with today's immunosuppressant drugs and technologies. The organs that may be transplanted from people who have died are the heart, intestines, kidneys, liver, lungs, and pancreas. Tissues that may be harvested for transfer include bone, cartilage, cornea, heart valves, pancreas islet cells, skin, tendons, and veins. Living persons may donate a kidney, parts of a lung or liver, or bone marrow. Typically, donated organs must be transplanted within six to forty-eight hours of harvest, while some tissue may be stored for future use.

Soon after organ transplantation began, the demand for donor organs exceeded the supply. In 1984 Congress passed the National Organ Transplant Act (PL 98–507) in order to create "a centralized network to match scarce donated organs with critically ill patients." (See Figure 4.5 for the process of matching organ donors and recipients.) Today, organ transplant is an accepted medical treatment for end-stage illnesses.

The United Network for Organ Sharing (UNOS), a private company under contract with the Division of Transplantation of the Department of Health and Human Services (HHS), manages the national transplant waiting list. It maintains data on all clinical organ transplants and distributes organ donor cards. (See Figure 4.6.) UNOS reported that 89,811 people were waiting for a transplant in the United States as of November 2005. In 2003, 7,147 people died while awaiting a transplant because donor organs were not available for them.

Table 4.5 shows the waiting list for organs at the end of the year, from 1994 through 2003. "Total

FIGURE 4.3

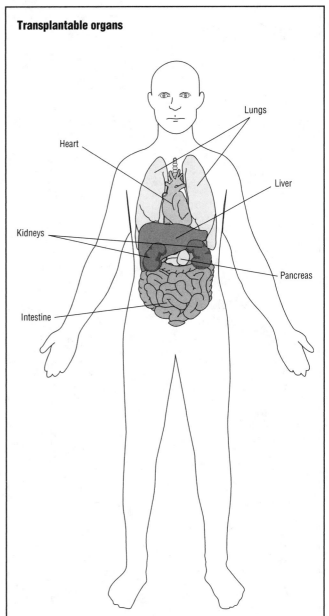

Transplantable organs

SOURCE: "3.1. Background: Transplantable Organs," in *Decision: Donation*, U.S. Department of Health and Human Services, Health Resources and Services Administration, Healthcare Systems Bureau, Division of Transplantation, 2004, http://www.organdonor.gov/student/docs/OrganDonorAllPages.pdf (accessed November 9, 2005)

registrations" refers to all the registrations from all transplant centers for all organs. Therefore, this figure is larger than "total patients," which is the number of patients waiting for a transplant. An individual may show up as more than one registration in the "registrations" category because that individual may be registered at more than one transplant center or for more than one organ. However, individuals waiting for transplants are counted only once in the "total patients" category, but they may show up more than once in the listing of organ types under that heading if they need more than one organ.

FIGURE 4.4

Transplantable tissues

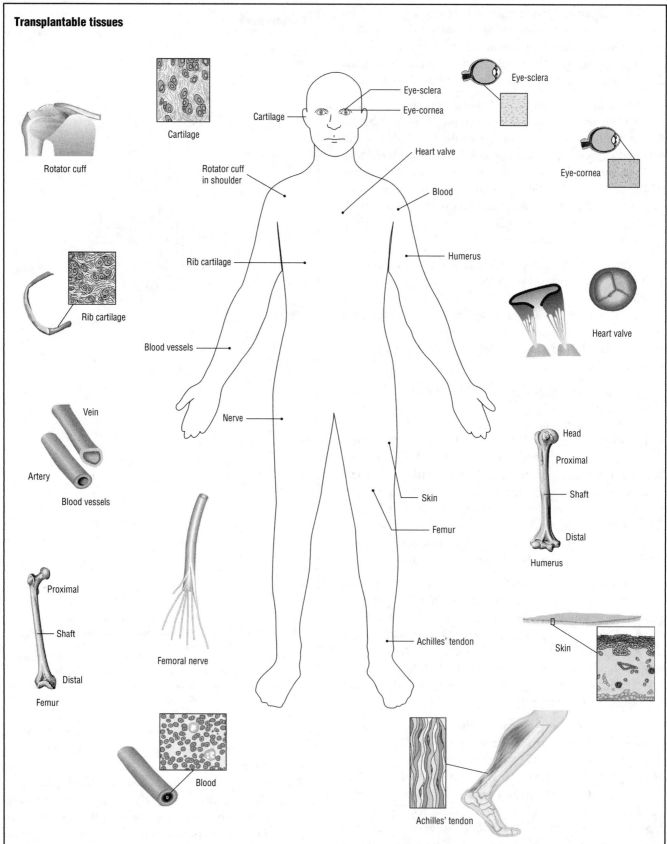

SOURCE: "3.2. Background: Transplantable Tissues," in *Decision: Donation*, U.S. Department of Health and Human Services, Healthcare Systems Bureau, Division of Transplantation, 2004, http://www.organdonor.gov/student/docs/OrganDonorAllPages.pdf (accessed November 9, 2005)

FIGURE 4.5

Matching donors and recipients: The Organ Procurement & Transplantation Network (OPTN) and the Scientific Registry of Transplant Recipients (SRTR)

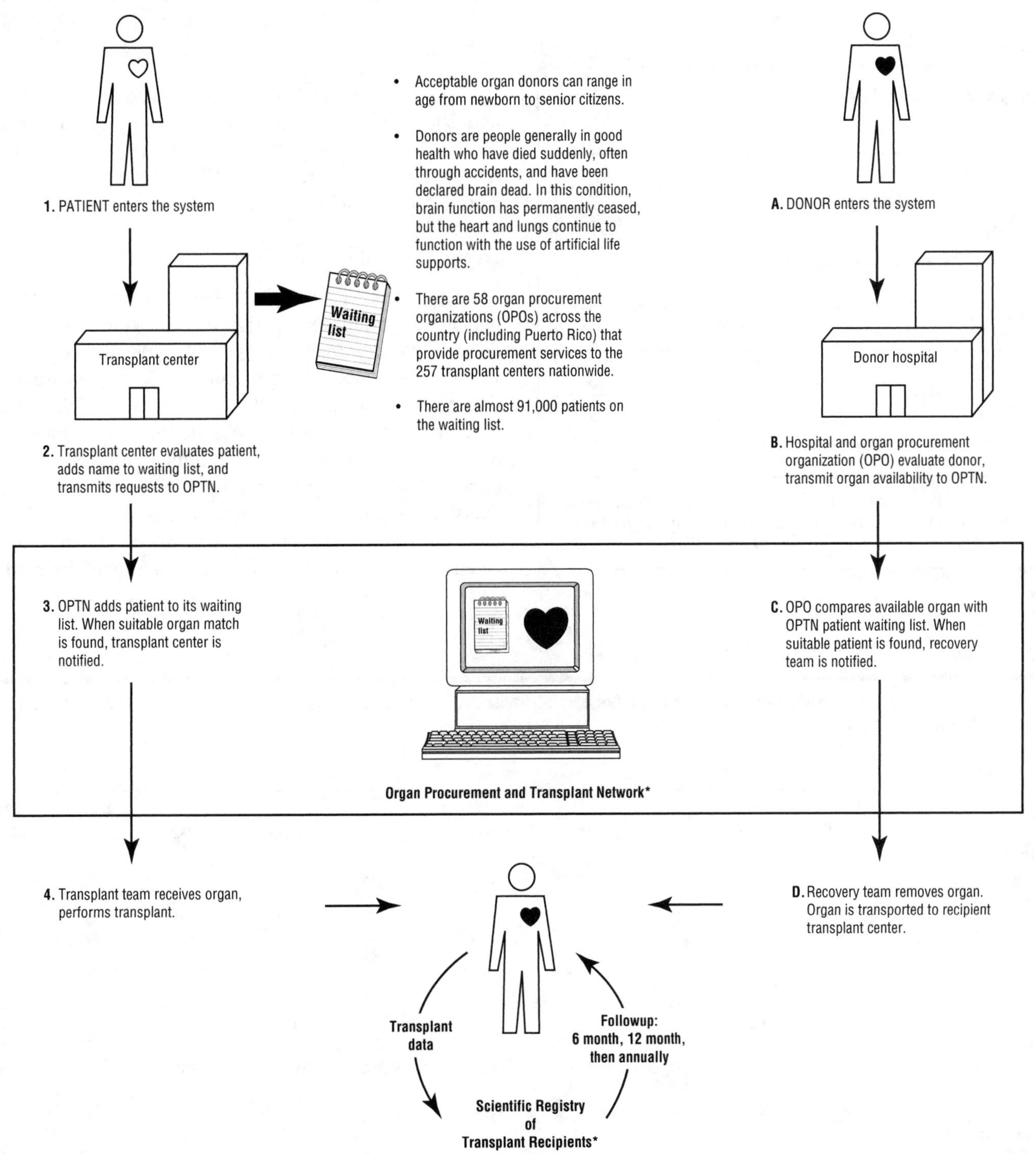

1. PATIENT enters the system

- Acceptable organ donors can range in age from newborn to senior citizens.

- Donors are people generally in good health who have died suddenly, often through accidents, and have been declared brain dead. In this condition, brain function has permanently ceased, but the heart and lungs continue to function with the use of artificial life supports.

- There are 58 organ procurement organizations (OPOs) across the country (including Puerto Rico) that provide procurement services to the 257 transplant centers nationwide.

- There are almost 91,000 patients on the waiting list.

A. DONOR enters the system

Transplant center

Waiting list

Donor hospital

2. Transplant center evaluates patient, adds name to waiting list, and transmits requests to OPTN.

B. Hospital and organ procurement organization (OPO) evaluate donor, transmit organ availability to OPTN.

3. OPTN adds patient to its waiting list. When suitable organ match is found, transplant center is notified.

Waiting list

C. OPO compares available organ with OPTN patient waiting list. When suitable patient is found, recovery team is notified.

Organ Procurement and Transplant Network*

4. Transplant team receives organ, performs transplant.

D. Recovery team removes organ. Organ is transported to recipient transplant center.

Transplant data

Followup: 6 month, 12 month, then annually

Scientific Registry of Transplant Recipients*

*Operated by the United Network for Organ Sharing (UNOS), Richmond, VA, under contract with the U.S. Department of Health and Human Services, Health Resources and Services Administration, Division of Transplantation.

SOURCE: *Questions and Answers about Organ Donation*, U.S. Department of Health and Human Services, Health Resources and Services Administration, Division of Transplantation, n.d. Data updated as of October 2005.

In 2003, 59.2% of all organs transplanted were kidneys, up slightly from 58.4% in 2000. Of the remainder, 21.4% were livers, up from 20.9% in 2000; 8.1% were hearts, down from 9.4% in 2000; 4.3% were lungs, nearly identical to 2000; nearly 0.5% were pancreas transplants alone, slightly less than in 2000; and only 0.2% were intestines, up from 0.1% in 2000. The remaining were multi-organ procedures, for a total of 25,076 transplants in 2003, up from 22,967 in 2000 and 18,172 in 1994. (See Table 4.6.)

The number of all donors rose 62% between 1994 and 2003, from 8,201 to 13,275. While the number of deceased donors increased 27%, from 5,099 to 6,455, living donors showed a significant increase of 120%, from 3,102 to 6,820. (See Table 4.7.)

Organ Donation

The Uniform Anatomical Gift Act of 1968 gives a person the opportunity to sign a donor card indicating a desire to donate organs or tissue after death. People who wish to be donors should complete a donor card (see Figure 4.6), which should be carried at all times. Alternatively, the wish to be a donor can be indicated on a driver's license or in a living will. Prospective donors should inform their family and physician of their decision. At the time of death, hospitals always ask for the family's consent, even if a donor has already indicated his or her wish to donate organs. Should the family

FIGURE 4.6

Organ/tissue donor card

Donate Life

Organ/Tissue Donor Card

I wish to donate my organs and tissues. I wish to give:

☐ any needed organs and tissues ☐ only the following organs and tissues:

____

Donor Signature ____________________ Date __________

Witness ______________________________

Witness ______________________________

SOURCE: U.S. Department of Health and Human Services, Healthcare Systems Bureau, Division of Transplantation, http://www.organdonor.gov/newdonorcard.pdf (accessed November 9, 2005)

TABLE 4.5

United Network for Organ Sharing (UNOS) and Scientific Registry of Transplant Recipients (SRTR) national patient waiting list for organ transplant, end of year, 1994–2003

	Year									
	1994	1995	1996	1997	1998	1999	2000	2001	2002	2003
Total registrations	**37,252**	**43,240**	**49,295**	**55,522**	**62,360**	**68,200**	**74,861**	**80,332**	**82,152**	**86,355**
Organ type										
Kidney	27,196	30,565	33,968	37,392	40,863	43,683	47,299	50,458	53,392	57,211
Pancreas transplant alone	166	183	204	225	278	248	313	391	406	455
Pancreas after kidney	89	137	159	157	186	283	460	685	796	935
Kidney-pancreas	1,015	1,166	1,377	1,530	1,756	2,136	2,453	2,476	2,514	2,472
Liver	3,993	5,576	7,346	9,438	11,744	14,183	16,448	18,285	17,122	17,515
Intestine	73	82	81	92	97	107	143	171	185	175
Heart	2,894	3,421	3,644	3,824	4,081	3,956	3,973	3,925	3,775	3,529
Lung	1,623	1,906	2,277	2,632	3,102	3,376	3,568	3,732	3,765	3,874
Heart-Lung	203	204	239	232	253	228	204	209	197	189
Total patients	**35,751**	**41,592**	**47,456**	**53,445**	**59,947**	**65,362**	**71,752**	**77,065**	**78,781**	**82,885**
Organ type										
Kidney	25,827	29,046	32,298	35,569	38,765	41,253	44,665	47,717	50,535	54,231
Pancreas transplant alone	164	181	201	221	272	246	312	383	403	452
Pancreas after kidney	89	136	155	153	182	280	456	674	784	925
Kidney-pancreas	989	1,145	1,351	1,492	1,697	2,051	2,366	2,371	2,412	2,390
Liver	3,955	5,526	7,261	9,297	11,562	13,958	16,133	17,953	16,790	17,171
Intestine	71	82	81	89	95	107	141	168	183	172
Heart	2,885	3,413	3,635	3,810	4,066	3,933	3,957	3,905	3,760	3,519
Lung	1,570	1,861	2,237	2,586	3,058	3,311	3,520	3,685	3,717	3,836
Heart-Lung	201	202	237	228	250	223	202	209	197	189

SOURCE: "Table 1.3. Waiting List at End of Year, 1994 to 2003," in *2004 OPTN/SRTR Annual Report 1994–2003*, Department of Health and Human Services, Health Resources and Services Administration, Healthcare Systems Bureau, Division of Transplantation, February 7, 2005, http://www.optn.org/AR2004/default.htm (accessed November 2, 2005)

TABLE 4.6

United Network for Organ Sharing (UNOS) and Scientific Registry of Transplant Recipients (SRTR) transplants, by organ and donor type, 1994–2003

					Year					
Organ/donor type	1994	1995	1996	1997	1998	1999	2000	2001	2002	2003
All organs										
Total	18,172	19,260	19,556	20,090	21,299	21,803	22,967	23,918	24,548	25,076
Deceased	15,085	15,790	15,794	16,049	16,766	16,817	17,094	17,360	17,936	18,270
Living	3,087	3,470	3,762	4,041	4,533	4,986	5,873	6,558	6,612	6,806
Kidney										
Total	10,540	10,980	11,255	11,557	12,298	12,612	13,407	14,076	14,524	14,853
Deceased	7,533	7,597	7,593	7,632	7,890	7,915	7,958	8,065	8,288	8,389
Living	3,007	3,383	3,662	3,925	4,408	4,697	5,449	6,011	6,236	6,464
Pancreas transplant alone										
Total	38	37	45	64	72	123	119	128	140	117
Deceased	38	36	45	64	72	123	118	127	139	117
Living	*	1	*	*	*	*	1	1	1	*
Pancreas after kidney										
Total	54	67	113	130	157	221	303	306	376	343
Deceased	54	67	112	130	157	221	303	306	376	343
Living	*	*	1	*	*	*	*	*	*	*
Kidney/pancreas										
Total	748	916	857	847	969	939	913	889	902	868
Deceased	746	910	847	841	967	931	907	886	902	865
Living	2	6	10	6	2	8	6	3	*	3
Liver										
Total	3,548	3,829	3,930	4,015	4,369	4,605	4,802	4,984	5,060	5,364
Deceased	3,488	3,775	3,868	3,929	4,277	4,354	4,407	4,466	4,699	5,044
Living	60	54	62	86	92	251	395	518	361	320
Intestine										
Total	6	22	15	23	28	31	30	42	42	52
Deceased	6	21	13	21	26	29	27	42	41	48
Living	*	1	2	2	2	2	3	*	1	4
Heart										
Total	2,321	2,346	2,319	2,267	2,310	2,157	2,167	2,171	2,112	2,024
Deceased	2,318	2,346	2,318	2,267	2,310	2,157	2,167	2,171	2,112	2,024
Living	3	*	1	*	*	*	*	*	*	*
Lung										
Total	722	871	812	930	866	891	959	1,059	1,041	1,080
Deceased	707	846	788	908	837	863	940	1,034	1,028	1,065
Living	15	25	24	22	29	28	19	25	13	15
Heart-lung										
Total	71	69	38	62	46	51	46	27	31	28
Deceased	71	69	38	62	46	51	46	27	31	28
Living	*	*	*	*	*	*	*	*	*	*
Multi-organ										
Total	124	123	172	195	184	173	221	236	320	347
Deceased	124	123	172	195	184	173	221	236	320	347
Living	*	*	*	*	*	*	*	*	*	*

*None in category.
Notes: An organ that is divided into segments (liver, lung, pancreas, intestine) is counted once per transplant. Kidney-pancreas and heart-lung transplants are counted as one transplant. Other multiple organ transplants are counted only in the multiple organ row.

SOURCE: "Table 1.7. Transplants by Organ and Donor Type, 1994 to 2003," in *2004 OPTN/SRTR Annual Report 1994–2003*, Department of Health and Human Services, Health Resources and Services Administration, Healthcare Systems Bureau, Division of Transplantation, February 7, 2005, http://www.optn.org/AR2004/default.htm (accessed November 2, 2005)

refuse, the doctors will not take the organs, despite the deceased's wish. In 2003 most organ donors whose cause of death was known died of a stroke (42.7%) or head trauma (40.5%). Anoxia (lack of oxygen) was the cause of death of 13.2% of organ donors. (See Table 4.8.)

In 1986 the Consolidated Omnibus Budget Reconciliation Act (PL 99–509) required all hospitals receiving federal funding to adopt procedures to identify potential organ donors and notify families of their option to donate. In June 1998 the government transferred this

TABLE 4.7

United Network for Organ Sharing (UNOS) and Scientific Registry of Transplant Recipients (SRTR) organ donors, by organ and donor type, 1994–2003

	Year									
	1994	1995	1996	1997	1998	1999	2000	2001	2002	2003
All organs										
Total	8,201	8,854	9,200	9,534	10,352	10,837	11,875	12,662	12,811	13,275
Deceased	5,099	5,363	5,418	5,479	5,794	5,824	5,985	6,080	6,187	6,455
Living	3,102	3,491	3,782	4,055	4,558	5,013	5,890	6,582	6,624	6,820
Kidney										
Total	7,806	8,393	8,709	9,014	9,749	10,090	10,944	11,542	11,872	12,221
Deceased	4,797	5,003	5,038	5,083	5,338	5,386	5,489	5,528	5,636	5,754
Living	3,009	3,390	3,671	3,931	4,411	4,704	5,455	6,014	6,236	6,467
Pancreas										
Total	1,362	1,296	1,302	1,328	1,464	1,636	1,710	1,822	1,873	1,777
Deceased	1,360	1,289	1,291	1,322	1,462	1,628	1,703	1,818	1,872	1,774
Living	2	7	11	6	2	8	7	4	1	3
Liver										
Total	4,153	4,390	4,525	4,685	4,936	5,198	5,392	5,624	5,654	6,000
Deceased	4,093	4,336	4,463	4,599	4,844	4,947	4,997	5,106	5,293	5,680
Living	60	54	62	86	92	251	395	518	361	320
Intestine										
Total	62	123	50	74	80	98	90	115	113	126
Deceased	62	122	48	72	78	96	87	115	112	122
Living	*	1	2	2	2	2	3	*	1	4
Heart										
Total	2,528	2,491	2,463	2,426	2,449	2,316	2,283	2,276	2,222	2,121
Deceased	2,525	2,491	2,462	2,426	2,449	2,316	2,283	2,276	2,222	2,121
Living	3	*	1	*	*	*	*	*	*	*
Lung										
Total	948	901	802	872	817	834	861	936	945	991
Deceased	918	856	757	836	764	778	825	887	920	962
Living	30	45	45	36	53	56	36	49	25	29
Donation after cardiac death										
Total	57	64	71	78	75	87	119	169	189	271
Deceased	57	64	71	78	75	87	119	169	189	271

*None in category

Notes: Includes only organs recovered for transplant. The number of transplants using living donors may be different from the number of living donors. This is because there is a small number of multi-organ living donors and multiple donors for one transplant. For example, a living donor might donate a kidney and pancreas segment; or two living donors might each donate a lung lobe for one transplant procedure. A donor of an organ divided into segments (liver, lung, pancreas, intestine) is counted only once for that organ. A donor of multiple organs is counted once for each organ recovered. Donors after cardiac death are included in the deceased donor counts as well and are counted separately on the last line.

SOURCE: "Table 1.1. U.S. Organ Donors by Organ and Donor Type, 1994 to 2003," in *2004 OPTN/SRTR Annual Report 1994–2003*, Department of Health and Human Services, Health Resources and Services Administration, Healthcare Systems Bureau, Division of Transplantation, February 7, 2005, http://www.optn.org/AR2004/default.htm (accessed November 2, 2005)

responsibility from hospitals to local organ procurement organizations because the hospitals were not doing the job well. The HHS estimates that twelve thousand to fifteen thousand potential organ donors die each year whose families are never asked to donate their loved ones' organs. Under the new procedure, hospitals are required to report every death to the procurement organizations.

To promote awareness of organ and tissue donation, Congress in 1997 authorized the Internal Revenue Service (IRS) to include organ and tissue donor information with federal tax refund checks. In another effort to increase public support for organ donation, the U.S. Postal Service introduced a new stamp in 1998 showing two intertwined figures, their hands reaching to touch each other's hearts.

By 2001 demand continued to outpace the supply of available organs and tissues for transplants. Governors of many states began a variety of programs aimed at increasing public awareness of the lack of donor organs and honoring people who have chosen to become donors. For example, Alabama Governor Don Siegelman created an Alabama Donor Registry; Georgia Governor Roy Barnes designated March 2001 as Eye Donor Month; and Utah Governor Michael O. Leavitt and his state's legislature adopted a resolution to improve public awareness about organ and tissue donation. Governors of at least nine states forged partnerships with local advocacy, medical, religious, and business groups to strengthen support for transplant programs.

TABLE 4.8

Deceased organ donor causes of death, 1994–2003, any organ

	Year									
	1994	**1995**	**1996**	**1997**	**1998**	**1999**	**2000**	**2001**	**2002**	**2003**
Total	**5,099**	**5,363**	**5,418**	**5,479**	**5,794**	**5,824**	**5,985**	**6,080**	**6,187**	**6,455**
Cause of death										
Anoxia	360	527	526	562	639	640	619	697	741	855
Cerebrovascular/stroke	1,417	2,052	2,270	2,236	2,478	2,509	2,612	2,631	2,627	2,757
Head trauma	2,019	2,618	2,456	2,489	2,497	2,429	2,520	2,545	2,610	2,614
Central nervous system tumor	42	53	50	63	57	61	62	52	56	48
Other	81	98	86	109	88	171	171	154	153	175
Unknown	4	15	30	20	35	14	1	1	b	6
Different coding pre 4/94	1,176	b	b	b	b	b	b	b	b	b
Cause of death (percentages)[a]										
Anoxia	7.1%	9.8%	9.7%	10.3%	11.0%	11.0%	10.3%	11.5%	12.0%	13.2%
Cerebrovascular/stroke	27.8%	38.3%	41.9%	40.8%	42.8%	43.1%	43.6%	43.3%	42.5%	42.7%
Head trauma	39.6%	48.8%	45.3%	45.4%	43.1%	41.7%	42.1%	41.9%	42.2%	40.5%
Central nervous system tumor	0.8%	1.0%	0.9%	1.1%	1.0%	1.0%	1.0%	0.9%	0.9%	0.7%
Other	1.6%	1.8%	1.6%	2.0%	1.5%	2.9%	2.9%	2.5%	2.5%	2.7%
Unknown	0.1%	0.3%	0.6%	0.4%	0.6%	0.2%	0.0%	0.0%	b	0.1%
Different coding pre 4/94	23.1%	b	b	b	b	b	b	b	b	b

[a]Percentages are calculated based on totals including missing and unknown cases.
[b]None in category.
Notes: Includes donors or organs recovered for transplant and not used, as well as those transplanted. Form changes on April 1, 1994 changed the way cause of death was calculated. Not all recovered organs are actually transplanted.

SOURCE: Adapted from "Table 2.1. Deceased Donor Characteristics, 1994 to 2003 Deceased Donors of Any Organ," in *2004 OPTN/SRTR Annual Report 1994–2003*, Department of Health and Human Services, Health Resources and Services Administration, Healthcare Systems Bureau, Division of Transplantation, February 7, 2005, http://www.optn.org/AR2004/default.htm (accessed November 2, 2005)

State programs were also reinforced by a national organ donation initiative announced by HHS Secretary Tommy G. Thompson in April 2001. Secretary Thompson called upon powerful alliances between employers and unions to promote donation. Called the "Workplace Partnership for Life," this coalition by 2004 was made up of hundreds of organizations and businesses, including some of the largest U.S. employers: Aetna, American Airlines, Bank of America, DaimlerChrysler, Ford Motor Company, General Motors Corporation, 3M, MetLife, and Verizon.

Transplant Regulations

In March 1998 the Clinton administration ordered UNOS to change its organ allocation policy. The network fought the new rules for two years in favor of the system already in place, which was based on geography. When an organ became available in a local area, that organ was offered to the sickest patient in that area. If no local patient needed the organ, it was then offered regionally, and last of all, nationally. The government, however, wanted organs to be given to the sickest patients first, regardless of geographic location. Secretary of HHS in the Clinton administration, Donna Shalala maintained, "People are dying unnecessarily, not because they don't have health insurance, not because they don't have access to care, but simply because of where they happen to live in the country. We need a level playing field for all patients."

A system based on need rather than location took effect in March 2000, although the issue of precisely who would decide the allocation of organs remained unresolved until April 2000, when the U.S. House of Representatives passed a proposal to restore decision making to UNOS, where it has remained.

CHAPTER 5
SERIOUSLY ILL CHILDREN

What greater pain could mortals have than this; To see their children dead before their eyes?

—Euripides

To a parent, the death of a child is an affront to the proper order of things. Children are supposed to outlive their parents, not the other way around. And when a child comes into the world irreparably ill, what is a parent to do—insist on continuous medical intervention, hoping against hope that a miracle happens, or let nature take its course and allow the newborn to die? When a five-year-old child has painful, life-threatening disabilities, the parent is faced with a similar agonizing decision. That decision is the parent's to make, preferably with the advice of a sensitive physician. But what if the ailing child is an adolescent who refuses further treatment for a terminal illness? Does a parent honor that wish?

INFANT MORTALITY

Since 1960 the infant mortality rate in the United States has declined 73%—from twenty-six deaths per one thousand live births in 1960 to seven deaths per one thousand live births in 2002, according to the Centers for Disease Control and Prevention (CDC). Table 5.1 shows the decline from 1983 to 2002, while Table 5.2 shows figures for 2002 and preliminary figures for 2003. The data in these two tables differ slightly due to the use of different data sets.

Advances in neonatology (the medical subspecialty concerned with the care of newborns, especially those at risk), which date back to the 1960s, have contributed to the huge drop in infant death rates. Infants born prematurely or with low birth weights, who were once likely to die, now can survive life-threatening conditions because of the development of neonatal intensive care units (NICUs). However, the improvements are not consistent for newborns of all races.

African-American infants are more than twice as likely as white and Hispanic infants to die before their first birthday. In 2002 the national death rate for African-American infants was 14.4 per one thousand live births, compared with 5.9 for non-Hispanic white infants per one thousand live births and 5.6 for Hispanic infants per one thousand live births. In 2003 the national death rate for African-American infants was 14.1 per one thousand live births, compared with 5.8 for non-Hispanic white infants per one thousand live births and 5.9 for Hispanic infants per one thousand live births. (See Table 5.2.) Additionally, the life expectancy at birth of African-American babies is less than that of white babies: African-American babies born in 2003 had a life expectancy of 72.7 years, while white babies born that same year had a life expectancy of seventy-eight years. (See Table 5.3.)

Leading Causes of Infant Mortality

Birth defects are the leading cause of infant mortality in the United States. Some of the more serious birth defects are anencephaly (a condition in which most of the brain and spinal cord are missing), spina bifida (a condition in which the spinal column does not close completely, leaving portions of the spinal cord exposed), and Down syndrome (a condition in which babies are born with an extra copy of chromosome 21 in their cells, which results in anatomical and developmental problems, along with cognitive deficits).

According to the CDC, one in every thirty-three babies born in the United States each year have birth defects. Babies born with birth defects have a greater chance of illness and long-term disability than babies without birth defects.

Birth defects, which are identified as "congenital malformations, deformations, and chromosomal abnormalities" by the *International Classification of Diseases*

TABLE 5.1

Infant, neonatal, and postneonatal mortality rates, by race and Hispanic origin of mother, selected years 1983–2002

[Data are based on linked birth and death certificates for infants]

Race and Hispanic origin of mother	1983[a]	1985[a]	1990[a]	1995[b]	1998[b]	1999[b]	2000[b]	2001[b]	2002[b]
	Infant[c] deaths per 1,000 live births								
All mothers	10.9	10.4	8.9	7.6	7.2	7.0	6.9	6.8	7.0
White	9.3	8.9	7.3	6.3	6.0	5.8	5.7	5.7	5.8
Black or African American	19.2	18.6	16.9	14.6	13.8	14.0	13.5	13.3	13.8
American Indian or Alaska Native	15.2	13.1	13.1	9.0	9.3	9.3	8.3	9.7	8.6
Asian or Pacific Islander	8.3	7.8	6.6	5.3	5.5	4.8	4.9	4.7	4.8
Chinese	9.5	5.8	4.3	3.8	4.0	2.9	3.5	3.2	3.0
Japanese	5.6*	6.0*	5.5*	5.3*	3.4*	3.5*	4.5*	4.0*	4.9*
Filipino	8.4	7.7	6.0	5.6	6.2	5.8	5.7	5.5	5.7
Hawaiian	11.2	9.9*	8.0*	6.5*	9.9	7.0*	9.0	7.3*	9.6
Other Asian or Pacific Islander	8.1	8.5	7.4	5.5	5.7	5.1	4.8	4.8	4.7
Hispanic or Latino[d, e]	9.5	8.8	7.5	6.3	5.8	5.7	5.6	5.4	5.6
Mexican	9.1	8.5	7.2	6.0	5.6	5.5	5.4	5.2	5.4
Puerto Rican	12.9	11.2	9.9	8.9	7.8	8.3	8.2	8.5	8.2
Cuban	7.5	8.5	7.2	5.3	3.7*	4.6	4.6	4.2	3.7
Central and South American	8.5	8.0	6.8	5.5	5.3	4.7	4.6	5.0	5.1
Other and unknown Hispanic or Latino	10.6	9.5	8.0	7.4	6.5	7.2	6.9	6.0	7.1
Not Hispanic or Latino:									
White[e]	9.2	8.6	7.2	6.3	6.0	5.8	5.7	5.7	5.8
Black or African American[e]	19.1	18.3	16.9	14.7	13.9	14.1	13.6	13.5	13.9
	Neonatal[c] deaths per 1,000 live births								
All mothers	7.1	6.8	5.7	4.9	4.8	4.7	4.6	4.5	4.7
White	6.1	5.8	4.6	4.1	4.0	3.9	3.8	3.8	3.9
Black or African American	12.5	12.3	11.1	9.6	9.4	9.5	9.1	8.9	9.3
American Indian or Alaska Native	7.5	6.1	6.1	4.0	5.0	5.0	4.4	4.2	4.6
Asian or Pacific Islander	5.2	4.8	3.9	3.4	3.9	3.2	3.4	3.1	3.4
Chinese	5.5	3.3	2.3	2.3	2.7	1.8	2.5	1.9	2.4
Japanese	3.7*	3.1*	3.5*	3.3*	2.5*	2.8*	2.6*	2.5*	3.7*
Filipino	5.6	5.1	3.5	3.4	4.6	3.9	4.1	4.0	4.1
Hawaiian	7.0*	5.7*	4.3*	4.0*	7.2*	4.9*	6.2*	3.6*	5.6*
Other Asian or Pacific Islander	5.0	5.4	4.4	3.7	3.9	3.3	3.4	3.2	3.3
Hispanic or Latino[d, e]	6.2	5.7	4.8	4.1	3.9	3.9	3.8	3.6	3.8
Mexican	5.9	5.4	4.5	3.9	3.7	3.7	3.6	3.5	3.6
Puerto Rican	8.7	7.6	6.9	6.1	5.2	5.9	5.8	6.0	5.8
Cuban	5.0*	6.2	5.3	3.6*	2.7*	3.5*	3.2*	2.5*	3.2*
Central and South American	5.8	5.6	4.4	3.7	3.6	3.3	3.3	3.4	3.5
Other and unknown Hispanic or Latino	6.4	5.6	5.0	4.8	4.5	4.8	4.6	3.9	5.1
Not Hispanic or Latino:									
White[e]	5.9	5.6	4.5	4.0	3.9	3.8	3.8	3.8	3.9
Black or African American[e]	12.0	11.9	11.0	9.6	9.4	9.6	9.2	9.0	9.3
	Postneonatal[c] deaths per 1,000 live births								
All mothers	3.8	3.6	3.2	2.6	2.4	2.3	2.3	2.3	2.3
White	3.2	3.1	2.7	2.2	2.0	1.9	1.9	1.9	1.9
Black or African American	6.7	6.3	5.9	5.0	4.4	4.5	4.3	4.4	4.5
American Indian or Alaska Native	7.7	7.0	7.0	5.1	4.4	4.3	3.9	5.4	4.0
Asian or Pacific Islander	3.1	2.9	2.7	1.9	1.7	1.7	1.4	1.6	1.4
Chinese	4.0	2.5*	2.0*	1.5*	1.3*	1.2*	1.0*	1.3*	0.7*
Japanese	*	2.9*	*	*	*	*	*	*	*
Filipino	2.8*	2.7	2.5	2.2	1.6	1.9	1.6	1.5*	1.7
Hawaiian	4.2*	4.3*	3.8*	*	*	*	*	3.7*	4.0*
Other Asian or Pacific Islander	3.0	3.0	3.0	1.9	1.8	1.8	1.4	1.6	1.4

(Tenth Revision, 1992), accounted for 20.1% of all infant deaths in 2003 (5,714 out of 28,422 total causes). (See Table 5.4.)

Disorders related to short gestation (premature birth) and low birth weight accounted for the second-leading cause of infant mortality (4,844 out of 28,422, or 17%). Among African-American infants, such disorders were the leading cause of death (22.7%; 1,903 out of 8,400 deaths from all causes). Other causes of infant deaths were sudden infant death syndrome (SIDS), maternal complications of pregnancy, and complications of the placenta, cord, and membranes. These five leading causes of infant mortality accounted for more than half (54.2%) of the total infant deaths in all races. (See Table 5.4.)

BIRTH DEFECTS

The March of Dimes Birth Defects Foundation, a national volunteer organization that seeks to improve infant health by preventing birth defects and lowering infant mortality rates, reported in its online quick references and fact sheets on birth defects (http://www.march ofdimes.com/pnhec/4439_1206.asp) that about 120,000

TABLE 5.1

Infant, neonatal, and postneonatal mortality rates, by race and Hispanic origin of mother, selected years 1983–2002 [CONTINUED]

[Data are based on linked birth and death certificates for infants]

Race and Hispanic origin of mother	1983[a]	1985[a]	1990[a]	1995[b]	1998[b]	1999[b]	2000[b]	2001[b]	2002[b]
Hispanic or Latino[d, e]	3.3	3.2	2.7	2.1	1.9	1.8	1.8	1.8	1.8
Mexican	3.2	3.2	2.7	2.1	1.9	1.8	1.8	1.7	1.8
Puerto Rican	4.2	3.5	3.0	2.8	2.6	2.4	2.4	2.5	2.4
Cuban	2.5*	2.3*	1.9*	1.7*	*	*	*	1.7*	*
Central and South American	2.6	2.4	2.4	1.9	1.7	1.4	1.4	1.6	1.6
Other and unknown Hispanic or Latino	4.2	3.9	3.0	2.6	2.0	2.5	2.3	2.1	2.0
Not Hispanic or Latino:									
White[e]	3.2	3.0	2.7	2.2	2.0	1.9	1.9	1.9	1.9
Black or African American[e]	7.0	6.4	5.9	5.0	4.5	4.6	4.4	4.5	4.6

*Estimates are considered unreliable. Rates preceded by an asterisk are based on fewer than 50 deaths in the numerator. Rates not shown are based on fewer than 20 deaths in the numerator.
[a]Rates based on unweighted birth cohort data.
[b]Rates based on a period file using weighted data.
[c]Infant (under 1 year of age), neonatal (under 28 days), and postneonatal (28 days–11 months).
[d]Persons of Hispanic origin may be of any race.
[e]Prior to 1995, data shown only for states with an Hispanic-origin item on their birth certificates.
Notes: The race groups white, black, American Indian or Alaska Native, and Asian or Pacific Islander include persons of Hispanic and non-Hispanic origin. National linked files do not exist for 1992–94. Data for additional years are available.

SOURCE: Adapted from "Table 19. Infant, Neonatal, and Postneonatal Mortality Rates, according to Detailed Race and Hispanic Origin of Mother: United States, Selected Years 1983–2002," in *Health, United States, 2005*, Centers for Disease Control and Prevention, National Center for Health Statistics, November 2005, http://www.cdc.gov/nchs/data/hus/hus05.pdf (accessed February 27, 2006)

---

babies are born annually in the United States with birth defects—a rate of one out of every thirty-three babies. The Foundation notes that birth defects are the leading cause of death for children younger than one year of age in the United States.

A birth defect may be a structural defect, a deficiency of function, or a disease present at birth. Some birth defects are genetic—inherited abnormalities such as Tay-Sachs disease (a fatal disease that generally affects children of Eastern European Jewish ancestry), or chromosomal irregularities such as Down syndrome. Other birth defects result from environmental factors—infections during pregnancy, such as rubella (German measles), or drugs used by the pregnant woman. Although the specific causes of many birth defects are unknown, scientists think that many result from a combination of genetic and environmental factors. Though many birth defects are impossible to prevent, some can be prevented, such as those caused by maternal alcohol and drug consumption during pregnancy.

Two birth defects that have been the subject of considerable ethical debate are neural tube defects (NTDs) and permanent disabilities coupled with operable but life-threatening factors. An example of the latter is Down syndrome, a genetic abnormality that causes mental retardation and, frequently, malformations of the heart or kidneys.

Neural Tube Defects

Neural tube defects are abnormalities of the brain and spinal cord resulting from the failure of the neural tube to develop properly during early pregnancy. The neural tube is the embryonic nerve tissue that develops into the brain and the spinal cord. In the period 1995–96, four thousand pregnancies were affected with NTDs. The number dropped to three thousand in 1999–2000. The Centers for Disease Control and Prevention, which reported these figures (*Morbidity and Mortality Weekly Report*, vol. 53, no. 17, May 7, 2004), suggested that the decline was due to an increase in folic acid consumption by pregnant women during those years.

Folic acid has been shown to prevent 50–70% of NTDs if women contemplating pregnancy consume sufficient folic acid before conception and then throughout the first trimester of pregnancy. Thus, in 1992, the U.S. Public Health Service recommended that all women capable of becoming pregnant consume four hundred micrograms of folic acid daily. In addition, the U.S. Food and Drug Administration (FDA) mandated that as of January 1998 all enriched cereal grain products be fortified with folic acid.

The two most common NTDs are anencephaly and spina bifida.

ANENCEPHALY. Anencephalic infants die before birth (in utero or stillborn) or shortly thereafter. The incidence of anencephaly dropped significantly from 1991 (0.018%) to 2003 (0.011%) in the states where data were reported. The largest drop during that time period was from 1991 to 1992. Since then, the general trend has been downward. (See Figure 5.1.)

Issues of brain death and organ donation sometimes surround anencephalic infants. One case that gained

TABLE 5.2

Infant deaths and infant mortality rates, by age, race, and Hispanic origin, 2002 and 2003

[Data are based on the continuous file of records received from the states. Rates per 1,000 live births. Figures for 2003 are based on weighted data rounded to the nearest individual, so categories may not add to totals. Rates for Hispanic origin should be interpreted with caution because of the inconsistencies between reporting Hispanic origin on birth and death certificates.]

Age and race and Hispanic origin	2003		2002	
	Number	Rate	Number	Rate
All races[a]				
Under 1 year	28,428	6.9	28,034	7.0
Under 28 days	19,108	4.7	18,747	4.7
28 days–11 months	9,320	2.3	9,287	2.3
Total white[b]				
Under 1 year	18,768	5.8	18,369	5.8
Under 28 days	12,698	3.9	12,354	3.9
28 days–11 months	6,070	1.9	6,015	1.9
Non-Hispanic white				
Under 1 year	13,450	5.8	13,463	5.9
Under 28 days	9,048	3.9	9,014	3.9
28 days–11 months	4,402	1.9	4,449	1.9
Total black[b]				
Under 1 year	8,437	14.1	8,524	14.4
Under 28 days	5,626	9.4	5,646	9.5
28 days–11 months	2,812	4.7	2,878	4.8
Hispanic[c]				
Under 1 year	5,389	5.9	4,943	5.6
Under 28 days	3,676	4.0	3,331	3.8
28 days–11 months	1,712	1.9	1,612	1.8

[a]Includes races other than white or black.
[b]Race and Hispanic origin are reported separately on both the birth and death certificate. Race categories are consistent with the 1977 Office of Management and Budget standards. California, Hawaii, Idaho, Maine, Montana, New York, and Wisconsin reported multiple-race data in 2003. The multiple-race data for these states were bridged to the single race categories of the 1977 Office of Management and Budget standards for comparability with other states. Data for persons of Hispanic origin are included in the data for each race group, according to the decedent's reported race.
[c]Includes all persons of Hispanic origin of any race.
Note: Data are subject to sampling or random variation.

SOURCE: Donna L. Hoyert, et al., "Table 4. Infant Deaths and Infant Mortality Rates, by Age and Race and Hispanic Origin: United States, Final 2002 and Preliminary 2003," in "Deaths, Preliminary Data for 2003," *National Vital Statistics Reports*, vol. 53, no. 15, February 28, 2005, http://www.cdc.gov/nchs/data/nvsr/nvsr53/nvsr53_15.pdf (accessed February 28, 2006)

national attention was that of Theresa Ann Campo in 1992. Prior to their daughter's birth, Theresa's parents (a Florida couple) discovered through prenatal testing that their baby would be born without a fully developed brain. They decided to carry the fetus to term and donate her organs for transplantation. When baby Theresa was born, her parents asked for her to be declared brain dead. But Theresa's brain stem was still functioning, so the court ruled against the parents' request. Baby Theresa died ten days later and her organs were not usable for transplant, having deteriorated as a result of oxygen deprivation.

Some physicians and ethicists agree that even if anencephalic babies have a brain stem, they should be considered brain dead. Lacking a functioning higher brain, these babies can feel nothing; they have no consciousness. Others fear that declaring anencephalic babies dead could be the start of a "slippery slope" that might eventually include babies with other birth defects, such as spina bifida, in the same category. Spina bifida defects range from mild to severe. Other people are concerned that anencephalic babies may be kept alive for the purpose of harvesting their organs for transplant at a later date.

SPINA BIFIDA. Spina bifida, which literally means "divided spine," is caused by the failure of the vertebrae (backbone) to completely cover the spinal cord early in fetal development, leaving the spinal cord exposed. Depending upon the amount of nerve tissue exposed, spina bifida defects range from minor developmental disabilities to paralysis.

Before the advent of antibiotics in the 1950s, most babies with severe spina bifida died soon after birth. With antibiotics and numerous medical advances, some of these newborns can be saved.

The treatment of newborns with spina bifida can pose serious ethical problems. Should an infant with a milder form of the disease be treated actively while another with severe defects is left untreated? In severe cases should the newborn be sedated and not be given nutrition and hydration until death occurs? Or should this seriously disabled infant be cared for while suffering from bladder and bowel malfunctions, infections, and paralysis? What if infants who have been left to die unexpectedly survive? Would they be more disabled than if they had been treated right away?

The development of fetal surgery to correct spina bifida before birth added another dimension to the debate. There are risks for both the mother and the fetus during and after fetal surgery, but techniques have improved since the first successful surgery of this type in 1997. In 2003 the National Institute of Child Health and Human Development (NICHD), a part of the National Institutes of Health (NIH), funded a study to compare how babies who have prenatal surgery do compared with those who have postnatal surgery. In 2006 the study was ongoing. The NICHD predicts that by the year 2020, routine diagnosis and treatment of congenital malformations by means of fetal surgery will be standard therapy for most disabling malformations that are currently treated in young infants.

In the United States the rates of spina bifida have been declining since 1960, and, though there was a slight increase in the mid-1990s, the rates decreased from nearly 0.025% in 1991 to about 0.019% in 2003. (See Figure 5.2; note that not all states participated in reporting spina bifida cases.) As mentioned previously, the decline is an early indicator of successful efforts to

TABLE 5.3

Deaths and life expectancy at birth, by race and sex; maternal and infant deaths and mortality rates, by race, 2002 and 2003

Measure and sex	All races[a]		White		Black	
	2003	2002	2003	2002	2003	2002
All deaths	2,448,288	2,443,387	2,103,714	2,102,589	291,300	290,051
Age-adjusted death rate[b]	832.7	845.3	817.0	829.0	1,065.9	1,083.3
Male	994.3	1,013.7	973.9	992.9	1,319.1	1,341.4
Female	706.2	715.2	693.1	701.3	885.6	901.8
Life expectancy at birth[c]	77.5	77.3	78.0	77.7	72.7	72.3
Male	74.8	74.5	75.3	75.1	69.0	68.8
Female	80.1	79.9	80.5	80.3	76.1	75.6
All maternal deaths	495	357	280	190	183	148
Maternal mortality rate	12.1	8.9	8.7	6.0	30.5	24.9
All infant deaths	28,025	28,034	18,440	18,369	8,402	8,524
Infant mortality rate[d]	6.85	6.97	5.72	5.79	14.01	14.36

[a]Includes races other than white and black.
[b]Age-adjusted death rates are per 100,000 U.S. standard population, based on the year 2000 standard.
[c]Life expectancy at birth stated in years.
[d]Infant mortality rates are deaths under 1 year per 1,000 live births in specified group.

SOURCE: Donna L. Hoyert, et al., "Table 1. Deaths, Age-Adjusted Death Rates, and Life Expectancy at Birth, by Race and Sex; Maternal and Infant Deaths and Mortality Rates, by Race: United States, 2002 and 2003," in *Deaths: Final Data for 2003, Health E-Stats*, Centers for Disease Control and Prevention, National Center for Health Statistics, January 19, 2006, http://www.cdc.gov/nchs/data/hestat/finaldeaths03_tables.pdf#2 (accessed February 27, 2006)

prevent this defect by increasing folic acid consumption among women of childbearing age.

Down Syndrome

Down syndrome is a birth defect caused by chromosomal irregularities. Instead of the normal forty-six chromosomes, Down syndrome newborns have an extra copy of chromosome 21, giving them a total of forty-seven chromosomes. Along with having certain anatomical differences from non-Down syndrome children, Down children have varying degrees of mental retardation, and approximately 40% have congenital heart diseases.

The CDC estimates prevalence of Down syndrome at birth as approximately ten cases per ten thousand live births. The occurrence of this birth defect rises with increasing maternal age, with a marked increase seen in children of women over thirty-five years of age.

In the past babies born with Down syndrome were usually institutionalized. Many died in infancy. Today, with the help of modern medical care, children with Down syndrome are typically raised at home and attain adulthood, although their life expectancy is shorter than average (approximately fifty-five years). Except for the most severe heart defects, many other malformations accompanying Down syndrome may be corrected by surgery. Depending on the degree of mental retardation, many people with Down syndrome are able to hold jobs and live independently.

Birth Defects Prevention Acts of 1998 and 2003

On April 21, 1998, President Bill Clinton signed into law the Birth Defects Prevention Act (PL 105–168), which authorized a nationwide network of birth defects research and prevention programs and called for a nationwide information clearinghouse on birth defects.

The Children's Health Act of 2000 (PL 106–310) authorized expanded research and services for a variety of childhood health problems. In addition, it created the National Center on Birth Defects and Developmental Disabilities (NCBDDD) at the CDC. Developmental disabilities are conditions that impair day-to-day functioning, such as difficulties with communication, learning, behavior, and motor skills. They are chronic conditions that initially appear in persons age eighteen years or younger.

The Birth Defects and Developmental Disabilities Prevention Act of 2003 revised and extended the Birth Defects Prevention Act of 1998. It also reauthorized the NCBDDD through 2007. The NCBDDD works with state health departments, academic institutions, and other public health partners to monitor birth defects and developmental disabilities, as well as to support research to identify their causes or risk factors. In addition, the center develops strategies and promotes programs to prevent birth defects and developmental disabilities.

The Economic Cost of Long-Term Care for Birth Defects and Developmental Disabilities

Research examining selected developmental disabilities associated with major birth defects was reported by Pierre Decoufle et al ("Increased Risk for Developmental Disabilities in Children Who Have Major Birth Defects: A Population-Based Study," *Pediatrics*, vol. 108, no. 3,

TABLE 5.4

Ten leading causes of infant deaths and infant mortality rates, by race and Hispanic origin, 2003

[Data are based on a continuous file of records received from the states. Rates are per 100,000 live births. Figures are based on weighted data rounded to the nearest individual, so categories may not add to totals or subtotals. Rates for Hispanic origin should be interpreted with caution because of inconsistencies between reporting Hispanic origin on birth and death certificates.]

Rank[a]	Cause of death and age	Number	Rate
All races[b]			
...	All causes	28,422	694.7
1	Congenital malformations, deformations and chromosomal abnormalities	5,714	139.7
2	Disorders related to short gestation and low birth weight, not elsewhere classified	4,844	118.4
3	Sudden infant death syndrome	1,994	48.7
4	Newborn affected by maternal complications of pregnancy	1,734	42.4
5	Newborn affected by complications of placenta, cord and membranes	1,112	27.2
6	Accidents (unintentional injuries)	928	22.7
7	Diseases of the circulatory system	834	20.4
8	Respiratory distress of newborn	819	20.0
9	Bacterial sepsis of newborn	766	18.7
10	Neonatal hemorrhage	648	15.8
...	All other causes	9,029	220.7
Total white[c]			
...	All causes	18,800	582.4
1	Congenital malformations, deformations and chromosomal abnormalities	4,378	135.6
2	Disorders related to short gestation and low birth weight, not elsewhere classified	2,769	85.8
3	Sudden infant death syndrome	1,246	38.6
4	Newborn affected by maternal complications of pregnancy	1,117	34.6
5	Newborn affected by complications of placenta, cord and membranes	756	23.4
6	Accidents (unintentional injuries)	621	19.2
7	Diseases of the circulatory system	539	16.7
8	Respiratory distress of newborn	537	16.6
9	Neonatal hemorrhage	476	14.8
10	Bacterial sepsis of newborn	465	14.4
...	All other causes	5,896	182.7
Non-Hispanic white			
...	All causes	13,454	579.7
1	Congenital malformations, deformations and chromosomal abnormalities	3,002	129.3
2	Disorders related to short gestation and low birth weight, not elsewhere classified	1,894	81.6
3	Sudden infant death syndrome	1,025	44.2
4	Newborn affected by maternal complications of pregnancy	803	34.6
5	Newborn affected by complications of placenta, cord and membranes	559	24.1
6	Accidents (unintentional injuries)	501	21.6
7	Diseases of the circulatory system	398	17.1
8	Respiratory distress of newborn	388	16.7
9	Neonatal hemorrhage	359	15.5
10	Bacterial sepsis of newborn	346	14.9
...	All other causes	4,179	180.1

TABLE 5.4

Ten leading causes of infant deaths and infant mortality rates, by race and Hispanic origin, 2003 [CONTINUED]

[Data are based on a continuous file of records received from the states. Rates are per 100,000 live births. Figures are based on weighted data rounded to the nearest individual, so categories may not add to totals or subtotals. Rates for Hispanic origin should be interpreted with caution because of inconsistencies between reporting Hispanic origin on birth and death certificates.]

Rank[a]	Cause of death and age	Number	Rate
Total black[c]			
...	All causes	8,400	1,401.4
1	Disorders related to short gestation and low birth weight, not elsewhere classified	1,903	317.4
2	Congenital malformations, deformations and chromosomal abnormalities	1,041	173.7
3	Sudden infant death syndrome	656	109.5
4	Newborn affected by maternal complications of pregnancy	563	93.9
5	Newborn affected by complications of placenta, cord and membranes	311	51.9
6	Bacterial sepsis of newborn	279	46.6
7	Accidents (unintentional injuries)	272	45.4
8	Respiratory distress of newborn	255	42.6
9	Diseases of the circulatory system	241	40.3
10	Necrotizing enterocolitis of newborn	158	26.4
...	All other causes	2,721	453.9
Hispanic[d]			
...	All causes	5,425	594.7
1	Congenital malformations, deformations and chromosomal abnormalities	1,381	151.4
2	Disorders related to short gestation and low birth weight, not elsewhere classified	888	97.4
3	Newborn affected by maternal complications of pregnancy	319	35.0
4	Sudden infant death syndrome	245	26.9
5	Newborn affected by complications of placenta, cord and membranes	201	22.1
6	Respiratory distress of newborn	152	16.6
7	Diseases of the circulatory system	142	15.5
8	Accidents (unintentional injuries)	123	13.5
9	Bacterial sepsis of newborn	120	13.1
10	Neonatal hemorrhage	120	13.1
...	All other causes	1,734	190.1

[a]Rank based on number of deaths.
[b]Includes races other than white and black.
[c]Race and Hispanic origin are reported separately on both the birth and death certificate. Race categories are consistent with the 1977 Office of Management and Budget standards. California, Hawaii, Idaho, Maine, Montana, New York, and Wisconsin reported multiple-race data in 2003. The multiple-race data for these states were bridged to the single race categories of the 1977 Office of Management and Budget standards for comparability with other states. Data for persons of Hispanic origin are included in the data for each race group, according to the decedent's reported race.
[d]Includes all persons of Hispanic origin of any race.
Notes: "..."=Category not applicable. Data are subject to sampling or random variation.

SOURCE: Donna L. Hoyert, et al., "Table 8. Infant Deaths and Infant Mortality Rates for the 10 Leading Causes of Infant Death, by Race and Hispanic Origin: United States, Preliminary 2003," in "Deaths, Preliminary Data for 2003," *National Vital Statistics Reports*, vol. 53, no. 15, February 28, 2005, http://www.cdc.gov/nchs/data/nvsr/nvsr53/nvsr53_15.pdf (accessed February 28, 2006)

September 2001). The investigators linked data from two independent population-based surveillance systems to find out if major birth defects were associated with serious developmental disabilities.

When compared with children who had no major birth defects, the prevalence of developmental disabilities among children with major birth defects was extremely high. The researchers observed that conditions such as mental retardation, cerebral palsy (a disorder marked by muscular impairment usually caused by brain damage), epilepsy (a disorder of the brain that results in seizures), autism (a brain disorder that affects communication, social interaction, and imaginative play), profound hearing loss, and legal blindness "prove costly in terms of special education services, medical and supportive care, demands on caregivers, and economic loss to society." They concluded, "Our data suggest that birth defects

FIGURE 5.1

Anencephalus rates and number of live births with anencephalus, 1991–2003

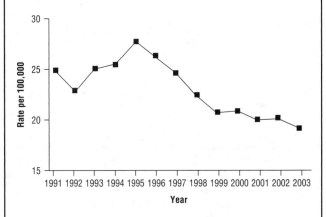

Year	Anencephalus cases	Total live births	Rate
2003	441	3,715,577	11.14
2002	348	3,645,770	9.55
2001	343	3,640,555	9.42
2000	376	3,640,376	10.33
1999	382	3,533,565	10.81
1998	349	3,519,240	9.92
1997	434	3,469,667	12.51
1996	416	3,478,723	11.96
1995	408	3,484,539	11.71
1994	387	3,527,482	10.97
1993	481	3,562,723	13.50
1992	457	3,572,890	12.79
1991	655	3,564,453	18.38

Note: Excludes data for Maryland, New Mexico, and New York, which did not require reporting for anencephalus for some years.

SOURCE: Adapted from "Figure 2. Anencephalus Rates, 1991–2002," and "Table 2. Number of Live Births and Anencephalus Cases and Rates per 100,000 Live Births for the United States, 1991–2002," *Trends in Spina Bifida and Anencephalus in the United States, 1991–2002*, Centers for Disease Control and Prevention, National Center for Health Statistics, 2004, http://www.cdc.gov/nchs/products/pubs/pubd/hestats/spine_anen.htm (accessed December 1, 2005). Data for 2003 are unpublished from the National Vital Statistics System, NCHS, CDC, December 1, 2005.

FIGURE 5.2

Spina bifida rates and number of live births with spina bifida, 1991–2003

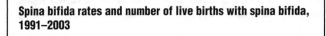

Year	Spina bifida cases	Total live births	Rate
2003	702	3,715,577	18.89
2002	734	3,645,770	20.13
2001	730	3,640,555	20.05
2000	759	3,640,367	20.85
1999	732	3,533,565	20.72
1998	790	3,519,240	22.45
1997	857	3,469,667	24.70
1996	917	3,478,723	26.36
1995	975	3,484,539	27.98
1994	900	3,527,482	25.51
1993	896	3,562,723	25.15
1992	816	3,572,890	22.84
1991	887	3,564,453	24.88

Note: Excludes data for Maryland, New Mexico, and New York, which did not require reporting for spina bifida for some years.

SOURCE: Adapted from "Figure 1. Spina Bifida Rates, 1991–2002," and "Table 1. Number of Live Births and Spina Bifida Cases and Rates per 100,000 Live Births for the United States, 1991–2002," *Trends in Spina Bifida and Anencephalus in the United States, 1991–2002*, Centers for Disease Control and Prevention, National Center for Health Statistics, 2004, http://www.cdc.gov/nchs/products/pubs/pubd/hestats/spine_anen.htm (accessed December 1, 2005). Data for 2003 are unpublished from the National Vital Statistics System, NCHS, CDC, December 1, 2005.

pose a greater burden on society than previously recognized."

The majority of people with birth defects and/or developmental disabilities require long-term care or services. Table 5.5 shows the economic costs of mental retardation, cerebral palsy, hearing loss, and vision impairment. Of these four developmental disabilities, mental retardation has the highest rate, at twelve affected children per one thousand, and the highest cost at more than $1 million per person.

LOW BIRTH WEIGHT AND PREMATURITY
Low Birth Weight

Infants who weigh less than twenty-five hundred grams (or five pounds, eight ounces) at birth are considered to be of low birth weight. Those born weighing less than fifteen hundred grams (three pounds, four ounces) have very low birth weight. Low birth weight may result from various causes, including premature birth, poor maternal nutrition, teen pregnancy, drug and alcohol use, smoking, or sexually transmitted diseases.

In 2003, 7.9% of the more than four million live births that year were low-birth-weight infants, the highest level reported in more than two decades. About 1.4% were very-low-birth-weight infants. African-American mothers were about twice as likely as white and Hispanic mothers to have low-birth-weight babies (13.6% of children born to non-Hispanic African-American birth mothers had low birth weight compared with 7% and 6.7%, respectively, born to non-Hispanic white and Hispanic mothers). (See Table 5.6 and Table 5.7.) The highest percentages of low-birth weight babies

TABLE 5.5

Estimated prevalence and lifetime economic costs for certain developmental disabilities, by cost category, 2003

Developmental disability	Rate[a]	Direct medical costs[b] (millions)	Direct nonmedical costs[c](millions)	Indirect costs[d] (millions)	Total costs (millions)	Average costs per person
Mental retardation	12.0	$7,061	$5,249	$38,927	**$51,237**	$1,014,000
Cerebral palsy	3.0	1,175	1,054	9,241	**11,470**	921,000
Hearing loss	1.2	132	640	1,330	**2,102**	417,000
Vision impairment	1.1	159	409	1,915	**2,484**	566,000

Note: Lifetime economic costs are present value estimates, in 2003 dollars, of lifetime costs for persons born in 2000, based on a 3% discount rate.

[a]Per 1,000 children aged 5–10 years, on the basis of Metropolitan Atlanta Developmental Disabilities Surveillance Program data for 1991–1994.

[b]Includes physician visits, prescription medications, hospital inpatient stays, assistive devices, therapy and rehabilitation (for persons aged <18 years), and long-term care (for persons aged 18–76 years), adjusted for age-specific survival.

[c]Includes costs of home and vehicle modifications for persons aged < 76 years and costs of special education for persons aged 3–17 years.

[d]Includes productivity losses from increased morbidity (i.e., inability to work or limitation in the amount or type of work performed) and premature mortality for persons aged ≤ 35 years with mental retardation, aged ≤ 25 years with cerebral palsy, and aged ≤ 17 years with hearing loss and vision impairment.

SOURCE: A. Honeycutt, et al., "Table. Estimated Prevalence and Lifetime Economic Costs for Mental Retardation, Cerebral Palsy, Hearing Loss, and Vision Impairment, by Cost Category—United States, 2003," in "Economic Costs Associated with Mental Retardation, Cerebral Palsy, Hearing Loss, and Vision Impairment—United States, 2003," *Morbidity & Mortality Weekly Report*, vol. 53, no. 3, January 30, 2004, http://www.cdc.gov/mmwr/PDF/wk/mm5303.pdf (accessed December 5, 2005)

are born to teenage mothers and to women over forty years of age. (See Table 5.7.)

Like the proportion of low-birth-weight babies, the proportion of very-low-birth-weight babies has also been increasing since the 1980s, although rates stabilized from the late 1990s through 2003. (See Table 5.8.) The increase in low- and very-low-birth-weight babies during the 1990s is attributed to the increase in the multiple birth rate. Babies born as part of a multiple birth are at much greater risk of low birth weight than babies born as a single birth.

Prematurity

The usual length of human pregnancy is forty weeks. Infants born before thirty-seven weeks of pregnancy are considered premature. A premature infant does not have fully formed organ systems. If the premature infant is born with a birth weight comparable to a full-term baby and has organ systems only slightly undeveloped, the chances of survival are great. Premature infants of very low birth weight are susceptible to numerous risks and are less likely to survive than full-term infants. If they survive, they may suffer from mental retardation and other abnormalities of the nervous system.

A severe medical condition called hyaline membrane disease, or respiratory distress syndrome (RDS), commonly affects premature infants. It is caused by the inability of the immature lungs to function properly. Occurring right after birth, it may cause infant death within hours. Intensive care includes the use of a mechanical ventilator to facilitate breathing. Also, premature infants' immature gastrointestinal systems preclude them from taking in nourishment properly. Unable to suck and swallow, they must be fed through a stomach tube.

WHO MAKES MEDICAL DECISIONS FOR INFANTS?

Prior to the 1980s in the United States, the courts were supportive of biologic parents making decisions regarding the medical care of their newborns. Parents often made these decisions in consultation with pediatricians. Medical advancements in the 1970s, however, allowed for the survival of infants who would have not had a chance for survival prior to that time. Parents' and physicians' decisions became more challenging and complex.

The history of federal and state laws pertaining to the medical care of infants began in 1982 with the "Baby Doe" regulations. These regulations created a standard of medical care for infants: the possibility of future handicaps in a child should play no role in his or her medical treatment decisions.

The "Baby Doe" Rules

In April 1982 an infant with Down syndrome was born at Bloomington Hospital in Indiana. The infant also had esophageal atresia, an obstruction in the esophagus that prevents the passage of food from the mouth to the stomach. Following their obstetrician's recommendation, the parents decided to forego surgery to repair the baby's esophagus. The baby would be kept pain-free with medication and allowed to die.

Disagreeing with the parents' decision, the hospital took them to the county court. The judge ruled that the parents had the legal right to their decision, which was based on a valid medical recommendation. The Indiana Supreme Court refused to hear the appeal. Before the county prosecutor could present the case to the U.S. Supreme Court, the six-day-old baby died.

TABLE 5.6

Percent of births with selected medical or health characteristics, by race, Hispanic origin, and birthplace of mother, 2003

Characteristic	All origins[a]	Origin of mother								
		Hispanic						Non-Hispanic		
		Total	Mexican	Puerto Rican	Cuban	Central and South American	Other and unknown Hispanic	Total[b]	White	Black
All births										
Mother										
Prenatal care beginning in the first trimester[c]	84.1	77.5	76.5	81.2	92.1	79.2	77.0	86.1	89.0	75.9
Late or no prenatal care[c]	3.5	5.3	5.6	3.7	1.3	4.7	5.4	3.0	2.1	6.0
Smoker[c, d]	10.7	2.7	2.0	7.9	2.4	1.1	6.6	12.6	14.3	8.3
Drinker[c, e]	0.7	0.4	0.4	0.6	0.3	0.3	0.9	0.8	0.9	0.8
Weight gain of less than 16 lbs[f]	12.3	15.2	16.9	12.8	7.8	12.3	13.2	11.6	10.2	17.7
Median weight gain[f]	30.5	28.7	27.3	30.7	31.9	30.1	30.3	30.7	31.0	29.8
Cesarean delivery rate	27.5	26.5	25.8	27.6	39.8	28.4	25.9	27.8	27.6	29.2
Infant										
Preterm births[g]	12.3	11.9	11.7	13.8	11.8	11.4	12.6	12.5	11.3	17.8
Birthweight										
Very low birthweight[h]	1.4	1.2	1.1	2.0	1.4	1.2	1.3	1.5	1.2	3.1
Low birthweight[i]	7.9	6.7	6.3	10.0	7.0	6.7	8.0	8.3	7.0	13.6
4,000 grams or more[j]	8.9	8.2	8.5	6.2	8.3	8.0	7.0	9.0	10.4	4.8
5-minute Apgar score of less than 7[k, l]	1.4	1.1	1.1	1.5	0.8	0.9	1.2	1.5	1.3	2.3
Births to mothers born in the 50 states and District of Columbia										
Mother										
Prenatal care beginning in the first trimester[c]	85.7	80.8	80.6	80.7	91.5	84.2	77.8	86.3	89.1	75.9
Late or no prenatal care[c]	3.0	4.1	4.1	3.9	1.4	3.1	5.2	2.9	2.1	5.8
Smoker[c, d]	13.1	5.8	4.7	9.1	3.5	3.5	8.7	13.8	14.9	9.3
Drinker[c, e]	0.9	0.8	0.8	0.6	0.5	0.5	1.1	0.9	0.9	0.8
Weight gain of less than 16 lbs[f]	11.9	13.6	14.7	12.2	7.9	9.0	13.1	11.7	10.2	18.0
Median weight gain[f]	30.7	30.3	30.1	30.8	32.6	31.0	30.5	30.8	31.0	30.0
Cesarean delivery rate	27.7	26.8	26.6	27.0	35.8	26.8	25.6	27.8	27.7	28.9
Infant										
Preterm births[g]	12.7	13.0	13.0	13.6	12.4	11.6	13.3	12.7	11.4	18.3
Birthweight										
Very low birthweight[h]	1.5	1.4	1.3	2.0	1.7	1.6	1.3	1.5	1.2	3.2
Low birthweight[i]	8.3	7.8	7.4	10.0	7.8	7.6	8.7	8.4	7.1	14.0
4,000 grams or more[j]	9.1	7.3	7.6	6.3	7.3	7.4	6.8	9.3	10.4	4.4
5-minute Apgar score of less than 7[k, l]	1.5	1.2	1.2	1.4	0.9	1.0	1.2	1.5	1.3	2.4
Births to mothers born outside the 50 states and District of Columbia										
Mother										
Prenatal care beginning in the first trimester[c]	79.1	75.6	74.1	82.3	92.6	78.5	75.2	84.5	86.9	76.5
Late or no prenatal care[c]	5.1	5.9	6.5	3.4	1.1	4.9	5.8	3.8	3.1	6.9
Smoker[c, d]	1.5	0.9	0.5	5.7	1.5	0.8	1.5	2.4	4.5	1.0
Drinker[c, e]	0.3	0.2	0.2	0.4	*	0.3	0.3	0.5	0.8	0.2
Weight gain of less than 16 lbs[f]	13.8	16.2	18.2	13.9	7.7	12.7	13.3	10.7	9.0	15.9
Median weight gain[f]	28.9	27.3	25.9	30.3	31.0	29.8	29.8	30.3	30.7	28.5
Cesarean delivery rate	26.9	26.4	25.3	28.9	43.3	28.6	26.8	27.6	26.0	31.7

The public outcry following the death of "Baby Doe" (the infant's court-designated name) brought immediate reaction from President Ronald Reagan's administration. The Department of Health and Human Services (HHS) informed all hospitals receiving federal funding that discrimination against handicapped newborns would violate Section 504 of the Rehabilitation Act of 1973 (PL 93–112). This section (nondiscrimination under federal grants and programs) states:

> No otherwise qualified individual with a disability in the United States ... shall, solely by reason of her or his disability, be excluded from the participation in, be denied the benefits of, or be subjected to discrimination under any program or activity receiving Federal financial assistance.

Furthermore, all hospital delivery rooms and nurseries were ordered to have posters warning that "DISCRIMINATORY FAILURE TO FEED AND CARE FOR HANDICAPPED INFANTS IN THIS FACILITY IS PROHIBITED BY FEDERAL LAW." The posters listed a toll-free hotline for anonymous reports of failure to comply.

Although government investigators (called "Baby Doe" squads) were summoned to many hospitals to verify claims of mistreatment (the hotline had five hundred calls in its first three weeks alone), no violation of the law could be found. On the contrary, the investigators found doctors resuscitating babies who were beyond treatment because they feared legal actions. Finally, a group led by the American Academy of Pediatrics filed

TABLE 5.6

Percent of births with selected medical or health characteristics, by race, Hispanic origin, and birthplace of mother, 2003 [CONTINUED]

		Origin of mother								
		Hispanic						Non-Hispanic		
Characteristic	All origins^a	Total	Mexican	Puerto Rican	Cuban	Central and South American	Other and unknown Hispanic	Total^b	White	Black
Infant										
Preterm births^g	11.0	11.2	11.0	14.2	11.3	11.4	10.5	10.7	9.5	14.2
Birthweight										
Very low birthweight^h	1.1	1.0	0.9	2.0	1.1	1.1	0.9	1.3	1.0	2.6
Low birthweight^i	6.6	6.0	5.7	10.0	6.3	6.6	5.9	7.5	6.2	10.0
4,000 grams or more^j	8.2	8.7	9.0	6.1	9.2	8.1	7.4	7.4	10.4	7.7
5-minute Apgar score of less than 7^k, l	1.1	1.0	1.1	1.6	0.8	0.9	1.0	1.2	0.9	1.9

*Figure does not meet standards of reliability or precision; based on fewer than 20 births in the numerator.
^aIncludes origin not stated.
^bIncludes races other than white and black.
^cExcludes data for Pennsylvania and Washington, which implemented the 2003 Revision to the U.S. Standard Certificate of Live Birth for data year 2003. This change has resulted in a lack of comparability between data based on the 2003 Revision and data based on the 1989 Revision to the U.S. Certificate of Live Birth.
^dExcludes data for California, which did not report tobacco use on the birth certificate.
^eExcludes data for California, which did not report alcohol use on the birth certificate.
^fExcludes data for California, which did not report weight gain on the birth certificate. Median weight gain shown in pounds.
^gBorn prior to 37 completed weeks of gestation.
^hBirthweight of less than 1,500 grams (3 lb 4 oz).
^iBirthweight of less than 2,500 grams (5 lb 8 oz).
^jEquivalent to 8 lb 14 oz.
^kThe Apgar score is one measure of a newborn's health immediately after birth. The best possible score is 10.
^lExcludes data for California and Texas, which did not report 5-minute Apgar score on the birth certificate.
Notes: Race and Hispanic origin are reported separately on birth certificates. Race categories are consistent with the 1977 Office of Management and Budget standards. Persons of Hispanic origin may be of any race. In this table Hispanic women are classified only by place of origin; non-Hispanic women are classified by race.

SOURCE: Joyce A. Martin, et al., "Table 25. Percentage of Births with Selected Medical or Health Characteristics, by Hispanic Origin of Mother and by Race for Mothers of Non-Hispanic Origin and by Place of Birth of Mother: United States, 2003," in "Births: Final Data for 2003," *National Vital Statistics Reports*, vol. 54, no. 2, September 8, 2005, http://www.cdc.gov/nchs/data/nvsr/nvsr54/nvsr54_02.pdf (accessed November 2, 2005)

suit in March 1983 to have the Baby Doe rules overturned because they believed them to be harsh, unreasonably intrusive, and not necessarily in the best interests of the child. After various legal battles, in 1986 the U.S. Supreme Court ruled that the HHS did not have the authority to require such regulations and invalidated them.

Child Abuse Amendments of 1984 and Their Legacy

As the Baby Doe regulations were being fought in the courts, Congress enacted and President Reagan signed the Child Abuse Amendments of 1984 (PL 98–457; CAA). The CAA extended and improved the provisions of the Child Abuse Prevention and Treatment Act and the Child Abuse Prevention and Treatment and Adoption Reform Act of 1978. The CAA established that states' child protection services systems would respond to complaints of medical neglect of children, including instances of withholding medically indicated treatment from disabled infants with life-threatening conditions. It noted that parents were the ones to make medical decisions for their disabled infants based on the advice of their physicians. These laws have been amended many times over the years, most recently by the Keeping Children and Families Safe Act of 2003 (PL 108–36), without voiding the states' and parents' responsibilities to disabled infants.

Born-Alive Infants Protection Act of 2001

The Born-Alive Infants Protection Act of 2001 (PL 107–207) was signed by President George W. Bush on August 5, 2002. The purpose of the law is to ensure that all infants born alive, whether developmentally able to survive long-term, are given legal protection as persons under federal law. The law neither prohibits nor requires medical care for newly born infants who are below a certain weight or developmental age.

The American Academy of Pediatrics Neonatal Resuscitation Program (NRP) Steering Committee has responded that the law "should not in any way affect the approach that physicians currently follow with respect to the extremely premature infant. . . . At the time of delivery, and regardless of the circumstances of the delivery, the medical condition and prognosis of the newly born infant should be assessed. At that point decisions about withholding or discontinuing medical treatment that is considered futile may be considered by the medical care providers in conjunction with the parents acting in the best interest of their child. Those newly born infants who are deemed appropriate to not resuscitate or to have medical support withdrawn should be treated with dignity and respect, and provided with 'comfort care' measures" (David Boyle et al, "Born-Alive Infants Protection Act of 2001, Public Law No. 107–207," *Pediatrics*, vol. 111, 2003, http://pediatrics. aappublications.org/cgi/reprint/111/3/680-a).

TABLE 5.7

Number and percent of low birthweight and number of live births by selected characteristics, 2003

Age and race and Hispanic origin of mother	Low birthweight[a] Number	Low birthweight[a] Percent	Total	Birthweight[b] Less than 500 grams	500–999 grams	1,000–1,499 grams	1,500–1,999 grams	2,000–2,499 grams	2,500–2,999 grams	3,000–3,499 grams	3,500–3,999 grams	4,000–4,499 grams	4,500–4,999 grams	5,000 grams or more	Not stated
All races[c]															
All ages	324,064	7.9	4,089,950	6,307	22,980	29,930	63,791	201,056	711,003	1,557,864	1,131,577	309,721	46,690	5,431	3,600
Under 15 years	848	12.7	6,661	32	85	87	149	495	1,698	2,694	1,220	179	14	1	7
15–19 years	40,211	9.7	414,580	804	3,152	3,637	7,462	25,156	92,531	169,390	91,699	18,154	2,014	178	403
15 years	2,103	11.5	18,238	50	191	210	412	1,240	4,423	7,548	3,524	553	59	2	26
16 years	4,402	10.7	41,344	77	381	414	825	2,705	9,843	16,996	8,390	1,502	146	19	46
17 years	7,549	10.1	74,802	161	622	670	1,383	4,713	16,990	30,720	16,087	3,053	295	32	76
18 years	11,268	9.6	117,750	234	858	981	2,066	7,129	26,522	48,060	26,044	5,127	574	43	112
19 years	14,889	9.2	162,446	282	1,100	1,362	2,776	9,369	34,753	66,066	37,654	7,919	940	82	143
20–24 years	82,494	8.0	1,032,305	1,604	5,732	7,084	15,167	52,907	199,835	412,228	264,313	63,142	8,526	878	889
25–29 years	76,631	7.1	1,086,366	1,522	5,399	6,943	14,862	47,905	178,150	415,463	314,316	86,511	12,886	1,477	932
30–34 years	71,477	7.3	975,546	1,454	4,944	6,822	14,636	43,621	148,022	357,144	293,569	88,696	14,155	1,701	782
35–39 years	40,550	8.7	467,642	685	2,863	4,059	8,797	24,146	72,708	164,600	137,185	43,764	7,397	991	447
40–44 years	10,655	10.6	101,005	194	730	1,151	2,403	6,177	16,858	34,639	27,995	8,908	1,626	198	126
45–54 years	1,198	20.5	5,845	12	75	147	315	649	1,201	1,706	1,280	367	72	7	14
White total[d]															
All ages	223,612	6.9	3,225,848	3,593	14,096	20,173	44,419	141,331	511,317	1,220,632	951,782	270,180	41,156	4,664	2,505
Under 15 years	378	10.3	3,677	8	41	42	68	219	838	1,573	752	124	10	1	1
15–19 years	24,774	8.3	298,347	409	1,771	2,193	4,604	15,797	61,144	123,409	72,095	14,884	1,666	138	237
15 years	1,107	9.6	11,484	26	93	107	221	660	2,503	4,899	2,522	396	45	2	10
16 years	2,536	9.0	28,151	30	199	247	482	1,578	6,120	11,844	6,301	1,197	119	12	22
17 years	4,669	8.8	52,941	78	357	418	849	2,967	11,026	21,981	12,452	2,487	249	27	50
18 years	7,054	8.2	85,734	127	496	596	1,281	4,554	17,756	35,474	20,627	4,246	467	33	77
19 years	9,408	7.8	120,037	148	626	825	1,771	6,038	23,739	49,211	30,193	6,558	786	64	78
20–24 years	53,600	6.8	790,910	824	3,323	4,447	9,751	35,255	140,299	316,971	217,687	53,701	7,340	717	595
25–29 years	54,143	6.2	871,496	901	3,401	4,750	10,617	34,474	130,541	330,559	267,011	75,912	11,397	1,267	666
30–34 years	52,407	6.6	795,902	882	3,209	4,927	10,888	32,501	110,515	287,041	252,401	78,817	12,650	1,503	568
35–39 years	29,593	7.8	379,773	435	1,791	2,878	6,520	17,969	54,448	132,207	117,123	38,636	6,593	854	319
40–44 years	7,751	9.6	81,031	125	500	824	1,718	4,584	12,592	27,513	23,658	7,799	1,436	177	105
45–54 years	966	20.6	4,712	9	60	112	253	532	940	1,359	1,055	307	64	7	14
Non-Hispanic white															
All ages	163,331	7.0	2,321,904	2,529	9,998	14,882	32,915	103,007	356,232	858,305	700,819	206,407	31,570	3,415	1,825
Under 15 years	144	10.3	1,399	3	19	18	30	74	309	551	323	67	5	0	0
15–19 years	14,904	8.6	172,620	258	1,122	1,369	2,811	9,344	33,960	69,160	43,514	9,726	1,120	75	161
15 years	525	10.8	4,878	10	46	53	113	303	994	1,973	1,152	208	21	0	5
16 years	1,266	9.5	13,375	16	111	119	232	788	2,703	5,432	3,208	684	68	4	10
17 years	2,666	9.3	28,550	49	218	253	509	1,637	5,654	11,474	6,991	1,556	159	16	34
18 years	4,316	8.6	50,484	88	321	380	789	2,738	10,061	20,199	12,708	2,795	323	21	61
19 years	6,131	8.1	75,333	95	426	564	1,168	3,878	14,548	30,082	19,455	4,483	549	34	51
20–24 years	36,764	7.0	522,275	571	2,273	3,141	6,777	24,002	91,307	204,117	146,151	37,745	5,273	497	421
25–29 years	39,730	6.3	627,437	615	2,438	3,503	7,900	25,274	92,116	233,898	194,930	56,873	8,508	904	478
30–34 years	41,263	6.6	626,315	661	2,383	3,849	8,613	25,757	85,088	223,247	201,188	63,791	10,175	1,132	431
35–39 years	23,634	7.8	303,354	319	1,334	2,282	5,231	14,468	42,777	104,440	94,704	31,608	5,284	665	242
40–44 years	6,083	9.4	64,600	95	380	628	1,340	3,640	9,895	21,760	19,149	6,344	1,152	137	80
45–54 years	809	20.8	3,904	7	49	92	213	448	780	1,132	860	253	53	5	12

TABLE 5.7

Number and percent of low birthweight and number of live births by selected characteristics, 2003 (CONTINUED)

Age and race and Hispanic origin of mother	Low birthweight[a]		Total	Birthweight[b]											
	Number	Percent		Less than 500 grams	500–999 grams	1,000–1,499 grams	1,500–1,999 grams	2,000–2,499 grams	2,500–2,999 grams	3,000–3,499 grams	3,500–3,999 grams	4,000–4,499 grams	4,500–4,999 grams	5,000 grams or more	Not stated
Black total[d]															
All ages	80,088	13.4	599,847	2,427	7,765	8,204	15,654	46,038	143,176	228,356	117,889	25,428	3,546	504	860
Under 15 years	437	16.1	2,726	20	42	41	76	258	807	1,016	416	41	3	0	6
15–19 years	14,092	14.0	100,951	359	1,281	1,328	2,620	8,504	27,963	39,811	16,167	2,493	246	33	146
15 years	913	15.1	6,056	21	92	93	178	529	1,777	2,361	852	125	13	0	15
16 years	1,686	14.5	11,654	41	172	154	312	1,007	3,374	4,565	1,739	243	20	6	21
17 years	2,648	13.8	19,145	74	249	238	483	1,604	5,349	7,643	3,020	436	22	4	23
18 years	3,861	13.9	27,817	100	329	348	729	2,355	7,808	10,877	4,474	678	81	8	30
19 years	4,984	13.8	36,279	123	439	495	918	3,009	9,655	14,365	6,082	1,011	110	15	57
20–24 years	25,500	13.0	196,268	730	2,228	2,386	4,856	15,300	49,599	76,813	36,184	6,970	838	114	250
25–29 years	17,182	12.3	139,947	557	1,733	1,816	3,341	9,735	31,287	53,465	29,962	6,744	958	146	203
30–34 years	13,021	13.4	97,529	495	1,431	1,471	2,601	7,023	20,197	35,739	21,850	5,546	907	120	149
35–39 years	7,712	15.5	49,889	200	865	904	1,652	4,091	10,553	17,226	10,784	2,965	476	76	97
40–44 years	2,007	16.9	11,895	64	171	237	470	1,065	2,632	4,086	2,400	632	114	15	9
45–54 years	137	21.3	642	2	14	21	38	62	138	200	126	37	4	0	0
Non-Hispanic black															
All ages	77,947	13.6	576,033	2,350	7,575	7,998	15,211	44,813	138,440	218,901	112,139	23,992	3,340	484	790
Under 15 years	423	16.0	2,642	20	40	40	75	248	784	986	402	38	3	0	6
15–19 years	13,738	14.1	97,509	342	1,250	1,296	2,562	8,288	27,154	38,392	15,462	2,364	229	32	138
15 years	884	15.1	5,852	21	90	88	175	510	1,726	2,279	818	120	13	0	12
16 years	1,637	14.6	11,247	37	165	151	307	977	3,277	4,396	1,660	234	17	6	20
17 years	2,575	14.0	18,431	70	238	230	472	1,565	5,169	7,352	2,884	406	20	3	22
18 years	3,779	14.1	26,915	98	323	343	710	2,305	7,601	10,502	4,282	639	76	8	28
19 years	4,863	13.9	35,064	116	434	484	898	2,931	9,381	13,863	5,818	965	103	15	56
20–24 years	24,899	13.2	189,020	707	2,179	2,333	4,735	14,945	48,011	73,795	34,567	6,620	786	109	233
25–29 years	16,668	12.5	133,821	544	1,694	1,772	3,228	9,430	30,194	51,072	28,330	6,332	895	142	188
30–34 years	12,667	13.6	93,346	480	1,396	1,432	2,523	6,836	19,462	34,164	20,738	5,202	865	112	136
35–39 years	7,484	15.7	47,661	195	837	872	1,606	3,974	10,166	16,383	10,230	2,798	446	74	80
40–44 years	1,933	16.9	11,419	60	165	232	445	1,031	2,532	3,923	2,290	605	112	15	9
45–54 years	135	22.0	615	2	14	21	37	61	137	186	120	33	4	0	0

TABLE 5.7

Number and percent of low birthweight and number of live births by selected characteristics, 2003 [CONTINUED]

Age and race and Hispanic origin of mother	Low birthweight[a] Number	Percent	Total	Birthweight[b] Less than 500 grams	500–999 grams	1,000–1,499 grams	1,500–1,999 grams	2,000–2,499 grams	2,500–2,999 grams	3,000–3,499 grams	3,500–3,999 grams	4,000–4,499 grams	4,500–4,999 grams	5,000 grams or more	Not stated
Hispanic[c]															
All ages	60,973	6.7	912,329	1,037	4,140	5,366	11,655	38,775	157,583	366,508	252,230	63,688	9,619	1,246	482
Under 15 years	244	10.4	2,356	5	24	24	36	155	556	1,045	444	61	5	0	1
15–19 years	10,120	7.9	128,524	160	669	853	1,834	6,604	27,891	55,455	29,109	5,255	565	60	69
15 years	610	9.0	6,818	16	50	60	110	374	1,552	3,021	1,409	194	25	2	5
16 years	1,303	8.6	15,151	15	91	129	256	812	3,520	6,566	3,163	524	57	8	10
17 years	2,054	8.2	24,986	28	147	171	348	1,360	5,533	10,756	5,573	952	93	11	14
18 years	2,791	7.8	35,927	40	174	226	503	1,848	7,866	15,574	8,050	1,472	146	12	16
19 years	3,362	7.4	45,642	61	207	267	617	2,210	9,420	19,538	10,914	2,113	244	27	24
20–24 years	17,173	6.3	273,311	254	1,075	1,339	3,052	11,453	50,176	114,882	72,521	16,079	2,105	225	150
25–29 years	14,624	5.9	246,361	274	975	1,266	2,780	9,329	38,964	97,748	72,557	19,065	2,921	364	118
30–34 years	11,122	6.6	169,054	209	813	1,075	2,277	6,748	25,497	63,815	50,866	14,839	2,460	370	85
35–39 years	5,914	7.8	75,801	104	455	601	1,272	3,482	11,665	27,649	22,118	6,939	1,281	190	45
40–44 years	1,641	10.2	16,172	29	119	190	374	929	2,692	5,689	4,432	1,399	272	35	12
45–54 years	135	18.0	750	2	10	18	30	75	142	225	183	51	10	2	2

[a]Less than 2,500 grams (5 lb 8 oz).

[b]Less than 500 grams=1 lb 1 oz or less
500–999 grams=1 lb 2 oz–2 lb 3 oz
1,000–1,499 grams=2 lb 4 oz–3 lb 4 oz
1,500–1,999 grams=3 lb 5 oz–4 lb 6 oz
2,000–2,499 grams=4 lb 7 oz–5 lb 8 oz
2,500–2,999 grams=5 lb 9 oz–6 lb 9 oz.

3,000–3,499 grams=6 lb 10 oz–7 lb 11 oz
3,500–3,999 grams=7 lb 12 oz–8 lb 13 oz
4,000–4,499 grams=8 lb 14 oz–9 lb 14 oz
4,500–4,999 grams=9 lb 15 oz–11 lb 0 oz
5,000 grams or more=11 lb 1 oz or more

[c]Includes races other than white and black and origin not stated.

[d]Race and Hispanic origin are reported separately on the birth certificate. Race categories are consistent with the 1977 Office of Management and Budget standards. Data for persons of Hispanic origin are included in the data for each group according to the mother's reported race.

[e]Includes all persons of Hispanic origin of any race.

SOURCE: Joyce A. Martin, et al., "Table 45. Number and Percentage Low Birthweight and Number of Live Births by Birthweight, by Age and Race and Hispanic Origin of Mother: United States, 2003," in "Births: Final Data for 2003," *National Vital Statistics Reports*, vol. 54, no. 2, September 8, 2005, http://www.cdc.gov/nchs/data/nvsr/nvsr54/nvsr54_02.pdf (accessed November 2, 2005)

TABLE 5.8

Low-birth-weight live births, by mother's race, Hispanic origin, and smoking status, selected years 1970–2003

[Data are based on birth certificates]

Birth-weight, race, Hispanic origin of mother, and smoking status of mother	1970	1975	1980	1985	1990	1995	1998	1999	2000	2001	2002	2003
Low birth-weight (less than 2,500 grams)					Percent of live births[a]							
All races	7.93	7.38	6.84	6.75	6.97	7.32	7.57	7.62	7.57	7.68	7.82	7.93
White	6.85	6.27	5.72	5.65	5.70	6.22	6.52	6.57	6.55	6.68	6.80	6.94
Black or African American	13.90	13.19	12.69	12.65	13.25	13.13	13.05	13.11	12.99	12.95	13.29	13.37
American Indian or Alaska Native	7.97	6.41	6.44	5.86	6.11	6.61	6.81	7.15	6.76	7.33	7.23	7.37
Asian or Pacific Islander[b]	—	—	6.68	6.16	6.45	6.90	7.42	7.45	7.31	7.51	7.78	7.78
Chinese	6.67	5.29	5.21	4.98	4.69	5.29	5.34	5.19	5.10	5.33	5.52	—
Japanese	9.03	7.47	6.60	6.21	6.16	7.26	7.50	7.95	7.14	7.28	7.57	—
Filipino	10.02	8.08	7.40	6.95	7.30	7.83	8.23	8.30	8.46	8.66	8.61	—
Hawaiian	—	—	7.23	6.49	7.24	6.84	7.15	7.69	6.76	7.91	8.14	—
Other Asian or Pacific Islander	—	—	6.83	6.19	6.65	7.05	7.76	7.76	7.67	7.76	8.16	—
Hispanic or Latino[c]	—	—	6.12	6.16	6.06	6.29	6.44	6.38	6.41	6.47	6.55	6.69
Mexican	—	—	5.62	5.77	5.55	5.81	5.97	5.94	6.01	6.08	6.16	6.28
Puerto Rican	—	—	8.95	8.69	8.99	9.41	9.68	9.30	9.30	9.34	9.68	10.01
Cuban	—	—	5.62	6.02	5.67	6.50	6.50	6.80	6.49	6.49	6.50	7.04
Central and South American	—	—	5.76	5.68	5.84	6.20	6.47	6.38	6.34	6.49	6.53	6.70
Other and unknown Hispanic or Latino	—	—	6.96	6.83	6.87	7.55	7.59	7.63	7.84	7.96	7.87	8.01
Not Hispanic or Latino:[c]												
White	—	—	5.69	5.61	5.61	6.20	6.55	6.64	6.60	6.76	6.91	7.04
Black or African American	—	—	12.71	12.62	13.32	13.21	13.17	13.23	13.13	13.07	13.39	13.55
Cigarette smoker[d]	—	—	—	—	11.25	12.18	12.01	12.06	11.88	11.90	12.15	12.40
Nonsmoker[d]	—	—	—	—	6.14	6.79	7.18	7.21	7.19	7.32	7.48	7.66
Very low birth-weight (less than 1,500 grams)												
All races	1.17	1.16	1.15	1.21	1.27	1.35	1.45	1.45	1.43	1.44	1.46	1.45
White	0.95	0.92	0.90	0.94	0.95	1.06	1.15	1.15	1.14	1.16	1.17	1.17
Black or African American	2.40	2.40	2.48	2.71	2.92	2.97	3.08	3.14	3.07	3.04	3.13	3.07
American Indian or Alaska Native	0.98	0.95	0.92	1.01	1.01	1.10	1.24	1.26	1.16	1.26	1.28	1.30
Asian or Pacific Islander[b]	—	—	0.92	0.85	0.87	0.91	1.10	1.08	1.05	1.03	1.12	1.09
Chinese	0.80	0.52	0.66	0.57	0.51	0.67	0.75	0.68	0.77	0.69	0.74	—
Japanese	1.48	0.89	0.94	0.84	0.73	0.87	0.84	0.86	0.75	0.71	0.97	—
Filipino	1.08	0.93	0.99	0.86	1.05	1.13	1.35	1.41	1.38	1.23	1.31	—
Hawaiian	—	—	1.05	1.03	0.97	0.94	1.53	1.41	1.39	1.50	1.55	—
Other Asian or Pacific Islander	—	—	0.96	0.91	0.92	0.91	1.12	1.09	1.04	1.06	1.17	—
Hispanic or Latino[c]	—	—	0.98	1.01	1.03	1.11	1.15	1.14	1.14	1.14	1.17	1.16
Mexican	—	—	0.92	0.97	0.92	1.01	1.02	1.04	1.03	1.05	1.06	1.06
Puerto Rican	—	—	1.29	1.30	1.62	1.79	1.86	1.86	1.93	1.85	1.96	2.01
Cuban	—	—	1.02	1.18	1.20	1.19	1.33	1.49	1.21	1.27	1.15	1.37
Central and South American	—	—	0.99	1.01	1.05	1.13	1.23	1.15	1.20	1.19	1.20	1.17
Other and unknown Hispanic or Latino	—	—	1.01	0.96	1.09	1.28	1.38	1.32	1.42	1.27	1.44	1.28
Not Hispanic or Latino:[c]												
White	—	—	0.87	0.91	0.93	1.04	1.15	1.15	1.14	1.17	1.17	1.18
Black or African American	—	—	2.47	2.67	2.93	2.98	3.11	3.18	3.10	3.08	3.15	3.12
Cigarette smoker[d]	—	—	—	—	1.73	1.85	1.87	1.91	1.91	1.88	1.88	1.92
Nonsmoker[d]	—	—	—	—	1.18	1.31	1.44	1.43	1.40	1.42	1.45	1.44

[a]Excludes live births with unknown birthweight. Percent based on live births with known birthweight.

[b]For 2003, data are not shown for Asian or Pacific Islander subgroups during the transition from single race to multiple race reporting.

[c]Prior to 1993, data from states lacking an Hispanic-origin item on the birth certificate were excluded. Data for non-Hispanic white and non-Hispanic black women for years prior to 1989 are not nationally representative and are provided for comparison with Hispanic data.

[d]Percent based on live births with known smoking status of mother and known birthweight. Data from states that did not require the reporting of mother's tobacco use during pregnancy on the birth certificate are not included. Reporting area for tobacco use increased from 43 states and the District of Columbia (DC) in 1989 to 49 states and DC in 2000–02. In 2003 California did not require reporting of tobacco use during pregnancy. Data for 2003 also exclude Pennsylvania and Washington that implemented the 2003 revision to the U.S. Standard Certificate of Live Birth. Tobacco use data based on the 2003 revision are not comparable with data based on the 1989 revision to the U.S. Standard Certificate of Live Birth.

Notes: "—"=Data not available. The race groups, white, black, American Indian or Alaska Native, and Asian or Pacific Islander, include persons of Hispanic and non-Hispanic origin. Persons of Hispanic origin may be of any race. Interpretation of trend data should take into consideration expansion of reporting areas and immigration.

SOURCE: "Table 13. Low-Birthweight Live Births, according to Mother's Detailed Race, Hispanic Origin, and Smoking Status: United States, Selected Years 1970–2003," in *Health, United States, 2005*, Centers for Disease Control and Prevention, National Center for Health Statistics, November 2005, http://www.cdc.gov/nchs/data/hus/hus05.pdf (accessed February 27, 2006).

MEDICAL DECISION-MAKING FOR OLDER CHILDREN

Under U.S. law, children under the age of eighteen cannot provide legally binding consent regarding their health care. Parents or guardians legally provide that consent, and, in most situations, physicians and the courts give parents wide latitude in the medical decisions they make for their children.

Religious Beliefs and Medical Treatment

When a parent's decisions are not in the best interests of the child, the state may intervene. Nonetheless, forty-six states exempt parents from child abuse and neglect laws if they rely on spiritual healing rather than seek medical treatment for their minor children. The states without these laws are Hawaii, Massachusetts, Nebraska, and North Carolina (Kenneth S. Hickey and Laurie Lyckholm, "Child Welfare versus Parental Autonomy: Medical Ethics, the Law, and Faith-Based Healing," *Theoretical Medicine*, vol. 25, no. 4, 2004). Confusing the issue, however, is the agreement of the courts that religious exemption laws are no defense against criminal neglect. The legal distinction between practicing one's religion and criminal conduct in the treatment of one's children remains unclear.

Adolescents

The United Nations defines adolescents as people between the ages of ten and nineteen. Early adolescence is from ten to fourteen years, while late adolescence is from fifteen to nineteen years.

More than three thousand U.S. adolescents die each year from chronic illnesses such as cancer, heart disease, AIDS, and metabolic disorders (David Freyer, "Care of the Dying Adolescent: Special Considerations," *Pediatrics*, vol. 113, no. 2, February 2004). While many laws concerning minors have changed, such as allowing minors to seek medical treatment for reproductive health and birth control services without parental consent, most states have no laws for end-of-life decisions by minors who are adolescents.

Freyer notes that although the law does not consider adolescents under the age of eighteen to be competent to make their own health care decisions, health care practitioners often do. A broad consensus has developed among pediatric health care practitioners, developmental psychologists, ethicists, and lawyers that by the age of fourteen years, terminally ill adolescents (unless they demonstrate otherwise) "have the functional competence to make binding medical decisions for themselves, including decision relating to the discontinuance of life-sustaining therapy and other end-of-life issues." According to Freyer, some experienced health care practitioners think that terminally ill children as young as ten years "often meet the criteria for having functional competence and should have substantial, if not decisive, input on major end-of-life care decisions, including the discontinuation of active therapy."

CHAPTER 6
SUICIDE, EUTHANASIA, AND PHYSICIAN-ASSISTED SUICIDE

BACKGROUND

The Merriam-Webster dictionary definition of euthanasia, which derives from the Greek for "easy death," is "the act or practice of killing or permitting the death of hopelessly sick or injured individuals...in a relatively painless way for reasons of mercy." This present-day definition differs from that of the classical Greeks, who considered euthanasia simply "one mode of dying." To the Greeks, euthanasia was a rational act by people who deemed their lives no longer useful. That these individuals sought the help of others to end their lives was considered morally acceptable.

The movement to legalize euthanasia in England began in 1935 with the founding of the Voluntary Euthanasia Society by such well-known figures as George Bernard Shaw, Bertrand Russell, and H. G. Wells. In 1936 the House of Lords (one of the houses in the British Parliament) defeated a bill that would have permitted euthanasia in cases of terminal illness. Nonetheless, it was common knowledge that physicians practiced euthanasia. The same year, it was rumored that King George V, who had been seriously ill for several years, was "relieved of his sufferings" by his physician, with the approval of his wife, Queen Mary.

The Euthanasia Society of America was established in 1938. In 1967 this group prepared the first living will. Renamed the Society for the Right to Die in 1974, it merged in 1991 with another organization called Concern for Dying, and the two became Choice in Dying (CID). While CID took no position on physician-assisted suicide (PAS), it "advocated for the rights of dying patients." It also educated the public about the importance of advance directives and end-of-life issues. In early 2000 CID dissolved, although many of its staff remained to found Partnership for Caring, Inc., which continues its programs. That organization's goal was to "ensure that everyone in this country soon has access to quality end-of-life care." Then, in early 2004, Partnership for Caring merged with Last Acts, a coalition of professional and consumer organizations that work to improve end-of-life care. The merged organization was named Last Acts Partnership, and its mission was to provide education, service, and counseling to people who needed accurate and reliable information about end-of-life care. Last Acts Partnership was also an advocate for policy reform in end-of-life issues. In 2005 Last Acts Partnership ceased its activities and all rights and copyrights to material produced by Partnership for Caring, Last Acts, and Last Acts Partnership were legally obtained by the National Hospice and Palliative Care Organization (NHPCO).

Euthanasia and the Nazis

The Nazis' version of euthanasia was a bizarre interpretation of an idea espoused by two German professors, Alfred Hoche and Karl Binding, in their 1920 book *The Permission to Destroy Life Unworthy of Life*. While initially advocating that it was ethical for physicians to assist in the death of those who requested an end to their suffering, the authors later argued that it was also permissible to end the lives of the mentally retarded and the mentally ill.

Some contemporary opponents of euthanasia fear that a society that allows physician-assisted suicide may eventually follow the path of Nazi dictator Adolf Hitler's euthanasia program, which began with the killing of physically and mentally impaired individuals and culminated in the annihilation of entire religious and ethnic groups considered by the Nazis to be unworthy of life. But those supporting euthanasia argue that unlike the murderous Nazi euthanasia program designed by Hitler and his followers, modern-day proposals are based upon voluntary requests by individuals in situations of physical suffering and would be sanctioned by laws passed by democratic governments.

Distinguishing between Euthanasia and Physician-Assisted Suicide

In the United States the debate over euthanasia distinguishes between active and passive euthanasia. Active euthanasia, also called voluntary active euthanasia by those who distinguish it from the kind of euthanasia practiced by the Nazis, involves the hastening of death through the administration of lethal drugs, as requested by the patient or another competent individual who represents the patient's wishes.

Passive euthanasia, on the other hand, involves foregoing medical treatment, knowing that such a decision will result in death. This action is not considered illegal because the underlying illness, permitted to run its natural course, will ultimately cause death. It is generally accepted in the United States that terminally ill individuals have a right to refuse medical treatment, as do those who are sick but not terminally so. But some people think that allowing patients to forego medical treatment is a practice tantamount to enabling suicide and is therefore morally reprehensible.

The debate about euthanasia in the United States has been expanded to include the question of whether a competent, terminally ill patient has the right to physician-assisted suicide, in which a physician provides the means (such as lethal drugs) for the patient to self-administer and commit suicide. The distinction between the two actions, euthanasia and physician-assisted suicide, is at times difficult to define: a patient in the latter stages of amyotrophic lateral sclerosis (ALS, or Lou Gehrig's disease), for example, is physically unable to kill him- or herself; therefore, a physician who aids in such a person's suicide would technically be committing euthanasia.

SUICIDE

Different Cultures and Religions

Different religions and cultures have viewed suicide in different ways. Ancient Romans who dishonored themselves or their families were expected to commit suicide in order to maintain their dignity and, frequently, the family property. Early Christians were quick to embrace martyrdom as a guarantee of eternal salvation, but during the fourth century St. Augustine discouraged the practice. He and later theologians were concerned that many Christians who were suffering in this world would see suicide as a reasonable and legitimate way to depart to a better place in the hereafter. The view of the Christian theologian St. Thomas Aquinas (circa 1225–74) is reflected in the contemporary Roman Catholic teaching that "suicide contradicts the natural inclination of the human being to preserve and perpetuate his life... and is contrary to love for the living God."

While Islam and Judaism also condemn the taking of one's own life, Buddhist monks and nuns have been known to commit suicide by self-immolation (burning themselves

alive) as a form of social protest. In a ritual called *suttee*, which is now outlawed, widows in India showed devotion to their deceased husbands by being cremated with them, sometimes throwing themselves on the funeral pyres, although it was not always voluntary. Widowers (men whose wives had died), however, did not follow this custom.

Quasi-religious reasons sometimes motivate mass suicide. In 1978 more than nine hundred members of a group known as the People's Temple killed themselves in Jonestown, Guyana. In 1997 a group called Heaven's Gate also committed mass suicide in California. The devastating terrorist attacks of September 11, 2001, were the result of a suicidal plot enacted by religious extremist groups. Suicide bombings in other parts of the world have also been attributed to extremist groups that have twisted or misinterpreted the fundamental tenets of Islam to further their political objectives.

The Japanese people have traditionally associated a certain idealism with suicide. During the twelfth century, samurai warriors practiced voluntary *seppuku* (more commonly known as *hara-kiri*) or ritual self-disembowelment, to avoid dishonor at the hands of their enemies. Some samurai committed this form of slow suicide to atone for wrongdoing or to express devotion to a superior who had died. Even as recently as 1970, famed author Yukio Mishima publicly committed *seppuku*. During World War II, Japanese kamikaze pilots inflicted serious casualties with suicidal assaults in which they would purposely crash their planes into enemy ships, killing themselves along with enemy troops.

Suicide is still commonly practiced in modern Japan. In early 1998 several government officials and businessmen hanged themselves in separate incidents involving scandals that attracted public attention. The reasons given for the suicides ranged from proclaiming innocence to assuming responsibility for wrongdoing. In November 2005 the *Daily Yomiuri* newspaper (Tokyo) reported that government statistics showed that more than thirty thousand suicides had occurred in Japan each year from 1998 to 2004.

Suicide in America

With the exception of certain desperate medical situations, suicide in the United States is generally considered an unacceptable act, the end result of irrationality or severe depression. It is often referred to as a permanent solution to a short-term problem.

In spite of this generally held belief, suicide was the eleventh-leading cause of death in America in 2003. There were almost twice as many suicides as homicides that year. (See Table 4.1 in Chapter 4.) Nevertheless, since 1950 the national suicide rate has dropped from 13.2 suicides per one hundred thousand people to 10.9 per one hundred thousand in 2002. However, that rate is up from a low of 10.4 suicides per one hundred thousand in 2000. (See Table 6.1.)

TABLE 6.1

Death rates for suicide, by sex, race, Hispanic origin, and age, selected years 1950–2002

[Data are based on death certificates]

Sex, race, Hispanic origin, and age	1950[a]	1960[a]	1970	1980	1990	2000	2001	2002
All persons				Deaths per 100,000 resident population				
All ages, age adjusted[b]	13.2	12.5	13.1	12.2	12.5	10.4	10.7	10.9
All ages, crude	11.4	10.6	11.6	11.9	12.4	10.4	10.8	11.0
Under 1 year	...	...	...	...	...	...	...	...
1–4 years	...	...	...	...	...	...	...	...
5–14 years	0.2	0.3	0.3	0.4	0.8	0.7	0.7	0.6
15–24 years	4.5	5.2	8.8	12.3	13.2	10.2	9.9	9.9
15–19 years	2.7	3.6	5.9	8.5	11.1	8.0	7.9	7.4
20–24 years	6.2	7.1	12.2	16.1	15.1	12.5	12.0	12.4
25–44 years	11.6	12.2	15.4	15.6	15.2	13.4	13.8	14.0
25–34 years	9.1	10.0	14.1	16.0	15.2	12.0	12.8	12.6
35–44 years	14.3	14.2	16.9	15.4	15.3	14.5	14.7	15.3
45–64 years	23.5	22.0	20.6	15.9	15.3	13.5	14.4	14.9
45–54 years	20.9	20.7	20.0	15.9	14.8	14.4	15.2	15.7
55–64 years	26.8	23.7	21.4	15.9	16.0	12.1	13.1	13.6
65 years and over	30.0	24.5	20.8	17.6	20.5	15.2	15.3	15.6
65–74 years	29.6	23.0	20.8	16.9	17.9	12.5	13.3	13.5
75–84 years	31.1	27.9	21.2	19.1	24.9	17.6	17.4	17.7
85 years and over	28.8	26.0	19.0	19.2	22.2	19.6	17.5	18.0
Male								
All ages, age adjusted[b]	21.2	20.0	19.8	19.9	21.5	17.7	18.2	18.4
All ages, crude	17.8	16.5	16.8	18.6	20.4	17.1	17.6	17.9
Under 1 year	...	...	...	...	...	...	...	...
1–4 years	...	...	...	...	...	...	...	...
5–14 years	0.3	0.4	0.5	0.6	1.1	1.2	1.0	0.9
15–24 years	6.5	8.2	13.5	20.2	22.0	17.1	16.6	16.5
15–19 years	3.5	5.6	8.8	13.8	18.1	13.0	12.9	12.2
20–24 years	9.3	11.5	19.3	26.8	25.7	21.4	20.5	20.8
25–44 years	17.2	17.9	20.9	24.0	24.4	21.3	22.1	22.2
25–34 years	13.4	14.7	19.8	25.0	24.8	19.6	21.0	20.5
35–44 years	21.3	21.0	22.1	22.5	23.9	22.8	23.1	23.7
45–64 years	37.1	34.4	30.0	23.7	24.3	21.3	22.5	23.5
45–54 years	32.0	31.6	27.9	22.9	23.2	22.4	23.4	24.4
55–64 years	43.6	38.1	32.7	24.5	25.7	19.4	21.1	22.2
65 years and over	52.8	44.0	38.4	35.0	41.6	31.1	31.5	31.8
65–74 years	50.5	39.6	36.0	30.4	32.2	22.7	24.6	24.7
75–84 years	58.3	52.5	42.8	42.3	56.1	38.6	37.8	38.1
85 years and over	58.3	57.4	42.4	50.6	65.9	57.5	51.1	50.7
Female								
All ages, age adjusted[b]	5.6	5.6	7.4	5.7	4.8	4.0	4.0	4.2
All ages, crude	5.1	4.9	6.6	5.5	4.8	4.0	4.1	4.3
Under 1 year	...	...	...	...	...	...	...	...
1–4 years	...	...	...	...	...	...	...	...
5–14 years	0.1	0.1	0.2	0.2	0.4	0.3	0.3	0.3
15–24 years	2.6	2.2	4.2	4.3	3.9	3.0	2.9	2.9
15–19 years	1.8	1.6	2.9	3.0	3.7	2.7	2.7	2.4
20–24 years	3.3	2.9	5.7	5.5	4.1	3.2	3.1	3.5
25–44 years	6.2	6.6	10.2	7.7	6.2	5.4	5.5	5.8
25–34 years	4.9	5.5	8.6	7.1	5.6	4.3	4.4	4.6
35–44 years	7.5	7.7	11.9	8.5	6.8	6.4	6.4	6.9
45–64 years	9.9	10.2	12.0	8.9	7.1	6.2	6.6	6.7
45–54 years	9.9	10.2	12.6	9.4	6.9	6.7	7.2	7.4
55–64 years	9.9	10.2	11.4	8.4	7.3	5.4	5.7	5.7
65 years and over	9.4	8.4	8.1	6.1	6.4	4.0	3.9	4.1
65–74 years	10.1	8.4	9.0	6.5	6.7	4.0	3.9	4.1
75–84 years	8.1	8.9	7.0	5.5	6.3	4.0	4.0	4.2
85 years and over	8.2	6.0	5.9	5.5	5.4	4.2	3.4	3.8
White male[c]								
All ages, age adjusted[b]	22.3	21.1	20.8	20.9	22.8	19.1	19.6	20.0
All ages, crude	19.0	17.6	18.0	19.9	22.0	18.8	19.5	19.9
15–24 years	6.6	8.6	13.9	21.4	23.2	17.9	17.6	17.7
25–44 years	17.9	18.5	21.5	24.6	25.4	22.9	24.0	24.0
45–64 years	39.3	36.5	31.9	25.0	26.0	23.2	24.7	25.9
65 years and over	55.8	46.7	41.1	37.2	44.2	33.3	33.7	34.2
65–74 years	53.2	42.0	38.7	32.5	34.2	24.3	26.3	26.8
75–84 years	61.9	55.7	45.5	45.5	60.2	41.1	40.2	40.6
85 years and over	61.9	61.3	45.8	52.8	70.3	61.6	55.0	53.9

TABLE 6.1

Death rates for suicide, by sex, race, Hispanic origin, and age, selected years 1950–2002 [CONTINUED]

[Data are based on death certificates]

Sex, race, Hispanic origin, and age	1950[a]	1960[a]	1970	1980	1990	2000	2001	2002
Black or African American male[c]								
All ages, age adjusted[b]	7.5	8.4	10.0	11.4	12.8	10.0	9.8	9.8
All ages, crude	6.3	6.4	8.0	10.3	12.0	9.4	9.2	9.1
15–24 years	4.9	4.1	10.5	12.3	15.1	14.2	13.0	11.3
25–44 years	9.8	12.6	16.1	19.2	19.6	14.3	14.4	15.1
45–64 years	12.7	13.0	12.4	11.8	13.1	9.9	9.7	9.6
65 years and over	9.0	9.9	8.7	11.4	14.9	11.5	11.5	11.7
65–74 years	10.0	11.3	8.7	11.1	14.7	11.1	10.7	9.7
75–84 years[d]	*	*	*	10.5	14.4	12.1	13.5	13.8
85 years and over	—	*	*	*	*	*	*	*
American Indian or Alaska Native male[c]								
All ages, age adjusted[b]	—	—	—	19.3	20.1	16.0	17.4	16.4
All ages, crude	—	—	—	20.9	20.9	15.9	17.0	16.8
15–24 years	—	—	—	45.3	49.1	26.2	24.7	27.9
25–44 years	—	—	—	31.2	27.8	24.5	27.6	26.8
45–64 years	—	—	—	*	*	15.4	17.0	14.1
65 years and over	—	—	—	*	*	*	*	*
Asian or Pacific male[c]	—	—	—	*	*	*	*	*
All ages, age adjusted[b]	—	—	—	10.7	9.6	8.6	8.4	8.0
All ages, crude	—	—	—	8.8	8.7	7.9	7.7	7.6
15–24 years	—	—	—	10.8	13.5	9.1	9.1	8.7
25–44 years	—	—	—	11.0	10.6	9.9	9.3	9.3
45–64 years	—	—	—	13.0	9.7	9.7	8.2	9.1
65 years and over	—	—	—	18.6	16.8	15.4	18.3	14.4
Hispanic or Latino male[c, e]								
All ages, age adjusted[b]	—	—	—	—	13.7	10.3	10.1	9.9
All ages, crude	—	—	—	—	11.4	8.4	8.3	8.3
15–24 years	—	—	—	—	14.7	10.9	9.5	10.6
25–24 years	—	—	—	—	16.2	11.2	11.8	10.9
45–64 years	—	—	—	—	16.1	12.0	11.4	11.9
65 years and over	—	—	—	—	23.4	19.5	18.5	17.5
White, not Hispanic or Latino male[e]								
All ages, age adjusted[b]	—	—	—	—	23.5	20.2	21.0	21.4
All ages, crude	—	—	—	—	23.1	20.4	21.4	21.9
15–24 years	—	—	—	—	24.4	19.5	19.6	19.3
25–44 years	—	—	—	—	26.4	25.1	26.4	26.9
45–64 years	—	—	—	—	26.8	24.0	25.9	27.2
65 years and over	—	—	—	—	45.4	33.9	34.4	35.1
White female[c]								
All ages, age adjusted[b]	6.0	5.9	7.9	6.1	5.2	4.3	4.5	4.7
All ages, crude	5.5	5.3	7.1	5.9	5.3	4.4	4.6	4.8
15–24 years	2.7	2.3	4.2	4.6	4.2	3.1	3.1	3.1
25–44 years	6.6	7.0	11.0	8.1	6.6	6.0	6.2	6.6
45–64 years	10.6	10.9	13.0	9.6	7.7	6.9	7.3	7.5
65 years and over	9.9	8.8	8.5	6.4	6.8	4.3	4.1	4.3
Black or African American female[c]								
All ages, age adjusted[b]	1.8	2.0	2.9	2.4	2.4	1.8	1.8	1.6
All ages, crude	1.5	1.6	2.6	2.2	2.3	1.7	1.7	1.5
15–24 years	1.8	*	3.8	2.3	2.3	2.2	1.3	1.7
25–44 years	2.3	3.0	4.8	4.3	3.8	2.6	2.6	2.4
45–64 years	2.7	3.1	2.9	2.5	2.9	2.1	2.6	2.1
65 years and over	*	*	2.6	*	1.9	1.3	1.6	1.1

The National Vital Statistics System (NVSS), which is a part of the Centers for Disease Control and Prevention (CDC), collects data from the fifty states, two cities (New York City and Washington, DC), and five territories (Puerto Rico, the Virgin Islands, Guam, American Samoa, and the Commonwealth of the Northern Mariana Islands). Each is responsible for registering vital events: births, deaths, marriages, divorces, and fetal deaths. Suicide data are compiled as part of the death data.

To add more specificity to violent death data, the CDC instituted the National Violent Death Reporting System (NVDRS) in 2003. The NVDRS is a state-based system that collects information on the numbers and

TABLE 6.1

Death rates for suicide, by sex, race, Hispanic origin, and age, selected years 1950–2002 [CONTINUED]

[Data are based on death certificates]

Sex, race, Hispanic origin, and age	1950[a]	1960[a]	1970	1980	1990	2000	2001	2002
American Indian or Alaska Native female[c]								
All ages, age adjusted[b]	—	—	—	4.7	3.6	3.8	4.0	4.1
All ages, crude	—	—	—	4.7	3.7	4.0	4.1	4.3
15–24 years	—	—	—	*	*	*	*	7.4
25–44 years	—	—	—	10.7	*	7.2	6.1	5.6
45–64 years	—	—	—	*	*	*	*	*
65 years and over	—	—	—	*	*	*	*	*
Asian or Pacific Islander female[c]								
All ages, age adjusted[b]	—	—	—	5.5	4.1	2.8	2.9	3.0
All ages, crude	—	—	—	4.7	3.4	2.7	2.8	2.9
15–24 years	—	—	—	*	3.9	2.7	3.6	
25–44 years	—	—	—	5.4	3.8	3.3	2.9	3.3
45–64 years	—	—	—	7.9	5.0	3.2	3.8	3.8
65 years and over	—	—	—	*	8.5	5.2	4.9	6.8
Hispanic or Latino female[c, e]								
All ages, age adjusted[b]	—	—	—	—	2.3	1.7	1.6	1.8
All ages, crude	—	—	—	—	2.2	1.5	1.5	1.6
15–24 years	—	—	—	—	3.1	2.0	2.3	2.1
25–44 years	—	—	—	—	3.1	2.1	2.0	2.0
45–64 years	—	—	—	—	2.5	2.5	2.3	2.5
65 years and over	—	—	—	—	*	*	*	1.9
White, not Hispanic or Latino female[e]								
All ages, age adjusted[b]	—	—	—	—	5.4	4.7	4.9	5.1
All ages, crude	—	—	—	—	5.6	4.9	5.0	5.3
15–24 years	—	—	—	—	4.3	3.3	3.3	3.4
25–44 years	—	—	—	—	7.0	6.7	6.9	7.5
45–64 years	—	—	—	—	8.0	7.3	7.8	8.0
65 years and over	—	—	—	—	7.0	4.4	4.3	4.5

*Rates based on fewer than 20 deaths are considered unreliable and are not shown.
[a]Includes deaths of persons who were not residents of the 50 states and the District of Columbia.
[b]Age-adjusted rates are calculated using the year 2000 standard population.
[c]The race groups, white, black, Asian or Pacific Islander, and American Indian or Alaska Native, include persons of Hispanic and non-Hispanic origin. Persons of Hispanic origin may be of any race. Death rates for the American Indian or Alaska Native and Asian or Pacific Islander populations are known to be underestimated.
[d]In 1950 rate is for the age group 75 years and over.
[e]Prior to 1997, excludes data from states lacking an Hispanic-origin item on the death certificate.
Notes: "..."=Category not applicable. "—"=Data not available. Starting with, 2003, rates for 1991–99 were revised using intercensal population estimates based on census 2000. Rates for 2000 were revised based on census 2000 counts. Rates for 2001 and 2002 were computed using 2000-based postcensal estimates. Figures for 2001 include September 11-related deaths for which death certificates were filed as of October 24, 2002. Age groups were selected to minimize the presentation of unstable age-specific death rates based on small numbers of deaths and for consistency among comparison groups.

SOURCE: "Table 46. Death Rates for Suicide, according to Sex, Race, Hispanic Origin, and Age: United States, Selected Years 1950–2002," in *Health, United States, 2005*, Centers for Disease Control and Prevention, National Center for Health Statistics, November 2005, http://www.cdc.gov/nchs/data/hus/hus05.pdf (accessed February 27, 2006)

kinds of violent deaths along with details regarding those deaths. Six states joined the NVDRS in 2003.

Figure 6.1 shows that suicide rates in the United States declined from 1993 to 1999, and then rose slightly between 2000 and 2002, falling again in 2003. (The 2003 data are not shown on Table 6.1.) The rate for the six NVDRS states is lower than the national rate, but rose from 2002 to 2003 when suicide rates were declining across the U.S.

Gopal K. Singh and Mohammad Siahpush compared the suicide rates in rural and urban populations in the United States. In "Increasing Rural-Urban Gradients in U.S. Suicide Mortality, 1970–1997" (*American Journal of Public Health*, vol. 92, no. 7, July 2002), Singh and Siahpush reported that the rate of suicide in rural populations of males increased between 1970 and 1997, while the rate of suicide in urban populations of males decreased over the same period. Although the rates are lower for females and the changes not as dramatic, a decrease was also noted in the suicide rate for urban females, while the suicide rate among rural females remained relatively stable.

In explaining these differences, Singh and Siahpush suggest that both rural and urban areas have experienced profound social and demographic changes during the past three decades. They contend, however, that change has affected life in rural areas more than in urban areas.

FIGURE 6.1

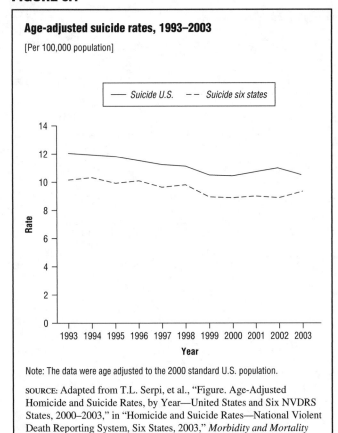

Age-adjusted suicide rates, 1993–2003

[Per 100,000 population]

Note: The data were age adjusted to the 2000 standard U.S. population.

SOURCE: Adapted from T.L. Serpi, et al., "Figure. Age-Adjusted Homicide and Suicide Rates, by Year—United States and Six NVDRS States, 2000–2003," in "Homicide and Suicide Rates—National Violent Death Reporting System, Six States, 2003," *Morbidity and Mortality Weekly Report*, vol. 54, no. 15, April 22, 2005, http://www.cdc.gov/mmwr/PDF/wk/mm5415.pdf (accessed December 7, 2005)

They note that high levels of social isolation, as often occurs in rural areas, are correlated with high suicide rates.

Suicide among Young People

According to the American Association of Suicidology, the rate of suicide among young people increased 200% between the 1950s and 1990s. During the 1990s death rates for suicide declined, but in some age groups the rate of suicide attempts actually rose. In 2003 suicide was the third-leading cause of death among people ages fifteen to twenty-four. (See Table 4.2 in Chapter 4.) While females are more likely to attempt suicide, males are more likely to die from their attempts ("Youth Risk Behavior Surveillance—United States, 2003," *Morbidity and Mortality Weekly Report*, vol. 53, No. SS–2, May 21, 2004).

While the overall suicide rate among African-American youths has been relatively low in comparison with that of white males, the rate rose among African-American males between 1950 and 1990. (See Table 6.1.) By 1990 the death rate for suicide among African-American males ages twenty-five to forty-four years had risen to a high of 19.6 suicides per one hundred thousand. After 1990 the suicide rate for young African-

American males steadily declined, and by 2000 it dropped to 14.3 per one hundred thousand. The rate rose slightly in 2001 to 14.4, and then rose more dramatically in 2002, to 15.1 per one hundred thousand.

Death rates for suicide rose for white males ages twenty-five to forty-four from 1950 through 1990. By 2000 the death rate had declined to 22.9, but it rose again to 24 in 2001 and 2002. (See Table 6.1.)

In 1990 the highest suicide death rate among youth ages fifteen to twenty-four was 49.1 suicides per one hundred thousand people among male American Indian or Alaska Natives. (See Table 6.1.) By 2001 this rate fell to 24.7 per one hundred thousand but rose again in 2002 to 27.9.

While death rates from suicide declined among young adults ages fifteen to nineteen between 1990 and 2002 (see Table 6.1), the percentage of high school students who attempted suicide increased from 7.3% in 1991 to 8.5% in 2003, peaking in 2001 at 8.8%. (See Table 6.2.) The percentage of students injured during a suicide attempt also rose from 1.7% in 1991 to 2.9% in 2003.

Table 6.3 shows that the percentage of high school students who attempted suicide was highest among ninth graders and decreased as grade level increased. The percentage of suicide attempts requiring medical attention followed the same pattern: a higher percentage of the suicide attempts of ninth graders required medical attention than did those of older students, and this percentage decreased as grade level increased. Hispanic students were the most likely to attempt suicide and white students the least likely. In addition, suicide attempts were highest among high school students living in Ohio, Texas, Michigan, and Kentucky. (See Table 6.4.)

The CDC also collects data on the percentage of high school students who feel sad or hopeless, who seriously consider attempting suicide, and who make a suicide plan. In 2003 nearly 30% of high school students in all grades felt sad or hopeless. Approximately 17% seriously considered attempting suicide, and 16% to 17% made a suicide plan. (See Table 6.5.) In 2003 the states in which more than 30% of high school students felt sad or hopeless were Arizona, Florida, Kentucky, Ohio, Texas, West Virginia, and Wyoming. (See Table 6.6.)

Figures 6.2 and 6.3 show the annual suicide rates among young people by method. The use of firearms was the method most frequently used by ten- to fourteen-year-olds from 1992 to 1996. In 1997 and from 1999 to 2001 suffocation (e.g. hanging) overtook firearms as the most frequently used method of suicide in this age group. Poisoning is the third most widely used method of suicide, although its use decreased from 1992 to 1996 and then somewhat stabilized by 2001. Other methods (for

TABLE 6.2

Suicide ideation, attempts, and injuries among students in grades 9–12, by sex, grade level, race, and Hispanic origin, selected years 1991–2003

[Data are based on a national sample of high school students, grades 9–12]

Sex, grade level, race, and Hispanic origin	1991	1993	1995	1997	1999	2001	2003
	Percent of students who seriously considered suicide[a]						
Total	**29.0**	**24.1**	**24.1**	**20.5**	**19.3**	**19.0**	**16.9**
Male							
Total	20.8	18.8	18.3	15.1	13.7	14.2	12.8
9th grade	17.6	17.7	18.2	16.1	11.9	14.7	11.9
10th grade	19.5	18.0	16.7	14.5	13.7	13.8	13.2
11th grade	25.3	20.6	21.7	16.6	13.7	14.1	12.9
12th grade	20.7	18.3	16.3	13.5	15.6	13.7	13.2
Not Hispanic or Latino:							
White	21.7	19.1	19.1	14.4	12.5	14.9	12.0
Black or African American	13.3	15.4	16.7	10.6	11.7	9.2	10.3
Hispanic or Latino	18.0	17.9	15.7	17.1	13.6	12.2	12.9
Female							
Total	37.2	29.6	30.4	27.1	24.9	23.6	21.3
9th grade	40.3	30.9	34.4	28.9	24.4	26.2	22.2
10th grade	39.7	31.6	32.8	30.0	30.1	24.1	23.8
11th grade	38.4	28.9	31.1	26.2	23.0	23.6	20.0
12th grade	30.7	27.3	23.9	23.6	21.2	18.9	18.0
Not Hispanic or Latino:							
White	38.6	29.7	31.6	26.1	23.2	24.2	21.2
Black or African American	29.4	24.5	22.2	22.0	18.8	17.2	14.7
Hispanic or Latino	34.6	34.1	34.1	30.3	26.1	26.5	23.4
	Percent of students who attempted suicide[a]						
Total	**7.3**	**8.6**	**8.7**	**7.7**	**8.3**	**8.8**	**8.5**
Male							
Total	3.9	5.0	5.6	4.5	5.7	6.2	5.4
9th grade	4.5	5.8	6.8	6.3	6.1	8.2	5.8
10th grade	3.3	5.9	5.4	3.8	6.2	6.7	5.5
11th grade	4.1	3.4	5.8	4.4	4.8	4.9	4.6
12th grade	3.8	4.5	4.7	3.7	5.4	4.4	5.2
Not Hispanic or Latino:							
White	3.3	4.4	5.2	3.2	4.5	5.3	3.7
Black or African American	3.3	5.4	7.0	5.6	7.1	7.5	7.7
Hispanic or Latino	3.7	7.4	5.8	7.2	6.6	8.0	6.1
Female							
Total	10.7	12.5	11.9	11.6	10.9	11.2	11.5
9th grade	13.8	14.4	14.9	15.1	14.0	13.2	14.7
10th grade	12.2	13.1	15.1	14.3	14.8	12.2	12.7
11th grade	8.7	13.6	11.4	11.3	7.5	11.5	10.0
12th grade	7.8	9.1	6.6	6.2	5.8	6.5	6.9
Not Hispanic or Latino:							
White	10.4	11.3	10.4	10.3	9.0	10.3	10.3
Black or African American	9.4	11.2	10.8	9.0	7.5	9.8	9.0
Hispanic or Latino	11.6	19.7	21.0	14.9	18.9	15.9	15.0

example, jumping from high places such as bridges) were used infrequently from 1992 to 2001.

Although the use of firearms to commit suicide dropped considerably in the fifteen- to nineteen-year-old age group, it was still the most frequently used method in 2001. (See Figure 6.3.) The use of suffocation to commit suicide increased slightly from 1992 to 2001. Poisoning and other methods of suicide ranked low in this age group during those years, as in the ten- to fourteen-year-old group. Poisoning declined in use from 1992 to 1997, and then stabilized. As a comparison, in the general population in 2002, 54% (17,108) of those who took their own lives used a firearm, 20% (6,462) used suffocation, and 17% (5,486) used poison.

Other methods were used much less frequently. (See Table 6.7.)

The statistics in this section underscore the urgent need for prevention, education, and support programs to help teens and young adults at risk. The National Center for Injury Prevention and Control (NCIPC) sponsors initiatives to raise public awareness of suicide and institutes strategies to reduce suicide deaths. Along with supporting research about risk factors for suicide in the general population, NCIPC develops programs for high-risk populations.

SUICIDE AMONG GAY AND LESBIAN ADOLESCENTS. The suicide rate for gay and lesbian adolescents is dramatically higher than for the general adolescent

TABLE 6.2

Suicide ideation, attempts, and injuries among students in grades 9–12, by sex, grade level, race, and Hispanic origin, selected years 1991–2003 [CONTINUED]

[Data are based on a national sample of high school students, grades 9–12]

Sex, grade level, race, and Hispanic origin	1991	1993	1995	1997	1999	2001	2003
	Percent of students with an injurious suicide attempt[a, b]						
Total	**1.7**	**2.7**	**2.8**	**2.6**	**2.6**	**2.6**	**2.9**
Male							
Total	1.0	1.6	2.2	2.0	2.1	2.1	2.4
9th grade	1.0	2.1	2.3	3.2	2.6	2.6	3.1
10th grade	0.5	1.3	2.4	1.4	1.8	2.5	2.1
11th grade	1.5	1.1	2.0	2.6	2.1	1.6	2.0
12th grade	0.9	1.5	2.2	1.0	1.7	1.5	1.8
Not Hispanic or Latino:							
White	1.0	1.4	2.1	1.5	1.6	1.7	1.1
Black or African American	0.4	2.0	2.8	1.8	3.4	3.6	5.2
Hispanic or Latino	0.5	2.0	2.9	2.1	1.4	2.5	4.2
Female							
Total	2.5	3.8	3.4	3.3	3.1	3.1	3.2
9th grade	2.8	3.5	6.3	5.0	3.8	3.8	3.9
10th grade	2.6	5.1	3.8	3.7	4.0	3.6	3.2
11th grade	2.1	3.9	2.9	2.8	2.8	2.8	2.9
12th grade	2.4	2.9	1.3	2.0	1.3	1.7	2.2
Not Hispanic or Latino:							
White	2.3	3.6	2.9	2.6	2.3	2.9	2.4
Black or African American	2.9	4.0	3.6	3.0	2.4	3.1	2.2
Hispanic or Latino	2.7	5.5	6.6	3.8	4.6	4.2	5.7

[a]Response is for the 12 months preceding the survey.
[b]A suicide attempt that required medical attention.
Notes: Only youths attending school participated in the survey. Persons of Hispanic origin may be of any race.

SOURCE: "Table 62. Suicidal Ideation, Suicide Attempts, and Injurious Suicide Attempts among Students in Grades 9–12, by Sex, Grade Level, Race, and Hispanic Origin: United States, Selected Years 1991–2003," in *Health, United States, 2005*, Centers for Disease Control and Prevention, National Center for Health Statistics, November 2005, http://www.cdc.gov/nchs/data/hus/hus05.pdf (accessed February 27, 2006)

TABLE 6.3

Percentage of high school students who actually attempted suicide and whose suicide attempt required medical attention, by sex, race/ethnicity, and grade, 2003

	Attempted suicide[a,b]			Suicide attempt required medical attention[a]		
	Female	Male	Total	Female	Male	Total
Category	Percent	Percent	Percent	Percent	Percent	Percent
Race/ethnicity						
White[c]	10.3	3.7	**6.9**	2.4	1.1	**1.7**
Black[c]	9.0	7.7	**8.4**	2.2	5.2	**3.7**
Hispanic	15.0	6.1	**10.6**	5.7	4.2	**5.0**
Grade						
9	14.7	5.8	**10.1**	3.9	3.1	**3.5**
10	12.7	5.5	**9.1**	3.2	2.1	**2.6**
11	10.0	4.6	**7.3**	2.9	2.0	**2.4**
12	6.9	5.2	**6.1**	2.2	1.8	**2.1**
Total	**11.5**	**5.4**	**8.5**	**3.2**	**2.4**	**2.9**

[a]During the 12 months preceding the survey.
[b]One or more times.
[c]Non-Hispanic.

SOURCE: Jo Anne Grunbaum, et al., "Table 18. Percentage of High School Students Who Actually Attempted Suicide and Whose Suicide Attempt Required Medical Attention, by Sex, Race/Ethnicity, and Grade—United States, Youth Risk Behavior Survey, 2003," in "Youth Risk Behavior Surveillance—United States, 2003," *Morbidity and Mortality Weekly Report*, vol. 53, no. SS-2, May 21, 2004, http://www.cdc.gov/mmwr/PDF/SS/SS5302.pdf (accessed November 9, 2005)

TABLE 6.4

Percentage of high school students who actually attempted suicide and whose suicide attempt required medical attention, by sex and selected U.S. sites, 2003

Site	Attempted suicide[a,b]			Suicide attempt required medical attention[a]		
	Female	Male	Total	Female	Male	Total
	Percent	Percent	Percent	Percent	Percent	Percent
State surveys						
Alabama	10.7	3.8	**7.3**	3.9	1.4	**2.6**
Alaska	10.0	6.1	**8.1**	1.5	2.6	**2.1**
Arizona	11.2	4.2	**7.8**	3.6	1.2	**2.5**
Delaware	11.5	5.5	**8.6**	3.5	2.0	**2.7**
Florida	11.8	6.2	**9.0**	3.9	2.9	**3.4**
Georgia	8.7	8.2	**8.5**	3.0	3.0	**3.0**
Idaho	11.3	5.8	**8.6**	3.3	1.9	**2.7**
Indiana	8.1	5.1	**6.6**	2.2	1.1	**1.6**
Kentucky	10.3	9.8	**10.3**	3.6	3.4	**3.7**
Maine	12.1	5.3	**9.0**	3.7	2.0	**2.9**
Massachusetts	9.4	7.3	**8.4**	2.7	2.8	**2.8**
Michigan	12.9	7.8	**10.5**	3.9	2.4	**3.2**
Mississippi	8.5	4.1	**6.6**	2.8	2.1	**2.5**
Missouri	9.8	4.8	**7.3**	2.7	1.4	**2.0**
Montana	12.3	6.8	**9.7**	3.8	2.3	**3.0**
Nebraska	11.3	6.4	**8.8**	3.7	3.2	**3.4**
Nevada	11.9	5.9	**8.8**	3.7	2.2	**2.9**
New Hampshire	11.4	3.9	**7.7**	4.0	0.9	**2.5**
New York	9.7	3.7	**6.8**	2.7	1.5	**2.1**
North Carolina	c	c	**c**	c	c	**c**
North Dakota	8.9	5.2	**7.2**	2.8	2.6	**2.8**
Ohio	12.8	10.8	**11.9**	5.7	4.2	**5.0**
Oklahoma	8.3	5.8	**7.0**	3.3	1.4	**2.4**
Rhode Island	9.5	6.9	**8.3**	2.5	3.1	**2.9**
South Dakota	12.4	6.3	**9.3**	3.1	2.4	**2.7**
Tennessee	11.5	6.4	**8.9**	3.8	2.5	**3.1**
Texas[d]	13.5	7.5	**10.6**	3.7	2.8	**3.3**
Utah	8.8	6.2	**7.5**	1.5	2.5	**2.0**
Vermont	9.9	4.6	**7.2**	2.8	1.7	**2.3**
West Virginia	12.8	6.0	**9.3**	2.6	2.5	**2.5**
Wisconsin	11.8	4.7	**8.2**	3.8	1.1	**2.5**
Wyoming	12.9	5.5	**9.1**	4.1	2.7	**3.4**
Median	**11.3**	**5.9**	**8.5**	**3.5**	**2.4**	**2.7**
Range	**8.1–13.5**	**3.7–10.8**	**6.6–11.9**	**1.5–5.7**	**0.9–4.2**	**1.6–5.0**
Local surveys[e]						
Boston PS, MA	9.1	8.6	**8.9**	2.9	2.4	**2.6**
Broward County PS, FL	10.7	6.0	**8.5**	3.3	2.3	**2.9**
Chicago PS, IL	13.4	10.4	**12.1**	3.7	5.4	**4.7**
Dallas ISD, TX	13.0	5.3	**9.5**	2.0	1.3	**1.7**
DeKalb County PS, GA	8.5	6.1	**7.4**	2.5	2.8	**2.6**
Detroit PS, MI	14.1	9.2	**12.0**	4.5	2.8	**3.7**
District of Columbia PS	12.2	12.0	**12.1**	2.2	4.8	**3.5**
Los Angeles USD, CA	17.5	5.0	**11.4**	4.5	1.4	**3.0**
Memphis PS, TN	11.2	7.1	**9.3**	3.8	2.7	**3.3**
Miami-Dade County PS, FL	12.5	5.9	**9.3**	3.7	1.8	**2.8**
Milwaukee PS, WI	11.4	10.3	**10.9**	3.8	3.0	**3.4**
New Orleans PS, LA	10.9	10.0	**10.4**	3.6	4.2	**3.9**
New York City PS, NY	11.3	5.1	**8.4**	2.2	1.5	**1.9**

population (S. McAndrew and R. Warne, "Ignoring the Evidence Dictating the Practice: Sexual Orientation, Suicidality and the Dichotomy of the Mental Health Nurse," *Journal of Psychiatric and Mental Health Nursing*, vol. 11, no. 4, 2004). Adolescence (the transition to adulthood) is often a difficult period. For gay and lesbian adolescents, this transition is compounded by having to come to terms with their sexuality in a society generally unaccepting of homosexuality.

At this period in their lives, when the need to confide in and gain acceptance from friends and family may be crucial, gay and lesbian adolescents are often torn between choices that do not necessarily meet either of these needs. Those who are open about their sexual orientation risk disappointing or even alienating their families and facing the hostility of their peers. Teens who choose not to disclose their homosexuality may suffer emotional distress because they have nowhere to turn for emotional support. In either scenario, despair, isolation, anger, guilt, and overwhelming depression may promote suicidal thoughts or actual suicide attempts.

TABLE 6.4

Percentage of high school students who actually attempted suicide and whose suicide attempt required medical attention, by sex and selected U.S. sites, 2003 [CONTINUED]

	Attempted suicide[a, b]			Suicide attempt required medical attention[a]		
	Female	Male	Total	Female	Male	Total
Site	Percent	Percent	Percent	Percent	Percent	Percent
Orange County PS, FL	12.1	6.4	**9.3**	4.1	2.8	**3.5**
Palm Beach County SD, FL	10.3	8.1	**9.4**	3.1	4.2	**3.8**
Philadelphia SD, PA	14.2	9.9	**12.3**	3.4	2.6	**3.1**
San Bernardino USD, CA	13.2	9.5	**11.5**	5.3	3.9	**4.8**
San Diego USD, CA	13.1	8.9	**10.9**	2.9	3.6	**3.3**
Median	**12.1**	**8.3**	**9.9**	**3.5**	**2.8**	3.3
Range	**8.5–17.5**	**5.0–12.0**	**7.4–12.3**	**2.0–5.3**	**1.3–5.4**	**1.7–4.8**

[a]During the 12 months preceding the survey.
[b]One or more times.
[c]Not available.
[d]Survey did not include students from one of the state's large school districts.
[e]PS=public school, SD=school district, ISD=independent school district, USD=unified school district.

SOURCE: Jo Anne Grunbaum, et al., "Table 19. Percentage of High School Students Who Actually Attempted Suicide and Whose Suicide Attempt Required Medical Attention, by Sex—Selected U.S. Sites, Youth Risk Behavior Survey, 2003," in "Youth Risk Behavior Surveillance—United States, 2003," *Morbidity and Mortality Weekly Report*, vol. 53, no. SS-2, May 21, 2004, http://www.cdc.gov/mmwr/PDF/SS/SS5302.pdf (accessed November 9, 2005)

TABLE 6.5

Percentage of high school students who felt sad or hopeless, who seriously considered attempting suicide, and who made a suicide plan, by sex, race/ethnicity, and grade, 2003

	Felt sad or hopeless[a, b]			Seriously considered attempting suicide[b]			Made a suicide plan[b]		
	Female	Male	Total	Female	Male	Total	Female	Male	Total
Category	Percent	Percent	Percent	Percent	Percent	Percent	Percent	Percent	Percent
Race/ethnicity									
White[c]	33.3	19.6	**26.2**	21.2	12.0	**16.5**	18.6	13.9	**16.2**
Black[c]	30.8	21.7	**26.3**	14.7	10.3	**12.5**	12.4	8.4	**10.4**
Hispanic	44.9	25.9	**35.4**	23.4	12.9	**18.1**	20.7	14.6	**17.6**
Grade									
9	35.7	21.0	**28.0**	22.2	11.9	**16.9**	20.9	14.8	**17.7**
10	36.9	22.7	**29.7**	23.8	13.2	**18.3**	19.5	13.1	**16.3**
11	35.9	22.1	**28.9**	20.0	12.9	**16.4**	17.9	14.4	**16.2**
12	32.6	22.0	**27.4**	18.0	13.2	**15.5**	16.2	13.7	**14.9**
Total	**35.5**	**21.9**	**28.6**	**21.3**	**12.8**	**16.9**	**18.9**	**14.1**	**16.5**

[a]Felt so sad or hopeless almost every day for ≥2 weeks in a row that they stopped doing some usual activities.
[b]During the 12 months preceding the survey.
[c]Non-Hispanic.

SOURCE: Anne Grunbaum, et al., "Table 16. Percentage of High School Students Who Felt Sad or Hopeless, Who Seriously Considered Attempting Suicide, and Who Made a Suicide Plan, by Sex, Race/Ethnicity, and Grade—Youth Risk Behavior Survey, 2003," in "Youth Risk Behavior Surveillance—United States, 2003," *Morbidity and Mortality Weekly Report*, vol. 53, no. SS-2, May 21, 2004, http://www.cdc.gov/mmwr/PDF/SS/SS5302.pdf (accessed November 9, 2005)

Exact data are not available for suicide rates of gay, lesbian, and bisexual teenagers because the sexual orientation of suicide victims often is unknown. But according to a 2006 study by the McCreary Center Society in British Columbia, Canada, lesbian teenagers are at particularly high risk of suicide ("Lesbian Teens Face Higher Risk of Suicide: Study," *Toronto Star*, June 2, 2006). In fact, the study found that suicide attempts among lesbian girls increased from one in five in 1992, to one in four in 1998, to one in three in 2003. In all, 38% of lesbian teenagers surveyed reported that they had attempted suicide in the past year, versus just 8.2% of heterosexual girls surveyed. Only 8.8% of gay male teenagers, and 3.3% of straight males, reported having attempted suicide in the past year, according to the survey.

EUTHANASIA AND PHYSICIAN-ASSISTED SUICIDE

The American Constitution does not guarantee the right to choose to die. The U.S. Supreme Court, however, recognized as of 2005 that Americans have a fundamental right to privacy, or what is sometimes called the "right to be left alone." While the right to

TABLE 6.6

Percentage of high school students who felt sad or hopeless, who seriously considered attempting suicide, and who made a suicide plan, by sex and selected U.S. sites, 2003

Site	Felt sad or hopeless[a, b]			Seriously considered attempting suicide[b]			Made a suicide plan[b]		
	Female	Male	Total	Female	Male	Total	Female	Male	Total
	Percent	Percent	Percent	Percent	Percent	Percent	Percent	Percent	Percent
State surveys									
Alabama	31.3	23.1	**27.1**	17.2	11.6	**14.4**	15.1	8.7	**11.9**
Alaska	30.1	20.8	**25.2**	21.1	12.7	**16.7**	16.6	8.6	**12.5**
Arizona	39.3	21.1	**30.4**	23.0	11.8	**17.6**	15.4	9.5	**12.6**
Delaware	33.7	21.0	**27.4**	20.0	11.0	**15.6**	14.0	9.2	**11.7**
Florida	37.6	22.7	**30.1**	20.4	11.3	**15.8**	14.8	10.3	**12.6**
Georgia	35.0	22.1	**28.5**	19.8	13.1	**16.4**	14.5	11.4	**13.0**
Idaho	35.9	21.9	**28.7**	22.4	13.4	**17.8**	17.4	12.4	**14.9**
Indiana	30.3	21.0	**25.5**	18.9	13.3	**16.0**	14.0	11.2	**12.6**
Kentucky	36.7	23.6	**30.1**	21.0	14.3	**17.6**	14.8	13.8	**14.5**
Maine	31.3	18.2	**24.7**	21.5	12.4	**17.1**	17.9	11.8	**15.0**
Massachusetts	35.0	21.1	**28.0**	20.0	12.7	**16.3**	15.0	10.0	**12.5**
Michigan	36.5	24.1	**30.2**	21.8	14.1	**18.1**	15.9	12.3	**14.2**
Mississippi	35.0	21.7	**28.7**	16.1	10.4	**13.5**	13.3	9.3	**11.6**
Missouri	32.1	20.2	**26.0**	21.5	12.2	**16.8**	15.9	9.9	**12.9**
Montana	33.1	20.2	**26.4**	24.2	13.8	**18.9**	18.0	11.7	**14.8**
Nebraska	31.6	19.2	**25.3**	24.0	12.2	**17.9**	20.1	14.5	**17.2**
Nevada	36.4	23.7	**29.9**	24.2	12.2	**18.1**	17.6	12.7	**15.1**
New Hampshire	34.2	21.6	**28.0**	22.5	12.9	**17.8**	16.9	9.6	**13.3**
New York	34.3	21.3	**27.8**	19.6	9.3	**14.4**	14.0	7.8	**10.9**
North Carolina	38.4	22.7	**30.6**	23.0	13.2	**18.1**	c	c	c
North Dakota	27.3	14.8	**20.8**	17.6	9.8	**13.6**	13.7	9.1	**11.3**
Ohio	37.4	23.9	**30.6**	21.3	15.2	**18.2**	16.5	11.8	**14.1**
Oklahoma	32.3	22.1	**27.1**	17.1	13.7	**15.4**	14.5	11.8	**13.3**
Rhode Island	29.4	19.4	**24.3**	16.5	11.9	**14.1**	13.2	9.3	**11.2**
South Dakota	31.4	18.1	**24.6**	21.8	15.9	**18.8**	18.0	12.1	**15.0**
Tennessee	37.4	19.6	**28.3**	21.6	13.6	**17.5**	17.7	10.6	**14.1**
Texas[d]	40.9	22.7	**31.7**	22.2	12.6	**17.3**	15.7	11.2	**13.4**
Utah	31.9	21.6	**26.6**	18.0	14.2	**16.1**	14.0	10.8	**12.4**
Vermont	29.4	18.4	**23.8**	c	c	c	16.7	10.6	**13.6**
West Virginia	41.7	22.6	**31.9**	24.0	12.1	**17.8**	19.4	10.5	**14.8**
Wisconsin	33.5	17.6	**25.3**	25.6	13.8	**19.6**	c	c	c
Wyoming	36.9	23.5	**30.2**	24.8	17.5	**21.0**	17.5	14.1	**15.8**
Median	**34.2**	**21.4**	**27.9**	**21.5**	**12.7**	**17.3**	**15.8**	**10.7**	**13.3**
Range	**27.3–41.7**	**14.8–24.1**	**20.8–31.9**	**16.1–25.6**	**9.3–17.5**	**13.5–21.0**	**13.2–20.1**	**7.8–14.5**	**10.9–17.2**
Local surveys[e]									
Boston PS, MA	36.7	21.4	**29.1**	17.2	8.3	**12.9**	15.7	7.7	**11.9**
Broward County PS, FL	38.8	23.0	**30.9**	18.9	10.0	**14.5**	13.3	8.6	**11.1**
Chicago PS, IL	35.6	26.0	**31.1**	15.7	11.0	**13.5**	13.0	9.3	**11.2**
Dallas ISD, TX	40.1	20.2	**30.4**	22.1	8.2	**15.3**	17.1	6.2	**11.7**
DeKalb County PS, GA	34.7	22.2	**28.5**	18.7	8.5	**13.7**	12.9	8.4	**10.7**
Detroit PS, MI	37.5	24.8	**31.4**	17.7	11.0	**14.6**	13.1	9.5	**11.4**
District of Columbia PS	36.4	25.6	**31.1**	18.5	9.6	**14.2**	15.9	10.8	**13.5**
Los Angeles USD, CA	44.2	25.1	**34.6**	22.9	9.2	**16.0**	18.9	10.4	**14.6**
Memphis PS, TN	34.7	20.3	**27.4**	15.0	10.1	**12.5**	12.3	9.4	**10.9**
Miami-Dade County PS, FL	37.9	23.3	**30.5**	17.2	8.8	**12.9**	13.7	8.0	**10.8**
Milwaukee PS, WI	39.0	23.2	**31.1**	20.3	13.0	**16.7**	c	c	c
New Orleans PS, LA	32.6	18.8	**25.9**	12.4	10.6	**11.5**	9.5	7.6	**8.6**
New York City PS, NY	39.3	24.9	**32.2**	17.8	9.3	**13.6**	13.5	7.9	**10.7**

privacy is not explicitly mentioned in the Constitution, the Supreme Court has interpreted several amendments as encompassing this right. In *Roe v. Wade* (410 US 113, 1973) the High Court ruled that the Fourteenth Amendment protects the right to privacy against state action, specifically a woman's right to abortion. In the landmark Karen Ann Quinlan case, the Court held that the right to privacy included the right to refuse unwanted medical treatment and, as a consequence, the right to die.

The Acceptability of Euthanasia and Physician-Assisted Suicide

In "When Is Physician Assisted Suicide or Euthanasia Acceptable?" (*Journal of Medical Ethics*, vol. 29, no. 6, December, 2003), S. Frileux and colleagues examined the opinion of the general public on euthanasia and physician-assisted suicide (PAS). Frileux and colleagues define these terms as follows: "In physician-assisted suicide, the physician provides the patient with the means to end his or her own life. In euthanasia, the

TABLE 6.6

Percentage of high school students who felt sad or hopeless, who seriously considered attempting suicide, and who made a suicide plan, by sex and selected U.S. sites, 2003 [CONTINUED]

Site	Felt sad or hopeless[a, b]			Seriously considered attempting suicide[b]			Made a suicide plan[b]		
	Female	Male	Total	Female	Male	Total	Female	Male	Total
	Percent	Percent	Percent	Percent	Percent	Percent	Percent	Percent	Percent
Orange County PS, FL	37.0	18.6	**27.8**	20.2	10.3	**15.3**	15.0	10.1	**12.6**
Palm Beach County SD, FL	39.9	24.9	**32.5**	22.2	13.1	**17.7**	15.4	9.7	**12.7**
Philadelphia SD, PA	38.9	28.5	**33.9**	18.7	9.1	**14.0**	15.6	9.2	**12.4**
San Bernardino USD, CA	38.9	24.7	**31.9**	20.1	12.6	**16.6**	16.4	13.4	**15.0**
San Diego USD, CA	40.7	22.0	**31.1**	24.6	14.4	**19.4**	21.7	11.8	**16.7**
Median	**38.3**	**23.2**	**31.1**	**18.7**	**10.0**	**14.3**	**15.0**	**9.3**	**11.7**
Range	**32.6–44.2**	**18.6–28.5**	**25.9–34.6**	**12.4–24.6**	**8.2–14.4**	**11.5–19.4**	**9.5–21.7**	**6.2–13.4**	**8.6–16.7**

[a]Felt so sad or hopeless almost every day for ≥2 weeks in a row that they stopped doing some usual activities.
[b]During the 12 months preceding the survey.
[c]Not available.
[d]Survey did not include students from one of the state's large school districts.
[e]PS=public school, SD=school district, ISD=independent school district, USD=unified school district.

SOURCE: Jo Anne Grunbaum, et al., "Table 17. Percentage of High School Students Who Felt Sad or Hopeless, Who Seriously Considered Attempting Suicide, and Who Made a Suicide Plan, by Sex—Selected U.S. Sites, Youth Risk Behavior Survey, 2003," in "Youth Risk Behavior Surveillance—United States, 2003," *Morbidity and Mortality Weekly Report*, vol. 53, no. SS-2, May 21, 2004, http://www.cdc.gov/mmwr/PDF/SS/SS5302.pdf (accessed November 9, 2005)

FIGURE 6.2

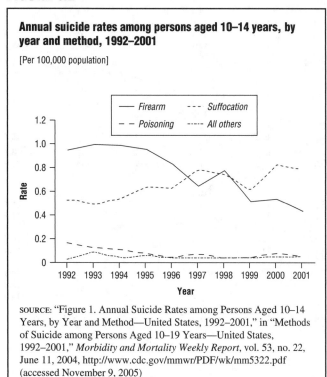

Annual suicide rates among persons aged 10–14 years, by year and method, 1992–2001

[Per 100,000 population]

SOURCE: "Figure 1. Annual Suicide Rates among Persons Aged 10–14 Years, by Year and Method—United States, 1992–2001," in "Methods of Suicide among Persons Aged 10–19 Years—United States, 1992–2001," *Morbidity and Mortality Weekly Report*, vol. 53, no. 22, June 11, 2004, http://www.cdc.gov/mmwr/PDF/wk/mm5322.pdf (accessed November 9, 2005)

FIGURE 6.3

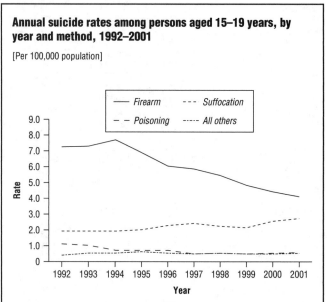

Annual suicide rates among persons aged 15–19 years, by year and method, 1992–2001

[Per 100,000 population]

SOURCE: "Figure 2. Annual Suicide Rates among Persons Aged 15–19 Years, by Year and Method—United States, 1992–2001," in "Methods of Suicide among Persons Aged 10–19 Years—United States, 1992–2001," *Morbidity and Mortality Weekly Report*, vol. 53, no. 22, June 11, 2004, http://www.cdc.gov/mmwr/PDF/wk/mm5322.pdf (accessed November 9, 2005)

physician deliberately and directly intervenes to end the patient's life; this is sometimes called 'active euthanasia' to distinguish it from withholding or withdrawing treatment needed to sustain life." Their study posed the questions: "Should a terminally ill patient be allowed to die? Should the medical profession have the option of helping such a patient to die?" The study found that acceptability of PAS or euthanasia appeared to depend

on four factors: the level of patient suffering, the extent to which the patient requested death, the age of the patient, and the degree of curability of the illness. In general, people judged euthanasia as less acceptable than PAS.

L. C. Kaldjian and colleagues conducted a study to determine the attitudes of internists (doctors specializing in internal medicine) towards PAS and other end-of-life

TABLE 6.7

Number of suicide deaths and suicide death rates, 2002

Mechanism of suicide	Number of deaths	Rate of death (per 100,000 population)
All mechanisms	31,655	11.0
Firearm	17,108	5.9
Suffocation	6,462	2.2
Poisoning	5,486	1.9
Fall	740	0.3
Cut/pierce	566	0.2
Drowning	368	0.1
Other specified, classifiable	315	0.1
Other specified, not elsewhere classified	200	0.1
Fire/flame	150	0.1
Unspecified	145	0.1
All transport	112	0.0
Motor vehicle traffic	112	0.0

SOURCE: Adapted from "Table 18. Number of Deaths, Death Rates, and Age-Adjusted Death Rates for Injury Deaths by Mechanism and Intent of Death: United States, 2002," in "Deaths: Final Data for 2002," *National Vital Statistics Reports*, vol. 53, no. 5, October 12, 2004, http://www.cdc.gov/nchs/data/nvsr53/nvsr53_05acc.pdf (accessed March 3, 2006)

care issues ("Internists' Attitudes toward Terminal Sedation in End of Life Care," *Journal of Medical Ethics*, vol. 30, no. 5, October 2004). Most physicians in the study (96%) agreed that it is appropriate to increase pain-reducing medication when needed in end-of-life care. More than three-quarters (78%) also agreed that if a terminally ill patient has pain that cannot be managed well, terminal sedation (TS) is appropriate. (TS means alleviating the pain and discomfort of dying people by sedating them or by providing medication that alleviates their painful or uncomfortable symptoms but that has complete sedation as a side effect. These patients are not usually given nutrition or fluids. TS is controversial because some feel it is tantamount to euthanasia, only slower, while still being perfectly legal.) One-third (33%) agreed that PAS is acceptable in some circumstances.

The results of the Kaldjian study also revealed that those who reported more experience with terminally ill patients were relatively more likely to support TS but not PAS than those who reported less or no experience with terminally ill patients. Those most likely to support both TS and PAS were those with no experience with terminally ill patients. In addition, the data showed that those who did not attend religious services or attended less than monthly were most likely to support both TS and PAS, while those who attended weekly were least likely to support both. No matter the number of terminal patients physicians cared for in the preceding year or the frequency with which they attended religious services, a large proportion supported TS but not PAS.

Assisted Suicide Funding Restriction Act of 1997

In April 1997 President Bill Clinton signed into law the Assisted Suicide Funding Restriction Act of 1997 (PL 105–12). The law bans federal funding of "active means

of causing death, such as by lethal injection or the provision of a lethal oral drug overdose." It does not, however, prohibit the use of federal funds for actions some consider to be passive euthanasia—withholding or withdrawing medical treatment or artificial nutrition and hydration, which may eventually lead to death. Neither does it prohibit "the use of items, goods, benefits, or services" to relieve pain or discomfort, even if they hasten death, so long as they are not intended to do so.

Patients Requesting Assisted Suicide and Euthanasia

Diane E. Meier et al studied various characteristics of patients requesting and receiving euthanasia and PAS and reported the results in "Characteristics of Patients Requesting and Receiving Physician-Assisted Death" (*Archives of Internal Medicine*, vol. 163, no. 13, July 14, 2003). The 1,902 physicians who responded to the researchers' survey reported 415 recent requests for aid in dying. Of these requests, 361 (89%) came from patients alone or in conjunction with their families. Only forty-six requests (11%) came from the family alone. Of the requests, 52% were for a lethal prescription, 25% for a lethal injection, and 23% for either a prescription or an injection.

Meier and her colleagues found that the patients requesting euthanasia or PAS were predominantly male (61%), forty-six to seventy-five years old (56%), and of white European descent (89%). Almost half (47%) were college graduates and had a primary diagnosis of cancer. A large number were experiencing severe pain (38%) or severe discomfort other than pain (42%). Many were described by their physicians as dependent (53%), bedridden (42%), and expected to live less than one month (28%).

Marijke C. Jansen-van der Weide, Bregje D. Onwuteaka-Philipsen, and Gerrit van der Wal published a study in 2005 that revealed characteristics of patients in the Netherlands who explicitly requested euthanasia or physician-assisted suicide from April 2000 to December 2002. As in the Meier study, more than half the patients requesting euthanasia and assisted suicide (EAS) were male (54%). Most of the patients were diagnosed with cancer (90%), a greater percentage than in the Meier study. Although only 9% were diagnosed with depression, 92% were "feeling bad."

Reasons for Assisted Suicide Requests

In an earlier study, "A National Survey of Physician Assisted Suicide and Euthanasia in the United States" (*New England Journal of Medicine*, vol. 338, no. 17, April 23, 1998), Meier and her colleagues surveyed physicians across medical specialties and throughout the country "to assess the prevalence of requests for assistance with suicide or euthanasia and of compliance with such requests." The physicians were asked to describe the reasons patients were requesting assistance to die.

The patients' reasons, as perceived by the physicians, were:

- Discomfort other than pain (reported by 79% of the physicians)

- Loss of dignity (53%)

- Fear of uncontrollable symptoms (52%)

- Actual pain (50%)

- Loss of meaning in life (47%)

- Being a burden (34%)

- Dependency (30%)

Interestingly, the patients' primary concerns were not physical (pain and suffering), but were more likely to be focused on loss of control, being a burden or dependent on others, and loss of dignity.

Results of the Jansen-van der Weide, Onwuteaka-Philipsen, and van der Wal study revealed some of the same reasons patients requested assistance in dying. The three most often cited reasons for requesting euthanasia or PAS were pointless suffering (75%), deterioration or loss of dignity (69%), and weakness or tiredness (60%). Depression was the reason most likely to have influenced a patient to request assistance in dying, while not wanting to burden his or her family was the second most influential factor.

PAIN NOT THE MAJOR REASON FOR REQUESTS TO DIE. Ezekiel Emanuel, an associate professor at Harvard Medical School and a member of the National Bioethics Advisory Commission, suggests that, contrary to popular belief, pain is not the major motivation behind a patient's request to die. In "Whose Right to Die?" (*Atlantic Monthly*, March 1997), Emanuel reported that empirical studies support this fact. Washington State physicians who received requests to assist in death or to perform euthanasia indicated that severe pain played a role in patient decisions in only about one-third of the requests. Emanuel's own study of cancer patients in Boston revealed that patients in pain were more likely to oppose euthanasia and physician-assisted suicide.

According to Emanuel, studies in the Netherlands—where assisted suicide and euthanasia have been practiced for many years—provide more evidence that pain is a minor factor in requests to end one's life. (The Netherlands, Belgium, and the state of Oregon in the United States are the only places in the world where physician-assisted suicide is legal.) A 1996 update of the Dutch government's landmark *Remmelink Report* illustrated that, while pain played some role in 32% of the requests, there was not a single case in which pain was the only reason for requesting assistance to die.

The findings of Emanuel's study are remarkably similar to those revealed by the Meier and Jansen-van

der Weide studies. Emanuel found that the major reasons for assisted suicide and euthanasia requests ranged from depression to hopelessness to fear of loss of dignity and being a burden. His Boston study also showed that depressed patients were more likely to discuss euthanasia, to stockpile drugs for future suicide, and to have read the suicide manual *Final Exit* by the Hemlock Society.

Nurses and Patient Requests for Assisted Suicide

According to a national survey, one in five nurses who worked in adult critical care units have hastened a patient's death. In this survey, "The Role of Critical Care Nurses in Euthanasia and Assisted Suicide" (*New England Journal of Medicine*, vol. 334, no. 21, May 23, 1996), David A. Asch, M.D., defined euthanasia and assisted suicide as circumstances in which a person performs an act with the specific intent of causing or hastening a patient's death. In this category Dr. Asch included intentional overdose of narcotics or other substances, or providing explicit advice to patients about how to commit suicide. Withholding and withdrawing life-sustaining treatment, such as removing a mechanical ventilator, were not included.

A total of 852 nurses responded to the survey. Sixteen percent (129 nurses) reported that they had participated in active euthanasia and assisted suicide at least once in their careers. Sixty-five percent of those nurses who participated at least once in active euthanasia or assisted suicide had done so three or fewer times, while 5% reported doing so more than twenty times.

Based on the responses, Dr. Asch estimated that at least 7% (fifty-eight nurses) had engaged in euthanasia or assisted suicide at least once without a request from either the patient or a surrogate. Eight percent (sixty-two nurses) indicated having done so at least once without a request from the attending physician. These sixty-two nurses further indicated some instances in which they practiced euthanasia or assisted suicide following an attending physician's explicit request, or with the physician's advance knowledge.

Reasons given by the nurses for practicing euthanasia or assisted suicide included concern about the overuse of life-sustaining technology; a sense of responsibility for the patient's welfare; a desire to relieve suffering; and a desire to overcome the perceived unresponsiveness of physicians toward that suffering.

Some experts questioned the accuracy of the survey's results and considered the survey questions ambiguous. Others claimed that the interpretation of euthanasia and assisted suicide was questionable in cases in which the dispensing of pain-relieving medicine resulted in death. Many nurses expressed concern that publicizing the results of the study would undermine the patients' and families' trust in nurses who work in intensive care units.

Individually and as members of professional associations, nurses continue to grapple with questions about end-of-life care and patient requests for assisted suicide. To assist all nurses in providing competent and compassionate care for the dying, the Oncology Nursing Society (ONS) published a position paper and practice guidelines, "The Nurse's Responsibility to the Patient Requesting Assisted Suicide," in January 2001. (Oncology nurses care for terminally ill patients more often than nurses in other clinical settings.)

The ONS guidelines encourage nurses to engage in frank discussions with patients requesting assisted suicide, while actively seeking to identify and address patients' previously unmet needs. Although ONS guidelines definitively prohibit nurse involvement in assisted suicide, the professional society also cautions nurses to "resist the inclination to abandon terminally ill patients who request assisted suicide." The guidelines advise, "In state(s) where assisted suicide is legal, the nurse may choose to continue to provide care or may withdraw from the situation after transferring responsibility for care to a nursing colleague."

SUPPORTERS OF ASSISTED SUICIDE

End-of-Life Choices

On July 21, 2003, the Hemlock Society officially became End-of-Life Choices. The organization advocates for legislation to allow Americans to live with the freedom of choosing a dignified death, and also informs and educates the public about the right to die.

End-Of-Life Choices was founded as the Hemlock Society in 1980 by Derek Humphry, a journalist from England. In 1975 Humphry helped his wife take her own life to end the pain and suffering caused by her terminal bone cancer. Humphry recounted this incident in *Jean's Way: A Love Story* (New York: Harper and Row, 1978). The book launched his career in the voluntary euthanasia movement two years later.

In 1991 Humphry published *Final Exit: The Practicalities of Self-Deliverance and Assisted Suicide for the Dying* (Eugene, OR: The Hemlock Society). The suicide manual, which was on the *New York Times* bestseller list for eighteen weeks, gives explicit instructions on how to commit suicide. While Humphry insisted that his how-to book was written only to those who were terminally ill, and not those suffering from depression, some physicians were concerned about how the book would affect those suffering from depression. Dr. Sherwin B. Nuland felt that depression was not a strong enough justification for teaching people how to kill themselves, to help them do it, or to bestow blessing on it (*How We Die*, New York: Alfred A. Knopf, 1994). In his opinion, no one with judgment impaired by depression is

in a position to make a critical decision about ending his or her life.

In October 1991, while *Final Exit* was selling out at bookstores, Humphry's second wife, Ann Wickett, whom he had divorced the year before, committed suicide. She had been diagnosed with cancer and was reportedly depressed.

Humphry retired from the Hemlock Society in 1992, but his more recent activities have also sparked controversy. In 1999 he recorded a video depicting a variety of methods for committing suicide. Though it had been available from the Hemlock Society USA for several months, the video drew even more criticism when it aired on public television in Oregon a number of times in 2000. Critics asserted that this airing provided dangerous information, particularly to people who were depressed or mentally ill and to children.

In 2004 Humphry published *The Good Euthanasia Guide 2005: Where, What, and Who in Choices in Dying*. Much of the book describes international suicide laws.

Dr. Jack Kevorkian

Dr. Jack Kevorkian first earned the nickname "Dr. Death" when, as a medical resident, he would photograph patients at the time of death to gather data that would help him differentiate death from coma, shock, and fainting. During his study and residency, he suggested unconventional ideas, such as the harvesting of organs from death row inmates. His career as a doctor was also "checkered" (Kevorkian's own word) and notable for controversy.

In the late 1980s Kevorkian retired from pathology work and pursued an interest in the concept of physician-assisted suicide, becoming one of its best-known and most passionate advocates. He constructed a machine that would allow a patient to press a red button and self-administer a lethal dose of poisonous potassium chloride, along with thiopental, a painkiller. With the use of this device, Kevorkian claims to have assisted in more than 130 suicides.

The first patient to commit suicide with Kevorkian's assistance and his suicide device, called Mercitron, was Janet Adkins. Adkins, a Hemlock Society member, sought Kevorkian's aid because she did not want to wait until she lost her cognitive abilities to Alzheimer's disease. In June 1990 Adkins committed suicide in Kevorkian's van in a public campground.

In 1991 Kevorkian assisted in the deaths of two Michigan women on the same day. Sherry Miller, age forty-three, had multiple sclerosis; Marjorie Wantz, age fifty-eight, complained of a painful pelvic disease. Neither one was terminally ill, but court findings showed that they both suffered from depression. In 1996 Dr. Kevorkian was tried for the assisted deaths of Miller and Wantz under the common law that considers assisted suicide illegal. He was acquitted.

Kevorkian continued to draw media attention with increasingly controversial actions. In February 1998 twenty-one-year-old Roosevelt Dawson, a paralyzed university student, became the youngest person to commit suicide with Kevorkian's help. In June 1998 Kevorkian announced that he was donating kidneys from Joseph Tushkowski, a quadriplegic whose death he had assisted. His actions were denounced by transplant program leaders, medical ethicists, and most of the public. The organs were refused by all medical centers and transplant teams.

In October 1998 Kevorkian euthanized fifty-two-year-old Thomas Youk, a man afflicted with Lou Gehrig's disease, at the patient's request. Dr. Kevorkian videotaped the death and gave the video to the CBS television show *60 Minutes* for broadcast. The death was televised nationwide in November 1998 during primetime and included an interview with Kevorkian. He taunted Oakland County, Michigan, prosecutors to file charges against him. They did, and Kevorkian was convicted of second-degree murder in March 1999. On April 13, 1999, the seventy-year-old retired pathologist was sentenced to ten to twenty-five years in prison. While in prison, Kevorkian has staged three hunger strikes and has been subjected to force-feeding by prison officials. As of February 2006, Kevorkian remained in prison. He will be eligible for parole in May 2007 but told the *Daily Oakland Press* in 2004 that he expects to die in prison.

ASSISTED SUICIDE'S DETRACTORS

In general, physician-assisted suicide is seen as being at odds with the work of doctors and nurses. In 2001 the American College of Physicians–American Society of Internal Medicine (ACP–ASIM) released its position on physician-assisted suicide in "Physician-Assisted Suicide" (*Annals of Internal Medicine*, vol. 135, no. 3, August 7, 2001). The organization stated that it does not support the legalization of physician-assisted suicide. In addition, the organization noted that not only would the routine practice of physician-assisted suicide raise serious ethical concerns, it "would undermine the patient-physician relationship and the trust necessary to sustain it."

In 2005 the ACP—the largest medical specialty society in the United States—again officially opposed physician-assisted suicide. The organization's formal position statement on this topic was published within the fifth edition of its "Ethics Manual" in the journal *Annals of Internal Medicine* (vol. 142, no. 7, April 5,

2005) and at http://www.acponline.org/ethics/ethicman 5th.htm. The statement reads:

> The College does not support legalization of physician-assisted suicide. After much consideration, the College concluded that making physician-assisted suicide legal raised serious ethical, clinical, and social concerns and that the practice might undermine patient trust and distract from reform in end of life care. The College was also concerned with the risks that legalization posed to vulnerable populations, including poor persons, patients with dementia, disabled persons, those from minority groups that have experienced discrimination, those confronting costly chronic illnesses, or very young children. One state, Oregon, has legalized the practice of physician-assisted suicide, and its experience is being reviewed. Other states might legalize this practice, but the major emphasis of the College and its members, including those who might lawfully participate in the practice, must focus on ensuring that all persons facing serious illness can count on good care through to the end of life, with prevention or relief of suffering, commitment to human dignity, and support for the burdens borne by family and friends. Physicians and patients must continue to search together for answers to the problems posed by the difficulties of living with serious illness before death, without violating the physician's personal and professional values, and without abandoning the patient to struggle alone.

In 1994 the American Nurses Association (ANA) position statement on assisted suicide was adopted by its board of directors. The ANA "believes that the nurse should not participate in assisted suicide. Such an act is in violation of the *Code for Nurses with Interpretive Statements (Code for Nurses)* and the ethical traditions of the profession. Nurses, individually and collectively, have an obligation to provide comprehensive and compassionate end-of-life care which includes the promotion of comfort and the relief of pain, and at times, foregoing life-sustaining treatments" (http://www.nursingworld.org/readroom/position/ethics/etsuic.htm).

The American Medical Association (AMA) updated its position statement on physician-assisted suicide in 1996. The AMA states: "Allowing physicians to participate in assisted suicide would cause more harm than good. Physician-assisted suicide is fundamentally incompatible with the physician's role as healer, would be difficult or impossible to control, and would pose serious societal risks" (http://www.ama-assn.org/ama/pub/cate gory/8459.html).

THE BATTLE OVER LEGALIZING PHYSICIAN-ASSISTED SUICIDE

In early 2006 Oregon was the only state with a law allowing physician-assisted suicide and then only in limited circumstances. Attempts to allow assisted suicide have been defeated in California, Washington, Michigan, Maine, and Wyoming. In addition, an assisted suicide proposal was shelved in the Hawaii legislature. In 2004 thirty-five states had explicit laws against assisted suicide. Nine states had "common law" provisions against assisted suicide. This means there was a precedent of customs, usage, and court decisions that would support prosecution of an individual assisting in a suicide. Three states (North Carolina, Utah, and Wyoming) have abolished their common law provisions and do not have statutes criminalizing assisted suicide, but they do not have laws allowing it either.

The Oregon Death with Dignity Act

In November 1994 Oregon voters approved Measure 16 by a vote of 51% to 49%, making Oregon the first jurisdiction in the United States to legalize physician-assisted suicide. Under the Oregon Death with Dignity Act (ODDA), a mentally competent adult resident of Oregon who is terminally ill (likely to die within six months) may request a prescription for a lethal dose of medication to end his or her life. (See Table 6.8 to see what the Oregon law does and does not do.) Critics charge that assisted death is now "state-subsidized" because Medicaid money may be used to pay for physician-assisted suicide for the poor.

Between 1994 and 1997 the ODDA was kept on hold due to legal challenges. In November 1997 Oregonians voted to defeat a measure to repeal the 1994 law. Immediately after this voter reaffirmation of the Death with Dignity Act, the Drug Enforcement Administration (DEA) warned Oregon doctors that they could be arrested or have their medical licenses revoked for prescribing lethal doses of drugs. DEA administrator Thomas Constantine, under pressure from some members of Congress, stated that prescribing a drug for suicide would be a violation of the Controlled Substances Act (PL 91–513) because assisted suicide was not a "legitimate

TABLE 6.8

Provisions of Oregon's Death with Dignity Act

What the law *does* do

The Death with Dignity law allows Oregon residents to obtain medication from their physicians after two explicit oral requests and a written request have been made.

Key facts

- At least two doctors must concur on diagnosis, prognosis and the patient's capability;
- The patient must provide a written request to their physician witnessed by two individuals who are not family members or primary caregivers;
- The patient must ultimately administer the prescription him/herself.

What the law *doesn't* do

- Allow non-Oregonians to use the law;
- Allow anyone other than the patient to make the request;
- Allow euthanasia. The law **explicitly prohibits** euthanasia, which is typically defined as having someone other than the patient administer a life-ending medication.

SOURCE: Adapted from "Death with Dignity Primer," Death with Dignity National Center

medical purpose." Janet Reno, who was then the U.S. Attorney General, overruled Constantine and decided that that portion of the Controlled Substances Act would not apply in states that legalize assisted suicide. Those opposed to the practice observed that Reno's ruling was inconsistent with other rulings, citing the government's opposite ruling in states that have legalized marijuana for medical use. (Reno maintained that the prescription of marijuana is still illegal, regardless of its medicinal value.)

In response to the DEA decision, Congress moved toward passage of the Pain Relief Promotion Act. This law would prevent the use of federally controlled drugs for the purpose of assisted suicide and euthanasia. It would also strengthen protections for doctors who use narcotics to manage patients' pain, provide research grants, and establish a program for palliative care. As of June 2000, the House had passed the measure (HR 2260) 271 to 156. In April 2000 it was favorably reported out of the Senate Judiciary Committee; however, a scheduled vote was stalled in the Senate, and as of June 2006 the Act had not been passed.

On November 6, 2001, John Ashcroft, who succeeded Janet Reno as U.S. Attorney General, overturned Reno's 1998 ruling that prohibited the DEA from acting against physicians who use drugs under Oregon's physician-assisted suicide law. Attorney General Ashcroft said that taking the life of terminally ill patients is not a "legitimate medical purpose" for federally controlled drugs. The Oregon Medical Association and Washington State Medical Association opposed Attorney General Ashcroft's ruling, and even physicians opposed to assisted suicide expressed concern that the ruling might compromise patient care and that any DEA investigation might discourage physicians from prescribing pain medication to patients in need.

The State of Oregon disagreed so vehemently with Attorney General Ashcroft's interpretation of the Controlled Substances Act that on November 7, 2001, Oregon's attorney general filed suit, claiming that Ashcroft was acting unconstitutionally. A November 8, 2001, restraining order allowed the Death with Dignity Act to remain in effect while the case was tried.

On April 17, 2002, U.S. District Judge Robert E. Jones ruled in favor of the Death with Dignity Act. His decision read, in part:

> State statutes, state medical boards, and state regulations control the practice of medicine. The [Controlled Substances Act] was never intended, and the [U.S. Department of Justice] and [Drug Enforcement Administration] were never authorized, to establish a national medical practice or act as a national medical board. To allow an attorney general—an appointed executive whose tenure depends entirely on whatever

administration occupies the White House—to determine the legitimacy of a particular medical practice without a specific congressional grant of such authority would be unprecedented and extraordinary.... Without doubt, there is tremendous disagreement among highly respected medical practitioners as to whether assisted suicide or hastened death is a legitimate medical practice, but opponents have been heard and, absent a specific prohibitive federal statute, the Oregon voters have made the legal, albeit controversial, decision that such a practice is legitimate in this sovereign state.

The Justice Department appealed the ruling to the Ninth Circuit Court of Appeals. On May 26, 2004, the court stopped Ashcroft's attempts to override the Oregon law. The divided three-judge panel ruled that Ashcroft overstepped his authority when he declared that physicians who prescribe lethal drug doses are in violation of the 1970 federal drug law and when he instructed the federal DEA to prosecute the physicians. In addition, the Court noted that Ashcroft's interpretation of the Controlled Substances Acts violated Congress's intent.

In February 2005 the U.S. Supreme Court agreed to hear the Bush administration's challenge of Oregon's physician-assisted suicide law. On January 17, 2006, the Supreme Court let stand Oregon's physician-assisted suicide law. The High Court held that the Controlled Substances Act "does not allow the Attorney General to prohibit doctors from prescribing regulated drugs for use in physician-assisted suicide under state law permitting the procedure." Writing for the majority, Justice Anthony Kennedy stated that both Ashcroft and Attorney General Alberto Gonzales did not have the power to override the Oregon physician-assisted suicide law. Kennedy also added that it should not be the attorney general who determines what is a "legitimate medical purpose" for the administration of drugs, because the job description for the attorney general does not include making health and medical policy.

ANALYSIS OF THE EFFECTS OF THE OREGON DEATH WITH DIGNITY ACT. In March 1998 an Oregon woman in her mid-eighties who had terminal breast cancer ended her life with a lethal dose of barbiturates. Hers was the first known death under Oregon's assisted-suicide law. By the end of 2004, a total of 208 people had reportedly committed suicide with a doctor's assistance under the ODDA. According to the Seventh Annual Report on Oregon's Death with Dignity Act (Oregon Department of Human Services, Office of Disease Prevention and Epidemiology, March 10, 2005, http://egov.oregon.gov/DHS/ph/pas/docs/year7.pdf), thirty-seven Oregon patients used legal physician-assisted suicide in 2004, and forty-two patients did so in 2003. The report also noted that sixty prescriptions for lethal medication were written in 2004, and sixty-eight in 2003. Prescriptions for lethal medication increased every year from 1998 to 2003. In 1998 twenty-four prescriptions were written.

The median age of people who took lethal medication in 2004 was sixty-four, and 78% percent suffered from end-stage cancer. Physicians were asked if patients voiced any of seven end-of-life concerns that might have contributed to their requests for lethal medication. In nearly all cases physicians reported that patients had multiple concerns contributing to the request. The most frequently cited concerns were losing autonomy (ability to make independent choices; 87%), a decreasing ability to participate in activities that make life enjoyable (92%), and loss of dignity (78%).

Based on the Oregon Health Division's annual reports, groups in favor of the legalization of assisted suicide conclude that the law is working as intended and without abuse. Opponents of the law continue to charge that the law discriminates against the elderly and seriously ill and express concern about reporting requirements. The Oregon Health Division admits, "Underreporting cannot be assessed, and noncompliance is difficult to assess because of the possible repercussions for noncompliant physicians reporting data to the division."

OREGON PHYSICIANS', NURSES', AND SOCIAL WORKERS' ATTITUDES TOWARD THE ODDA. Bioethicists, physicians, legislators, and patient advocacy groups have watched with interest to learn whether the attitudes and practices of Oregon physicians and other health care practitioners would change in response to the passage of the Death with Dignity Act. In early 1999 researchers mailed questionnaires to 3,981 Oregon physicians to find out about their experiences with the Act. The responses of the 2,641 physicians who returned the survey by August 1999 were reported by Linda Ganzini, M.D., et al in "Oregon Physicians' Attitudes about and Experiences with End-of-Life Care since Passage of the Oregon Death with Dignity Act" (*Journal of the American Medical Association*, vol. 285, no. 18, May 9, 2001).

Ganzini and her colleagues found that 51% of responding physicians supported the Act, 32% opposed it, and 17% neither supported nor opposed it. Four out of five respondents said their attitude about the law was unchanged since it passed; however, among those whose feelings had changed, nearly twice as many supported the Act as opposed it. Thirty percent considered prescribing lethal medication under the Act immoral or unethical, and 46% were unwilling to prescribe lethal medication. Despite their reluctance to assist patients to die, more than half of the respondents (53%) reported that if terminally ill, they would consider seeking physician assistance to end their own lives.

The researchers found that more than three-quarters of physicians who had cared for a terminally ill patient in the prior year had sought to improve their knowledge of depression, their ability to recognize and treat the illness, as well as prescribing pain medication. Nearly all respondents (91%) indicated some degree of comfort discussing the Act with patients and 36% said patients had asked them whether they would be willing to prescribe lethal medication. Nearly 60% of physicians who were not morally opposed to prescribing lethal medication expressed concerns about adhering to federal DEA law and feared public scrutiny and hospital sanction.

In 2001 Lois L. Miller, along with Ganzini and colleagues (see previous paragraphs) researched the attitudes of Oregon hospice nurses and social workers to legalized assisted suicide (Miller et al, "Attitudes and Experiences of Oregon Hospice Nurses and Social Workers Regarding Assisted Suicide," *Palliative Medicine*, vol. 18, no. 8, 2004). They found that 48% of the 306 hospice nurses who responded to the survey and 72% of the eighty-five social workers who responded supported the ODDA.

Miller noted that results showed a much higher percentage of social workers (78%) supported the ODDA than did hospice nurses (48%). The researchers suggested that this dissimilarity reflects different emphases in the nurses and social workers professional organizations' codes of ethics and position statements on assisted suicide. The American Nurses Association's position statement emphasizes the patient, while that of the U.S. National Association of Social Workers views client self-determination as a primary guiding principle. Table 6.9 summarizes the differences in the attitudes toward the ODDA among Oregon physicians, nurses, and social workers.

TABLE 6.9

Proportion of Oregon physicians, nurses, and social workers in support of and opposition to the Oregon Death with Dignity Act, 1999 and 2001

	1999 survey	2001 survey	
	Physicians (percent)	Nurses (percent)	Social workers (percent)
Support ODDA*	51	48	72
Oppose ODDA*	32	36	13
Neutral on ODDA*	17	16	15
More supportive since 1994	13	16	24
More opposed since 1994	7	9	5

*ODDA is Oregon Death with Dignity Act.

SOURCE: Lois L. Miller, et al., "Table 3. Proportion of Physicians, Nurses, Social Workers in Support of and Opposition to ODDA," in "Attitudes and Experiences of Oregon Hospice Nurses and Social Workers Regarding Assisted Suicide," *Palliative Medicine*, vol. 18, no. 8, 2004

EUTHANASIA AND PHYSICIAN-ASSISTED SUICIDE IN EUROPE

The Netherlands

Euthanasia became legal in the Netherlands on April 10, 2001. Prior to that date, active euthanasia was a criminal offense under Article 293 of the Dutch Penal Code, which read, "He who takes the life of another person on this person's explicit and serious request will be punished with imprisonment of up to twelve years or a fine of the fifth category." At the same time, however, Section 40 of the same penal code stated that an individual was not punishable if he or she was driven by "an irresistible force" (legally known as force majeure) to put another person's welfare above the law. This might include a circumstance in which a physician is confronted with the conflict between the legal duty of not taking a life and the humane duty to end a patient's intolerable suffering.

ORIGIN OF OPEN PRACTICE. In 1971 Dr. Geertruida Postma granted an elderly nursing home patient's request to die by injecting the patient with morphine and ending her life. The patient was her seventy-eight-year-old mother, who was partially paralyzed and was tied to a chair to keep her from falling. Dr. Postma was found guilty of murder, but her penalty consisted of a one-week suspended jail sentence and one-year probation. This light sentence encouraged other physicians to come forward, admitting they had also assisted in patients' suicides.

Two years later the Royal Dutch Medical Association announced that, should a physician assist in the death of a terminally ill patient, it was up to the court to decide if the physician's action could be justified by "a conflict of duties." In Alkmaar, Netherlands, Dr. Schoonheim helped Marie Barendregt to die in 1982, using a lethal injection. The ninety-five-year-old, severely disabled Barendregt had initially signed an advance directive refusing artificial (life-prolonging) treatment. Schoonheim assisted in Barendregt's death with the knowledge of the patient's son and after consultation with two independent physicians. In 1984 the Dutch Supreme Court, ruling on this well-known Alkmaar case (the court case is referred to by the name of the city where the trial took place), found Schoonheim not guilty of murder.

Since then, until euthanasia was legalized, each euthanasia case brought under prosecution was judged on its individual circumstances. The force majeure defense ensured acquittal, while compliance with certain guidelines for performing euthanasia laid down by the Royal Dutch Medical Association and the Dutch courts in 1984 protected physicians from prosecution.

On April 10, 2001, the Dutch Parliament voted forty-six to twenty-eight to legalize physician-assisted suicide by passing the Termination of Life on Request and Assisted Suicide (Review Procedures) Act. Arguments in favor of the bill included public approval ratings of 90%. In May 2001 the results of a Dutch public opinion poll revealed that nearly half of respondents favored making lethal drugs available to older adults who no longer wanted to live.

MONITORING OF EUTHANASIA AND PHYSICIAN-ASSISTED SUICIDE. Euthanasia and physician-assisted suicide have been monitored in the Netherlands since 1994, with the first review procedure given approval by the Dutch government in 1991. Although euthanasia and PAS were not yet legal in that country, physicians were required to report cases and would not be prosecuted if they met the requirements for prudent practice that had been developed. The substantive requirements asserted that "the patient's request must be voluntary and well considered"; "the patient's condition must be unbearable and hopeless"; "no acceptable alternatives for treatment are available"; and "the method is medically and technically appropriate." The procedural requirements asserted that "another doctor is consulted before proceeding" and "the case is reported as an unnatural death" (Bregje D. Onwuteaka-Philipsen et al, "Dutch Requirements for Prudent Practice in Euthanasia and Physician Assisted Suicide," in "Dutch Experience of Monitoring Euthanasia," *British Medical Journal*, vol. 331, no. 7518, September 24, 2005). The procedure was evaluated in 1996, and a new system was introduced in 1998, but euthanasia and PAS remained illegal.

The Termination of Life on Request and Assisted Suicide (Review Procedures) Act was passed in 2001 and enacted in 2002. Along with legalizing euthanasia and PAS, this law established a revised review procedure (as suggested in its name). Throughout the review changes, the requirements for prudent practice did not change and were the main focus of review. The purpose of the review process was to have physicians report on euthanasia and PAS, and to follow prudent practice.

Success of the review process depends on whether physicians report euthanasia and PAS. Onwuteaka-Philipsen and colleagues reported that cases increased from 480 in 1990 (before the review procedure) to 1460 in 1995 and to 2216 in 1999. The numbers decreased during 2001 to 2003 but rose in 2004. The researchers also compared the reported cases with the total number of cases, which they determined by large-scale anonymous survey research of Dutch physicians in 1990, 1995, and

2001. The researchers determined that the notification rate increased from 18% in 1990 to 54% in 2001. Thus, the review process appears to have been successful in increasing the reporting of euthanasia and PAS. Research is ongoing to determine whether the decrease in reported cases since 1999 is due to a decrease in reporting or to a decrease in the occurrence of euthanasia and PAS.

Euthanasia in Belgium

The Belgian Act on Euthanasia passed in 2002 after the Netherlands law, making Belgium the second country to legalize euthanasia. The law applies to competent adults who have an incurable illness causing unbearable, constant suffering and patients in a persistent vegetative state who made their wishes known within the prior five years in front of two witnesses. It allows someone to terminate the life of another at their "voluntary, well-considered, and repeated" request, but does not allow PAS. All acts of euthanasia must be reported.

Switzerland Allows Assisted Suicide but Not Euthanasia

Euthanasia is not legal in Switzerland, but the country allows suicide assisted by physicians or people with no medical training. Suicide and assisted suicide has been legal in Switzerland since 1937. The Swiss criminal code states that suicide may be assisted for altruistic reasons, but that assisted suicide is a crime if motivated for financial gain or for what it deems "negative" reasons.

Although legal, assisted suicide is not considered an appropriate part of medical practice by the Swiss Academy of Medical Sciences, so physicians do not assist in suicides of the terminally ill. Members of EXIT (the Swiss Society for Humane Dying) are allowed to help terminally ill Swiss residents commit suicide in their homes. In January 2006 the Vaud University Hospital Center in Lausanne began allowing EXIT to help patients already admitted to the hospital and who could no longer go home to take their own lives.

Great Britain Considers Euthanasia and Physician-Assisted Suicide

In November 2005 a bill was introduced in the House of Lords that would allow both assisted suicide and euthanasia. It sets requirements for either procedure, including assessment by a physician that the adult patient is likely to die within a few months, is competent to make a request to die, and is suffering unbearably. The patient must sign a declaration of intent to choose death. If the declaration is not revoked by the patient within fourteen days, then the patient can receive the means to take his or her own life.

CHAPTER 7
ADVANCE DIRECTIVES

The movement toward greater patient participation in health care that began in the 1960s and 1970s focused increasing attention on the desire for control over nearly all aspects of medical care, including critical care. Dramatic medical and technological advances further underscored the importance of planning ahead for end-of-life care. Baby boomers (the generation of people born between 1946 and 1964), on the threshold of aging and faced with caring for elderly parents, have become increasingly aware of the need to make provisions for their own future medical treatment. Some hope that executing advance directives will help protect their right to self-determination (the right to make one's own medical decisions, including the right to accept or refuse treatments).

A BRIEF HISTORY OF ADVANCE DIRECTIVES

Advance directive is the general term that refers to a person's request (oral and/or written) concerning health care, should he or she become incompetent. There are two main documents in an advance directive: a living will and a durable power of attorney for health care. Many states have special forms or specific procedures for creating an advance directive. Some people think it is sufficient to tell a loved one or a physician what they desire. But the National Health Lawyers Association stresses that although courts have enforced oral instructions, and physicians often consider the information that family members offer about a patient's requests, the wishes of the terminally ill are more likely to be honored if they are written down. In 1967 the Euthanasia Society of America and attorney Luis Kutner, cofounder of Amnesty International, devised the first living will (later called an advance directive).

California was the first state to recognize the legality of living wills (1976) and the durable power of attorney for health care (1984). The California Natural Death Act of 1976 states that to preserve "dignity and privacy . . . any adult person may execute a directive directing the withholding or withdrawal of life-sustaining procedures in a terminal condition."

All fifty states and the District of Columbia passed laws recognizing the use of living wills and durable power of attorney for health care, although the provisions of these laws vary from state to state. As of January 2004, forty-six states and the District of Columbia had laws authorizing both living wills and the appointment of a health care proxy or agent. Alaska's law permits living wills only; even if a patient has a health care agent, that agent is not permitted to order the termination of life-sustaining treatment. While Massachusetts, Michigan, and New York laws only authorize the appointment of a health care agent, their laws do permit the inclusion of specific instructions about medical care at the end of life within the appointment of the agent. (See Figure 7.1.)

LIVING WILLS

As mentioned previously, a living will is one part of an advance directive. It is a document that outlines a patient's preferences about end-of-life medical treatments in the event that he or she is unable to communicate or make his or her own decisions. Laws regulating living wills vary from state to state. For example, thirty-one states did not allow the withdrawal of life support from pregnant patients in 2004. Thus, a pregnant woman's living will could not be honored in those states if the living will asked for the withholding or withdrawal of life support. (See Figure 7.2.)

Living wills enable people to list the types of medical treatments they want or do not want. It is therefore important for an individual contemplating a living will to know what these treatments involve. Some examples of life-prolonging treatments patients should consider

FIGURE 7.1

State laws governing living wills and appointment of health care agents, 2004

☐ Jurisdictions with legislation that authorizes both living wills and the appointment of a health care agent (the District of Columbia and 46 states: Alabama, Arizona, Arkansas, California, Colorado, Connecticut, Delaware, Florida, Georgia, Hawaii, Idaho, Illinois, Indiana, Iowa, Kansas, Kentucky, Louisiana, Maine, Maryland, Minnesota, Mississippi, Missouri, Montana, Nebraska, Nevada, New Hampshire, New Jersey, New Mexico, North Carolina, North Dakota, Ohio, Oklahoma, Oregon, Pennsylvania, Rhode Island, South Carolina, South Dakota, Tennessee, Texas, Utah, Vermont, Virginia, Washington, West Virginia, Wisconsin and Wyoming).

☐ Alaska's Power of Attorney Act precludes health care agent authority to terminate life-sustaining medical procedures. The act does provide that the health care agent may enforce a declaration.

☐ States with legislation that authorizes only the appointment of a health care agent (3 states: Massachusetts, Michigan and New York).

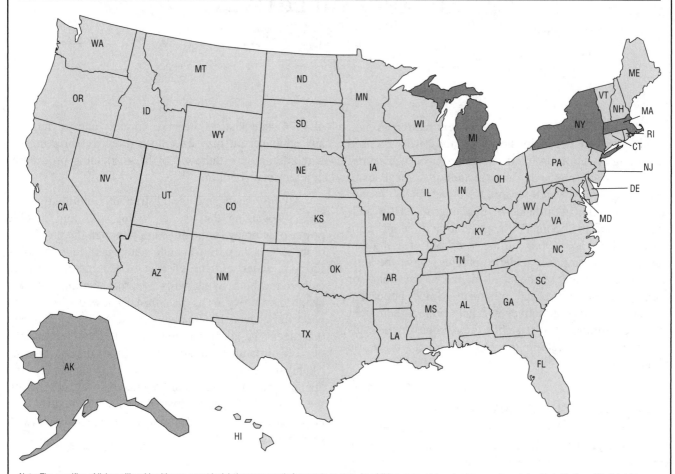

Note: The specifics of living will and health care agent legislation vary greatly from state to state. In addition, many states also have court-made law that affects residents' rights.

SOURCE: "State Statutes Governing Living Wills and Appointment of Health Care Agents," in *End-of-Life Law Digest*, The National Hospice and Palliative Care Organization, 2004

when preparing a living will include cardiopulmonary resuscitation (CPR), mechanical ventilation, artificial nutrition and hydration, and kidney dialysis.

An advance directive form included in the model Uniform Health Care Decisions Act (UHCDA) offers several options that include treatments to prolong life. (See Table 7.1, Part 2: Instructions for Health Care.) This model law was approved by the National Conference of Commissioners on Uniform State Laws in 1993 to provide some consistency among state advance directives and remained a model law as of June 2006.

Another form, called "Five Wishes," was developed in Florida by a nonprofit organization called Aging with Dignity and is now distributed nationwide. The document probes legal and medical issues as well as spiritual and emotional ones. It even outlines small details, such as requests for favorite music to be played and poems to be read, and provides space for individuals to record their wishes for funeral arrangements. The document is relatively easy to complete because it uses simplified language rather than legal or medical jargon. As of June 2005, "Five Wishes" met living will or advance directive criteria in thirty-seven states and the District of

FIGURE 7.2

State laws governing the withdrawal of life support from pregnant patients, 2004

☐ States with living will statutes that explicitly forbid the withholding or withdrawal of life support from pregnant patients (31 states: Alabama, Alaska[a], Arkansas[a], Colorado[b], Connecticut, Delaware, Georgia[c], Idaho, Illinois[a], Indiana, Iowa[a], Kansas[a], Kentucky[a], Mississippi, Missouri, Montana[a], Nebraska[a], Nevada[a], New Hampshire, North Dakota, Ohio, Oklahoma, Pennsylvania[a], Rhode Island[a], South Carolina, South Dakota[a], Texas, Utah, Washington, Wisconsin and Wyoming).

☐ States with living will statutes that permit the principal to choose to refuse life support if she is pregnant (4 states: Arizona, Maryland, Minnesota and New Jersey).

☐ Jurisdictions whose living will statutes make no mention of pregnancy (the District of Columbia and 12 states: California, Florida, Hawaii, Louisiana, Maine, New Mexico, North Carolina, Oregon, Tennessee, Vermont, Virginia and West Virginia).

☐ States without a living will statute (3 states: Massachusetts, Michigan and New York).

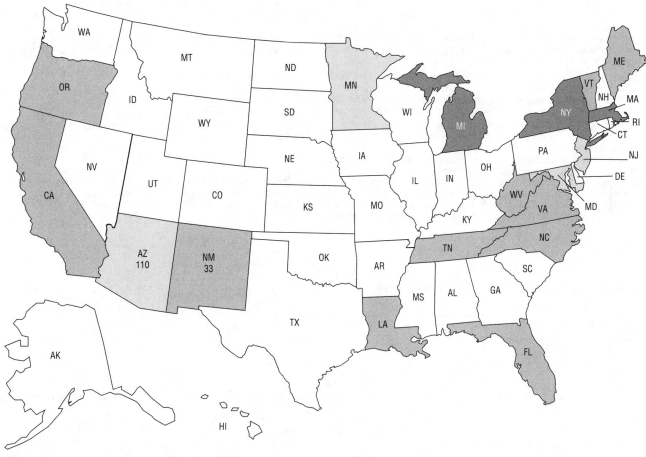

[a]Life support cannot be withheld/withdrawn if the fetus can develop to the point of live birth with continued life support.
[b]Life support cannot be withheld/withdrawn if the fetus is viable.
[c]Explicitly permits individuals to choose to have living will honored during pregnancy, but only until the point of viability.

SOURCE: "Pregnancy Restrictions in Living Will Statutes," in *End-of-Life Law Digest*, The National Hospice and Palliative Care Organization, 2004

Columbia. It did not meet advance directive criteria in these thirteen states: Oregon, Nevada, Utah, Texas, Oklahoma, Kansas, Alabama, Kentucky, Indiana, Ohio, Wisconsin, Vermont, and New Hampshire. Other forms were necessary in those states, although the "Five Wishes" document can still serve as a guide for family and physicians.

Pro-Life Alternative to Living Wills

The National Right to Life Committee (NRLC) opposes active and passive euthanasia and offers an alternative to the standard living will. Called the "Will to Live," it does not consider artificial nutrition and hydration as forms of medical treatment but as basic necessities for the preservation of life.

DURABLE POWER OF ATTORNEY FOR HEALTH CARE

A durable power of attorney for health care, also called a medical power of attorney, is another part of an advance directive. It designates a health care agent or proxy authorized to make medical treatment decisions on behalf of a patient who can no longer make these decisions

TABLE 7.1

Advance health-care directive

Optional Form

The following form may, but need not, be used to create an advance health-care directive. The other sections of this [Act] govern the effect of this or any other writing used to create an advance health-care directive. An individual may complete or modify all or any part of the following form:

ADVANCE HEALTH-CARE DIRECTIVE

Explanation

You have the right to give instructions about your own health care. You also have the right to name someone else to make health-care decisions for you. This form lets you do either or both of these things. It also lets you express your wishes regarding donation of organs and the designation of your primary physician. If you use this form, you may complete or modify all or any part of it. You are free to use a different form.

Part 1 of this form is a power of attorney for health care. Part 1 lets you name another individual as agent to make health-care decisions for you if you become incapable of making your own decisions or if you want someone else to make those decisions for you now even though you are still capable. You may also name an alternate agent to act for you if your first choice is not willing, able, or reasonably available to make decisions for you. Unless related to you, your agent may not be an owner, operator, or employee of [a residential long-term health-care institution] at which you are receiving care.

Unless the form you sign limits the authority of your agent, your agent may make all health-care decisions for you. This form has a place for you to limit the authority of your agent. You need not limit the authority of your agent if you wish to rely on your agent for all health-care decisions that may have to be made. If you choose not to limit the authority of your agent, your agent will have the right to:

(a) consent or refuse consent to any care, treatment, service, or procedure to maintain, diagnose, or otherwise affect a physical or mental condition;

(b) select or discharge health-care providers and institution;

(c) approve or disapprove diagnostic tests, surgical procedures, programs of medication, and orders not to resuscitate; and

(d) direct the provision, withholding, or withdrawal of artificial nutrition and hydration and all other forms of health care.

Part 2 of this form lets you give specific instructions about any aspect of your health care. Choices are provided for you to express your wishes regarding the provision, withholding, or withdrawal of treatment to keep you alive, including the provision of artificial nutrition and hydration, as well as the provision of pain relief. Space is also provided for you to add to the choices you have made or for you to write out any additional wishes.

Part 3 of this form lets you express an intention to donate your bodily organs and tissues following your death.

Part 4 of this form lets you designate a physician to have primary responsibility for your health care.

After completing this form, sign and date the form at the end. It is recommended but not required that you request two other individuals to sign as witnesses. Give a copy of the signed and completed form to your physician, to any other health-care providers you may have, to any health-care institution at which you are receiving care, and to any health-care agents you have named. You should talk to the person you have named as agent to make sure that he or she understands your wishes and is willing to take the responsibility.

You have the right to revoke this advance health-care directive or replace this form at any time.

* * * * * * * * *

PART 1

POWER OF ATTORNEY FOR HEALTH CARE

1. DESIGNATION OF AGENT: I designate the following individual as my agent to make health-care decisions for me:

_____

(name of individual you choose as agent)

| (address) | (city) | (state) | (zip code) |

| (home phone) | (work phone) |

OPTIONAL: If I revoke my agent's authority or if my agent is not willing, able, or reasonably available to make a health-care decision for me, I designate as my first alternate agent:

_____

(name of individual you choose as first alternate agent)

| (address) | (city) | (state) | (zip code) |

| (home phone) | (work phone) |

OPTIONAL: If I revoke the authority of my agent and first alternate agent or if neither is willing, able, or reasonably available to make a health-care decision for me, I designate as my second alternate agent:

_____

(name of individual you choose as first alternate agent)

| (address) | (city) | (state) | (zip code) |

| (home phone) | (work phone) |

(Add additional sheets if needed.)

for himself or herself. (See Table 7.1, Part 1: Power of Attorney for Health Care.) The role of this agent or proxy begins as soon as the physician certifies that a patient is incompetent to make his or her own decisions. The agent's role may or may not be limited to end-of-life care.

While a living will provides specific directions about medical treatment, it cannot address every possible future medical situation. Most standard living wills apply only to limited circumstances, such as terminal illness or permanent coma. There are, however, many medical

TABLE 7.1

Advance health-care directive [CONTINUED]

2. AGENT'S AUTHORITY: My agent is authorized to make all health-care decisions for me, including decisions to provide, withhold, or withdraw artificial nutrition and hydration and other forms of health care to keep me alive, except as I state here:

_____

_____

_____

3. WHEN AGENT'S AUTHORITY BECOMES EFFECTIVE: My agent's authority becomes effective when my primary physician determines that I am unable to make my own health-care decisions unless I mark the following box. If I mark this box [ ], my agent's authority to make health-care decisions for me takes effect immediately.

4. AGENT'S OBLIGATION: My agent shall make health-care decisions for me in accordance with this power of attorney for health care, any instructions I give in Part 2 of this form, and my other wishes to the extent known to my agent. To the extent my wishes are unknown, my agent shall make health-care decisions for me in accordance with what my agent determines to be in my best interest. In determining my best interest, my agent shall consider my personal values to the extent known to my agent.

NOMINATION OF GUARDIAN: If a guardian of my person needs to be appointed for me by a court, I nominate the agent designated in this form. If that agent is not willing, able, or reasonably available to act as guardian, I nominate the alternate agents whom I have named, in the order designated.

PART 2

INSTRUCTIONS FOR HEALTH CARE

If you are satisfied to allow your agent to determine what is best for you in making end-of-life decisions, you need not fill out this part of the form. If you do fill out this part of the form, you may strike any wording you do not want.

6. END-OF-LIFE DECISIONS: I direct that my health-care providers and others involved in my care provide, withhold, or withdraw treatment in accordance with the choice I have marked below:

[ ] (a) Choice Not To Prolong Life
I do not want my life to be prolonged if (i) I have an incurable and irreversible condition that will result in my death within a relatively short time, (ii) I become unconscious and, to a reasonable degree of medical certainty, I will not regain consciousness, or (iii) the likely risks and burdens of treatment would outweigh the expected benefits, OR

[ ] (b) Choice To Prolong Life
I want my life to be prolonged as long as possible within the limits of generally accepted health-care standards.

7. ARTIFICIAL NUTRITION AND HYDRATION: Artificial nutrition and hydration must be provided, withheld, or withdrawn in accordance with the choice I have made in paragraph (6) unless I mark the following box. If I mark this box [ ], artificial nutrition and hydration must be provided regardless of my condition and regardless of the choice I have made in paragraph (6).

8. RELIEF FROM PAIN: Except as I state in the following space, I direct that treatment for alleviation of pain or discomfort be provided at all times, even if it hastens my death:

_____

_____

9. OTHER WISHES: (If you do not agree with any of the optional choices above and wish to write your own, or if you wish to add to the instructions you have given above, you may do so here.) I direct that:

_____

_____

(Add additional sheets if needed.)

PART 3

DONATION OF ORGANS AT DEATH (OPTIONAL)

10. Upon my death (mark applicable box)

[ ] (a) I give any needed organs, tissues, or parts, OR
[ ] (b) I give the following organs, tissues, or parts only

_____

[ ] (c) My gift is for the following purposes (strike any of the following you do not want)

(i) Transplant
(ii) Therapy
(iii) Research
(iv) Education

treatments that require decision making. Examples of these are surgical procedures, diagnostic tests, blood transfusion, the use of antibiotics, radiation therapy, and chemotherapy.

A durable power of attorney for health care is generally more flexible than a living will. It allows individuals to appoint proxies (agents) who will use their judgment to respond to unforeseen situations based on

TABLE 7.1

Advance health-care directive [CONTINUED]

PART 4
PRIMARY PHYSICIAN (OPTIONAL)

11. I designate the following physician as my primary physician:

_____
(name of physician)

_____
(address)   (city)   (state)   (zip code)

_____
(phone)

OPTIONAL: If the physician I have designated above is not willing, able, or reasonably available to act as my primary physician, I designate the following physician as my primary physician:

_____
(name of physician)

_____
(address)   (city)   (state)   (zip code)

_____
(phone)

* * * * * * * * * *

EFFECT OF COPY: A copy of this form has the same effect as the original.

12. SIGNATURES: Sign and date the form here:

_____   _____
(date)   (sign your name)

_____   _____
(address)   (print name)

_____
(city)   (state)

Optional SIGNATURES OF WITNESSES:

_____   _____
(First witness)   (Second witness)

_____   _____
(print name)   (print name)

_____   _____
(address)   (address)

_____   _____
(city)   (state)   (city)   (state)

_____   _____
(signature of witness)   (signature of witness)

_____   _____
(date)   (date)

SOURCE: "Advance Health-Care Directive," in *Patient Self-Determination Act: Providers Offer Information on Advance Directives but Effectiveness Uncertain*, U.S. General Accounting Office, August 1995, http://www.gao.gov/archive/1995/he95135.pdf (accessed November 7, 2005)

their knowledge of the patient and the patient's values and beliefs. Because there is no uniform advance directive statute nationally, the rights of health care agents vary across states. Limits on agent's powers in each state and the District of Columbia as of September 1, 2004, are shown in Table 7.2.

In the Absence of Durable Power of Attorney for Health Care

Physicians usually involve family members in medical decisions when the patient has not designated a health care proxy in advance. Many states have family consent or surrogate consent laws for this purpose. (See Figure 7.3.) Some have laws that designate the order in which family members may assume the role of surrogates or decision makers. For example, the spouse may be the prime surrogate, followed by an adult child, then the patient's parent, etc.

ADDITIONAL INSTRUCTIONS IN ADVANCE DIRECTIVES

Artificial Nutrition and Hydration

Some living wills contain a provision for the withdrawal of nutrition and hydration. (See Table 7.1, Part 2: Instructions for Health Care.) Artificial nutrition and

TABLE 7.2

Health care power of attorney and combined advance directive legislation, September 2004

State	Type	Form	Limits on agent's powers	Prohibited agents	Formalities of execution	Prohibited witnesses	Authority over autopsy, organ donation or remains	Comity provision
1. Alabama Alabama statutes §22-8A-2to-10 (West 2004). "Natural Death Act" *See also* durable power of attorney act, §26-1-2 *Separate living will statute: No*	Combined advance directive *[modeled on Uniform Health Care Decisions Act (modified)]**	*Yes* Must be substantially followed	• Mental health facility admission and treatments • Psycho-surgery • Sterilization • Abortion • Pregnancy limitation • Nutrition & hydration–refusal permitted if expressly authorized	• Individual provider* *Exception for relatives employed by the provider	• 2 or more witnesses age 19 or older	• Minor=18 • Agent • Proxy signor • Relative • Heir • Person responsible for care costs	*No*	*Yes*
2. Alaska Effective 1/1/05: Alaska statutes §13.52.010 to .395 (West 2004) "Health Care Decisions Act" *Separate living will statute: No*	Combined advance directive *[modeled on Uniform Health Care Decisions Act (modified)]** plus incorporates mental health directive	*Yes* Optional	• Psycho-surgery* • Sterilization* • Abortion* • Removal of bodily organs* • Temporary admission to mental health facility* • Electro-convulsive therapy* • Psychotropic mediation* • Life-sustaining procedures* • Pregnancy limitation *Consent/refusal permitted only if expressly authorized.	• Facility provider* *Exception for relatives	• 2 witness or notarized	• Agent • Facility provider One may not be: • Relative • Heir	Organ donation	*Yes*
3. Arizona Arizona revised statutes annotated §36-3201 to 3262 (West 2004)	Combined advance directive	*Yes* Optional	None specified	None specified	• 1 witness or notarized	• Agent • Provider If only *one* witness, person may not be: • Relative • Heir	Autopsy Organ donation	*Yes*
4. Arkansas Arkansas code annotated §20-13-104 (1999) "Durable Power of Attorney for Health Care Act" *See also* Arkansas code annotated §20-17-201 to –218 (proxy appointment in living will declaration)	Special durable power of attorney	*No* (but proxy appointment in living will declaration does have optional form)	• Life-sustaining treatment—unless the durable power of attorney incorporates a proxy authorization from the living will declaration statute, §20-17-202 • Pregnancy limitation	None specified	• 2 witnesses	None specified	*No*	*Yes,* if part of a (living will) declaration
5. California California probate code §4600 to 4948 (west 2004) *Separate living will statute: No*	Combined advance directive	*Yes* Optional	• Civil commitment • Electro-convulsive therapy • Psycho-surgery • Sterilization • Abortion	• Supervising individual provider • Facility provider • Conservator—unless conditions are met.	• 2 witnesses or notarized • Special institutional requirements	• Agent • Individual provider • Facility provider One may not be: • Relative • Heir	Autopsy Organ donation Disposition of remains	*Yes*

TABLE 7.2

Health care power of attorney and combined advance directive legislation, September 2004 [CONTINUED]

State	Type	Form	Limits on agent's powers	Prohibited agents	Formalities of execution	Prohibited witnesses	Authority over autopsy, organ donation or remains	Comity provision
6. Colorado Colorado revised statutes §15-14-503 to –509 (West 2004) "Colorado Patient Autonomy Act" See also §15-14-501 to –502 and §15-14-601 to –611 re durable power of attorney *Separate living will statute:* Colorado revised statutes §15-18-101 to –113	Special durable power of attorney	*No*	None specified	None specified	None specified	n/a	*No*	*Yes*
7. Connecticut Connecticut general statutes §19a-570 to –580d (West 2004) See also Connecticut general statutes §1-43 et seq. (2004) (statutory short form durable power of attorney) *Separate living will statute: No*	Combined advance directive	*Yes* Optional	• None specified (but authority is described as authority to "convey" principal's wishes, rather than to make decisions for principal.) • Pregnancy limitation	• Facility provider* • Attending physician • Administrator or employee of government agency financially responsible for care* *Exception for relatives	• 2 witnesses • Special institutional requirements	• Agent	*No*	*No*
8. Delaware Delaware code annotated title 16, §2501 to 2518 (2004) *Separate living will statute: No*	Combined advance directive *[modeled on Uniform Health Care Decisions Act (modified)]**	*Yes* Optional	• Pregnancy limitation	• Residential long term care facility provider* *Exception for relatives	• 2 witnesses • Special institutional requirements	• Facility provider • Relative • Heir • Creditor • Person responsible for care costs	*No*	*Yes*
9. District of Columbia District of Columbia codes annotated §21-2201 to –2213 (2004) *Separate living will statute:* District of Columbia code annotated §7-621 to –630 (2004)	Special durable power of attorney	*Yes* Optional	• Decision to medicate defendant to render him/her competent to stand trial	• Individual provider • Facility provider	• 2 witnesses	• Principal • Individual provider • Facility provider • *One may not be relative or heir*	*No*	*No*
10. Florida Florida statutes annotated § 765.101 to –404 (West 2004) *Separate living will statute: No*	Combined advance directive	*Yes* Optional	• Mental health facility admission* • Electro-convulsive therapy* • Psycho-surgery* • Sterilization* • Abortion* • Experimental treatments not approved by institutional review board (IRB)* • Life-sustaining procedures while pregnant* • Pregnancy limitation* *Consent/refusal permissible if expressly authorized	None specified	• 2 witnesses	• Agent • *One may not be spouse or relative*	Autopsy (see Florida statute ann. §872.04) Organ donation	*Yes*

TABLE 7.2

Health care power of attorney and combined advance directive legislation, September 2004 [CONTINUED]

State	Type	Form	Limits on agent's powers	Prohibited agents	Formalities of execution	Prohibited witnesses	Authority over autopsy, organ donation or remains	Comity provision
11. Georgia Georgia code annotated §31-36-1 to –13 (West 2004) *Separate living will statute:*	Special durable power of attorney	*Yes* Optional	• Mental health facility admission or treatment under Title 37 of code • Psycho-surgery • Sterilization	• Individual provider directly or indirectly involved	• 2 witnesses • Special institutional requirements	None	Autopsy Organ donation Disposition of remains	*No*
12. Hawaii Hawaii revised statutes §327E-1 to –16 (2004) *See also* Hawaii revised statutes §551D-2.5 re durable power of attorney for health care *Separate living will statute: No*	Combined advance directive *[modeled on Uniform Health Care Decisions Act (modified)]**	*Yes* Optional	None specified	• Facility provider* *Exception for relatives	• 2 witnesses *or* notarized	• Individual provider • Facility provider • Agent *One* may not be • Relative • Heir	*No*	*Yes*
13. Idaho Idaho code §39-4501 to –4509 (West 2004), specifically §39-4505. *Separate living will statute: No*	Combined advance directive	*Yes* Optional	None specified	• Individual provider* • Community care facility provider* *Exception for relatives who are employees of.	• 2 witnesses *or* notarized	• Agent • Individual provider • Community care facility • *One* may not be relative or heir	*No*	*No*
14. Illinois 755 Illinois code statutes 45/4-1 through 4-12 (West 2004) *Separate living will statute:* 755 Illinois code statutes 35/1 to 35/10	Special durable power of attorney	*Yes* Optional	None specified	• Individual provider	None specified	None specified	Autopsy Organ donation Disposition of remains	*Yes*
15. Indiana Indiana code annotated §30-5-1 to 30-5-10 (West 2004), specifically §30-5-5-16 and –17. *Separate living will statute:* Indiana code annotated §16-36-4-1 to –15 Indiana code annotated §16-36-1-1 to –14 (West 2004)	General durable power of attorney with health powers.	*No* but mandatory language for authority re life-sustaining treatment (§30-5-5-17)	None specified	None specified	• Notarized	n/a	Autopsy Organ donation Disposition of remains (but powers terminate upon death of principal)	*Yes*
	Health care consent statute including appointment of health care representative	*No* but mandatory language above is incorporated by reference at § 16-36-1-14	None specified	None specified	• 1 witness	• Agent	*No*	*No*
16. Iowa Iowa code annotated §144B.1 to 12 (West 2004) *Separate living will statute:* Iowa code annotated §144A.1 to .12	Special durable power of attorney	*Yes* optional	None specified	• Individual provider* *Exception for relatives	• 2 witnesses *or* notarized	• Agent • Individual provider *One* may not be relative	*No*	*Yes*

TABLE 7.2

Health care power of attorney and combined advance directive legislation, September 2004 [CONTINUED]

State	Type	Form	Limits on agent's powers	Prohibited agents	Prohibited witnesses	Formalities of execution	Authority over autopsy, organ donation or remains	Comity provision
17. Kansas Kansas statutes annotated §58-625 to –632 (2003) *Separate living will statute:* Kansas statutes annotated §65-28,101 to 28,109	Special durable power of attorney	*Yes* Must be substantially followed	• Cannot revoke previous living will	• Individual provider* • Facility provider* *Exception for relatives & religious community members	• Agent • Relative • Heir • Person responsible for care costs	• 2 witnesses *or* notarized	Autopsy Organ donation Disposition of remains	*Yes*
18. Kentucky Kentucky revised statutes §311.621 to –643 (Baldwin 2004) *Separate living will statute: No*	Combined advanced directive (but called "living will directive")	*Yes* Must be substantially followed	• Nutrition & hydration* • Pregnancy limitation *Refusal permissible if specified conditions are met	• Facility provider* *Exception for relatives	• Relative • Facility provider • Attending physician • Heir • Person responsible for care costs	• 2 witnesses *or* notarized	*No*	*No*
19. Louisiana Louisiana revised statutes annotated 40:1299.58.1 to .10 (West 2004) See also durable power of attorney ("Procuration") statute: Louisiana civic code annotated articles 2985 to 3034 (West 2004), specifically article 2997 *Separate living will statute: No*	Proxy contained in living will statute	*Yes* Optional	• Powers implicitly limited to executing a living will declaration on behalf of principal. However, a durable power of attorney (a "procuration") may confer health care decision powers generally on an agent (a "mandatary")	None specified	• Relative • Heir	2 witnesses	*No*	*Yes*
20. Maine Maine revised statutes annotated titles 18A, §5-801 to §5-817 (West 2004) *Separate living will statute: No*	Combined advance directive [modeled on *Uniform Health Care Decisions Act (modified)*]*	*Yes* Optional	• Mental health facility admission, consent permissible if expressly authorized	• Long term care facility provider* *Exception for relatives	None specified	• 2 witnesses	*No*	*Yes*
21. Maryland Maryland code annotated [Health-Gen.] §5-601 to –608 (2004) *Separate living will statute: No*	Combined advance directive	*Yes* Optional	• None specified	• Facility provider* *Exception for relatives	• Agent • *One* must not be: heir, or have any other financial interest in person's death	• 2 witnesses Also recognizes oral directive to a physician with one witness	*No*	*Yes*
22. Massachusetts Massachusettes general laws annotated chapter 201D (West 2004) *Separate living will statute: None*	Special durable power of attorney	*No*	• None specified	• Facility provider* *Exception for relatives	• Agent	• 2 witnesses	*No*	Yes

TABLE 7.2

Health care power of attorney and combined advance directive legislation, September 2004 [CONTINUED]

State	Type	Form	Limits on agent's powers	Prohibited agents	Formalities of execution	Prohibited witnesses	Authority over autopsy, organ donation or remains	Comity provision
23. Michigan Michigan compiled laws annotated §700.5506 to 5513 (West 2004) *Separate living will statute: none*	Special durable power of attorney	Only for agent's acceptance	• Pregnancy limitation • Life-sustaining procedures* *Refusal permissible if expressly authorized	None specified	• 2 witnesses Agent must accept in writing before acting as agent ("patient advocate")	• Agent • Relative • Heir • Individual provider • Facility provider • Employee of life/health insurance provider for patient	Organ donation	No
24. Minnesota Minnesota statutes annotated §145C.01 to .16 (West 2004) *Separate living will statute:* Minnesota statute §145B.01 to .17 (West 2004)	Combined advance directive	Yes Optional	• None specified	• Individual provider* • Facility provider* *Exception for relatives	• 2 witnesses *or* notarized	• Agent *One may not be provider*	Organ donation Disposition of remains	Yes
25. Mississippi Mississippi code annotated §41-41-201 to −229 (West 2004) *Separate living will statute: no*	Combined advance directive *[modeled on Uniform Health Care Decisions Act (modified)]**	Yes Optional	• Mental health facility admission, consent permissible if expressly authorized	• Long term care facility *Exception for relatives	• 2 witnesses *or* notarized	• Agent • Individual provider • Facility provider *One may not be relative or heir*	No	Yes, but only if directive complies with this act
26. Missouri Missouri annotated statute §404.800–.872 (West 2004) and cross-referenced parts of §404.700 to .735 (durable power of attorney statute) *Separate living will statute:* Missouri annotated statute §459.010 to 459.055 (West 2004)	Special durable power of attorney	No	• Nutrition & hydration* *Refusal permissible if expressly authorized	• Attending physician* • Facility provider* *Exception for relatives and members of same religious community	• Must contain language of durability and be acknowledged as conveyance of real estate (§404.705)	None specified	No	Yes
27. Montana Montana code annotated §50-9-101 to −206 (2004). Also incorporates by reference §72-5-501 and −502 (durable power of attorney statute) *Separate living will statute: no*	Proxy contained in living will statute	Yes Optional	• Pregnancy limitation	None specified	• 2 witnesses under living will statute • Durable power of attorney statute: none, although customarily notarized	None specified	No	Yes
28. Nebraska Nebraska revised statutes §30-3401 to −3432 (2004) *Separate living will statute:* Nebraska revised statutes §20-401 to −416 (2004)	Special durable power of attorney	Yes Optional	• Life-sustaining procedures* • Nutrition & hydration* • Pregnancy limitation *Refusal permissible if expressly authorized	• Provider • Facility • Any agent serving 10 or more principals	• 2 witnesses *or* notarized	• Agent • Spouse • Relative • Heir • Attending physician • Insurer *One may not be facility provider*	No	Yes

TABLE 7.2

Health care power of attorney and combined advance directive legislation, September 2004 [CONTINUED]

State	Type	Form	Limits on agent's powers	Prohibited agents	Formalities of execution	Prohibited witnesses	Authority over autopsy, organ donation or remains	Comity provision
29. Nevada Nevada revised statutes §449.800 to .860 (2004) *Separate living will statute:* Nevada revised statutes 449.535 to 690 (2004) with proxy designation. NB. living will statute recognizes an agent under a regular DPA with authority to withold or withdraw life-sustaining treatment.	Special durable power of attorney (DPA)	*Yes* Form with disclosure statement must be substantially followed	• Mental health facility admission • Electro-convulsive therapy • Aversive intervention • Psycho-surgery • Sterilization • Abortion	• Individual provider* • Facility provider* *Exception for relatives	• 2 witnesses *or* notarized	• Agent • Individual provider • Facility provider • *One* may not be relative or heir	*No*	*No*
30. New Hampshire New Hampshire revised statutes annotated §137-J:1 to -J:16 (2004) *Separate living will statute:* New Hampshire revised statutes annotated §137-H:1 to -H:16 (2004)	Special durable power of attorney	Form and disclosure statement must be substantially followed.	• Mental health facility admission • Sterilization • Pregnancy limitation • Nutrition & hydration* *Refusal permissible if expressly authorized	• Individual provider* • Facility provider* *Exception for relatives who are employees of	• 2 witnesses • Principal must acknowledge receipt of mandatory notice	• Agent • Spouse • Heir • *One* may not be provider or facility	*No*	*Yes*
31. New Jersey New Jersey statutes annotated §26:2H-53 to –81 (West 2004) *Separate living will statute: no*	Combined advance directive	*No*	• None specified	• Attending physician • Facility provider *	• 2 witnesses *or* notarized	• Agent	*No*	*Yes*
32. New Mexico New Mexico statutes annotated §24-7A-1 to –18 (West 2004) *Separate living will statute: no*	Combined advance directive [modeled on *Uniform Health Care Decisions Act (modified)]**	*Yes* Optional	• Mental health facility admission	• Long term care facility provider * Exception for relatives	• 2 witnesses recommended but not required	None specified	*No*	*Yes, but only if directive complies with this act*
33. New York New York public health law §2980 to 2994 (McKinney 2004) *Separate living will statute: none*	Special durable power of attorney	*Yes* Optional	• Nutrition & hydration* *Principal must make his/her wishes "reasonably known"	• Attending physician • Facility provider* • Any agent serving 10 or more principals* * Exception for relatives	• 2 witnesses • Special institutional requirements	• Agent	*No*	*Yes*
34. North Carolina General statutes of North Carolina §32A-15 to –26 (2004) *Separate living will statute:* general statutes of North Carolina §90-320 to –322(2004)	Special durable power of attorney	*Yes* Optional	• None specified	• Individual provider	• 2 witnesses *and* notarized	• Relative • Heir • Attending physician • Facility provider • Creditor	*Yes* (but authority terminates on death of principal)	*No*

TABLE 7.2

Health care power of attorney and combined advance directive legislation, September 2004 [CONTINUED]

State	Type	Form	Limits on agent's powers	Prohibited agents	Formalities of execution	Prohibited witnesses	Authority over autopsy, organ donation or remains	Comity provision
35. North Dakota North Dakota century code §23-06.5-01 to –18 (2004) *Separate living will statute:* North Dakota century code §23-06.4-01 to –14 (2004)	Special durable power of attorney *Yes*	Optional	• Mental health facility admission > 45 days • Psycho-surgery • Abortion • Sterilization	• Individual provider* • Facility provider* * Exception for relatives who are employees of	• 2 witnesses *or* notarized • Agent must accept in writing	• Agent* • Spouse* • Heir* • Relative* • Creditor* One may *not* be: • Individual provider* • Facility provider* *Also disqualifies notary	*No*	*Yes*
36. Ohio Ohio revised code §1337.11 to .17 (West 2004) *Separate living will statute:* to .15 Ohio revised code §2133.01 (West 2004)	Special durable power of attorney *Yes*	Only for mandatory disclosure statement	• Life-sustaining procedures* • Nutrition & hydration* • Pregnancy limitation *Refusal permissible if specified conditions are met	• Attending physician • Nursing home administrator* * Exception for relatives who are employees of	• 2 witnesses *or* notarized	• Agent • Relative • Att. Physician • Nursing home administrator	*No*	*Yes*
37. Oklahoma Oklahoma statutes annotated title 63, §3101.1 to .16 (West 2004) *Separate living will statute: no*	Combined advance directive *Yes*	Must be substantially followed	• Nutrition & hydration* • Pregnancy limitation *Refusal permissible if expressly authorized	None specified	• 2 witnesses	• Heir	*No*	*Yes*
38. Oregon Oregon revised statutes §127.505 to .660 and 127.995 (2004) *Separate living will statute: no* (2004)	Combined advance directive *Yes*	Must be followed but recognizes that any other form "constitutes evidence of the patient's desires and interests"	• Mental health facility admission • Electro-convulsive therapy • Psycho-surgery • Sterilization • Abortion • Life-sustaining procedures* • Nutrition & hydration* *Refusal permissible if expressly authorized or if specified conditions are met	• Attending physician* • Facility provider* * Exception for relatives	• 2 witnesses • Agent must accept in writing • Special institutional requirements	• Agent • Att. physician *One* may not be relative, heir, or facility provider	*No*	*Yes*
39. Pennsylvania Pennsylvania statutes annotated title 20, §5401 to 5416 (West 2004), *and* 20 Pennsylvania consolidated statutes annotated §5601 5611 (durable power of attorney)	Living will statute *Yes* Statutory form durable power of attorney health decision powers	Optional	Living will: Unclear whether agent is permitted to act *only* if principal is in a: • Terminal condition, or • State of permanent unconsciousness • Nutrition & hydration* • Pregnancy limitation *Refusal permissible if expressly authorized Statutory form durable power of attorney defines powers specifically	None specified	Living will: 2 witnesses Statutory form durable power of attorney: None required	LW: person who signs declaration on declarant's behalf Statutory form DPA: none specified	• Living will: none • Statutory form durable power of attorney: organ donation	• Living will: *no* • Statutory form durable power of attorney: *yes*
40. Rhode Island Rhode Island general laws §23-4.10-1 to –12 (2004) *Separate living will statute:* Rhode Island general laws §23-4.11-1 to –15 (2004)	Special durable power of attorney *Yes*	Not clear whether optional or mandatory	• None specified	• Individual provider* • Community care facility* * Exception for relatives who are employees of	• 2 witnesses • Principal must be Rhode Island resident	• Agent • Individual provider • Community care facility *One* may not be relative or heir	*No*	*Yes*

TABLE 7.2

Health care power of attorney and combined advance directive legislation, September 2004 [CONTINUED]

State	Type	Form	Limits on agent's powers	Prohibited agents	Formalities of execution	Prohibited witnesses	Authority over autopsy, organ donation or remains	Comity provision
41. South Carolina South Carolina code §62-5-501 to –505 (2004), particularly §62-5-504 *Separate living will statute:* South Carolina code § 44-77-10 to –160 (also permits appointment of agent)	Special durable power of attorney (within general durable power of attorney statute)	*Yes* Must be substantially followed (but conventional durable powers of attorney contain health powers)	• Nutrition & hydration "necessary for comfort care or alleviation of pain"* • Pregnancy limitation *Refusal permissible if expressly authorized	• Individual provider* • Facility provider* • Spouse of a provider* *Exception for relatives	• 2 witnesses	• Agent • Spouse • Relative • Heir • Attending physician • Creditor • Life insurance beneficiary • Person responsible for care costs • One may not be facility provider	Organ donation	*Yes*
42. South Dakota South Dakota codified laws §59-7-9 (2004) See also §34-12C-1 to – 8 (health care consent procedures) *Separate living will statute:* South Dakota codified laws §34-12D–l to –22(2004)	General durable power of attorney that permits health decisions authority	*No*	• Pregnancy limitation • Nutrition & hydration* *Refusal permissible if expressly authorized or other conditions are met	None specified	None specified	None specified	*No*	*Yes*
43. Tennessee Tennessee code annotated §68-11-1801 to –1815 (2004) *Separate living will statute: no*	Combined advance directive	*No*	None specified	None specified	• 2 witnesses *or* notarized	• Agent • Provider • Facility *One may not be relative or heir*	*No*	*Yes*
44. Texas Texas [health & safety] code annotated §166.001 to –.166 (Vernon 2004) *Separate living will statute: no*	(1) Special durable power of attorney (medical power of attorney): *yes.* Must be substantially followed plus mandatory disclosure statement. (2) Living will: *yes* optional		• Mental health facility admission • Electro-convulsive therapy • Psycho-surgery • Abortion • Comfort care	• Individual provider* • Facility provider* *Exception for relatives who are employees of	• 2 witnesses	*One* may not be: • Agent • Attending physician • Relative • Facility • Heir • Creditor	*No*	*Yes*
45. Utah Utah code annotated §75-2-1101 to –1119 (2004) *Separate living will statute: no*	Special durable power of attorney	*Yes* Must be substantially followed	• Life-sustaining procedures* • Pregnancy limitation *Agent makes health care decisions by executing a medical directive.	None specified	• Notarized	None specified	*No*	*Yes*

TABLE 7.2

Health care power of attorney and combined advance directive legislation, September 2004 [CONTINUED]

State	Type	Form	Limits on agent's powers	Prohibited agents	Formalities of execution	Prohibited witnesses	Authority over autopsy, organ donation or remains	Comity provision
46. Vermont Vermont statutes annotated title 18, §§263 to 5278 (2004) *Separate living will statute:* Vermont statutes annotated title 18, §5251 to 5262 (2004)	Combined advance directive	Yes Disclosure statement must be substantially followed Form optional	• Mental health facility admission • Sterilization	• Individual provider* • Residential care provider* • Funeral/crematory/ cemetery representative (if authorized to dispose of remains or donate organs) *Exception for relatives who are employees of	• Warning disclosure • 2 witnesses • Special institutional requirements	• Agent • Individual provider* • Residential care provider • Spouse • Heir • Creditor • Funeral/crematory/ cemetery representative	Organ donation Disposition of remains	Yes
47. Virginia Virginia code §54.1-2981 to −2993 (West 2004) *Separate living will statute: no*	Combined advance directive	Yes Optional	• Mental health facility admission • Psycho-surgery • Sterilization • Abortion • Decisions about "visitation" unless expressly authorized	None specified	• 2 witnesses	• Spouse • Relative	Organ donation	Yes
48. Washington Revised code of Washington annotated §11.94.010 to .900 (West 2004) *Separate living will statute:* revised code of Washington annotated §70.122.010 to −.920 (West 2004)	General durable power of attorney	No	Cross reference to guardianship law [RCWA 11.92.043(5)]: • Electro-convulsive therapy • Psycho-surgery • Other psychiatric • Amputation	• Individual provider* • Facility provider* *Exception for relatives	None specified	n/a	No	Yes
49. West Virginia West Virginia code annotated §16-30-1 to −25 (West 2004) *Separate living will statute: no*	Combined advance directive(but maintains separate living will and medical power of attorney documents)	Yes Optional	• Limit on agent's authority to revoke a pre-need funeral contract	• Individual provider* • Facility provider* *Exception for relatives who are employees of	• 2 witnesses *and* notarized	• Agent • Attending physician • Principal's signatory • Relative • Heir • Person responsible for care costs	Autopsy Organ donation Disposition of remains	Yes
50. Wisconsin Wisconsin statutes annotated §155.01 to .80 (west 2004) See durable power of attorney cross reference §243.07(6m) (west 2004) *Separate living will statute:* Wisconsin statutes annotated §§l54.0l to −.15 (West 2004)	Special durable power of attorney	Yes Optional, but disclosure statement is mandatory	• Admission to facility for mental health/retardation or other listed conditions • Electro-convulsive therapy • Mental health research • Drastic mental health treatment • Admission to nursing home or residential facility—very limited unless expressly authorized in the document • Nutrition & hydration* • Pregnancy limitation *Refusal permissible only if specified conditions are met	• Individual provider* • Facility provider* *Exception for relatives	• 2 witnesses	• Agent • Individual provider • Facility provider* • Relative • Heir • Person responsible for care costs *Exception for chaplains & social workers	Organ donation	Yes

TABLE 7.2

Health care power of attorney and combined advance directive legislation, September 2004 [CONTINUED]

State	Type	Form	Limits on agent's powers	Prohibited agents	Formalities of execution	Prohibited witnesses	Authority over autopsy, organ donation or remains	Comity provision
51. Wyoming Wyoming statutes §3-5-201 to –213 (2004) *Separate living will statute:* Wyoming statutes §§35-22-101 to –109 (2004)	Special durable power of attorney	*No*	• Mental health facility admission • Electro-convulsive therapy • Psycho-surgery	• Individual provider* • Facility provider* *Exception for relatives who are employees of	• 2 witnesses *or* notarized	• Agent • Individual provider • Facility provider • *One* may not be relative or heir	Organ donation Disposition of remains	*Yes*
Uniform Health-Care Decision Act *Separate living will statute: No*	Comprehensive Health Care Decisions Act	*Yes* Optional	• Mental health facility admission, consent permissible if expressly authorized	• Long term care facility provider	2 witnesses recommended, but not required	None	*No*	Yes, but only if directive complies with this act

Notes: LW is living will. DPA is durable power of attorney. The descriptions and limitations listed in this chart are broad characterizations for comparison purposes and not precise quotations from legislative language.

SOURCE: "Health Care Power of Attorney and Combined Advance Directive Legislation September 1, 2004," American Bar Association, Commission on Legal Problems of the Elderly, 2004, http://www.abanet.org/aging/HCPA-CHT04.doc (accessed December 1, 2005). Reprinted with permission.

FIGURE 7.3

State laws governing surrogate decision-making for terminally ill patients in the absence of advance directives, 2004

■ *Jurisdictions with statutes authorizing surrogate decision-making in the absence of advance directives (the District of Columbia and 29 states: Alabama, Arizona, Arkansas, Colorado, Connecticut, Delaware, Florida, Hawaii, Illinois, Indiana, Iowa, Kentucky, Louisiana, Maine, Maryland, Mississippi, Montana, Nevada, New Mexico, North Carolina, Ohio, Oklahoma, Oregon, South Carolina, Texas, Utah, Virginia, West Virginia and Wyoming).*

□ *States without statutes authorizing surrogate decision making (21 states: Alaska, California, Georgia, Idaho, Kansas, Massachusetts, Michigan, Minnesota, Missouri, Nebraska, New Hampshire, New Jersey, New York[a], North Dakota, Pennsylvania, Rhode Island, South Dakota, Tennessee, Vermont, Washington and Wisconsin[b]).*

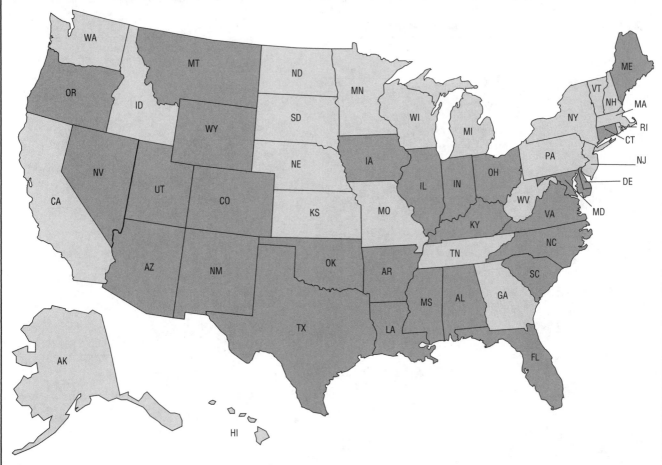

[a]New York does authorize surrogate decision-making for do-not-resuscitate order decisions.
[b]Wisconsin does authorize surrogate decision-making for the sole purpose of admittance of a terminally ill incapacitated patient to hospice.

SOURCE: "State Statutes Governing Surrogate Decision-Making," in *End-of-Life Law Digest*, The National Hospice and Palliative Care Organization, 2004

hydration are legally considered medical treatments and may, therefore, be refused. But this form of treatment remains controversial in the right-to-die issue because food and drink are the most basic forms of life sustenance yet they are not usually needed by dying persons and may make them less comfortable. The unresolved problem is mirrored in the fact that not all states' advance directive statutes (laws) address this issue. (See Figure 7.4 and Figure 7.5.)

Relief from Pain

Some living wills also enable an individual to give instructions about the management of pain. While a number of studies have shown that pain is not the primary motivation for assisted suicide requests, many people have seen family and friends suffer painful deaths, and they fear the same fate. Experts advise that advance directives should expressly indicate desires for pain control and comfort care, even when individuals have chosen to forego life-sustaining treatments.

In the past, patient pain may not have been adequately treated because medical professionals lacked training or feared overprescribing pain medications. A variety of legislative and education initiatives by states and medical professional societies have dramatically improved pain management. The Federation of State Medical Boards has developed guidelines to help

FIGURE 7.4

State laws governing the refusal of artificial nutrition and hydration in living wills, 2004

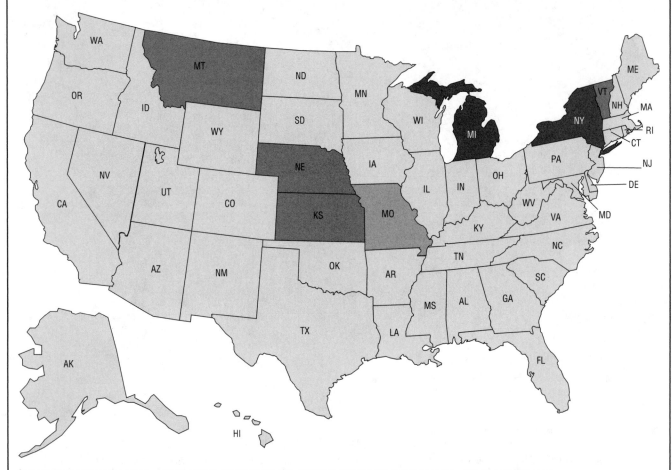

☐ *States with living will statutes that permit individuals to refuse artificial nutrition and hydration through their living wills (42 states: Alabama, Alaska, Arkansas, Arizona[a], California, Colorado, Connecticut, Delaware, Florida, Georgia, Hawaii, Idaho, Illinois[b], Indiana, Iowa, Kentucky, Louisiana, Maine, Maryland, Minnesota, Mississippi, Nevada, New Jersey, New Hampshire, New Mexico, North Carolina, North Dakota, Ohio, Oklahoma, Oregon, Pennsylvania, Rhode Island, South Carolina, South Dakota, Tennessee, Texas, Utah, Virginia, Washington, West Virginia, Wisconsin and Wyoming).*

▨ *States with living will statutes that require the provision of nutrition and hydration except in very limited circumstances (1 state: Missouri[c]).*

▩ *Jurisdictions whose living will statutes do not explicitly address the issue of artificial nutrition and hydration (the District of Columbia and 4 states: Kansas, Montana, Nebraska, and Vermont).*

■ *States without living will statutes (3 states: Massachusetts, Michigan and New York).*

[a]The authority to withhold or withdraw artificial nutrition and hydration is only explicitly mentioned in the sample document, not in the text of the statute.
[b]Artificial nutrition and hydration cannot be withheld or withdrawn if the resulting death is due to starvation or dehydration.
[c]The medical power of attorney statute in Missouri permits appointed agents to refuse artificial nutrition and hydration on behalf of the principal.

SOURCE: "Artificial Nutrition and Hydration in Living Will Statutes," in *End-of-Life Law Digest*, The National Hospice and Palliative Care Organization, 2004

physicians use medication to manage pain safely and effectively. Special instruction in pain management for patients with life-limiting illnesses is now offered in many medical and nursing schools.

Further pressure to improve pain management can come from patients and their families. In December 2000 a California jury held a physician liable for prescribing too little pain medication for a patient dying from lung cancer. The children of eighty-five-year-old William Bergman sued his physician for elder abuse on the grounds that the doctor failed to prescribe strong enough medication to control their father's pain before, during, and after his hospitalization in 1998. The jury awarded the family $1.5 million, but to comply with the state limit on such awards, the sum was reduced to $250,000. Advocates for improved end-of-life care hoped the verdict would remind physicians about the importance of pain management.

FIGURE 7.5

State laws governing the refusal of artificial nutrition and hydration by health care agents, 2004

☐ *States with statutes that permit health care agents to order the withholding or withdrawal of artificial nutrition and hydration (41 states: Alabama, Arizona, California, Colorado, Connecticut, Delaware, Florida, Georgia, Hawaii, Idaho, Illinois, Indiana, Iowa, Kentucky, Louisiana, Maine, Maryland, Minnesota, Mississippi, Missouri, Nebraska, Nevada, New Hampshire, New Jersey, New Mexico, New York, North Carolina, Ohio, Oklahoma, Oregon, Pennsylvania, South Carolina, South Dakota, Tennessee, Texas, Utah, Virginia, Vermont, Washington, West Virginia, and Wisconsin).*

▨ *Jurisdictions whose medical power of attorney statutes do not explicitly address the issue of artificial nutrition and hydration (the District of Columbia and 9 states: Arkansas, California, Kansas, Massachusetts, Michigan, Montana, North Dakota, Rhode Island, and Wyoming).*

▦ *Alaska's Power of Attorney Act precludes health care agent authority to terminate life-sustaining medical procedures. The act does provide that the agent may enforce a declaration.*

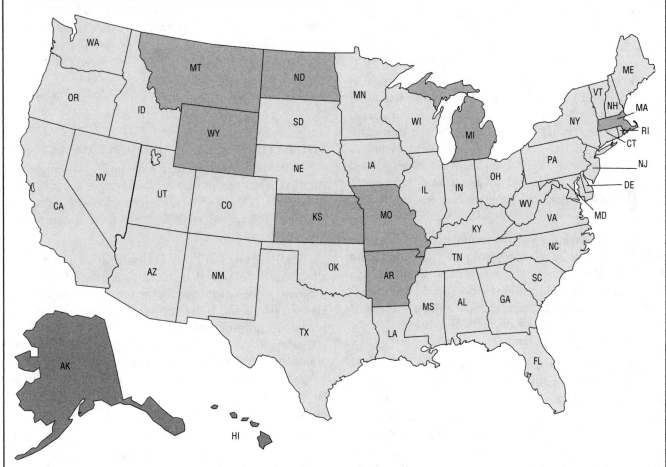

SOURCE: "Artificial Nutrition and Hydration in Statutes Authorizing Health Care Agents," in *End-of-Life Law Digest*, The National Hospice and Palliative Care Organization, 2004

COMBINED ADVANCE DIRECTIVE LAWS

Some states have separate laws that govern living wills and durable powers of attorney for health care. The National Conference of State Legislatures (NCSL) and the Center to Improve Care of the Dying (CICD) believe that rather than having separate laws for these two documents, states should combine right-to-die laws into a single statute. By September 2004, twenty-two states had done just that. (See Table 7.2.) Of these states, Alabama, Alaska, Delaware, Hawaii, Maine, Mississippi, and New Mexico had also adopted the Uniform Health-Care Decisions Act (UHCDA) as a model.

The UHCDA has been recommended by the NCSL and the CICD as a model law because it is simple and comprehensive. It contains provisions governing living wills and durable powers of attorney, as well as limits on an agent's powers. The law permits instructions regarding one's future health care to be either written or oral. States using the law as a model may adopt the optional combined directive, which does not require witnesses to the document. It further enables individuals to express their preferences about organ donation and to designate a primary physician. (See Table 7.1, Part 3 and Part 4.)

Along with showing the type of health care power of attorney and combined advance directive legislation in each state, Table 7.2 shows other related information, including the comity provision. If a state has a comity provision, it has legislation specifically requiring that another state's living will, a health care power of attorney, or both, be honored within their borders.

IMPORTANCE OF COMMUNICATION FOR END-OF-LIFE CARE

The consideration of an advance directive should be the start of an ongoing discussion among the individual, family members, and the family doctor about end-of-life health care. Discussions about one's advance directive do not have to be limited to treatment preferences and medical circumstances. Sometimes knowing things such as the patient's religious beliefs and values can be important for the proxy when speaking for the patient's interests. The Center for Health Law and Ethics at the University of New Mexico has devised a values questionnaire to help people examine their attitudes about issues related to illness, health care, and dying. It may serve as a valuable tool to guide discussions between the patient and the proxy, as well as among family members.

When preparing an advance directive, it is vitally important for the family and proxy to fully understand the care and measures that are wanted. Even when a patient has a living will calling for no "heroic measures," if the family demands such medical intervention, it is likely that the hospital or doctor will comply with the family's wishes rather than risk a lawsuit.

Highlighting the need for communication, a 1998 study of 250 terminally ill patients and their families showed that only 66% of the families surveyed accurately predicted the level of treatment their dying family member would want. Researchers from the Georgetown University Center for Clinical Bioethics separately questioned the patient and the patient's likely surrogate about the treatment that the patient would desire in three different end-of-life scenarios. One-third of the surrogates chose differently than the patient, evenly divided between picking too much and too little treatment.

Bernard Lo and Robert Steinbrook also highlight the need for patient-physician communication regarding end-of-life matters in "Resuscitating Advance Directives" (*Archives of Internal Medicine*, vol. 164, no. 14, July 26, 2004). The authors state that "Advance directives have not fulfilled their promise of facilitating decisions about end-of-life care for incompetent patients," and explain that legal requirements and restrictions make it difficult for patients to complete advance directives during visits to their doctors. They suggest that the patient's discussion with the physician is probably more important to the patient's end-of-life care than is the legal document. Lo and Steinbrook thus conclude that the procedures for the written advance directives should be simplified to foster this discussion.

The National Conference of State Legislatures and the Center to Improve Care of the Dying also recognize that standard advance directives may not be applicable to specific medical conditions and to medical conditions that may evolve over time. Thus, if patients have had end-of-life care discussions with their physicians, Lo and Steinbrook suggest, then "physicians can identify and correct misunderstandings about the medical situation, options, and outcomes." The NCSL and the CICD believe that—in addition to patient-physician discussions—patients should have access to advance directives that are flexible enough to allow for changes in their medical conditions and end-of-life education as was initially intended in the Patient Self-Determination Act of 1990.

THE PATIENT SELF-DETERMINATION ACT

In 1990 Congress enacted the Patient Self-Determination Act (PSDA) as part of the Omnibus Budget Reconciliation Act of 1990 (PL 101–508). This legislation was intended to "reinforce individuals' constitutional right to determine their final health care."

The PSDA took effect on December 1, 1991. It requires all health care providers participating in Medicare (a program of the federal government through which people age sixty-five and older receive health insurance) and Medicaid (a program run by the federal and state governments to provide health insurance to people younger than sixty-five years of age who cannot afford to pay for private health insurance) to provide all patients over age eighteen with the following written information:

- The patient's rights under the law to participate in decisions about his or her medical care, including the right to accept or refuse treatments

- The patient's right under state law to complete advance directives, which will be documented in his or her medical records

- The health care provider's policies honoring these rights

Providers include hospitals, nursing homes, home health care providers, hospices, and health maintenance organizations (HMOs), but not outpatient-service providers or emergency medical personnel. The PSDA requires health care providers to educate their staff and the community about advance directives. It also prohibits hospital personnel from discriminating against patients based on whether they have an advance directive. (Patients are informed that having an advance directive is not a prerequisite to receiving medical care.)

CHAPTER 8
COURTS AND THE END OF LIFE

Traditionally, death was defined as the total cessation of circulatory and respiratory functions. In 1968 the Ad Hoc Committee of the Harvard Medical School defined irreversible coma, or brain death, as a new criterion for death. As medical technology has become increasingly able to maintain patients who would otherwise die from severe injuries or illnesses, the debate about defining death, and about whether patients have the right to choose to die, has intensified.

THE RIGHT TO PRIVACY: KAREN ANN QUINLAN

The landmark case of Karen Ann Quinlan was the first to deal with the dilemma of withdrawing life-sustaining treatment from a patient who was not terminally ill but who was not really "alive." The decision to terminate life support, which was once a private matter between the patient's family and doctor, became an issue to be decided by the courts. The New Jersey Supreme Court ruling on this case became the precedent for nearly all right-to-die cases nationwide.

In 1975 twenty-one-year-old Karen Ann Quinlan suffered cardiopulmonary arrest after ingesting a combination of alcohol and drugs. She subsequently went into a persistent vegetative state (PVS). Dr. Fred Plum, a neurologist, described her as no longer having any cognitive function but retaining the capacity to maintain the vegetative parts of neurological function. She grimaced, made chewing movements, uttered sounds, and maintained a normal blood pressure, but she was entirely unaware of anyone or anything. The medical opinion was that Quinlan had some brainstem function, but that in her case it could not support breathing. She had been on a respirator since her admission to the hospital.

Quinlan's parents asked that her respirator be removed and that she be allowed to die. Quinlan's doctor refused, claiming that his patient did not meet the Harvard Criteria for brain death. Based on the existing

medical standards and practices, a doctor could not terminate a patient's life support if that patient did not meet the legal definitions for brain death. According to the Harvard Criteria, Quinlan could not be declared legally dead, and medical experts believed she would die if the respirator were removed.

Quinlan's father, Joseph Quinlan, went to court to seek appointment as his daughter's guardian (because she was of legal age) and to gain the power to authorize "the discontinuance of all extraordinary procedures for sustaining Quinlan's vital processes." The court denied his petition to have Quinlan's respirator turned off and also refused to grant him guardianship over his daughter.

First and Eighth Amendments Are Irrelevant to Case

Joseph Quinlan subsequently appealed to the Supreme Court of New Jersey (*Quinlan*, 70 N.J. 10, 355 A.2d 647, 1976). He requested, as a parent, to have Quinlan's life support removed based on the U.S. Constitution's First Amendment—the right to religious freedom. The court rejected his request. It also considered the Eighth Amendment—protection against cruel and unusual punishment—inapplicable in Quinlan's case, stating that this amendment applied to protection from excessive criminal punishment. The court considered Quinlan's cruel and unusual circumstances not punishment inflicted by the law or state, but the result of "an accident of fate and nature."

The Right to Privacy

The New Jersey Supreme Court stated, however, that an individual's right to privacy was most relevant to the case. Although the U.S. Constitution does not expressly indicate a right to privacy, U.S. Supreme Court rulings in past cases had not only recognized this right but had also determined that some areas of the right to privacy are guaranteed by the Constitution. For example, the

Supreme Court had upheld the right to privacy in *Griswold v. Connecticut* (the right to marital privacy, or the right to use contraception, 381 US 479, 1965) and in *Roe v. Wade* (the right to abortion, 410 US 113, 1973). The U.S. Supreme Court had further presumed that the right to privacy included a patient's right to refuse medical treatment in some situations.

Based on these U.S. Supreme Court rulings, the New Jersey Supreme Court ruled that "Karen's right of privacy may be asserted on her behalf by her guardian under the peculiar circumstances here present," and further noted:

> We have no doubt...that if Karen were herself miraculously lucid for an interval (not altering the existing prognosis of the condition to which she would soon return) and perceptive of her irreversible condition, she could effectively decide upon discontinuance of the life-support apparatus, even if it meant the prospect of natural death.

The State's Interest

Balanced against Quinlan's constitutional right to privacy was the state's interest in preserving life. Judge Hughes of the New Jersey Supreme Court noted that in many cases the court had ordered medical treatment continued because the minimal bodily invasion (usually blood transfusion) resulted in recovery. He indicated that, in Quinlan's case, bodily invasion was far greater than minimal, consisting of twenty-four-hour nursing care, antibiotics, respirator, catheter, and feeding tube. Judge Hughes further noted:

> We think that the State's interest...weakens and the individual's right to privacy grows as the degree of bodily invasion increases and the prognosis dims. Ultimately there comes a point at which the individual's rights overcome the State's interest.

Prevailing Medical Standards and Practices

Quinlan's physicians had refused to remove the respirator because they did not want to violate the prevailing medical standards and practices. Even though Quinlan's physicians assured the court that the possibility of lawsuits and criminal sanctions did not influence their decision in this specific case, the court believed that the threat of legal ramifications strongly influenced the existing medical standards and practices of health care providers.

The court also observed that life-prolongation advances had rendered the existing medical standards ambiguous (unclear), leaving doctors in a quandary. Moreover, modern devices used for prolonging life, such as respirators, had confused the issue of "ordinary" and "extraordinary" measures. Therefore, the court suggested that respirators could be considered "ordinary" care for a curable patient, but "extraordinary" care for irreversibly unconscious patients.

The court also suggested that hospitals form ethics committees to assist physicians with difficult cases like Quinlan's. These committees would be similar to a multi-judge panel exploring different solutions to an appeal. The committees would not only diffuse professional responsibility, but also eliminate any possibly unscrupulous motives of physicians or families. The justices considered the court's intervention on medical decisions an infringement on the physicians' field of competence.

Is It Homicide?

The state had promised to prosecute anyone who terminated Quinlan's life support because such an act would constitute homicide. The New Jersey Supreme Court, however, rejected this consequence because the resulting death would be from natural causes. The court stated:

> The exercise of a constitutional right, such as we have here found, is protected from criminal prosecution....The constitutional protection extends to third parties whose action is necessary to effectuate the exercise of that right.

After the Respirator Was Removed

In March 1976 the New Jersey Supreme Court ruled that, if the hospital ethics committee agreed that Quinlan would not recover from irreversible coma, her respirator could be removed. Furthermore, all parties involved would be legally immune from criminal and civil prosecution. However, after Quinlan's respirator was removed, she continued to breathe on her own and remained in a PVS until she died of multiple infections in 1985.

Some people wondered why the Quinlans did not request permission to discontinue Karen's artificial nutrition and hydration. In *Karen Ann: The Quinlans Tell Their Story* (New York: Doubleday and Company, 1977) the Quinlans stated that they would have had moral problems with depriving their daughter of food and antibiotics.

SUBSTITUTED JUDGMENT

Superintendent of Belchertown State School et al v. Joseph Saikewicz

Joseph Saikewicz was a mentally incompetent resident of the Belchertown State School of the Massachusetts Department of Mental Health. In April 1976 Saikewicz was diagnosed with acute myeloblastic monocytic leukemia. He was sixty-seven years old but had the mental age of about two years and eight months. The superintendent of the mental institution petitioned the court for a guardian *ad litem* (a temporary guardian for the duration of the trial). The court-appointed guardian recommended that it would be in the patient's best interests that he not undergo chemotherapy.

In May 1976 the probate judge ordered nontreatment of the disease based in part on findings of medical experts who indicated that chemotherapy might produce remission of leukemia in 30 to 50% of the cases. If remission occurred, it would last between two and thirteen months. Chemotherapy, however, would make Saikewicz suffer adverse side effects that he would not understand. Without chemotherapy, the patient might live for several weeks or months, but would die without the pain or discomfort associated with chemotherapy.

In fact, Saikewicz died on September 4, 1976, from pneumonia, a complication of the leukemia. Nevertheless, his case was heard by the Supreme Court of Massachusetts in order to establish a precedent on the question of substituted judgment (*Superintendent of Belchertown State School et al v. Joseph Saikewicz*, Mass., 370 N.E.2d 417, 1977).

The court agreed that extraordinary measures should not be used if the patient would not recover from the disease. The court also ruled that a person has a right to the preservation of his or her bodily integrity and can refuse medical invasion. The Massachusetts Supreme Court turned to *Quinlan* for support of its right of privacy argument.

THE RIGHTS OF AN INCOMPETENT PATIENT. Once the right to refuse treatment had been established, the court declared that everyone, including an incompetent person, has the right of choice:

> To presume that the incompetent person must always be subjected to what many rational and intelligent persons may decline is to downgrade the status of the incompetent person by placing a lesser value on his intrinsic human worth and vitality.

Referring to *Quinlan*, the *Saikewicz* court recommended that the patient not receive the treatment most people with leukemia would choose. (Unlike some later courts, the *Quinlan* court accepted the premise that a vegetative patient would not want to remain "alive.") The *Saikewicz* court believed that the "substituted judgment" standard would best preserve respect for the integrity and autonomy of the patient. In other words, the decision maker—in this case, the court—would put itself in Saikewicz's position and make the treatment decision the patient most likely would make were he competent. The court believed Saikewicz would have refused treatment.

In evaluating the role of the hospital and the guardian in the decision-making process, the *Saikewicz* court rejected the *Quinlan* court's recommendation that an ethics committee should be the source of the decision. The court instead concluded:

We do not view the judicial resolution of this most difficult and awesome question—whether potentially life-prolonging treatment should be withheld from a person incapable of making his own decision—as constituting a "gratuitous encroachment" on the domain of medical expertise. Rather, such questions of life and death seem to us to require the process of detached but passionate investigation and decision that forms the ideal on which the judicial branch of government was created.

The Case of John Storar

John Storar, a fifty-two-year-old mentally retarded man with a mental age of about eighteen months, was diagnosed with terminal cancer. His mother, Dorothy Storar, petitioned the court to discontinue blood transfusions that were delaying her son's death, which would probably occur within three to six months.

At the time of the hearing, Storar required two units of blood every week or two. He found the transfusions disagreeable and had to be given a sedative before the procedure. He also had to be restrained during the transfusions. Without the blood transfusions, however, there would be insufficient oxygen in his blood, causing his heart to beat faster and his respiratory rate to increase. After transfusions, the doctor reported, Storar had more energy and was able to resume most of his normal activities.

The probate court granted Mrs. Storar the right to terminate the treatments, but the order was stayed and treatment continued pending the appeal to the New York Appellate Division (or appellate court) (*Charles S. Soper, as Director of Newark Developmental Center et al v. Dorothy Storar*, N.Y., 420 N.E.2d 64, 1981). Storar died before the case could be heard, rendering the decision moot, but because the issue was considered to be of public importance, the appellate court proceeded to hear the case.

The appellate court agreed with the probate court that a guardian can make medical decisions for an incompetent patient. However, the parent/guardian "may not deprive a child of life-saving treatment." In this case there were two threats to Storar's life—the incurable cancer and the loss of blood that could be remedied with transfusions. Because the transfusions did not, in the eyes of the majority opinion written by Judge Wachtler, cause much pain, the appellate court overturned the probate court's ruling.

Judge Jones, dissenting from the determination, believed the treatments did not serve Storar's best interests. They did not relieve his pain and, in fact, caused him additional pain. Since the blood transfusions would not cure his cancer, they could be considered extraordinary treatments. Finally, the judge reasoned that Storar's mother had cared for him for a long time and knew best how he felt, and therefore the court should respect her decision.

COMPETENT PATIENTS' WISHES

Satz v. Perlmutter

Not all the cases of patients seeking to terminate life support concern incompetent people. Abe Perlmutter, seventy-three years old, was suffering from amyotrophic lateral sclerosis (ALS; sometimes called Lou Gehrig's disease). ALS is always fatal after prolonged physical degeneration, but it does not affect mental functions.

Perlmutter's 1978 request to have his respirator removed was approved by the Circuit Court of Broward County, Florida. At a bedside hearing, the court questioned whether the patient truly understood the consequences of his request. Perlmutter told the judge that, if the respirator were removed, "It can't be worse than what I'm going through now."

The state appealed the case before the Florida District Court of Appeals (appellate court), citing the state's duty to preserve life and to prevent the unlawful killing of a human being. The state also noted the hospital's and the doctors' fear of criminal prosecution and civil liability. In *Michael J. Satz, State Attorney for Broward County, Florida v. Abe Perlmutter* (Fla. App., 362 So.2d, 160, 1978) the appellate court concluded that Perlmutter's right to refuse treatment overrode the state's interests, and found in Perlmutter's favor.

THE STATE'S INTERESTS. An individual's right to refuse medical treatment is generally honored as long as it is consistent with the state's interests, which include:

• Interest in the preservation of life

• Need to protect innocent third parties

• Duty to prevent suicide

• Requirement that it help maintain the ethical integrity of medical practice

In the Perlmutter case the Florida District Court of Appeals found that the preservation of life is an important goal, but not when the disease is incurable and causes the patient to suffer. The need to protect innocent third parties refers to cases in which a parent refuses treatment and a third party suffers, such as the abandonment of a minor child. Perlmutter's children were all adults and Perlmutter was not committing suicide. Were it not for the respirator, he would be dead; therefore, disconnecting it would not cause his death but would result in the disease running its natural course. Finally, the court turned to *Quinlan* and *Saikewicz* to support its finding that there are times when medical ethics dictates that a dying person needs comfort more than treatment. The court concluded:

Abe Perlmutter should be allowed to make his choice to die with dignity.... It is all very convenient to insist on continuing Mr. Perlmutter's life so that there can be no question of foul play, no resulting civil liability and no possible trespass on medical ethics. However, it is quite another matter to do so at the patient's sole expense and against his competent will, thus inflicting never-ending physical torture on his body until the inevitable, but artificially suspended, moment of death. Such a course of conduct invades the patient's constitutional right of privacy, removes his freedom of choice and invades his right to self-determine.

The state again appealed the case, this time to the Supreme Court of Florida, which, in *Michael J. Satz, etc. v. Abe Perlmutter* (Fla., 379 So.2d 359, 1980), supported the decision by the Florida District Court of Appeals.

THE SUBJECTIVE, LIMITED-OBJECTIVE, AND PURE-OBJECTIVE TESTS

In the Matter of Claire C. Conroy

Claire Conroy was an eighty-four-year-old nursing-home patient suffering from "serious and irreversible mental and physical impairments with a limited life expectancy." In March 1984 her nephew (her guardian and only living relative) petitioned the Superior Court of Essex County, New Jersey, for removal of her nasogastric feeding tube. Conroy's guardian *ad litem*, appointed by the court, opposed the petition. The Superior Court approved the nephew's request, and the guardian *ad litem* appealed. Claire Conroy died with the nasogastric tube in place while the appeal was pending. Nonetheless, the appellate court chose to hear the case (*In the Matter of Claire C. Conroy*, 486 A.2d 1209, [N.J. 1985]). The court reasoned that this was an important case and that its ruling could influence future cases with comparable circumstances.

Conroy suffered from heart disease, hypertension, and diabetes. She also had a gangrenous leg, bedsores, and an eye problem that required irrigation. She lacked bowel control, could not speak, and had a limited swallowing ability. In the appeals trial one medical expert testified that Conroy, although awake, was seriously demented. Another doctor testified that "although she was confused and unaware, 'she responds somehow.'"

Both experts were not sure if the patient could feel pain, although she had moaned when subjected to painful stimuli. They agreed, though, that if the nasogastric tube were removed, Conroy would die a painful death.

Conroy's nephew testified that his aunt would never have wanted to be maintained in this manner. She feared doctors and had avoided them all her life. Because she was Roman Catholic, a priest was brought in to testify. In his judgment the removal of the tube would be ethical and moral even though her death might be painful.

The appeals court held that:

The right to terminate life-sustaining treatment based on a guardian's judgment was limited to incurable and terminally ill patients who are brain dead, irreversibly comatose, or vegetative, and who would gain no medical benefit from continued treatment.

Furthermore, a guardian's decision did not apply to food withdrawal, which hastens death. The court considered this active euthanasia, which it did not consider ethically permissible.

THE THREE TESTS. The court proposed three tests to determine if Conroy's feeding tube should have been removed. The subjective test served to clarify what Conroy would have decided about her tube feeding if she were able to do so. The court listed acceptable expressions of intent that should be considered by surrogates or the court—spoken expressions, living wills, durable power of attorney, oral directives, prior behavior, and religious beliefs.

If the court determines that patients in Conroy's circumstance have not explicitly expressed their wishes, two other "best interests" tests may be used: the limited-objective and the pure-objective tests. The limited-objective test permits discontinuing life-sustaining treatment if medical evidence shows that the patient would reject treatment that would only prolong suffering and that medication would not alleviate pain. Under this test, the court requires the additional evidence from the subjective test.

The pure-objective test applies when there is no trustworthy evidence, or any evidence at all, to help guide a decision. The burden imposed on the patient's life by the treatment should outweigh whatever benefit would result from the treatment. "Further, the recurring, unavoidable and severe pain of the patient's life with the treatment should be such that the effect of administering life-sustaining treatment would be inhumane."

Conroy, the court concluded in January 1985, failed the tests. Her intentions, while perhaps clear enough to help support a limited-objective test (she had shown some evidence of a desire to reject treatment) were not strong enough for the subjective test (clear expressions of her intent). In addition, the information on her possible pain versus benefits of remaining alive was not sufficient for either the limited-objective test (her pain might outweigh her pleasure in life) or the pure-objective test (her pain would be so great it would be inhumane to continue treatment). Had Conroy survived the appellate court's decision, the court would have required her guardian to investigate these matters further before reaching a decision.

Judge Handler, dissenting in part, disagreed with the majority's decision to measure Conroy's "best interests" in terms of the possible pain she could have been experiencing. First, in many cases pain can be controlled through medication. Second, pain levels cannot always be determined, as was shown in Conroy's case. Finally, not all patients make a decision based on pain. Some fear being dependent on others, especially when their bodily functions deteriorate; others value personal privacy and dignity. Bodily integrity may be more important than simply prolonging life. Judge Handler supported reliance on knowledgeable, responsible surrogates as opposed to standards set in a series of tests.

CAN DOCTORS BE HELD LIABLE?

Barber v. Superior Court of the State of California

Historically, physicians have been free from prosecution for terminating life support. A precedent was set in 1983, however, when two doctors were charged with murder and conspiracy to commit murder after agreeing to requests from a patient's family to discontinue life support (*Barber v. Superior Court of the State of California*, 195 Cal.Rptr. 484 [Cal.App. 2 Dist. 1983]). The two physicians were Drs. Neil Barber and Robert Nejdl.

Clarence Herbert suffered cardio-respiratory arrest following surgery. He was revived and placed on a respirator. Three days later his doctors diagnosed him as deeply comatose. The prognosis was that he would likely never recover. The family requested in writing that Herbert's respirator and other life-sustaining equipment be removed. The doctors complied, but Herbert continued to breathe on his own. After two days the family asked the doctors to remove the intravenous tubes that provided nutrition and hydration. The request was honored. From that point until his death, Mr. Herbert received care that provided a clean and hygienic environment and allowed for preservation of his dignity.

A superior court judge ruled that because the doctors' behavior intentionally shortened the patient's life, they had committed murder. The Court of Appeals, however, found that a patient's right to refuse treatment, and a surrogate's right to refuse treatment for an incompetent, superseded any liability that could be attributed to the physicians.

In ruling that the physicians' compliance with the request of Herbert's family did not constitute murder, the Court of Appeals stated that "cessation of 'heroic' life support measures is not an affirmative act but rather a withdrawal or omission of further treatment." In addition, artificial nutrition and hydration also constituted a medical treatment.

WHAT ARE THE HOSPITAL'S RIGHTS?

Patricia E. Brophy v. New England Sinai Hospital, Inc.

In 1983 Paul E. Brophy, Sr., suffered an aneurysm (a blood-filled sac formed by dilation of a blood vessel with a weak wall, which makes the vessel more prone to burst) that left him in a PVS. He was not brain dead, nor was he terminal. He had been a fireman and emergency medical technician and often expressed the opinion that he never wanted to be kept alive artificially.

Patricia Brophy brought suit when physicians refused to remove or clamp a gastrostomy tube (g-tube) that supplied nutrition and hydration to her husband. The Massachusetts Appeals Court ruled against Mrs. Brophy, but the Massachusetts Supreme Court allowed substituted judgment for a comatose patient who had previously made his intentions clear.

The Massachusetts Supreme Court, however, did agree with the Massachusetts Appeals Court ruling that the hospital could not be forced to withhold food and water, which went against the hospital's ethical beliefs. Consequently, the Massachusetts Supreme Court ordered New England Sinai Hospital to facilitate Brophy's transfer to another facility or to his home where his wife could carry out his wishes (*Patricia E. Brophy v. New England Sinai Hospital, Inc.*, 497 N.E.2d 626, [Mass. 1986]).

VITALIST DISSENSIONS. Justices Nolan and Lynch of the Massachusetts Supreme Court strongly disagreed with the majority opinion to allow removal of the gastrostomy tube. Justice Nolan argued that food and water were not medical treatments that could be refused. In his view food and water are basic human needs, and by permitting removal of the g-tube, the court gave its stamp of approval to euthanasia and suicide.

Justice Lynch believed the Massachusetts Supreme Court majority had ignored what he considered valid findings by the Massachusetts Appeals Court which found that Brophy's wishes, as expressed in his wife's substituted-judgment decision of withholding food and water, did not concern intrusive medical treatment. Rather, Brophy's decision, if he were competent to make it, was to knowingly terminate his life by declining food and water. This was suicide and the state was, therefore, condoning suicide. Justice Lynch concluded:

> This case raises for the first time in this Commonwealth the question whether an individual has a legal right to choose to die, and to enlist the assistance of others to effectuate that choice on the ground that, irrespective of the nature of available life-prolonging treatment, life in any event is not worth living and its continuation is intolerable.

In the Matter of Beverly Requena

Beverly Requena was a competent fifty-five-year-old woman with ALS (Lou Gehrig's disease). She informed St. Clare's/Riverside Medical Center—a Roman Catholic hospital—that when she lost the ability to swallow, she would refuse artificial feeding. The hospital filed a suit to force Requena to leave the hospital, citing its policy against withholding food or fluids from a patient.

Time was running out for Requena. She was paralyzed from the neck down, and unable to make sounds, although she could form words with her lips. At the time of the hearing, she could not eat but could suck some nutrient liquids through a straw. Soon she would not even be able to do that. Judge Stanton described the patient:

> Requena seems to have significant pain.... Her body is now almost totally useless. She is trapped within it. Most understandably, she feels enormous frustration and experiences a pervasive sense of helplessness and hopelessness. Her situation is desperately sad.

The court did not question Requena's right to refuse nutrition, nor did the hospital question that right. That was a right that had been upheld in many prior cases. But reasserting its policy of refusing to participate in the withholding or withdrawal of artificial nutrition and hydration, the hospital offered to help transfer Requena to another facility that was willing to fulfill her wishes.

Requena did not want to transfer to another hospital. In the last seventeen months, she had formed a relationship of trust in, and affection for, the staff. She also liked the familiar surroundings. The court found that being forced to leave would upset her emotionally and psychologically. The hospital staff was feeling stress as well. They were fond of Requena and did not want to see her die a presumably painful death from dehydration.

Judge Stanton ruled that Requena could not be removed from the hospital without her consent, and that the hospital would have to accede to her wishes (*In the Matter of Beverly Requena*, 517 A.2d 869 [N.J.Super.A.D. 1986]). He stressed the importance of preserving the personal worth, dignity, and integrity of the patient. The hospital may provide her information about her prognosis and treatment options, but Requena alone had the right to decide what was best for her.

WHAT ARE THE NURSING HOME'S RIGHTS?

In the Matter of Nancy Ellen Jobes

In 1980 twenty-four-year-old Nancy Ellen Jobes was in a car accident. At the time, she was four-and-a-half months pregnant. Doctors who treated her determined that her fetus was dead. During the surgery to remove the fetus, Jobes suffered loss of oxygen and blood flow to the brain. Never regaining consciousness, she was moved to the Lincoln Park Nursing Home several months later.

The nursing home provided nourishment to Jobes through a jejunostomy tube (j-tube) inserted into the jejunum of her small intestine. Five years later, Jobes's husband, John H. Jobes, asked the nursing home to stop his wife's artificial feeding. The nursing home refused, citing moral considerations.

The trial court appointed a guardian *ad litem*, who, after reviewing the case, filed in favor of Mr. Jobes. The nursing home moved to appoint a "life advocate" (a person who would support retaining the feeding tube), which was turned down by the trial court. The Supreme Court of New Jersey heard the case (*In the Matter of Nancy Ellen Jobes*, 529 A.2d 434 [N.J. 1987]).

DIFFERING INTERPRETATIONS OF PERSISTENT VEGETATIVE STATE. Whether Jobes was in a PVS was hotly debated, revealing how different medical interpretations of the same patient's condition can produce different conclusions. After Mr. Jobes initiated the suit, his wife was transferred to Cornell Medical Center for four days of observation and testing. Dr. Fred Plum, a world-renowned neurologist who had coined the term "persistent vegetative state," and his associate Dr. David Levy concluded, after extensive examination and testing, that Jobes was indeed in a PVS and would never recover.

On the other hand, Drs. Maurice Victor and Allan Ropper testified for the nursing home. Having examined Jobes for about one-and-a-half hours, Dr. Victor reported that, although the patient was severely brain-damaged, he did not believe she was in a PVS. She had responded to his commands, such as to pick up her head or to stick out her tongue. However, he could not back up his testimony with any written record of his examination.

Dr. Ropper had also examined Jobes for about an hour and a half. He testified that some of the patient's motions, such as lifting an arm off the bed, excluded her from his definition of PVS. (His definition of PVS differed from Dr. Plum's in that it excluded patients who made reflexive responses to outside stimuli—a definition that would have also excluded Karen Quinlan.) Testimony from the nurses who had cared for Jobes over the past years was also contradictory, with some asserting she smiled or responded to their care and others saying they saw no cognitive responses.

The New Jersey Supreme Court concluded that the neurological experts, especially Drs. Plum and Levy, "offered sufficiently clear and convincing evidence to support the trial court's finding that Jobes is in an irreversibly vegetative state." However, the court could find no "clear and convincing" evidence that Jobes, if she were competent, would want the j-tube removed. Jobes's family and friends, including her minister, had testified that in general conversation she had mentioned that she would not want to be kept alive with artificial life supports. The court did not accept these past remarks as clear evidence of the patient's intent.

With no clear and convincing evidence of Jobes's beliefs about artificial feeding, the New Jersey Supreme Court turned to *In re Quinlan* for guidance. The court stated:

Our review of these cases and medical authorities confirms our conclusion that we should continue to defer, as we did in *Quinlan*, to family members' substituted judgments about medical treatment for irreversibly vegetative patients who did not clearly express their medical preferences while they were competent. Those decisions are best made because the family is best able to decide what the patient would want.

THE NURSING HOME'S RESPONSIBILITY. The New Jersey Supreme Court reversed the trial court decision that had allowed the nursing home to refuse to participate in the withdrawal of the feeding tube. The court noted, "Mrs. Jobes's family had no reason to believe that they were surrendering the right to choose among medical alternatives when they placed her in the nursing home." The court pointed out that it was not until 1985, five years after Jobes's admission to the Lincoln Park Nursing Home, and only after her family requested the removal of her feeding tube, that her family learned of the policy. The court ordered the nursing home to comply with the family's request.

Justice O'Hern dissented on both issues. He claimed that not all families may be as loving as Jobes's. He was concerned for other individuals whose family might not be so caring, but who would still have the authority to order the withdrawal of life-sustaining treatments. He also disagreed with the order given the nursing home to comply with the family's request to discontinue Jobes's feeding. "I believe a proper balance could be obtained by adhering to the procedure adopted [in] *In re Quinlan*, that would have allowed the nonconsenting physician not to participate in the life-terminating process."

CLEAR AND CONVINCING EVIDENCE

Throughout the history of right-to-die cases, there has been considerable debate about how to determine a patient's wishes. How clearly must a patient have expressed his or her wishes before becoming incompetent? Does a parent or other family member best represent the patient? Are casual conversations sufficient to reveal intentions, or must there be written instructions?

In the Matter of Philip K. Eichner, on Behalf of Joseph C. Fox

Eighty-three-year-old Joseph Fox went into a PVS after a hernia operation. He was a member of a Roman Catholic religious order, the Society of Mary. The local director of the society, Philip Eichner, filed suit, asking for permission to have Fox's respirator removed.

The court reasoned that "the highest burden of proof beyond a reasonable doubt should be required when granting the relief that may result in the patient's death." The need for high standards "forbids relief whenever the evidence is loose, equivocal, or contradictory." Fox, however, had discussed his feelings in the context of formal religious discussions. Only two months before his final hospitalization, he had stated he would not want his life prolonged if his condition were hopeless. The court argued, "These were obviously solemn pronouncements and not casual remarks made at some social gathering, nor can it be said that he was too young to realize or feel the consequences of his statements" (*In the Matter of Philip K. Eichner, on Behalf of Joseph C. Fox v. Denis Dillon, as District Attorney of Nassau County*, N.Y., 420 N.E.2d 64, 1981).

The case of Joseph Fox was the first where the reported attitudes of an incompetent patient were accepted as "clear and convincing."

In the Matter of Westchester County Medical Center, on Behalf of Mary O'Connor

Not all patients express their attitudes about the use of life-sustaining treatments in serious religious discussions as did Joseph Fox. Nonetheless, courts have accepted evidence of "best interests" or "substituted judgments" in allowing the termination of life-sustaining treatments.

In 1985 Mary O'Connor had a stroke that rendered her mentally and physically incompetent. More than two years later she suffered a second major stroke, after which she had additional disabilities and difficulty swallowing. O'Connor's two daughters moved her to a long-term geriatric facility associated with the Westchester County Medical Center. During her hospital admission, her daughters submitted a signed statement to be added to their mother's medical records. The document stated that O'Connor had indicated in many conversations that "no artificial life support be started or maintained in order to continue to sustain her life."

In June 1988, when Mary O'Connor's condition deteriorated, she was admitted to Westchester County Medical Center. Because she was unable to swallow, her physician prescribed a nasogastric tube. The daughters objected to the procedure, citing their mother's expressed wish. The hospital petitioned the court for permission to provide artificial feeding, without which O'Connor would starve to death within seven to ten days. The lower court found in favor of O'Connor's daughters. The hospital subsequently brought the case of the seventy-seven-year-old woman before the Court of Appeals of New York (*In the Matter of Westchester County Medical Center, on Behalf of Mary O'Connor*, 531 N.E.2d 607 [N.Y. 1988]).

O'Connor's physician testified that she was not in a coma. While he anticipated that O'Connor's awareness might improve in the future, he believed she would never regain the mental ability to understand complex matters. This included the issue of her medical condition and treatment. The physician further indicated that, if his patient were allowed to starve to death, she would experience pain and "extreme, intense discomfort."

A neurologist testifying for the daughters reported that O'Connor's brain damage would keep her from experiencing pain. If she did have pain in the process of starving to death, she could be given medication. However, the doctor admitted he could not be "medically certain" because he had never had a patient die under the same circumstances.

The New York Court of Appeals majority concluded that, although family and friends testified that Mary O'Connor "felt that nature should take its course and not use artificial means" and that it is "monstrous" to keep someone alive by "machinery," these expressions did not constitute clear and convincing evidence of her present desire to die. Also, she had never specifically discussed the issue of artificial nutrition and hydration. Nor had she ever expressed her wish to refuse artificial medical treatment should such refusal result in a painful death.

The court further noted that O'Connor's statements about refusing artificial treatments had generally been made in situations involving terminal illness, specifically cancer—her husband had died of cancer and so did two of her brothers, her stepmother, and a close friend. Judge Wachtler, speaking for the Court of Appeals majority, stressed that O'Connor was not terminally ill, was conscious, and could interact with others, albeit minimally. Her main problem was that she could not eat on her own, and her physician could help her with that. Writing for the majority, Judge Wachtler stated:

> Every person has a right to life, and no one should be denied essential medical care unless the evidence clearly and convincingly shows that the patient intended to decline the treatment under some particular circumstances.... This is a demanding standard, the most rigorous burden of proof in civil cases. It is appropriate here because if an error occurs it should be made on the side of life.

THIS IS TOO RESTRICTIVE. New York Court of Appeals' Judge Simons differed from the majority in his opinion of O'Connor's condition. O'Connor's "conversations" were actually limited to saying her name and the words okay, all right, and yes. Neither the hospital doctor nor the neurologist who testified for her daughters could say for sure that she understood their questions. The court majority mentioned the patient's squeezing her doctor's hand in response to some questions, but failed to add that she did not respond to most questions.

While it was true the patient was not terminally ill, her severe mental and physical injuries—should nature take its course—would result in her death. Judge Simons believed the artificial feeding would not cure or improve her deteriorating condition.

The Court of Appeals' Judge Wachtler had noted that O'Connor talked about refusing artificial treatment in the aftermath of the deaths of loved ones from cancer. He claimed this had no bearing on her present condition, which was not terminal. Judge Simons pointed out that O'Connor had worked for twenty years in a hospital emergency room and pathology laboratory. She was no casual observer of death, and her "remarks" about not wanting artificial treatment for herself carried a lot of weight. Her expressed wishes to her daughters, who were nurses and coworkers in the same hospital, could not be considered "casual," as the majority observed. Judge Simons stated:

> Until today, under New York law, decisions concerning medical treatment remained the right of the patient. Today's opinion narrowly circumscribes our rule to a degree that makes it all but useless. Few, if any, patients can meet the demanding standard the majority has adopted....
>
> The majority, disguising its action as an application of the rule on self-determination, has made its own substituted judgment by improperly finding facts and drawing inferences contrary to the facts found by the courts below. Judges, the persons least qualified by training, experience, or affinity to reject the patient's instructions, have overridden Mrs. O'Connor's wishes, negated her long-held values on life and death, and imposed on her and her family their ideas of what her best interests require.

THE CASE OF NANCY CRUZAN

While *O'Connor* set a rigorous standard of proof for the state of New York, *Cruzan* was the first right-to-die case heard by the U.S. Supreme Court. It confirmed the legality of such strict standards for the entire country.

Cruzan, by Cruzan v. Harmon

In January 1983 twenty-five-year-old Nancy Beth Cruzan lost control of her car. A state trooper found her lying face-down in a ditch. She was in cardiac and respiratory arrest. Paramedics were able to revive her, but a neurosurgeon diagnosed "a probable cerebral contusion compounded by significant anoxia." The final diagnosis estimated she suffered anoxia (deprivation of oxygen) for twelve to fourteen minutes. At the trial the judge stated that after six minutes of oxygen deprivation, the brain generally suffers permanent damage.

At the time of the U.S. Supreme Court hearing in 1990, Cruzan was able to breathe on her own but was being nourished with a gastrostomy feeding tube. Doctors had surgically implanted the feeding tube about a month after the accident, following the consent of her then-husband. Medical experts diagnosed the thirty-three-year-old patient to be in a PVS, capable of living

another thirty years. Cruzan had been a ward of the state of Missouri since January 1986.

Cruzan's case was first heard by a Missouri trial court, which gave her parents, Joyce and Lester Cruzan, Jr., the right to terminate artificial nutrition and hydration. The state and the court-appointed guardian *ad litem* appealed to the Missouri Supreme Court (*Nancy Beth Cruzan, By Co-guardians, Lester L. Cruzan, Jr., and Joyce Cruzan v. Robert Harmon*, 760 S.W.2d 408 [Mo.banc 1988]). The guardian *ad litem* believed it was in Cruzan's best interests to have the artificial feeding tube removed. However, he felt it was his duty as her attorney to take the case to the state supreme court because "this is a case of first impression in the state of Missouri." (A case of first impression is one without a precedent.)

THE RIGHT TO PRIVACY. The Missouri Supreme Court stressed that the state Constitution did not expressly provide for the right of privacy, which would support an individual's right to refuse medical treatment. While the U.S. Supreme Court had recognized the right of privacy in such cases as *Roe v. Wade* and *Griswold v. Connecticut*, this right did not extend to the withdrawal of food and water. In fact, the U.S. Supreme Court, in *Roe v. Wade*, stressed that it "has refused to recognize an unlimited right of this kind in the past."

THE STATE'S INTEREST IN LIFE. In Cruzan's case the Missouri Supreme Court majority confirmed that the state's interest in life encompassed the sanctity of life and the prolongation of life. The state's interest in the prolongation of life was especially valid in Cruzan's case. She was not terminally ill and, based on medical evidence, would "continue a life of relatively normal duration if allowed basic sustenance." Furthermore, the state was not interested in the quality of life. The court was mindful that its decision would apply not only to Cruzan and feared treading a slippery slope. "Were the quality of life at issue, persons with all manner of handicaps might find the state seeking to terminate their lives. Instead, the state's interest is in life; that interest is unqualified."

THE GUARDIANS' RIGHTS. The Missouri Supreme Court ruled that Cruzan had no constitutional right to die and that there was no clear and convincing evidence that she would not wish to continue her vegetative existence. The majority further found that her parents, or guardians, had no right to exercise substituted judgment on their daughter's behalf. The court concluded:

> We find no principled legal basis which permits the co-guardians in this case to choose the death of their ward. In the absence of such a legal basis for that decision and in the face of this State's strongly stated policy in favor of life, we choose to err on the side of life, respecting the rights of incompetent persons who may wish to live despite a severely diminished quality of life.

The Missouri Supreme Court, therefore, reversed the judgment of the Missouri trial court that had allowed discontinuance of Cruzan's artificial feeding.

THE STATE DOES NOT HAVE AN OVERRIDING INTEREST. In his dissent Missouri Supreme Court Judge Blackmar indicated that the state should not be involved in cases such as Cruzan's. He was not convinced that the state had spoken better for Cruzan's interests than did her parents. The judge also questioned the state's interest in life in the context of espousing capital punishment, which clearly establishes "the proposition that some lives are not worth preserving."

Judge Blackmar did not share the majority's opinion that acceding to the guardians' request would lead to the mass euthanasia of handicapped people whose conditions did not come close to Cruzan's. He stressed that a court ruling is precedent only for the facts of that specific case. Besides, one of the very purposes of courts is to protect incompetent people against abuse. He claimed:

> The principal opinion attempts to establish absolutes, but does so at the expense of human factors. In so doing, it unnecessarily subjects Nancy and those close to her to continuous torture, which no family should be forced to endure.

"ERRONEOUS DECLARATION OF LAW." Missouri Supreme Court's Judge Higgins, also dissenting, mainly disagreed with the majority's basic premise that the more than fifty precedent-setting cases from sixteen other states were based on an "erroneous declaration of law." And yet, Judge Higgins noted, all cases cited by the majority upheld an individual's right to refuse life-sustaining treatment, either personally or through the substituted judgment of a guardian. The judge could not understand the majority's contradiction of its own argument.

Cruzan v. Director, Missouri Department of Health

Cruzan's father appealed the Missouri Supreme Court's decision and, in December 1989, the U.S. Supreme Court heard arguments in the case (*Nancy Beth Cruzan, by her Parents and Co-Guardians, Lester L. Cruzan et ux v. Director, Missouri Department of Health et al*, 497 US 261, 1990). This was the first time the right-to-die issue had been brought before the U.S. Supreme Court, which chose not to rule on whether Cruzan's parents could have her feeding tube removed. Instead, it considered whether the U.S. Constitution prohibited the state of Missouri from requiring clear and convincing evidence that an incompetent person desires withdrawal of life-sustaining treatment. In a five-to-four decision the Supreme Court held that the U.S. Constitution did not prohibit the state of Missouri from requiring convincing evidence that an incompetent person wants life-sustaining treatment withdrawn.

Chief Justice William Rehnquist wrote the opinion, with Justices White, O'Connor, Scalia, and Kennedy joining. (Justices Brennan, Marshall, Blackmun, and Stevens dissented.) The court majority believed that its rigorous requirement of clear and convincing evidence that Cruzan had refused termination of life-sustaining treatment was justified. An erroneous decision not to withdraw the patient's feeding tube meant that the patient would continue to be sustained artificially. Possible medical advances or new evidence of the patient's intent could correct the error. An erroneous decision to terminate the artificial feeding could not be corrected, because the result of that decision—death—is irrevocable. The chief justice concluded:

> No doubt is engendered by anything in this record but that Nancy Cruzan's mother and father are loving and caring parents. If the State were required by the United States Constitution to repose a right of "substituted judgment" with anyone, the Cruzans would surely qualify. But we do not think the Due Process Clause requires the State to repose judgment on these matters with anyone but the patient herself. [The Due Process clause of the Fourteenth Amendment provides that no state shall "deprive any person of life, liberty, or property, without due process of law."]

STATE INTEREST SHOULD NOT OUTWEIGH THE FREEDOM OF CHOICE. Justice Brennan, dissenting, pointed out that the state of Missouri's general interest in the preservation of Cruzan's life in no way outweighed her freedom of choice—in this case the choice to refuse medical treatment. "The regulation of constitutionally protected decisions...must be predicated on legitimate state concerns other than disagreement with the choice the individual has made....Otherwise, the interest in liberty protected by the Due Process Clause would be a nullity."

Justice Brennan believed the state of Missouri had imposed an uneven burden of proof. The state would only accept clear and convincing evidence that the patient had made explicit statements refusing artificial nutrition and hydration. However, it did not require any proof that she had made specific statements desiring continuance of such treatment. Hence, it could not be said that the state had accurately determined Cruzan's wishes.

Justice Brennan disagreed that it is better to err on the side of life than death. He argued that, to the patient, erring from either side is "irrevocable." He explained:

> An erroneous decision to terminate artificial nutrition and hydration, to be sure, will lead to failure of that last remnant of physiological life, the brain stem, and result in complete brain death. An erroneous decision not to terminate life support, however, robs a patient of the very qualities protected by the right to avoid unwanted medical treatment. His own degraded existence is

perpetuated; his family's suffering is protracted; the memory he leaves behind becomes more and more distorted.

STATE USES NANCY CRUZAN FOR "SYMBOLIC EFFECT." Justice Stevens, in a separate dissenting opinion, believed the state of Missouri was using Cruzan for the "symbolic effect" of defining life. The state sought to equate Nancy's physical existence with life. But Justice Stevens pointed out that life is more than physiological functions. In fact, life connotes a person's experiences that make up his or her whole history, as well as "the practical manifestation of the human spirit."

Justice Stevens viewed the state's refusal to let Cruzan's guardians terminate her artificial feeding as ignoring their daughter's interests, and therefore, "unconscionable":

> Insofar as Nancy Cruzan has an interest in being remembered for how she lived rather than how she died, the damage done to those memories by the prolongation of her death is irreversible. Insofar as Nancy Cruzan has an interest in the cessation of any pain, the continuation of her pain is irreversible. Insofar as Nancy Cruzan has an interest in a closure to her life consistent with her own beliefs rather than those of the Missouri legislature, the State's imposition of its contrary view is irreversible. To deny the importance of these consequences is in effect to deny that Nancy Cruzan has interests at all, and thereby to deny her personhood in the name of preserving the sanctity of her life.

CRUZAN CASE FINALLY RESOLVED. On December 14, 1990, nearly eight years after Cruzan's car accident, a Missouri circuit court ruled that new evidence presented by three more friends constituted "clear and convincing" evidence that she would not want to continue existing in a persistent vegetative state. The court allowed the removal of her artificial feeding. Within two hours of the ruling, Cruzan's doctor removed the tube. Cruzan's family kept a twenty-four-hour vigil with her, until she died on December 26, 1990. Cruzan's family, however, believed she had left them many years earlier.

THE TERRI SCHIAVO CASE

Like Cruzan, the case of Terri Schiavo involved a young woman in a persistent vegetative state and the question of whether her nutrition and hydration could be discontinued.

In 1990 Schiavo suffered a loss of potassium in her body due to an eating disorder. This physiological imbalance caused her heart to stop beating, which deprived her brain of oxygen and resulted in a coma. She underwent surgery to implant a stimulator in her brain, an experimental treatment. The brain stimulator implant appeared to be a success, and the young woman appeared to be slowly emerging from her coma.

Years later, even though Schiavo was continually provided with appropriate stimulation to recover, she remained in a persistent vegetative state. Her husband, Michael Schiavo, believing that she would never recover and saying that his wife did not want to be kept alive by artificial means, petitioned a Florida court to remove her feeding tube. Her parents, however, believed that she could feel, understand, and respond. They opposed the idea of removing the feeding tube.

In 2000 a Florida trial court determined that Schiavo did not wish to be kept alive by artificial means based on her clear and direct statement to that effect to her husband. However, Schiavo's parents appealed the ruling, based on their belief that their daughter responded to their voices and could improve with therapy. They also contested the assertion that their daughter did not want to be kept alive by artificial means. Schiavo had left no living will to clarify her position, but under Florida's Health Care Advance Directives Law, a patient's spouse is second in line to make a decision about whether life support should be suspended (after a court-appointed guardian), adult children are third, and parents are fourth.

Constitutional Breach?

By October 2003 Schiavo's parents had exhausted their appeals; the Florida appellate courts upheld the ruling of the trial court. At that time, a Florida judge ruled that removal of the tube take place. However, Schiavo's parents requested that Florida Governor Jeb Bush intervene. In response, the Florida legislature developed House Bill 35–E ("Terri's Law") and passed this bill on October 21, 2003. The law gave Governor Bush the authority to order Schiavo's feeding tube reinserted, and he did that by issuing Executive Order No. 03–201 that same day, six days after the feeding tube had been removed.

Legal experts noted that the Florida legislature, in passing Terri's Law, appeared to have taken judicial powers away from the judicial branch of the Florida government and had given them to the executive branch. If this were the case, then the law was unconstitutional under Article 2, Section III, of the Florida constitution, which states: "No person belonging to one branch shall exercise any powers appertaining to either of the other branches unless expressly provided herein." Thus, Michael Schiavo challenged the law's constitutionality in Pinellas County Circuit Court. Governor Bush requested that the Pinellas County Circuit Court Judge dismiss Michael Schiavo's lawsuit arguing against Terri's Law. On April 30, 2004, Judge Charles A. Davis rejected the Governor's technical challenges, denying the Governor's motion to dismiss. In May 2004 the law that allowed Governor Bush to intervene in the case was ruled unconstitutional by a Florida appeals court.

Continued Appeals

Schiavo's parents then appealed the case to the Florida Supreme Court, which heard the case in September 2004. The High Court upheld the ruling of the lower court, with the seven justices ruling unanimously and writing that Terri's Law was "an unconstitutional encroachment on the power that has been reserved for the independent judiciary." Nonetheless, Schiavo's parents continued their legal fight to keep her alive, and a stay on the tube's removal was put in place while their appeals were pending. Shortly thereafter, in October 2004, Governor Bush asked the Florida Supreme Court to reconsider its decision. The court refused the request.

Attorneys for the Florida governor then asked the U.S. Supreme Court to hear the Schiavo case. The Supreme Court rejected the request, which essentially affirmed lower court rulings that the governor had no legal right to intervene in the matter. In February 2005 a Florida judge ruled that Michael Schiavo could remove his wife's feeding tube in March of that year. On March 18, 2005, the tube was removed. Days later, in an unprecedented action, the United States House and Senate approved legislation, which was quickly signed by President George W. Bush, granting Terri Schiavo's parents the right to sue in federal court. In effect, this legislation allowed the court to intervene in the case and restore Terri's feeding tube. When Schiavo's parents appealed to the court, however, a federal judge refused to order the feeding tube reinserted. They then filed an appeal with the U.S. Supreme Court. Once again the High Court refused to hear the case.

The Effect of the Schiavo Situation on End-of-Life Decision Making

Terri Schiavo died on April 1, 2005. Her death and the events leading up to her death resulted in an intense debate among Americans over end-of-life decisions and brought new attention to the question of who should make the decision to stop life support. By the time of Terri Schiavo's death, new end-of-life legislation has been introduced in about ten states. Nonetheless, it was unclear how many of these proposals were likely to become law.

The medical examiners who conducted Terri Schiavo's autopsy found her brain "profoundly atrophied," only half the normal size, and noted that "no amount of therapy or treatment would have regenerated the massive loss of neurons." An autopsy cannot definitively establish a persistent vegetative state, but the Schiavo findings were seen as "very consistent" with a PVS.

THE CONSTITUTIONALITY OF ASSISTED SUICIDE

Washington v. Glucksberg

FOURTH AMENDMENT PROTECTION. In January 1994 four Washington State doctors, three terminally ill patients, and the organization Compassion in Dying filed a suit in the U.S. District Court. The plaintiffs sought to have the Washington Revised Code 9A.36.060(1) (1994) declared unconstitutional. This Washington law states: "A person is guilty of promoting a suicide attempt when he knowingly causes or aids another person to attempt suicide."

According to the plaintiffs, mentally competent terminally ill adults have the right, under the Equal Protection Clause of the Fourteenth Amendment, to a physician's assistance in determining the time and manner of their death. In *Compassion in Dying v. Washington* (850 F. Supp. 1454, 1459, [WD Wash. 1994]), the U.S. District Court agreed, stating that the Washington Revised Code violated the Equal Protection Clause's provision that "all persons similarly situated . . . be treated alike."

In its decision the District Court relied on *Planned Parenthood of Southeastern Pennsylvania v. Casey* (a reaffirmation of *Roe v. Wade*'s holding of the right to abortion, 505 US 833, 1992) and *Cruzan v. Director, Missouri Department of Health* (the right to refuse unwanted life-sustaining treatment, 497 US 261, 1990). The court found Washington's statute against assisted suicide unconstitutional because the law "places an undue burden on the exercise of [that] constitutionally protected liberty interest."

In 1995 a panel (three or more judges but not the full court) of the Court of Appeals for the Ninth Circuit Court reversed the District Court's decision, stressing that in the 205 years of United States history, no court had ever recognized the right to assisted suicide (*Compassion in Dying v. Washington*, 49 F. 3d 586, 591, 1995). In 1996 the Ninth Circuit Court reheard the case en banc (by the full court), reversed the panel's decision, and affirmed the U.S. District Court's ruling (*Compassion in Dying v. Washington*, 79 F. 3d 790, 798, 1996).

The en banc Court of Appeals for the Ninth Circuit Court did not mention the Equal Protection Clause violation as indicated by the District Court; however, it referred to *Casey* and *Cruzan*, adding that the U.S. Constitution recognizes the right to die. Quoting from *Casey*, Judge Stephen Reinhardt wrote:

> Like the decision of whether or not to have an abortion, the decision how and when to die is one of "the most intimate and personal choices a person may make in a lifetime, . . . central to personal dignity and autonomy."

THE U.S. SUPREME COURT DECIDES. The state of Washington and its attorney general appealed to the U.S. Supreme Court (*Washington et al v. Harold Glucksberg et al*, 117 S.Ct 2258, 1997). U.S. Supreme Court Chief Justice William Rehnquist, instead of addressing the plaintiffs' initial question of whether mentally competent terminally ill adults have the right to physician-assisted suicide, reframed the issue, focusing on "whether Washington's prohibition against 'caus[ing]' or 'aid[ing]' a suicide offends the Fourteenth Amendment to the United States Constitution."

Chief Justice Rehnquist recalled the more than seven hundred years of Anglo-American common-law tradition disapproving of suicide and assisted suicide. He added that assisted suicide is considered a crime in almost every state, with no exceptions granted to mentally competent terminally ill adults.

PRIOR SUBSTANTIVE DUE-PROCESS CASES. The plaintiffs argued that in prior substantive due-process cases, such as *Cruzan*, the U.S. Supreme Court had acknowledged the principle of self-autonomy by ruling "that competent dying persons have the right to direct the removal of life-sustaining medical treatment and thus hasten death." Chief Justice Rehnquist claimed that, although committing suicide with another's help is just as personal as refusing life-sustaining treatment, it is not similar to refusing unwanted medical treatment. In fact, according to the chief justice, in *Cruzan*, the court specifically stressed that most states ban assisted suicide.

STATE'S INTEREST. The U.S. Supreme Court pointed out that Washington's interest in preserving human life includes the entire spectrum of that life, from birth to death, regardless of a person's physical or mental condition. The court agreed with the state that allowing assisted suicide might imperil the lives of vulnerable populations such as the poor, the elderly, and the disabled. The state included the terminally ill in this group.

The U.S. Supreme Court justices agreed with the state of Washington that legalizing physician-assisted suicide would eventually lead to voluntary and involuntary euthanasia. Because a health care proxy's decision is legally accepted as an incompetent patient's decision, what if the patient cannot self-administer the lethal medication? In such a case a physician or a family member would have to administer the drug, thus committing euthanasia.

The U.S. Supreme Court unanimously ruled that:

> [The Washington Revised] Code ... does not violate the Fourteenth Amendment, either on its face (in all or most cases in which it might be applied) or "as applied to competent terminally ill adults who wish to hasten their deaths by obtaining medication prescribed by their doctors." Our holding permits this debate to continue, as it should in a democratic society. The decision of the en banc Court of Appeals is reversed, and the case is remanded [sent back] for further proceedings consistent with this opinion.

PROVISION OF PALLIATIVE CARE. U.S. Supreme Court Justices Sandra Day O'Connor and Stephen Breyer, concurring, wrote that "terminally ill patients in

New York and Washington ... can obtain palliative care (care that relieves pain but does not cure the illness), even potentially lethal doses of drugs that are foreseen to result in death." Hence, the justices did not see the need to address a dying person's constitutional right to obtain relief from pain. Justice O'Connor believed the court was justified in banning assisted suicide for two reasons: "The difficulty of defining terminal illness and the risk that a dying patient's request for assistance in ending his or her life might not be truly voluntary."

Vacco v. Quill

REFUSING LIFE-SUSTAINING TREATMENT ESSENTIALLY THE SAME AS ASSISTED SUICIDE. In 1994 three New York physicians and three terminally ill patients sued the state attorney general. They claimed, before the U.S. District Court, that New York violated the Equal Protection Clause by prohibiting physician-assisted suicide. The state permits a competent patient to refuse life-sustaining treatment, but not to obtain physician-assisted suicide. These, claimed the plaintiffs, are "essentially the same thing" (*Quill v. Koppell*, 870 F. Supp. 78, 84–85 [SDNY 1994]). The court disagreed, stating that withdrawing life support to let nature run its course differs from intentionally using lethal drugs to cause death.

The plaintiffs brought their case to the Court of Appeals for the Second Circuit (appellate court), which reversed the District Court's ruling (*Quill v. Vacco*, 80 F. 3d 716, 1996). The appellate court found that the New York statute does not treat equally all competent terminally ill patients wishing to hasten their deaths. The court stated:

> The ending of life by [the withdrawal of life-support systems] is *nothing more or less* than assisted suicide. ... To the extent that [New York's statutes] prohibit a physician from prescribing medications to be self-administered by a mentally competent, terminally ill person in the final stages of his terminal illness, they are not rationally related to any legitimate state interest.

REFUSING LIFE-SUSTAINING TREATMENT DIFFERS FROM ASSISTED SUICIDE. New York's attorney general appealed the case to the U.S. Supreme Court (*Dennis C. Vacco, Attorney General of New York et al v. Timothy E. Quill et al*, 117 S.Ct 2293, 1997). The Supreme Court distinguished between withdrawing life-sustaining medical treatment and assisted suicide. The court contended that when a patient refuses life support, he or she dies because the disease has run its natural course. On the other hand, if a patient self-administers lethal drugs, death results from that medication.

The court also distinguished between the physician's role in both scenarios. A physician who complies with a patient's request to withdraw life support does so to honor a patient's wish because the treatment no longer benefits the patient. Likewise, when a physician prescribes pain-killing drugs, the needed drug dosage might hasten death, although the physician's only intent is to ease pain. However, when a physician assists in suicide, his or her prime intention is to hasten death. The U.S. Supreme Court, therefore, reversed the ruling made by the Court of Appeals for the Second Circuit.

STATE LEGISLATURES REJECT PHYSICIAN-ASSISTED SUICIDE

U.S. Supreme Court justices John Paul Stevens and David Souter issued opinions encouraging individual states to enact legislation to permit physician-assisted suicide in selected cases. At the state level, more than thirty bills to legalize physician-assisted suicide have been introduced. As of February 2006, Oregon remained the only state with a law that legalizes the practice. The Oregon legislation was approved in 1994 and reaffirmed by voters in 1997.

Many state ballot initiatives failed to garner enough votes to legalize physician-assisted suicide. Voters in California in 1988 and again in 1992 rejected the initiative. Assembly Bill 651, a measure that would permit doctors to prescribe lethal drugs to terminally ill patients, was to be discussed in the California legislature in March 2006. Washington State voters rejected a physician-assisted initiative in 1991, Michigan in 1998, Maine in 2000, and Wyoming in 2004. In addition, an assisted suicide proposal was shelved in the Hawaii legislature in 2004 and unsuccessful in another try in 2005, and it was being discussed in the Vermont and Arizona legislatures in 2006.

THE SUPREME COURT RULING ON PHYSICIAN-ASSISTED SUICIDE IN OREGON

In late 2001 Attorney General John Ashcroft reversed a decision made by his predecessor Janet Reno by asserting that the federal Controlled Substances Act could be used against Oregon physicians who helped patients commit suicide by prescribing lethal drugs. If that were the case, then the federal Drug Enforcement Administration (DEA) could disallow the prescription-writing privileges of any Oregon physician who prescribed drugs commonly used for assisted suicide. The possibility would also exist for those physicians to be criminally prosecuted as well. In response, the state of Oregon filed a lawsuit against Ashcroft's decision.

In May 2004 a federal appeals court upheld Oregon's Death with Dignity Act. The decision, by a divided three-judge panel of the United States Court of Appeals for the Ninth Circuit in San Francisco, said the Justice Department did not have the power to punish physicians for prescribing medication for the purpose of assisted suicide. The majority opinion stated that Ashcroft overstepped his authority in trying to block enforcement of Oregon's law.

In February 2005 the U.S. Supreme Court agreed to hear the Bush administration's challenge of Oregon's physician-assisted suicide law. On January 17, 2006, the Supreme Court let stand Oregon's physician-assisted suicide law. The High Court held that the Controlled Substances Act "does not allow the Attorney General to prohibit doctors from prescribing regulated drugs for use in physician-assisted suicide under state law permitting the procedure." Writing for the majority, Justice Anthony Kennedy stated that both Ashcroft and Attorney General Alberto Gonzales did not have the power to override the Oregon physician-assisted suicide law. Kennedy also added that it should not be the attorney general who determines what is a "legitimate medical purpose" for the administration of drugs, because the job description for the attorney general does not include making health and medical policy.

CHAPTER 9
THE COST OF HEALTH CARE

INCREASING COSTS

Americans want quality medical care despite its increasingly high cost. In 1960 the United States spent 5.2% of its gross domestic product (GDP—the total value of all the goods and services produced by the nation) on health care. In 1970 this percentage had risen 2% to 7.2%, and by 1980 it had risen to 9.1%—almost another 2%. But in the next thirteen years, health care expenditures rose 4.7%, to 13.8% ($916.5 billion) of the GDP. During the next few years that percentage dropped slightly (although actual dollars continued to rise), but it was back to 13.8% of the GDP by the year 2000. Then in 2001 through 2004 the cost of health care increased dramatically, to 14.6% of the GDP in 2001, 15.4% in 2002, 15.9% in 2003, and 16% in 2004. Table 9.1 compares the growth in national health care expenditures and in GDP, and presents the national health expenditures as a percentage of the GDP (1960–2004).

The Consumer Price Index (CPI) is a measure of the average change in prices paid by consumers. For many years the medical component of the CPI increased at a greater rate than any other component, even food and housing. Between 1960 and 2002 the average annual percent change from the previous year shown in the overall CPI ("All items" in the "average annual percent change from previous year shown" portion of Table 9.2) was well below the average annual percent change for medical care. From 2003 to 2004 the overall CPI increased by 2.7%, while medical care increased by 4.4%.

In 2004, fifty-five cents (55%) of every dollar spent for health care came from private funds, including private health insurance (thirty-five cents), out-of-pocket expenses (thirteen cents), and other private sources (seven cents). The remaining forty-six cents came from federal or state government sources. (The

numbers do not add to 100 because of rounding; see Figure 9.1.)

In 2004 hospital and physician costs, traditionally composing the greater part of health care expenses, were 30% and 21%, respectively, while prescription drug costs were 10% of all health care expenses. (See Figure 9.1.)

GOVERNMENT HEALTH CARE PROGRAMS

Unlike most developed countries, the United States does not have a universal health care program. Two government entitlement programs that provide health care coverage for older adults (age sixty-five and older), the poor, and the disabled are Medicare and Medicaid. Enacted in 1965 as amendments to the Social Security Act of 1935 (PL 89–97), these programs went into effect in 1966. In 1972 amendments to Medicare extended medical insurance coverage to those disabled long term and those with chronic kidney disease or end-stage renal disease. In 2004 nearly forty-two million older adults and people with disabilities were enrolled in Medicare, with total expenditures of nearly $309 billion. (See Table 9.3.)

The Original Medicare Plan

The Original Medicare Plan, enacted under Title XVIII ("Health Insurance for the Aged") of the Social Security Act, comprises two health-related insurance plans:

- Part A (hospital insurance) is funded by Social Security payroll taxes. It pays for inpatient hospital care, which includes physicians' fees, nursing services, meals, a semiprivate room, special care units, operating room costs, laboratory tests, and some drugs and supplies. It also pays for skilled nursing facility care after hospitalization, home health care visits by

TABLE 9.1

National health expenditures, selected calendar years 1960–2004

Item	1960	1970	1980	1990	1993	1997	1998	1999	2000	2001	2002	2003	2004
Amount in billions													
National health expenditures	$27.6	$75.1	$254.9	$717.3	$916.5	$1,129.7	$1,195.6	$1,270.3	$1,358.5	$1,474.2	$1,607.9	$1,740.6	$1,877.6
Private	20.7	46.8	147.6	427.3	514.2	614.1	662.3	710.2	756.3	807.2	881.4	957.2	1,030.3
Public	6.8	28.3	107.3	290.0	402.3	515.6	533.2	560.1	602.2	667.0	726.5	783.4	847.3
Federal	2.9	17.7	71.6	193.9	277.7	365.1	372.5	390.0	418.4	465.0	509.5	554.4	600.0
State and local	4.0	10.6	35.7	96.2	124.7	150.5	160.7	170.1	183.8	202.0	217.1	229.0	247.3
U.S. population*	186	210	230	254	265	278	281	284	287	290	293	296	299
Gross domestic product	$526	$1,039	$2,790	$5,803	$6,657	$8,304	$8,747	$9,268	$9,817	$10,128	$10,470	$10,971	$11,734
Per capita amount													
National health expenditures	$148	$357	$1,106	$2,821	$3,461	$4,070	$4,257	$4,471	$4,729	$5,079	$5,485	$5,879	$6,280
Private	111	222	640	1,680	1,942	2,212	2,358	2,500	2,633	2,781	3,007	3,233	3,446
Public	37	135	466	1,140	1,520	1,857	1,899	1,971	2,096	2,298	2,478	2,646	2,834
Federal	15	84	311	762	1,049	1,315	1,326	1,373	1,456	1,602	1,738	1,873	2,007
State and local	21	50	155	378	471	542	572	599	640	696	740	774	827
Percent distribution													
National health expenditures	100.0	100.0	100.0	100.0	100.0	100.0	100.0	100.0	100.0	100.0	100.0	100.0	100.0
Private	75.2	62.3	57.9	59.6	56.1	54.4	55.4	55.9	55.7	54.8	54.8	55.0	54.9
Public	24.8	37.7	42.1	40.4	43.9	45.6	44.6	44.1	44.3	45.2	45.2	45.0	45.1
Federal	10.4	23.6	28.1	27.0	30.3	32.3	31.2	30.7	30.8	31.5	31.7	31.9	32.0
State and local	14.4	14.1	14.0	13.4	13.6	13.3	13.4	13.4	13.5	13.7	13.5	13.2	13.2
Percent of gross domestic product													
National health expenditures	5.2	7.2	9.1	12.4	13.8	13.6	13.7	13.7	13.8	14.6	15.4	15.9	16.0
Average annual percent growth from previous year shown													
National health expenditures		10.5	13.0	10.9	8.5	5.4	5.8	6.3	6.9	8.5	9.1	8.2	7.9
Private		8.5	12.2	11.2	6.4	4.5	7.9	7.2	6.5	6.7	9.2	8.6	7.6
Public		15.3	14.2	10.5	11.5	6.4	3.4	5.0	7.5	10.8	8.9	7.8	8.2
Federal		20.0	15.0	10.5	12.7	7.1	2.0	4.7	7.3	11.1	9.6	8.8	8.2
State and local		10.3	12.9	10.4	9.0	4.8	6.8	5.8	8.1	9.9	7.4	5.5	8.0
U.S. population		1.2	0.9	1.0	1.4	1.2	1.2	1.1	1.0	1.0	1.0	1.0	1.0
Gross domestic product		7.0	10.4	7.6	4.7	5.7	5.3	6.0	5.9	3.2	3.4	4.8	7.0

*Census resident based population less armed forces overseas and less the population of outlying areas.
Note: Numbers and percents may not add to totals because of rounding. Dollar amounts shown are in current dollars.

SOURCE: "Table 1. National Health Expenditures Aggregate and Per Capita Amounts, Percent Distribution, and Average Annual Percent Growth, by Source of Funds: Selected Calendar Years 1960–2004," in *NHE Web Tables*, Centers for Medicare and Medicaid Services, Office of the Actuary, http://www.cms.hhs.gov/NationalHealthExpendData/downloads/tables.pdf (accessed February 28, 2006)

TABLE 9.2

Consumer price index and average annual percent change for general items and medical care components, selected years 1960–2004

[Data are based on reporting by samples of providers and other retail outlets]

Items and medical care components	1960	1970	1980	1990	1995	2000	2001	2002	2003	2004
					Consumer price index (CPI)					
All items	29.6	38.8	82.4	130.7	152.4	172.2	177.1	179.9	184.0	188.9
All items excluding medical care	30.2	39.2	82.8	128.8	148.6	167.3	171.9	174.3	178.1	182.7
All services	24.1	35.0	77.9	139.2	168.7	195.3	203.4	209.8	216.5	222.8
Food	30.0	39.2	86.8	132.4	148.4	167.8	173.1	176.2	180.0	186.2
Apparel	45.7	59.2	90.9	124.1	132.0	129.6	127.3	124.0	120.9	120.4
Housing	—	36.4	81.1	128.5	148.5	169.6	176.4	180.3	184.8	189.5
Energy	22.4	25.5	86.0	102.1	105.2	124.6	129.3	121.7	136.5	151.4
Medical care	22.3	34.0	74.9	162.8	220.5	260.8	272.8	285.6	297.1	310.1
Components of medical care										
Medical care services	19.5	32.3	74.8	162.7	224.2	266.0	278.8	292.9	306.0	321.3
Professional services	—	37.0	77.9	156.1	201.0	237.7	246.5	253.9	261.2	271.5
Physicians' services	21.9	34.5	76.5	160.8	208.8	244.7	253.6	260.6	267.7	278.3
Dental services	27.0	39.2	78.9	155.8	206.8	258.5	269.0	281.0	292.5	306.9
Eye glasses and eye care[a]	—	—	—	117.3	137.0	149.7	154.5	155.5	155.9	159.3
Services by other medical professionals[a]	—	—	—	120.2	143.9	161.9	167.3	171.8	177.1	181.9
Hospital and related services	—	—	69.2	178.0	257.8	317.3	338.3	367.8	394.8	417.9
Hospital services[b]	—	—	—	—	—	115.9	123.6	134.7	144.7	153.4
Inpatient hospital services[b, c]	—	—	—	—	—	113.8	121.0	131.2	140.1	148.1
Outpatient hospital services[a, c]	—	—	—	138.7	204.6	263.8	281.1	309.8	337.9	356.3
Hospital rooms	9.3	23.6	68.0	175.4	251.2	—	—	—	—	—
Other inpatient services[a]	—	—	—	142.7	206.8	—	—	—	—	—
Nursing homes and adult day care[b]	—	—	—	—	—	117.0	121.8	127.9	135.2	140.4
Medical care commodities	46.9	46.5	75.4	163.4	204.5	238.1	247.6	256.4	262.8	269.3
Prescription drugs and medical supplies	54.0	47.4	72.5	181.7	235.0	285.4	300.9	316.5	326.3	337.1
Nonprescription drugs and medical supplies[a]	—	—	—	120.6	140.5	149.5	150.6	150.4	152.0	152.3
Internal and respiratory over-the-counter drugs	—	42.3	74.9	145.9	167.0	176.9	178.9	178.8	181.2	180.9
Nonprescription medical equipment and supplies	—	—	79.2	138.0	166.3	178.1	178.2	177.5	178.1	179.7
					Average annual percent change from previous year shown					
All items	...	2.7	7.8	4.7	3.1	2.5	2.8	1.6	2.3	2.7
All items excluding medical care	...	2.6	7.8	4.5	2.9	2.4	2.7	1.4	2.2	2.6
All services	...	3.8	8.3	6.0	3.9	3.0	4.1	3.1	3.2	2.9
Food	...	2.7	8.3	4.3	2.3	2.5	3.2	1.8	2.2	3.4
Apparel	...	2.6	4.4	3.2	1.2	−0.4	−1.8	−2.6	−2.5	−0.4
Housing	...	—	8.3	4.7	2.9	2.7	4.0	2.2	2.5	2.5
Energy	...	1.3	12.9	1.7	0.6	3.4	3.8	−5.9	12.2	10.9
Medical care	...	4.3	8.2	8.1	6.3	3.4	4.6	4.7	4.0	4.4
Components of medical care										
Medical care services	...	5.2	8.8	8.1	6.6	3.5	4.8	5.1	4.5	5.0
Professional services	...	—	7.7	7.2	5.2	3.4	3.7	3.0	2.9	3.9
Physicians' services	...	4.6	8.3	7.7	5.4	3.2	3.6	2.8	2.7	4.0
Dental services	...	3.8	7.2	7.0	5.8	4.6	4.1	4.5	4.1	4.9
Eye glasses and eye care[a]	...	—	—	—	3.2	1.8	3.2	0.6	0.3	2.2
Services by other medical professionals[a]	...	—	—	—	3.7	2.4	3.3	2.7	3.1	2.7
Hospital and related services	...	—	—	9.9	7.7	4.2	6.6	8.7	7.3	5.9
Hospital services[b]	...	—	—	—	—	—	6.6	9.0	7.4	6.0
Inpatient hospital services[b, c]	...	—	—	—	—	—	6.3	8.4	6.8	5.7
Outpatient hospital services[a, c]	...	—	—	—	8.1	5.2	6.6	10.2	9.1	5.4
Hospital rooms	...	9.8	11.2	9.9	7.4	—	—	—	—	—
Other inpatient services[a]	...	—	—	—	7.7	—	—	—	—	—
Nursing homes and adult day care[b]	...	—	—	—	—	—	4.1	5.0	5.7	3.8

nurses or medical technicians, and hospice care for the terminally ill.

- Part B (medical insurance) is an elective medical insurance. Because Part A does not pay all health care costs and other expenses associated with hospitalization, many beneficiaries enroll in the Part B plan. Most people pay a monthly premium for this coverage. Those monthly premiums and general federal revenues finance Part B. Coverage includes physicians' and surgeons' services, diagnostic and laboratory tests, outpatient hospital services, outpatient physical therapy, speech pathology services, home health care services, and medical equipment and supplies.

The Original Medicare Plan coverage (Part A and Part B) has "gaps," which means that it does not cover all medical costs and services. Medigap insurance is supplemental Medicare insurance sold by private

TABLE 9.2

Consumer price index and average annual percent change for general items and medical care components, selected years 1960–2004 [CONTINUED]

[Data are based on reporting by samples of providers and other retail outlets]

Items and medical care components	1960	1970	1980	1990	1995	2000	2001	2002	2003	2004
Medical care commodities	...	−0.1	5.0	8.0	4.6	3.1	4.0	3.6	2.5	2.5
Prescription drugs and medical supplies	...	−1.3	4.3	9.6	5.3	4.0	5.4	5.2	3.1	3.3
Nonprescription drugs and medical supplies[a]	...	—	—	—	3.1	1.2	0.7	−0.1	1.1	0.2
Internal and respiratory over-the-counter drugs	...	—	5.9	6.9	2.7	1.2	1.1	−0.1	1.3	−0.2
Nonprescription medical equipment and supplies	...	—	—	5.7	3.8	1.4	0.1	−0.4	0.3	0.9

[a]December 1986=100.
[b]December 1996=100.
[c]Special index based on a substantially smaller sample.
Notes: "—"=Data not available. "..."=Category not applicable. Consumer price index for all urban consumers (CPI-U) U.S. city average, detailed expenditure categories. 1982–84=100, except where noted. Data are not seasonally adjusted.

SOURCE: "Table 120. Consumer Price Index and Average Annual Percent Change for All Items, Selected Items, and Medical Care Components: United States, Selected Years 1960–2004," in *Health, United States, 2005*, Centers for Disease Control and Prevention, National Center for Health Statistics, November 2005, http://www.cdc.gov/nchs/data/hus/hus05.pdf (accessed February 27, 2006)

insurance companies to pay these gaps in Original Medicare Plan coverage. Except in Massachusetts, Minnesota, and Wisconsin, there are ten standardized plans labeled Plan A through Plan J. Medigap policies only work with the Original Medicare Plan.

Medicare Advantage Plans

Medicare Advantage Plans are offered by private companies that have contracts with Medicare to provide Medicare services. Although there are generally lower copayments (the amounts patients pay for each medical service) and extra benefits with Medicare Advantage Plans versus the Original Medicare Plan, patients generally must see physicians that belong to the plan and go to certain hospitals to get services. Medicare Advantage Plans include Medicare Health Maintenance Organizations (HMOs), Medicare Preferred Provider Organizations (PPOs), Medicare Special Needs Plans (designed for specific groups of people), and Medicare Private Fee-for-Service Plans (PFFS).

Other Medicare Health Plans

Other types of Medicare Health Plans include Medicare Cost Plans, Demonstrations, and Programs of All-inclusive Care for the Elderly (PACE). Medicare Cost Plans are limited in number and combine features of both Medicare Advantage Plans and the Original Medicare Plan. Demonstrations are special projects that test possible future improvements in Medicare costs, coverage, and quality of care. PACE provides services for frail elderly Americans.

Medicare Prescription Drug Plans

On January 1, 2006, Medicare began to offer insurance coverage for prescription drugs to everyone with Medicare. Its Medicare Prescription Drug Plans typically pay half a person's prescription drug costs. Most people pay a monthly premium for this coverage. Medicare Prescription Drug Plans are available with the Original Medicare Plan, Medicare Advantage Plans, and the other Medicare health plans.

Medicaid

The Medicaid health insurance program, enacted under Title XIX ("Grants to States for Medical Assistance Programs") of the Social Security Act, provides medical assistance to low-income people, including those with disabilities and members of families with dependent children. Jointly financed by federal and state governments, Medicaid coverage includes hospitalization, physicians' services, laboratory fees, diagnostic screenings, and long-term nursing home care.

In 2001, while people age sixty-five and older made up only 8.3% of all Medicaid recipients, they received slightly more than one-fourth (25.9%) of all Medicaid benefits. The average payment was $12,725 per older adult, compared with $11.318 for the blind and disabled, $2,059 for adults in families with dependent children, and $1,448 for children under the age of twenty-one. (See Table 9.4.)

WHO PAYS FOR END-OF-LIFE CARE?

The Committee on Care at the End of Life of the Institute of Medicine (IOM) noted in its 1997 report *Approaching Death: Improving Care at the End of Life* (Washington, DC) that nearly three-fourths (74.7%) of those who die each year are age sixty-five or older. Medicare covers these older adults during the terminal stage of their lives. Medicaid further covers 13% of

FIGURE 9.1

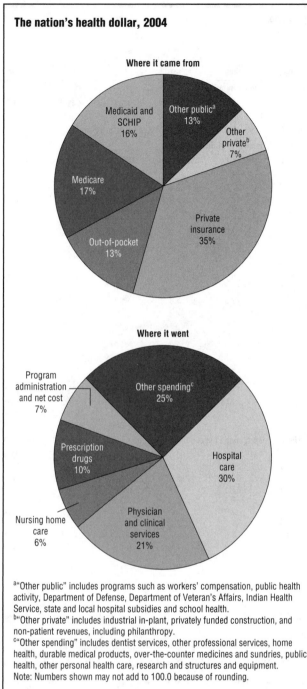

The nation's health dollar, 2004

Where it came from

- Other public[a] 13%
- Other private[b] 7%
- Private insurance 35%
- Out-of-pocket 13%
- Medicare 17%
- Medicaid and SCHIP 16%

Where it went

- Other spending[c] 25%
- Hospital care 30%
- Physician and clinical services 21%
- Nursing home care 6%
- Prescription drugs 10%
- Program administration and net cost 7%

[a]"Other public" includes programs such as workers' compensation, public health activity, Department of Defense, Department of Veteran's Affairs, Indian Health Service, state and local hospital subsidies and school health.
[b]"Other private" includes industrial in-plant, privately funded construction, and non-patient revenues, including philanthropy.
[c]"Other spending" includes dentist services, other professional services, home health, durable medical products, over-the-counter medicines and sundries, public health, other personal health care, research and structures and equipment.
Note: Numbers shown may not add to 100.0 because of rounding.

SOURCE: "The Nation's Health Dollar, Calendar Year 2004: Where It Came From, Where It Went," Centers for Medicare and Medicaid Services, Office of the Actuary, http://www.cms.hhs.gov/NationalHealth ExpendData/downloads/PieChartSourcesExpenditures2004.pdf (accessed February 28, 2006)

those older adults who have exhausted their Medicare benefits, as well as poor and disabled younger patients. Health programs under the Department of Veterans Affairs and the Department of Defense also pay for terminal care.

In his June 11, 2003, testimony to the U.S. Senate Committee on Appropriations, Donald Hoover of the Rutgers Institute for Health, Health Care Policy, and Aging Research presented data on medical expenditures during the last year of life for Americans age sixty-five and older. Hoover noted that Medicare currently pays most end-of-life medical costs for individuals in this age group but stated that the elderly may be expected to pay an increasing proportion of end-of-life costs as the number of elderly individuals in the population increases and end-of-life costs increase as a result. The results of Hoover's research are also published in the report "Medical Expenditures during the Last Year of Life: Findings from the 1992–1996 Medicare Current Beneficiary Survey," (*Health Services Research*, vol. 37, no. 6, December 2002).

The research results of Hoover and his colleagues showed that an average person over age sixty-five who died between 1992 and 1996 created approximately $40,000 of medical expenditures in his or her last year of life. Of this amount, Medicare paid approximately $32,800 (82%), supplemental/private insurance paid about $2,000 (5%), and the individual paid approximately $5,200 (13%). Hoover noted that several initiatives such as hospice and advanced directives have attempted to reduce end-of-life medical costs. However, those costs have not decreased notably as a fraction of Medicare expenditures over the past twenty-five years. Currently about 25% of Medicare expenditures and about 20% of all health care expenditures for the elderly go to those in their last year of life.

No specific information about the cost of end-of-life care exists for the one-fourth of those who die every year who are under age sixty-five. Such care is more than likely financed by employer health insurance, personal funds, Medicare, and Medicaid. Nonetheless, aside from funds paid out for hospice services, the government has no other information about this group's terminal health care.

Medicare Hospice Benefits

In 1982 Congress created a Medicare hospice benefit program (Tax Equity and Fiscal Responsibility Act, PL 97–248, 122) to provide services to terminally ill patients with six months or less to live. In 1989 the Government Accounting Office (GAO; now called the Government Accountability Office) reported that only 35% of eligible hospices were Medicare-certified, in part due to the Health Care Financing Administration's low rates of reimbursement to hospices. That same year Congress gave hospices a 20% increase in reimbursement rates through a provision in the Omnibus Budget Reconciliation Act (PL 101–239, 6005).

Under the Balanced Budget Act of 1997 (PL 105–33), Medicare hospice benefits are divided into three benefit periods:

TABLE 9.3

Medicare enrollees and expenditures, by type of service, selected years 1970–2004

[Data are compiled from various sources by the Centers for Medicare & Medicaid Services]

Type of service	1970	1980	1990	1995	2000	2001	2002	2003	2004[a]
Enrollees					**Number in millions**				
Total[b]	**20.4**	**28.4**	**34.3**	**37.6**	**39.7**	**40.1**	**40.5**	**41.1**	**41.7**
Hospital insurance	20.1	28.0	33.7	37.2	39.3	39.7	40.1	40.6	41.2
Supplementary medical insurance	19.5	27.3	32.6	35.6	37.3	37.7	38.0	38.4	38.8
Expenditures					**Amount in billions**				
Total	**$7.5**	**$36.8**	**$110.8**	**$184.0**	**$221.8**	**$244.8**	**$265.7**	**$280.8**	**$308.9**
Total hospital insurance (HI)	5.3	25.6	66.8	117.4	131.1	143.4	152.5	154.6	170.6
HI payments to managed care organizations[c]	—	0.0	2.7	6.7	21.4	20.8	19.2	19.5	20.8
HI payments for fee-for-service utilization	5.3	25.5	64.2	110.7	109.7	122.6	133.3	135.1	149.8
Inpatient hospital	4.8	24.1	56.9	82.3	87.1	95.6	104.1	108.6	116.2
Skilled nursing facility	0.2	0.4	2.5	9.1	11.1	13.4	15.3	14.8	16.9
Home health agency	0.1	0.5	3.7	16.2	3.8	4.2	5.0	4.8	5.8
Home health agency transfer[d]	—	—	—	—	1.7	3.1	1.2	−2.2	—
Hospice	—	—	0.3	1.9	3.0	3.7	4.9	6.2	7.6
Administrative expenses[e]	0.2	0.5	0.8	1.2	2.9	2.5	2.8	2.8	3.3
Total supplementary medical insurance (SMI)	2.2	11.2	44.0	66.6	90.7	101.4	113.2	126.1	138.3
SMI payments to managed care organizations[c]	0.0	0.2	2.8	6.6	18.4	17.6	17.5	17.3	18.7
SMI payments for fee-for-service utilization[f]	2.2	11.0	41.2	60.0	72.3	83.8	95.7	108.9	119.6
Physician/supplies[g]	1.8	8.2	29.6	—	—	—	—	—	—
Outpatient hospital[h]	0.1	1.9	8.5	—	—	—	—	—	—
Independent laboratory[i]	0.0	0.1	1.5	—	—	—	—	—	—
Physician fee schedule	—	—	—	31.7	37.0	42.0	44.8	48.2	53.8
Durable medical equipment	—	—	—	3.7	4.7	5.4	6.6	7.7	8.0
Laboratory[j]	—	—	—	4.3	4.0	4.4	5.0	5.5	6.0
Other[k]	—	—	—	9.9	13.7	16.0	19.6	22.6	25.0
Hospital[l]	—	—	—	8.7	8.5	12.8	13.5	15.3	17.4
Home health agency	—	0.2	0.1	0.2	4.4	4.4	5.1	5.1	5.9
Home health agency transfer[d]	—	—	—	—	−1.7	−3.1	−1.2	2.2	—
Administrative expenses[e]	0.2	0.6	1.5	1.6	1.8	1.8	2.3	2.4	3.4
					Percent distribution of expenditures				
Total hospital insurance (HI)	100.0	100.0	100.0	100.0	100.0	100.0	100.0	100.0	100.0
HI payments to managed care organizations[c]	—	0.0	4.0	5.7	16.3	14.5	12.6	12.6	12.2
HI payments for fee-for-service utilization	100.0	99.6	96.1	94.3	83.7	85.5	87.4	87.4	87.8
Inpatient hospital	90.6	94.5	85.1	70.1	66.5	66.7	68.2	70.3	68.1
Skilled nursing facility	3.8	1.6	3.7	7.8	8.5	9.4	10.1	9.6	9.9
Home health agency	1.9	2.0	5.5	13.8	2.9	2.9	3.3	3.1	3.4
Home health agency transfer[d]	—	—	—	—	1.3	2.2	0.8	−1.4	—
Hospice	—	—	0.4	1.6	2.3	2.6	3.2	4.0	4.4
Administrative expenses[e]	3.8	2.0	1.2	1.0	2.2	1.7	1.9	1.8	2.0

- An initial ninety-day period

- A subsequent ninety-day period

- An unlimited number of subsequent sixty-day periods, based on a patient's satisfying the program eligibility requirements

At the start of each period the Medicare patient must be recertified as terminally ill. After the patient's death, the patient's family receives up to thirteen months of bereavement service.

In 2004 there were 2,670 Medicare-certified hospices, a substantial increase from thirty-one hospices in 1984. This growth was stimulated in part by increased reimbursement rates established by Congress in 1989. Of the 2,670 hospices, 656 were with home health agencies (HHA), 562 were affiliated with hospitals (HOSP), 14 were with skilled nursing facilities (SNF), and 1,438 were freestanding hospices (FSTG). (See

Table 9.5.) Medicare pays most of the cost of hospice care.

Terminally ill Medicare patients who stayed in a hospice incurred less Medicare cost than those who stayed in a hospital or skilled nursing facility. In 2004 a one-day stay in a hospice cost Medicare $127, compared with $493 for a skilled nursing facility and $3,502 for a hospital. (See Table 9.6.)

The Hospice Association of America (HAA) contends that terminally ill patients often wait too long to enter hospice care. The HAA believes that the difficulty of predicting when death may occur could account for part of the delay, along with the reticence of caregivers, patients, and family to accept a terminal prognosis.

While terminal care is often associated with hospice, the hospice Medicare benefit represents a small

TABLE 9.3

Medicare enrollees and expenditures, by type of service, selected years 1970–2004 [CONTINUED]

[Data are compiled from various sources by the Centers for Medicare & Medicaid Services]

Type of service	1970	1980	1990	1995	2000	2001	2002	2003	2004[a]
				Percent distribution of expenditures					
Total supplementary medical insurance (SMI)	100.0	100.0	100.0	100.0	100.0	100.0	100.0	100.0	100.0
SMI payments to managed care organizations[c]	0.0	1.8	6.4	9.9	20.3	17.3	15.5	13.7	13.5
SMI payments for fee-for-service utilization[f]	100.0	98.2	93.6	90.1	79.8	82.7	84.5	86.3	86.5
Physician/supplies[g]	85.7	73.2	67.3	—	—	—	—	—	—
Outpatient hospital[h]	4.8	17.0	19.3	—	—	—	—	—	—
Independent laboratory[i]	0.0	0.9	3.4	—	—	—	—	—	—
Physician fee schedule	—	—	—	47.5	40.8	41.5	39.6	38.2	38.9
Durable medical equipment	—	—	—	5.5	5.2	5.4	5.8	6.1	5.8
Laboratory[j]	—	—	—	6.4	4.4	4.3	4.4	4.3	4.3
Other[k]	—	—	—	14.8	15.1	15.8	17.3	17.9	18.1
Hospital[l]	—	—	—	13.0	9.4	12.6	12.0	12.2	12.6
Home health agency	0.0	1.8	0.2	0.3	4.8	4.4	4.5	4.0	4.2
Home health agency transfer[d]	—	—	—	0.0	−1.9	−3.1	−1.1	1.7	—
Administrative expenses[e]	9.5	5.4	3.4	2.4	2.0	1.8	2.0	1.9	2.5

[a]Preliminary figures.
[b]Average number enrolled in the hospital insurance (HI) and/or supplementary medical insurance (SMI) programs for the calendar year.
[c]Medicare-approved managed care organizations.
[d]Reflects home health transfer amounts between HI and SMI.
[e]Includes research, costs of experiments and demonstration projects, and peer review activity.
[f]Type of service reporting categories for fee-for-service reimbursement differ before and after 1991.
[g]Includes payment for physicians, practitioners, durable medical equipment, and all suppliers other than independent laboratory, which is shown separately through 1990. Beginning in 1991, those physician services subject to the physician fee schedule are so broken out. Payments for laboratory services paid under the laboratory fee schedule and performed in a physician office are included under "laboratory" beginning in 1991. Payments for durable medical equipment are broken out and so labeled beginning in 1991. The remaining services from the "physician" category are included in "other."
[h]Includes payments for hospital outpatient department services, for skilled nursing facility outpatient services, for Part B services received as an inpatient in a hospital or skilled nursing facility setting, and for other types of outpatient facilities. Beginning in 1991, payments for hospital outpatient department services, except for laboratory services, are listed under "hospital." Hospital outpatient laboratory services are included in the "laboratory" line.
[i]Beginning in 1991, those independent laboratory services that were paid under the laboratory fee schedule (most of "independent lab") are included in the "laboratory" line; the remaining services are included in "physician fee schedule" and "other" lines.
[j]Payments for laboratory services paid under the laboratory fee schedule performed in a physician office, independent lab, or in a hospital outpatient department.
[k]Includes payments for physician-administered drugs; free-standing ambulatory surgical center facility services; ambulance services; supplies; free-standing end-stage renal disease (ESRD) dialysis facility services; rural health clinics; outpatient rehabilitation facilities; psychiatric hospitals; and federally qualified health centers.
[l]Includes the hospital facility costs for Medicare Part B services that are predominantly in the outpatient department, with the exception of hospital outpatient laboratory services, which are included on the "laboratory" line. Physician reimbursement is included on the "physician fee schedule" line.
Notes: "—"=Data not available. 0.0 quantity greater than 0 but less than 0.05. "—"=Quantity zero. Percents are calculated using unrounded data. Table includes service disbursements as of February 2005 for Medicare enrollees residing in Puerto Rico, Virgin Islands, Guam, other outlying areas, foreign countries, and unknown residence. Totals do not necessarily equal the sum of rounded components.

SOURCE: "Table 139. Medicare Enrollees and Expenditures and Percent Distribution, according to Type of Service: United States and Other Areas, Selected Years 1970–2004," in *Health, United States, 2005*, Centers for Disease Control and Prevention, National Center for Health Statistics, November 2005, http://www.cdc.gov/nchs/data/hus/hus05.pdf (accessed February 27, 2006).

---

proportion of the total Medicare dollars spent. In 2004 only about 2.5% ($7.2 billion) of all Medicare benefit payments went to hospice care. The 2005 projected hospice spending was comparably small ($8.6 billion, or 2.6% of the projected $326 billion total Medicare expenditures). (See Table 9.7.)

Medicaid Hospice Benefits

Hospice services also comprise a small portion of Medicaid reimbursements. In 2002 Medicaid reimbursements for hospice accounted for only 0.3% ($706.2 million) of the $214.2 billion total expenditures. (See Table 9.8.) Providing hospice care under Medicaid is optional for each state. In 2002 forty-seven states and Washington, D.C., offered hospice benefits. (See Table 9.9.)

LONG-TERM HEALTH CARE

Longer life spans and life-sustaining technologies have created an increasing need for long-term care. For some older people, relatives provide the long-term care; but those who require labor-intensive, round-the-clock care often stay in nursing homes.

Home Health Care

The concept of home health care began as post–acute care after hospitalization, an alternative to longer, costlier hospital stays. Home health care services have grown tremendously since the 1980s. In 1997 the U.S. Department of Census estimated that approximately twenty thousand home care agencies existed. In 2003 the National Association for Home Care and Hospice (NAHC) reported that 7,265 home care agencies were Medicare certified.

In 1972 Medicare extended home care coverage to people under sixty-five only if they were disabled or suffered from end-stage renal disease. By the year 2000 Medicare coverage for home health care was limited to patients immediately following discharge

TABLE 9.4

Medicaid recipients and medical vendor payments, by eligibility, race, and ethnicity, selected fiscal years 1972–2001

[Data are compiled by the Centers for Medicare & Medicaid Services from the Medicaid data system]

Basis of eligibility and race and ethnicity	1972	1980	1990	1995	1997	1998[a]	1999[b]	2000	2001
Recipients					Number in millions				
All recipients	17.6	21.6	25.3	36.3	34.9	40.6	40.1	42.8	46.0
					Percent of recipients				
Basis of eligibility:[c]									
Aged (65 years and over)	18.8	15.9	12.7	11.4	11.3	9.8	9.4	8.7	8.3
Blind and disabled	9.8	13.5	14.7	16.1	17.6	16.3	16.7	16.1	15.4
Adults in families with dependent children[d]	17.8	22.6	23.8	21.0	19.5	19.5	18.7	20.5	21.1
Children under age 21[e]	44.5	43.2	44.4	47.3	45.3	46.7	46.9	46.1	45.7
Other Title XIX[f]	9.0	6.9	3.9	1.7	6.3	7.8	8.4	8.6	9.5
Race and ethnicity:[g]									
White	—	—	42.8	45.5	44.4	41.3	—	—	40.2
Black or African American	—	—	25.1	24.7	23.5	24.2	—	—	23.1
American Indian or Alaska Native	—	—	1.0	0.8	1.0	0.8	—	—	1.3
Asian or Pacific Islander	—	—	2.0	2.2	1.9	2.5	—	—	3.0
Hispanic or Latino	—	—	15.2	17.2	14.3	15.6	—	—	17.9
Unknown	—	—	14.0	9.6	14.9	15.5	—	—	14.6
Vendor payments[h]					Amount in billions				
All payments	$6.3	$23.3	$64.9	$120.1	$124.4	$142.3	$153.5	$168.3	$186.3
					Percent distribution				
Total	100.0	100.0	100.0	100.0	100.0	100.0	100.0	100.0	100.0
Basis of eligibility:									
Aged (65 years and over)	30.6	37.5	33.2	30.4	30.3	28.5	27.7	26.4	25.9
Blind and disabled	22.2	32.7	37.6	41.1	43.5	42.4	42.9	43.2	43.1
Adults in families with dependent children[d]	15.3	13.9	13.2	11.2	9.9	10.4	10.3	10.6	10.7
Children under age 21[e]	18.1	13.4	14.0	15.0	14.1	16.0	15.7	15.9	16.3
Other Title XIX[f]	13.9	2.6	1.6	1.2	2.2	2.6	3.4	3.9	3.9
Race and ethnicity:[g]									
White	—	—	53.4	54.3	55.0	54.3	—	—	54.4
Black or African American	—	—	18.3	19.2	18.5	19.6	—	—	19.8
American Indian or Alaska Native	—	—	0.6	0.5	0.6	0.8	—	—	1.1
Asian or Pacific Islander	—	—	1.0	1.2	0.9	1.4	—	—	2.5
Hispanic or Latino	—	—	5.3	7.3	6.8	8.2	—	—	9.4
Unknown	—	—	21.3	17.6	18.2	15.7	—	—	12.9

from the hospital. As of 2003 Medicare covered beneficiaries' home health care services with no requirement for prior hospitalization. There were also no limits to the number of professional visits or to the length of coverage. As long as the patient's condition warranted it, the following services were provided:

- Part-time or intermittent skilled nursing and home health aide services
- Speech-language pathology services
- Physical and occupational therapy
- Medical social services
- Medical supplies
- Durable medical equipment (with a 20% co-pay)

Over time, the population receiving home care services has changed. Today much of home health care is associated with rehabilitation from critical illnesses, and fewer users are long-term patients with chronic conditions. In 2000, 75% (1,017,900) of home health users received medical/skilled nursing services, 44% (600,900) received personal care, 37% (502,600) received therapy, and 12% (160,000) received psychosocial services. (See Table 9.10.)

Medicare payments for home health care peaked in 1997 and began to decline in 1998. From 1998 to 1999 Medicare spending for home health care dropped nearly 33%. (See Table 9.11.) Likewise, the number of home care agencies that were Medicare certified declined from a high of 10,444 in 1997, to 8,080 in 1998, then to 7,747 in 1999. (See Table 9.12.) NAHC believes that the decline in agencies since 1997 is the direct result of changes in Medicare home health reimbursement enacted as part of the Balanced Budget Act of 1997 (PL 105–33; see next section).

Relaxed eligibility criteria for home health care, including elimination of the requirement of an acute hospitalization before receiving home care in 2003, enabled an increased number of beneficiaries to use home

TABLE 9.4

Medicaid recipients and medical vendor payments, by eligibility, race, and ethnicity, selected fiscal years 1972–2001 [CONTINUED]

[Data are compiled by the Centers for Medicare & Medicaid Services from the Medicaid data system]

Basis of eligibility and race and ethnicity	1972	1980	1990	1995	1997	1998[a]	1999[b]	2000	2001
Vendor payments per recipient[h]					Amount				
All recipients	$358	$1,079	$2,568	$3,311	$3,568	$3,501	$ 3,819	$3,936	$ 4,053
Basis of eligibility:									
Aged (65 years and over)	580	2,540	6,717	8,868	9,538	10,242	11,268	11,929	12,725
Blind and disabled	807	2,618	6,564	8,435	8,832	9,095	9,832	10,559	11,318
Adults in families with dependent children[d]	307	662	1,429	1,777	1,809	1,876	2,104	2,030	2,059
Children under age 21[e]	145	335	811	1,047	1,111	1,203	1,282	1,358	1,448
Other Title XIX[f]	555	398	1,062	2,380	1,242	1,166	1,532	1,778	1,680
Race and ethnicity:[g]									
White	—	—	3,207	3,953	4,421	4,609	—	—	5,489
Black or African American	—	—	1,878	2,568	2,798	2,836	—	—	3,480
American Indian or Alaska Native	—	—	1,706	2,142	2,500	3,297	—	—	3,452
Asian or Pacific Islander	—	—	1,257	1,713	1,610	1,924	—	—	3,283
Hispanic or Latino	—	—	903	1,400	1,699	1,842	—	—	2,126
Unknown	—	—	3,909	6,099	4,356	3,531	—	—	3,576

[a]Prior to 1999 recipient counts exclude those individuals who only received coverage under prepaid health care and for whom no direct vendor payments were made during the year; and vendor payments exclude payments to health maintenance organizations and other prepaid health plans ($19.3 billion in 1998 and $18 billion in 1997). The total number of persons who were Medicaid eligible and enrolled was 41.4 million in 1998, 41.6 million in 1997, and 41.2 million in 1996.
[b]Starting in 1999, the Medicaid data system was changed.
[c]In 1980 and 1985 recipients are included in more than one category. In 1990–96, 0.2–2.5 percent of recipients have unknown basis of eligibility. From 1997 onwards, unknowns are included in "Other Title XIX."
[d]Includes adults in the Aid to Families with Dependent Children (AFDC) program. From 1997 onwards includes adults in the Temporary Assistance for Needy Families (TANF) program. From 2001 onwards includes women in the Breast and Cervical Cancer Prevention and Treatment Program.
[e]Includes children in the AFDC program. From 1997 onwards includes children and foster care children in the TANF program.
[f]Includes some participants in the supplemental security income program and other people deemed medically needy in participating states. From 1997 onwards excludes foster care children and includes unknown eligibility.
[g]Race and ethnicity as determined on initial Medicaid application. Categories are mutually exclusive. Starting in 2001, Hispanic category included Hispanic persons regardless of race. Persons indicating more than one race were included in the unknown category.
[h]Vendor payments exclude disproportionate share hospital payments ($15.5 billion in fiscal year 2001).
Notes: "—"=Data not available. 1972 data are for fiscal year ending June 30. All other years are for fiscal year ending September 30.

SOURCE: "Table 142. Medicaid Recipients and Medical Vendor Payments, according to Basis of Eligibility, and Race and Ethnicity: United States, Selected Fiscal Years 1972–2001," in *Health, United States, 2005*, Centers for Disease Control and Prevention, National Center for Health Statistics, November 2005, http://www.cdc.gov/nchs/data/hus/hus05.pdf (accessed February 27, 2006).

health services. Table 9.12 shows that the number of Medicare-certified home care agencies increased from a low of 6,861 in 2001 to 7,265 in 2003. In addition, Medicare payments for home health care increased by 7.5% in 2002 over 2001. In 2004 and 2005 payments increased 10.9% and 11.6% over the prior year, respectively. (See Table 9.11.)

MEDICARE LIMITS HOME CARE SERVICES. The Balanced Budget Act of 1997 (PL 105–33) aimed to cut approximately $16.2 billion from Medicare home care expenditures over a period of five years. The federal government sought to return home health care to its original concept of short-term care plus skilled nursing and therapy services. Medicare beneficiaries who received home health care would lose certain personal care services, such as assistance with bathing, dressing, and eating.

The Balanced Budget Act sharply curtailed the growth of home care spending, greatly affecting health care providers. As mentioned in the prior section, annual Medicare home health care spending fell nearly 33% between 1998 and 1999 in response to tightened

eligibility requirements for skilled nursing services, limited per-visit payments, and increasingly stringent claims review. (See Table 9.11.) The changes forced many agencies to close and transfer their patients to other home health care companies. In addition, the number of current home health care patients declined (see Figure 9.2), in large part due to decreased funding. However, the decline began one year prior to the Balanced Budget Act, so more factors than decreased Medicare funding are likely to be playing a role in the decline.

Nursing Home Care

Growth of the home health care industry in the 1980s and early to mid-1990s is only partly responsible for the decline in the rate of Americans entering nursing homes (residents per one thousand population), as shown in Table 9.13. Declines also occurred in years when numbers of home health care patients declined as well. Another reason for the decline in the rate of nursing home residents may be that the elderly are choosing assisted living and continuing-care retirement communities that offer alternatives to nursing home care. There is also a

TABLE 9.5

Medicare-certified hospices, by type, 1984–2004

Year	Home health agency-based	Hospital-based	Skilled nursing facility-based	Freestanding	Total
1984	n/a	n/a	n/a	n/a	31
1985	n/a	n/a	n/a	n/a	158
1986	113	54	10	68	245
1987	155	101	11	122	389
1988	213	138	11	191	553
1989	286	182	13	220	701
1990	313	221	12	260	806
1991	325	282	10	394	1,011
1992	334	291	10	404	1,039
1993	438	341	10	499	1,288
1994	583	401	12	608	1,604
1995	699	460	19	679	1,857
1996	815	526	22	791	2,154
1997	823	561	22	868	2,274
1998	763	553	21	878	2,215
1999	762	562	22	928	2,274
2000	739	554	20	960	2,273
2001	690	552	20	1,003	2,265
2002	676	557	17	1,072	2,322
2003	653	561	16	1,214	2,444
2004	656	562	14	1,438	2,670

Notes: Home health agency-based (HHA) hospices are owned and operated by freestanding proprietary and nonprofit home care agencies. Hospital-based (HOSP) hospices are operating units or departments of a hospital.

SOURCE: "Table 1. Number of Medicare-Certified Hospices, by Auspice, 1984–2004," in *Hospice Facts & Statistics*, National Association for Home Care & Hospice, March 2005, http://www.nahc.org/hospicefands.pdf (accessed November 10, 2005)

TABLE 9.6

Comparison of hospital, SNF, and hospice Medicare charges, 1998–2004

	1998	1999	2000	2001	2002	2003	2004
Hospital inpatient charges per day	$2,177	$2,583	$2,762	$3,069	$3,164	$3,354	$3,502
Skilled nursing facility charges per day	482	424	413	422	444	465	493
Hospice charges per covered day of care	113	116	121	125	128	123	127

SOURCE: "Table 13. Comparison of Hospital, SNF, and Hospice Medicare Charges, 1998–2004," in *Hospice Facts & Statistics*, National Association for Home Care & Hospice, March 2005, http://www.nahc.org/hospicefands.pdf (accessed November 10, 2005)

trend toward healthy aging—more older adults are living longer with fewer disabilities.

Still, in 1999 (the latest data available) nearly 1.5 million adults age sixty-five and older were nursing home residents. Most were white (87.1%) and female (74.3%), and more than half (51.5%) were eighty-five years and older. (See Table 9.13.)

Nursing homes provide terminally ill residents with end-of-life services in different ways:

• Caring for patients in the nursing home

• Transferring patients who request it to hospitals or hospices

• Contracting with hospices to provide palliative care (care that relieves the pain but does not cure the illness) within the nursing home

A combination of federal, state, and private monies finance nursing home care. According to the Administration on Aging, in 2000 almost half of the funds came from Medicaid, one-third came from private payment, 10% from Medicare, and 5% from private insurance.

Patients in a Persistent Vegetative State

The precise number of patients in a persistent vegetative state (PVS) is unknown because no system is in place to count them. The costs to maintain such patients range from $2,000 to $10,000 per month, depending on the acuity of care needed (the type, degree, or extent of required services).

The End-Stage Renal Disease Program

End-stage renal disease (ESRD) is the final phase of irreversible kidney disease and requires either kidney

TABLE 9.7

Medicare benefit payments, fiscal years 2004 and 2005

	2004 (estimated)		2005 (projected)	
	Amount ($ millions)	Percent of total	Amount ($ millions)	Percent of total
Total Medicare benefit payments*	**295,334**	**100.0**	**326,019**	**100.0**
Part A				
Hospital care	113,624	38.5	119,398	36.6
Skilled nursing facility	16,468	5.6	16,976	5.2
Home health	5,501	1.9	6,152	1.9
Hospice	7,238	2.5	8,599	2.6
Managed care	20,932	7.1	27,764	8.5
Total	**163,764**	**55.5**	**178,889**	**54.9**
Part B				
Physician	52,022	17.6	56,096	17.2
Durable medical equipment	7,868	2.7	8,136	2.5
Carrier lab	3,202	1.1	3,447	1.1
Other carrier	13,821	4.7	14,731	4.5
Hospital	16,883	5.7	18,573	5.7
Home health	5,689	1.9	6,370	2.0
Intermediary lab	2,651	0.9	2,834	0.9
Other intermediary	10,414	3.5	11,213	3.4
Managed care	18,830	6.4	24,573	7.5
Total	**131,379**	**44.5**	**145,975**	**44.8**

*Part A total does not include peer review organization payments. Figures may not add to totals due to rounding.

SOURCE: "Table 4. Medicare Benefit Payments, FY2004 and FY2005," in *Hospice Facts & Statistics*, National Association for Home Care & Hospice, March 2005, http://www.nahc.org/hospicefands.pdf (accessed November 10, 2005)

TABLE 9.8

Medicaid payments, by type of service, fiscal years 2001 and 2002

	2001 ($ millions)	Percent of total	2002 ($ millions)	Percent of total
Inpatient hospital	25,943.1	13.8	29,127.1	13.6
Nursing home	37,322.7	19.9	39,282.2	18.3
Physician	7,438.7	4.0	8,354.6	3.9
Outpatient hospital	7,496.1	4.0	8,470.6	4.0
Home health[d]	16,655.4	8.9	19,287.8	9.0
Hospice[b]	546.1	0.3	706.2	0.3
Prescription drugs	23,764.4	12.7	28,408.2	13.3
ICF (MR) services[c]	9,700.9	5.2	10,681.3	5.0
Other	58,592.5	31.3	69,879.5	32.6
Total payments[a]	**187,459.9**	**100.0**	**214,197.5**	**100.0**

[a]Total outlays include hospice outlays from the Form CMS-64 plus payments for all service types included in the Medicaid Statistical Information System (MSIS), not just the eight service types listed.
[b]Hospice outlays come from Form CMS-64 and do not include Medicaid State Children's Health Insurance Program (SCHIP). All other expenditures come from the MSIS. The federal share of Medicaid's hospice spending in 2001 was $314.6 million, or 57.6% of the total. In fiscal year 2002, it was $404.7 million, or 57.3% of total Medicaid hospice payments.
[c]ICF is intermediate care facilities. MR is Medicaid reimbursed.
[d]Home health includes both home health and personal support services.

SOURCE: "Table 9. Medicaid Payments, by Type of Service, FY 2001 & FY 2002," in *Hospice Facts & Statistics*, National Association for Home Care & Hospice, March 2005, http://www.nahc.org/hospicefands.pdf (accessed November 10, 2005)

TABLE 9.9

Number of states offering hospice under Medicaid, selected years 1987–2002

Year	Total number	States added	States dropped
1987	6	FL, KY, MI, MN, ND, VT	
1988	15	DE, HI, IL, MA, NE, NY, NC, RI, TX, WI	MN
1989	24	AZ, CA, GA, ID, KS, MO, MT, PA, TN, UT	NE
1990	32	AL, AK, IA, MD, MN, NM, OH, VA, WA	TN
1991	34	CO, MS, TN	AK
1992	35	NJ	
1993	36	DC, WV	AZ
1994	38	OR, WY	
1995	40	AK, SC	
1996	41	AR	
1997	42	IN	
1998	44	AZ, NV	
1999	44		
2002	47	TN, MN, ME	

SOURCE: "Table 10. Number of States Offering Hospice under Medicaid, Selected Years, 1987–2002," in *Hospice Facts & Statistics*, National Association for Home Care & Hospice, March 2005, http://www.nahc.org/hospicefands.pdf (accessed November 10, 2005)

transplantation or dialysis to maintain life. Dialysis is a medical procedure in which a machine takes over the function of the kidneys by removing waste products from the blood. Medicare beneficiaries with ESRD are high-cost users of Medicare services. Amendments to the Social Security Act in 1972 extended Medicare coverage to include ESRD patients. According to the Centers for Medicare and Medicaid's *2005 CMS Statistics*, Medicare enrollees with end-stage renal disease increased from 66,700 in 1980 to 359,400 in 2004, an increase of 439%.

TABLE 9.10

Number of current home health care patients by services received, 2000

Selected services[a]	Number
All patients[b]	1,355,300
Medical/skilled nursing	
Total medical and/or skilled nursing	1,017,900
Physician	32,300
Skilled nursing	1,016,500
Equipment and/or medication	
Total equipment/medication	174,800
Durable medical equipment and supplies	109,500
Medications	88,900
Personal care	
Total personal care	600,900
Continuous home care	53,100
Companion	40,400
Homemaker-household[c]	329,400
Personal care	476,400
Transportation	25,300*
Respite care	17,000*
Therapeutic	
Total therapeutic	502,600
Dietary and/or nutritional	60,200
Enterostomal therapy	17,700*
IV therapy[d]	52,700
Occupational therapy	112,300
Physical therapy	360,700
Respiratory therapy	29,500
Speech therapy and/or audiology	30,600
Other high tech care[e]	11,000*
Psychosocial	
Total psychosocial	160,000
Counseling	22,400
Psychological	14,700*
Social	117,500
Spiritual and/or pastoral care	15,300*
Referral	34,800
Other[e,f]	46,300

*Figure does not meet standard of reliability or precision because the sample size is between 30 and 59.
[a]Numbers will not add to totals because a patient may be included in more than one category.
[b]Total number of home health care patients.
[c]Includes Meals on Wheels.
[d]IV is intravenous.
[e]Includes enteral nutrition and dialysis.
[f]Includes dental, vocational therapy, volunteers, and other services.

SOURCE: Adapted from "Table 6. Number of Current Home Health Care Patients by Services Received, by Sex and Race: United States, 2000," in *National Home and Hospice Care Data*, Centers for Disease Control and Prevention, National Center for Health Statistics, http://www.cdc.gov/nchs/data/nhhcsd/curhomecare00.pdf (accessed November 7, 2005)

The segment of Medicare beneficiaries with a disability or ESRD rose from 3% of all Medicare beneficiaries in 1980 to 5.4% in 2000. This group is projected to grow to 8.7% by the year 2020 and level off in the next decade. (See Figure 9.3.)

PATIENTS WITH TERMINAL DISEASES

Terminal patients often receive high-technology intensive care that simply prolongs the dying process. Studies by the Health Care Financing Administration (HCFA; now the CMS) found that "medical services generally become much more intense as death approaches." In the United States the fear of malpractice suits, physicians trained to fight death to the end, and government reimbursement encourage continued medical care at all costs.

Acquired Immunodeficiency Syndrome

Acquired immunodeficiency syndrome (AIDS) is a set of signs, symptoms, and certain diseases occurring together when the immune system of a person infected with the human immunodeficiency virus (HIV) becomes extremely weakened. According to the Centers for Disease Control and Prevention (CDC), advances in treatment during the mid- to late 1990s slowed the progression of HIV infection to AIDS and led to dramatic decreases in AIDS deaths. The decrease in AIDS deaths continued from 1999 to 2003 with a 3% decrease in deaths. Nonetheless, the number of AIDS diagnoses increased an estimated 4% from 1999 to 2003. In 2003 an estimated 43,171 people became infected with HIV. The CDC estimated that in 2003 18,017 people died of AIDS. Cumulatively through 2003, 929,985 people had been diagnosed with AIDS, 524,060 people had died from the syndrome, and 405,926 were living with it.

In 2003 the federal government spent $16.7 billion on research, education and prevention, medical care, and cash assistance for HIV/AIDS patients—a nearly ninety-nine-fold increase over the $209 million spent in 1985. More than half (61.3%, or $10.2 billion) was spent on medical care. (See Table 9.14.)

In 2006 the per-person cost of AIDS medication in the U.S. was approximately $10,000 annually. In other parts of the world costs have been brought down to as low as $140 per person per year. Former President Bill Clinton suggested that those lower prices could drive down prices in the U.S. as well ("Clinton: Worlds AIDS Fight May Lower Drug Costs," ABC News, February 19, 2006, http://abcnews.go.com/GMA/Health/story?id=1637770&page=1&CMP=OTC-RSSFeeds0312).

MEDICAID ASSISTANCE. The financing of health care for AIDS patients has increasingly become the responsibility of Medicaid, the entitlement program that provides medical assistance to low-income Americans. This is due, in large part, to the rising incidence of AIDS among poor people and intravenous drug users—the groups least likely to have private health insurance. Further, many patients who might once have had private insurance through their employers lose their coverage when they become too ill to work. These individuals eventually turn to Medicaid and other public programs for medical assistance.

Some people, whose employment and economic condition previously afforded the insurance coverage

TABLE 9.11

Medicare payments and annual percent change, by benefit type, fiscal years 1998–2005

Benefit type	1998	1999	2000	2001	2002	2003	2004	2005*
					Amount ($ billions)			
Managed care	31.9	37.4	39.8	42.1	33.9	36.5	39.8	52.3
Inpatient hospitals	87.0	85.7	86.5	93.2	102.1	108.6	113.6	119.4
Skilled nursing facilities	13.6	11.5	10.6	12.4	14.7	14.5	16.5	17.0
Home health	14.0	9.4	9.2	9.3	10.0	10.1	11.2	12.5
Hospice	2.1	2.5	2.8	3.4	4.5	5.9	7.2	8.6
Physicians	32.3	33.4	36.0	40.4	44.2	47.3	52.0	56.1
Outpatient hospitals	10.5	8.5	8.4	10.1	12.8	14.7	16.9	18.6
Other	14.6	15.7	17.2	20.3	23.7	27.4	30.0	35.2
Durable medical equipment	4.1	4.3	4.6	5.3	6.2	7.6	7.9	8.1
Prescription drugs	n/a	n/a	n/a	n/a	n/a	n/a	0.2	1.2
Total, part A	134.3	129.3	126.2	136.0	144.1	153.1	163.8	178.9
Total, part B	75.8	79.1	88.9	100.5	108.1	119.5	131.4	146.0
Total, part D	n/a	n/a	n/a	n/a	n/a	n/a	0.2	1.2
Total Medicare	210.1	208.4	215.1	236.5	252.1	272.6	295.3	329.0
					Percent change from previous year by benefit type			
Managed care		17.2	6.4	5.8	−19.5	7.7	9.0	31.4
Inpatient hospitals		−1.5	0.9	7.7	9.5	6.4	4.6	5.1
Skilled nursing facilities		−15.4	−7.8	17.0	18.5	−1.4	13.8	3.0
Home health		−32.9	−2.1	1.1	7.5	1.0	10.9	11.6
Hospice		19.1	12.0	21.4	32.4	31.1	22.0	19.4
Physicians		3.4	7.8	12.2	9.4	7.0	9.9	7.9
Outpatient hospitals		−19.1	−1.2	20.2	26.7	14.8	15.0	10.1
Other		7.5	9.6	18.0	16.7	15.6	9.5	17.3
Durable medical equipment		4.9	7.0	15.2	17.0	22.6	3.9	2.5

Notes: *Fiscal year 2005 numbers are estimated.

SOURCE: "Table 4. Medicare Payments and Annual Percent Change, by Benefit Type, Fiscal Years 1998–2005," in *Basic Statistics about Home Care*, National Association for Home Care & Hospice, January 2006, unpublished data

they needed, find their situation changed once they test positive for HIV. Some may become virtually ineligible for private health insurance coverage. Others require government assistance because insurance companies can declare HIV infection a "pre-existing condition," making it ineligible for payment of insurance claims. In addition, some insurance companies limit AIDS coverage to relatively small amounts.

THE RYAN WHITE COMPREHENSIVE AIDS RESOURCES EMERGENCY (CARE) ACT. Currently, the CARE Act (PL 101–381) is the only federal program providing funds specifically for medical and support services for HIV/AIDS patients. It was initially passed in 1990 and was reauthorized in 1996 and 2000. Appropriations of CARE funds follow one of four formulas:

- Under the Title I formula, the federal government provides emergency assistance to metropolitan areas disproportionately affected by the HIV epidemic. To qualify for Title I financing, eligible metropolitan areas (EMAs) must have more than two thousand cumulative AIDS cases reported during the preceding five years and a population of at least five hundred thousand. In fiscal year (FY) 2005, fifty-one EMAs in twenty-one states, the District of Columbia, and Puerto Rico received $587.4 million. (See Table 9.15.)

- Under the Title II formula, funds are provided to state governments. Ninety percent of Title II funds are allocated based on AIDS patient counts, while 10% are distributed through competitive grants to public and nonprofit agencies. In addition, states receive funding to support AIDS Drug Assistance Programs (ADAPs), which provide medication to low-income HIV patients who are uninsured or underinsured. In 2005 alone the federal government provided nearly $1.1 billion for ADAPs funds and for improved health care and support services for HIV/AIDS patients. (See Table 9.16.)

- Title III funds are designated for Early Intervention Services (EIS) and Planning. EIS grants support outpatient HIV services for low-income people in existing primary care systems, and Planning grants aid those working to develop HIV primary care.

- Title IV programs focus on the development of assistance for women, infants, and children.

Cancer

Cancer, in all its forms, is very expensive to treat. Compared with other diseases, there are more options for cancer treatment, more adverse side effects that require treatment, and a greater potential for unrelieved pain. According to the American Cancer Society's *2006 Cancer Facts & Figures*, the overall estimated cost of

TABLE 9.12

Number of Medicare-certified home care agencies, by type, selected years 1967–2003

Year	Freestanding agencies						Facility-based agencies			Total
	Visiting nurse associations[a]	Combination agencies[b]	Public agencies[c]	Proprietary agencies[d]	Private not-for-profit agencies[e]	Other freestanding agencies[f]	Hospital-based agencies[g]	Rehabilitation facilities[h]	Skilled nursing facilities[i]	
1967	549	93	939	0	0	39	133	0	0	1,753
1975	525	46	1,228	47	0	109	273	9	5	2,242
1980	515	63	1,260	186	484	40	359	8	9	2,924
1985	514	59	1,205	1,943	832	4	1,277	20	129	5,983
1990	474	47	985	1,884	710	0	1,486	8	101	5,695
1991	476	41	941	1,970	701	0	1,537	9	105	5,780
1992	530	52	1,083	1,962	637	28	1,623	3	86	6,004
1993	594	46	1,196	2,146	558	41	1,809	1	106	6,497
1994	586	45	1,146	2,892	597	48	2,081	3	123	7,521
1995	575	40	1,182	3,951	667	65	2,470	4	166	9,120
1996	576	34	1,177	4,658	695	58	2,634	4	191	10,027
1997	553	33	1,149	5,024	715	65	2,698	3	204	10,444
1998	460	35	968	3,414	610	69	2,356	2	166	8,080
1999	452	35	918	3,192	621	65	2,300	1	163	7,747
2000	436	31	909	2,863	560	56	2,151	1	150	7,152
2001	425	23	867	2,835	543	68	1,976	1	123	6,861
2002	430	27	850	3,027	563	79	1,907	1	119	7,007
2003	439	27	888	3,402	546	74	1,776	0	113	7,265

Note: 2003 data obtained in January, 2004.
[a]Visiting nurse associations are freestanding, voluntary, nonprofit organizations governed by a board of directors and usually financed by tax-deductible contributions as well as by earnings.
[b]Combination agencies are combined government and voluntary agencies. These agencies are sometimes included with counts for visiting nurse associations.
[c]Public agencies are government agencies operated by a state, county, city, or other unit of local government having a major responsibility for preventing disease and for community health education.
[d]Proprietary agencies are freestanding, for-profit home care agencies.
[e]Private not-for-profit agencies are freestanding and privately developed, governed, and owned nonprofit home care agencies. These agencies were not counted separately prior to 1980.
[f]Other freestanding agencies that do not fit one of the categories for freestanding agencies listed above.
[g]Hospital-based agencies are operating units or departments of a hospital. Agencies that have working arrangements with a hospital, or perhaps are even owned by a hospital but operated as separate entities, are classified as freestanding agencies under one of the categories listed above.
[h]Refers to agencies based in rehabilitation facilities.
[i]Refers to agencies based in skilled nursing facilities.

SOURCE: "Table 1. Number of Medicare-Certified Home Care Agencies, by Auspice, for Selected Years, 1967–2003," in *Basic Statistics about Home Care*, National Association for Home Care & Hospice, updated 2004, http://www.nahc.org/04HC_Stats.pdf (accessed March 1, 2006)

FIGURE 9.2

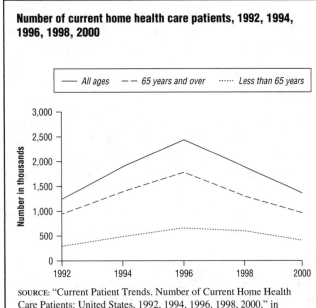

Number of current home health care patients, 1992, 1994, 1996, 1998, 2000

— All ages   – – 65 years and over   ····· Less than 65 years

SOURCE: "Current Patient Trends. Number of Current Home Health Care Patients: United States, 1992, 1994, 1996, 1998, 2000," in *National Home and Hospice Care Data*, Centers for Disease Control and Prevention, National Center for Health Statistics, http://www.cdc.gov/nchs/about/major/nhhcsd/nhhcschart.htm (accessed November 7, 2005)

cancer to the nation in 2005 was $209.9 billion. Of this amount, $74 billion was due to direct medical costs—the total of all health expenditures. Of the remainder, $17.5 billion was the cost of lost productivity due to illness, and $118.4 billion was the cost of lost productivity due to premature death.

MEDICARE, CLINICAL TRIALS, AND CANCER. Some health insurance plans cover all or a portion of the costs associated with clinical trials (research studies that offer promising new anticancer drugs and treatment to patients enrolled). Policies vary, and some plans decide whether they will pay for clinical trials on a case-by-case basis. Some health plans limit coverage to patients for whom no standard therapy is available. Others cover clinical trials only if they are not much more expensive than standard treatment, and many choose not to cover any costs involved with clinical trials.

On June 7, 2000, President Clinton revised Medicare payment policies to enable beneficiaries to participate in clinical trials. Prior to this policy change, many older adults were prevented from participating in clinical trials because they could not afford the costs associated with the trials.

TABLE 9.13

Nursing home residents 65 years of age and over, by age, sex, and race, 1973–74, 1985, 1995, and 1999

[Data are based on a sample of nursing home residents]

Age, sex, and race	Residents				Residents per 1,000 population			
	1973–74	1985	1995	1999	1973–74	1985	1995	1999
Age								
65 years and over, age adjusted[a]	...	...	...	...	58.5	54.0	45.9	43.3
65 years and over, crude	961,500	1,318,300	1,422,600	1,469,500	44.7	46.2	42.4	42.9
65–74 years	163,100	212,100	190,200	194,800	12.3	12.5	10.1	10.8
75–84 years	384,900	509,000	511,900	517,600	57.7	57.7	45.9	43.0
85 years and over	413,600	597,300	720,400	757,100	257.3	220.3	198.6	182.5
Male								
65 years and over, age adjusted[a]	...	...	...	...	42.5	38.8	32.8	30.6
65 years and over, crude	265,700	334,400	356,800	377,800	30.0	29.0	26.1	26.5
65–74 years	65,100	80,600	79,300	84,100	11.3	10.8	9.5	10.3
75–84 years	102,300	141,300	144,300	149,500	39.9	43.0	33.3	30.8
85 years and over	98,300	112,600	133,100	144,200	182.7	145.7	130.8	116.5
Female								
65 years and over, age adjusted[a]	...	...	...	...	67.5	61.5	52.3	49.8
65 years and over, crude	695,800	983,900	1,065,800	1,091,700	54.9	57.9	53.7	54.6
65–74 years	98,000	131,500	110,900	110,700	13.1	13.8	10.6	11.2
75–84 years	282,600	367,700	367,600	368,100	68.9	66.4	53.9	51.2
85 years and over	315,300	484,700	587,300	612,900	294.9	250.1	224.9	210.5
White[b]								
65 years and over, age adjusted[a]	...	...	...	...	61.2	55.5	45.4	41.9
65 years and over, crude	920,600	1,227,400	1,271,200	1,279,600	46.9	47.7	42.3	42.1
65–74 years	150,100	187,800	154,400	157,200	12.5	12.3	9.3	10.0
75–84 years	369,700	473,600	453,800	440,600	60.3	59.1	44.9	40.5
85 years and over	400,800	566,000	663,000	681,700	270.8	228.7	200.7	181.8
Black or African American[b]								
65 years and over, age adjusted[a]	...	...	...	...	28.2	41.5	50.4	55.6
65 years and over, crude	37,700	82,000	122,900	145,900	22.0	35.0	45.2	51.1
65–74 years	12,200	22,500	29,700	30,300	11.1	15.4	18.4	18.2
75–84 years	13,400	30,600	47,300	58,700	26.7	45.3	57.2	66.5
85 years and over	12,100	29,000	45,800	56,900	105.7	141.5	167.1	183.1

[a]Age adjusted by the direct method to the year 2000 population standard using the following three age groups: 65–74 years, 75–84 years, and 85 years and over.
[b]Beginning in 1999 the instruction for the race item on the questionnaire was changed so that more than one race could be recorded. In previous years only one racial category could be checked. Estimates for racial groups presented in this table are for residents for whom only one race was recorded. Estimates for residents where multiple races were checked are unreliable due to small sample sizes and are not shown.
Notes: "..."=Category not applicable. Excludes residents in personal care or domiciliary care homes. Age refers to age at time of interview. Civilian population estimates used to compute rates for the 1990s are 1990-based postcensal estimates, as of July 1.

SOURCE: "Table 102. Nursing Home Residents 65 Years of Age and Over, according to Age, Sex, and Race: United States, 1973–74, 1985, 1995, and 1999," in *Health, United States, 2006*, Centers for Disease Control and Prevention, National Center for Health Statistics, November 2005, http://www.cdc.gov/nchs/data/hus/hus05.pdf (accessed February 27, 2006)

Alzheimer's Disease

Liesi E. Hebert et al, in "Alzheimer Disease in the U.S. Population: Prevalence Estimates Using the 2000 Census" (*Archives of Neurology*, vol. 60, no. 8, August 2003), estimate that in 2000 there were 4.5 million people with Alzheimer's disease (AD) in the U.S. population. AD is a form of dementia characterized by memory loss, behavior and personality changes, and decreasing thinking abilities. Care and treatment of those suffering from dementia cost the United States as much as $100 billion each year.

THE COST OF DYING

The Canadian Health Services Research Foundation (CHSRF), in "Myth: The Cost of Dying Is an Increasing Strain on the Healthcare System" (CHSRF, 2003), reported that treating the dying is not growing and overwhelming health care systems. The report describes research conducted in North America and Europe, showing that thirty years of research debunk the myth that health care costs in the last year of life are extraordinarily high and are increasing. Research spanning countries and continents, the report notes, shows that treating the dying accounts for only about 10% to 12% of many countries' total health care budgets.

In "Medicare Expenditures during the Last Year of Life: Findings from the 1992–1996 Medicare Current Beneficiary Survey—Cost of Care" (Donald R. Hoover et al, *Health Services Research*, vol. 37, no. 6, December, 2002), the authors show that approximately 22% of total annual U.S. health care expenditures is spent during the last year of life. This figure is higher than noted in the previous paragraph. These expenses consume about 26% of the Medicare budget and about

FIGURE 9.3

Growth in the number and percent of Medicare beneficiaries with disabilities or end stage renal disease, selected years 1970–2030

[The number of people Medicare serves will nearly double by 2030]

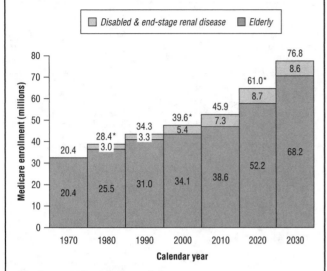

*Numbers may not sum due to rounding.

SOURCE: "Number of Medicare Beneficiaries," in *Program Information on Medicare, Medicaid, SCHIP, and Other Programs of the Centers for Medicare and Medicaid Services*, Centers for Medicare and Medicaid Services, June 2002, http://www.cms.hhs.gov/TheChartSeries/ (accessed February 28, 2006)

18% of non-Medicare budgets. The researchers note, however, that end-of-life Medicare expenses grew at the same rate as did other Medicare expenses in the early 1990s and are not growing more quickly than other Medicare expenses.

Why aren't health care costs in the last year of life rising? The CHSRF report comments that most people die without using costly high-tech equipment, and many die after only two weeks or less in a hospital. In the United States nearly half (46%) of Medicare recipients were not hospitalized before they died. Hospitalization dramatically drives up the cost of dying in America, and many terminally ill patients are choosing alternatives to hospitalization, such as hospice and home health care.

TABLE 9.14

Federal spending for human immunodeficiency virus (HIV)-related activities, by agency and type of activity, selected fiscal years 1985–2003

[Data are compiled from federal government appropriations]

Agency and type of activity	1985	1990	1995	1999	2000	2001	2002	2003[a]
Agency				**Amount in millions**				
All federal spending	$209	$3,070	$7,019	$10,779	$12,025	$14,184	$14,988	$16,677
Department of Health and Human Services, total	201	2,372	5,200	8,494	9,621	11,406	12,039	13,292
Department of Health and Human Services discretionary spending, total[b]	109	1,592	2,700	4,094	4,546	5,226	5,789	6,142
National Institutes of Health	66	908	1,334	1,793	2,004	2,247	2,499	2,717
Substance Abuse and Mental Health Services Administration	—	50	24	92	110	157	169	171
Centers for Disease Control and Prevention	33	443	590	657	687	859	931	936
Food and Drug Administration	9	57	73	70	76	76	76	80
Health Resources and Services Administration (HRSA)	—	113	661	1,416	1,599	1,815	1,917	2,025
Agency for Healthcare Research and Quality	—	8	9	2	2	3	3	2
Office of the Secretary[c]	—	10	6	12	13	15	14	18
Indian Health Service	—	3	4	4	4	4	4	4
Emergency Fund	...	...	...	50	50	50	50	50
Global AIDS Trust Fund	...	...	...	...	...	...	125	99
The International Mother and Child HIV Prevention Initiative[d]	...	...	...	...	...	...	...	40
Centers for Medicare & Medicaid Services	75	780	2,500	4,400	5,000	5,600	6,250	7,150
Social Security Administration[e]	17	...	...	...	...	...	...	...
Ricky Ray Hemophilia Relief Fund (HRSA)[f]	...	...	...	...	75	580	...	...
Social Security Administration[e]	...	239	881	1,158	1,240	1,259	1,351	1,395
Department of Veterans Affairs	8	220	317	401	345	405	391	396
Department of Defense	—	124	110	86	97	108	96	78
Agency for International Development	—	71	120	139	200	430	510	873
Department of Housing and Urban Development	—	—	171	225	232	257	277	292
Office of Personnel Management	—	37	212	266	279	292	297	321
Other departments	—	7	8	10	11	27	27	30
Activity				**Amount in millions**				
Research	75	1,013	1,460	1,900	2,125	2,368	2,614	2,821
Department of Health and Human Services discretionary spending[b]	75	974	1,417	1,869	2,085	2,328	2,580	2,800
Department of Veterans Affairs	—	6	5	7	7	7	8	8
Department of Defense	—	33	38	24	33	33	26	13
Education and prevention	33	591	770	902	998	1,396	1,629	1,940
Department of Health and Human Services discretionary spending[b]	33	460	604	719	751	950	1,091	1,130
Department of Veterans Affairs	—	29	31	30	33	35	35	
Department of Defense	—	28	12	10	10	17	17	11
Agency for International Development	—	71	120	139	200	380	473	749
Other	—	3	3	4	4	14	13	15
Medical care	83	1,227	3,738	6,595	7,356	8,324	9,117	10,229
Centers for Medicare & Medicaid Services: Medicaid (federal share)	70	670	1,500	2,900	3,300	3,700	4,200	4,800
Medicare	5	110	1,000	1,500	1,700	1,900	2,050	2,350
Department of Health and Human Services discretionary spending[b]	—	158	680	1,507	1,711	1,948	2,118	2,212
Department of Veterans Affairs	8	185	281	364	305	363	348	353
Department of Defense	—	63	60	52	54	58	53	54
Agency for International Development	—	—	—	—	—	50	38	124
Office of Personnel Management	—	37	212	266	279	292	297	321
Other	—	4	5	6	7	13	14	15

TABLE 9.14

Federal spending for human immunodeficiency virus (HIV)-related activities, by agency and type of activity, selected fiscal years 1985–2003 [CONTINUED]

Agency and type of activity	1985	1990	1995	1999	2000	2001	2002	2003[a]
Cash assistance	17	239	1,052	1,383	1,547	2,096	1,628	1,687
Social Security Administration:								
Disability insurance	12	184	631	828	870	919	961	985
Supplemental security income	5	55	250	330	370	340	390	410
Department of Housing and Urban Development	—	—	171	225	232	257	277	292
Ricky Ray Hemophilia Relief Fund[f]	. . .	. . .	. . .	. . .	75	580	. . .	. . .

Notes: "—"=Quantity zero. ". . ."=Category not applicable.
[a]Preliminary figures.
[b]Discretionary spending is contrasted with entitlement spending. Medicare and Medicaid are examples of entitlement spending.
[c]The Office of the Assistant Secretary for Health prior to fiscal year 1996 (FY1996).
[d]The International Mother and Child HIV Prevention Initiative was introduced in 2002 with funding starting in fiscal year 2003 (FY2003).
[e]Prior to 1995 the Social Security Administration was part of the Department of Health and Human Services.
[f]The Ricky Ray Hemophilia Relief Fund was established by the U.S. Congress in 1998 to make compassionate payments to certain individuals who were treated with antihemophilic factor between July 1, 1982 and December 31, 1987, and who contracted HIV. Some family members may also be covered by the fund.

SOURCE: "Table 128. Federal Spending for Human Immunodeficiency Virus (HIV)-Related Activities, according to Agency and Type of Activity, United States, Selected Fiscal Years 1985–2003," in *Health, United States, 2004*, Centers for Disease Control and Prevention, National Center for Health Statistics, September 2004, ftp://ftp.cdc.gov/pub/Health_Statistics/NCHS/Publications/Health_US/hus04tables/ (accessed February 27, 2006)

TABLE 9.15

Ryan White CARE (Comprehensive AIDS Resources Emergency) Act Title I Grant Awards, 1992–2005

Eligible metropolitan areas	1992	1993	1994	1995	1996	1997	1998	1999	2000	2001	2002	2003	2004	2005
Atlanta, GA	$3,130,126	$5,490,571	$7,488,801	$9,091,331	$9,208,162	$12,632,117	$12,021,454	$13,147,268	$15,507,832	$15,992,692	$17,554,590	$18,751,178	$18,339,732	$19,126,568
Austin, TX	$2,124,274	$2,398,671	$3,337,861	$2,856,752	$3,175,509	$3,575,995	$3,922,582	$3,946,480	$3,995,912	$3,800,520	$3,851,321			
Baltimore, MD	$1,898,561	$3,250,343	$3,923,438	$4,715,150	$8,364,074	$10,033,688	$12,184,481	$13,478,549	$15,351,112	$16,698,367	$17,986,832	21,458,791	19,710,879	19,179,964
Bergen-Passaic, NJ			$2,019,121	$2,847,639	$3,369,095	$4,292,593	$4,354,291	$4,320,176	$4,626,995	$5,234,104	$5,313,602	5,203,065	4,814,704	4,376,432
Boston, MA	$2,823,768	$4,154,744	$6,955,035	$7,079,242	$8,360,436	$9,033,443	$9,463,130	$10,647,381	$12,469,255	$15,363,160	$15,198,508	15,398,403	14,848,697	13,651,229
Caguas, PR				$902,928	$1,064,876	$1,431,210	$1,405,197	$1,610,314	$1,713,686	$1,750,404	$1,768,847	1,623,395	1,816,647	1,816,497
Chicago, IL	$4,327,603	$7,390,763	$9,625,451	$12,099,865	$13,164,930	$15,741,071	$15,995,512	$18,227,884	$19,003,954	$22,963,079	$23,005,863	23,225,285	25,426,760	24,992,277
Cleveland, OH					$1,384,956	$1,877,513	$2,459,443	$2,933,058	$3,107,796	$3,384,855	$3,535,615	3,593,703	3,486,936	3,464,211
Dallas, TX	$3,119,688	$4,542,034	$6,935,644	$8,176,385	$7,820,653	$8,129,583	$9,082,217	$10,164,078	$11,077,000	$12,098,406	$12,001,240	13,205,009	12,820,583	13,038,882
Denver, CO		$2,091,739	$3,375,884	$3,092,041	$3,549,707	$4,668,572	$4,278,161	$4,150,341	$4,581,734	$4,840,128	$4,741,353	5,035,812	4,529,097	4,305,958
Detroit, MI			$2,849,559	$2,406,902	$4,405,380	$6,087,121	$5,628,350	$6,585,744	$7,234,813	$7,612,631	$8,363,876	8,766,530	8,590,281	8,605,663
Dutchess County, NY			$581,761	$776,847	$854,481	$1,220,662	$1,208,858	$1,362,331	$1,271,442	$1,337,041	$1,231,242	1,222,865		
Ft. Lauderdale, FL	$3,065,827	$4,591,215	$6,814,599	$5,091,994	$6,584,204	$8,312,185	$10,128,631	$10,810,324	$11,437,539	$13,816,037	$14,872,845	14,695,524	14,749,550	14,611,634
Ft. Worth, TX					$2,255,398	$1,902,232	$2,618,024	$2,935,543	$2,968,606	$3,298,024	$3,376,074	3,503,726	3,373,450	3,502,064
Hartford, CT					$3,048,467	$2,661,473	$3,613,029	$4,019,409	$4,417,574	$4,868,180	$4,648,410	4,679,151	4,552,237	4,498,360
Houston, TX	$5,826,845	$7,820,319	$10,133,592	$10,233,981	$10,312,524	$10,768,697	$12,722,479	$15,489,996	$17,665,434	$19,283,756	$19,720,190	20,526,823	19,128,572	19,911,575
Hudson	$2,181,853	$3,618,220	$4,140,141	$2,418,868	$3,767,874	$4,600,103	$5,320,300	$5,015,785	$5,541,714	$6,167,889	$6,278,761	6,426,456	5,884,194	5,644,838
Jacksonville, FL					$2,725,251	$3,762,713	$3,443,168	$3,683,146	$4,175,873	$4,799,813	$5,019,332	5,166,800	4,863,093	5,025,194
Jersey City, NJ				$2,726,195	$2,514,291	$2,884,537	$2,622,409	$2,952,910	$3,064,120	$3,386,127	$3,328,170	3,138,000	3,240,813	2,786,392
Kansas City, MO							$75,000	$3,402,697	$3,689,337	$4,455,787	$4,231,997	4,658,661	4,473,401	4,531,754
Las Vegas, NV														
Los Angeles, CA	$9,788,087	$19,190,269	$25,568,865	$31,216,202	$26,555,597	$30,227,298	$30,637,106	$33,540,737	$34,683,327	$35,020,216	$37,962,755	39,994,550	36,644,121	36,834,089
Miami, FL	$5,923,065	$9,716,264	$15,258,563	$19,195,347	$15,156,078	$18,863,208	$18,472,153	$21,248,387	$23,450,383	$25,385,904	$27,097,189	27,024,359	25,540,011	24,551,236
Middlesex-Somerset-Hunterdon, NJ					$2,198,883	$1,919,076	$2,597,923	$2,555,029	$2,750,975	$2,888,808	$2,925,300	2,991,173	2,723,697	2,689,723
Minneapolis-St. Paul, MN				$1,370,726	$1,990,700	$2,548,603	$2,570,712	$2,826,949	$3,216,026	$3,220,400	$3,255,148	3,093,915	3,011,747	
Nassau-Suffolk, NY		$2,012,809	$2,886,968	$3,895,849	$3,683,885	$4,697,795	$4,939,871	$5,632,012	$6,118,736	$6,532,144	$6,242,641	6,470,593	5,951,789	5,805,121
New Haven, CT			$2,136,872	$2,711,634	$4,002,182	$5,336,678	$5,348,730	$6,100,471	$6,261,941	$6,944,353	$6,644,351	7,545,500	7,069,348	7,050,669
New Orleans, LA		$1,796,972	$3,243,332	$3,503,009	$2,087,199	$4,727,682	$4,921,857	$5,695,360	$5,935,834	$6,942,652	$7,066,837	7,326,105	6,787,028	7,323,546
New York, NY	$35,894,688	$44,469,219	$100,054,267	$93,587,184	$92,241,697	$92,459,373	$95,325,334	$96,961,856	$107,560,148	$119,256,891	$117,739,488	103,875,412	122,103,117	117,906,710
Newark, NJ	$5,363,563	$3,542,848	$7,009,180	$11,791,405	$9,725,848	$11,612,530	$12,630,257	$14,390,269	$14,554,092	$16,254,538	$17,467,481	17,706,875	15,312,104	15,412,565
Norfolk, VA							$75,000	$3,665,087	$4,089,698	$4,736,759	$4,906,134	5,168,622	4,820,201	4,726,063
Oakland, CA	$2,123,466	$2,602,816	$3,929,287	$4,148,299	$4,741,595	$5,905,961	$5,926,194	$6,218,532	$6,704,657	$6,776,406	$6,987,208	7,024,473	6,611,607	6,092,561
Orange County, CA		$1,839,726	$2,702,937	$3,319,282	$3,629,317	$4,401,330	$3,810,759	$4,300,690	$4,670,880	$4,956,671	$5,564,004	5,683,092	5,233,329	5,041,476
Orlando, FL			$2,715,587	$3,194,835	$3,599,489	$4,319,349	$4,609,839	$4,907,180	$6,007,600	$6,497,014	$7,225,978	7,329,133	7,821,786	7,963,150
Philadelphia, PA	$3,671,248	$4,729,230	$7,374,936	$9,836,096	$10,345,478	$13,465,328	$14,081,773	$16,011,451	$18,134,011	$22,114,655	$23,522,981	24,744,350	24,448,485	24,051,724
Phoenix, AZ			$2,217,471	$2,447,784	$2,901,602	$3,380,053	$3,412,037	$3,865,319	$5,001,568	$6,575,645	$6,422,556	6,867,905	6,814,427	6,467,107
Ponce, PR		$1,280,364	$1,176,793	$1,908,071	$1,685,036	$2,183,463	$2,200,114	$2,487,768	$2,460,695	$2,607,961	$2,858,721	2,611,677	2,718,331	2,431,319
Portland, OR				$2,402,734	$2,688,924	$3,472,480	$3,057,466	$3,115,251	$3,216,312	$3,513,044	$3,649,120	3,687,601	3,567,475	3,445,252
Riverside-San Bernardino, CA			$2,402,010	$2,656,331	$4,687,432	$5,986,979	$5,634,427	$6,463,388	$6,913,948	$6,940,381	$7,428,435	7,199,843	6,823,183	6,362,841
Sacramento, CA			$2,248,247		$2,463,814	$2,038,827	$2,389,370	$2,578,873	$2,744,171	$2,899,765	$2,840,714	2,660,029	2,968,051	2,782,514
St. Louis, MO				$2,581,330	$2,587,364	$3,506,350	$3,561,850	$3,664,771	$4,239,080	$4,432,316	$4,767,604	5,068,856	4,371,154	4,494,789

TABLE 9.15

Ryan White CARE (Comprehensive AIDS Resources Emergency) Act Title I Grant Awards, 1992–2005 [CONTINUED]

Eligible metropolitan areas	1992	1993	1994	1995	1996	1997	1998	1999	2000	2001	2002	2003	2004	2005
San Antonio, TX	$2,778,724			$1,731,222	$2,396,426	$3,014,191	$2,952,239	$3,014,654	$3,163,374	$3,862,398	$3,876,586	3,806,139	3,833,443	3,893,845
San Diego, CA		$3,761,979	$5,233,574	$5,628,252	$6,592,104	$8,198,109	$8,452,437	$8,872,685	$9,071,625	$10,577,352	$10,436,496	10,765,303	10,287,797	9,741,708
San Francisco, CA	$19,043,763	$27,217,076	$39,275,384	$32,119,914	$35,397,274	$37,194,634	$36,394,914	$36,218,513	$35,246,477	$35,771,651	$33,561,470	33,941,235	29,849,780	28,297,777
San Jose, CA					$2,275,044	$1,992,602	$2,445,480	$2,486,136	$2,612,060	$2,866,655	$2,754,005	2,798,524	2,656,550	2,497,465
San Juan, PR	$3,579,982	$4,679,777	$8,456,057	$10,269,416	$8,199,506	$10,550,845	$11,658,912	$11,912,865	$13,558,330	$15,094,482	$16,235,174	14,772,898	14,732,565	14,695,304
Santa Rosa, CA				$1,207,605	$1,142,456	$1,330,630	$1,225,807	$1,127,018	$1,152,406	$1,206,194	$1,131,226	1,106,742	1,107,428	1,049,715
Seattle, WA		$2,824,570	$3,233,903	$4,048,484	$4,289,545	$5,481,431	$5,060,533	$5,303,343	$5,488,688	$5,852,286	$5,978,779	6,286,678	5,842,615	5,631,611
Tampa, St. Petersburg, FL		$2,265,553	$3,304,312	$4,231,119	$4,610,201	$6,548,952	$6,536,189	$7,236,728	$8,016,131	$8,595,830	$8,530,778	8,856,949	8,719,669	9,196,277
Vineland-Millville Bridgeton, NJ				$340,644	$454,338	$677,001	$594,001	$688,648	$684,897	$807,157	$910,779	810,259	847,898	875,354
Washington, DC	$5,127,184	$7,447,578	$9,408,935	$10,787,072	$12,849,067	$15,838,868	$16,710,726	$18,322,558	$19,903,750	$24,507,346	$25,980,259	27,871,807	26,951,014	29,431,967
West Palm Beach, FL			$3,582,542	$3,770,641	$3,390,914	$5,122,618	$5,965,481	$6,711,944	$7,169,030	$7,795,848	$9,156,524	9,871,953	9,408,695	9,526,597
Total	**$119,668,041**	**$182,326,998**	**$320,336,851**	**$349,916,505**	**$372,829,731**	**$429,377,900**	**$445,326,000**	**$485,816,900**	**$526,811,000**	**$582,727,700**	**$597,256,000**	**$599,513,000**	**$595,342,001**	**$587,425,500**

SOURCE: Adapted from "Title I Funding History," and "Ryan White CARE Act: Fiscal Year 2003 Title I Awards," in "HHS Awards $600 Million for AIDS Care in Major Urban Areas," *HHS News*, and "Ryan White CARE Act: Fiscal Year 2004 Title I Awards," in "HHS Awards $595 Million for AIDS Care in Major Urban Areas," in *News Release*, and "Ryan White CARE Act: Fiscal Year 2005 Title I Awards," in "HHS Awards Almost $1.7 Billion for HIV/AIDS Care," in *HHS News*, March 2, 2005, Health Resources and Services Administration, HIV/AIDS Bureau, http://www.hhs.gov/news/press/2005pres/20050302.html (accessed November 7, 2005)

TABLE 9.16

Ryan White CARE (Comprehensive AIDS Resources Emergency) Act Title II Grant Awards, 1996–2005

State	Fiscal year 1996	Fiscal year 1997	Fiscal year 1998	Fiscal year 1999	Fiscal year 2000	Fiscal year 2001	Fiscal year 2002	Fiscal year 2003	Fiscal year 2004	Fiscal year 2005
AL	$2,756,823	$4,167,971	$5,110,076	$7,294,833	$8,223,550	$10,100,107	$11,005,960	$10,867,008	$11,317,534	$11,881,914
AK	$288,443	$362,917	$444,562	$593,491	$644,658	$863,456	$898,686	$926,023	$974,705	1,006,313
AZ	$2,260,259	$3,496,214	$4,553,503	$6,281,940	$7,876,550	$9,267,392	$10,130,689	$11,255,601	$11,648,614	12,732,077
AR	$1,369,814	$2,050,008	$2,505,494	$3,313,331	$3,729,267	$3,970,060	$4,397,016	$4,933,831	$4,933,831	5,161,119
CA	$36,282,354	$57,920,029	$73,677,524	$95,937,546	$106,594,028	$108,968,671	$115,580,982	$118,274,998	$121,425,527	121,734,064
CO	$2,509,154	$3,734,969	$4,614,053	$5,755,742	$6,501,977	$7,988,712	$7,384,159	$7,447,255	$7,759,634	7,759,634
CT	$3,651,778	$6,120,430	$8,267,209	$11,422,933	$12,473,062	$13,071,734	$13,873,014	$14,915,598	$15,175,723	15,746,598
DE	$1,259,006	$1,942,410	$2,429,055	$3,065,717	$3,444,082	$3,952,853	$4,549,172	$5,129,211	$5,340,795	5,432,326
DC	$3,332,588	$5,490,772	$7,719,573	$11,009,761	$12,208,813	$13,851,117	$15,492,398	$16,875,124	$18,323,488	18,951,519
FL	$25,220,349	$41,314,996	$53,845,136	$73,482,287	$84,151,932	$90,768,728	$99,913,339	$108,800,440	$111,668,948	116,883,905
GA	$7,394,151	$12,340,139	$16,211,799	$21,473,723	$24,609,445	$29,063,413	$31,581,983	$32,523,811	$33,354,271	36,312,311
HI	$1,180,678	$1,701,733	$1,933,618	$2,425,061	$2,714,578	$2,973,119	$2,879,231	$3,134,711	$3,298,130	3,298,130
ID	$285,657	$362,917	$444,562	$581,700	$637,862	$946,929	$977,028	$940,179	$964,689	965,496
IL	$7,260,236	$12,033,969	$15,478,545	$21,516,441	$23,741,440	$26,962,344	$29,041,633	$32,061,756	$34,870,568	36,007,864
IN	$2,762,555	$4,301,051	$5,362,040	$7,161,199	$7,813,244	$8,888,172	$9,607,370	$10,080,837	$11,402,950	11,631,445
IA	$613,264	$917,406	$1,104,116	$1,450,320	$1,597,254	$1,684,688	$1,886,371	$2,046,335	$2,067,375	2,111,150
KS	$1,050,840	$1,565,364	$1,888,481	$2,407,272	$2,680,639	$2,856,155	$2,993,080	$3,061,160	$3,061,160	3,130,712
KY	$1,344,978	$2,078,323	$2,882,026	$4,075,831	$4,679,465	$5,757,688	$6,377,776	$6,566,479	$6,688,723	6,962,984
LA	$4,080,447	$6,969,329	$9,199,630	$13,072,061	$14,659,595	$16,282,740	$19,462,270	$19,165,624	$21,324,721	23,096,176
ME	$536,845	$719,201	$806,854	$970,811	$1,053,098	$1,165,524	$1,222,848	$1,291,963	$1,333,909	1,333,909
MD	$6,521,685	$10,948,524	$14,847,982	$20,672,553	$23,625,388	$25,567,961	$28,539,346	$33,236,307	$34,509,971	36,055,252
MA	$4,836,051	$7,528,256	$9,780,533	$12,626,775	$15,135,145	$17,849,167	$19,027,859	$20,165,312	$20,190,874	20,190,874
MI	$3,897,084	$5,814,246	$7,690,514	$10,452,742	$11,836,551	$12,389,033	$13,817,447	$14,902,329	$15,455,849	15,983,050
MN	$1,249,617	$1,878,085	$2,365,346	$2,995,477	$3,429,038	$3,583,168	$3,930,918	$4,041,505	$4,059,707	4,183,467
MS	$1,868,450	$2,760,714	$3,623,766	$4,995,545	$5,940,732	$7,005,955	$7,994,828	$8,927,096	$9,454,950	10,514,013
MO	$3,131,126	$4,586,448	$5,952,010	$7,811,393	$8,842,764	$9,100,570	$10,041,335	$10,231,106	$10,250,137	10,500,632
MT	$129,912	$201,037	$375,524	$477,324	$493,995	$766,328	$784,249	$798,932	$810,671	810,671
NE	$506,277	$733,358	$931,421	$1,206,634	$1,363,635	$1,556,845	$1,752,274	$1,735,366	$1,757,215	1,757,215
NV	$2,049,946	$3,001,392	$3,898,380	$4,647,952	$4,962,828	$5,341,517	$5,768,265	$6,248,392	$6,456,309	6,654,115
NH	$332,092	$529,197	$651,190	$861,790	$927,722	$1,137,986	$1,170,914	$1,225,589	$1,257,028	1,281,115
NJ	$13,135,111	$21,380,789	$28,345,926	$37,702,846	$40,762,441	$43,471,413	$45,652,579	$47,117,129	$47,641,537	47,641,537
NM	$882,641	$1,183,568	$1,687,316	$2,476,155	$2,684,197	$2,842,890	$3,042,298	$3,338,463	$3,338,463	3,489,677
NY	$38,324,520	$64,354,160	$87,884,362	$127,095,837	$138,462,204	$147,829,027	$153,793,751	$166,416,534	$169,263,213	171,786,592
NC	$4,810,589	$7,053,271	$8,657,402	$11,672,934	$13,337,097	$16,397,641	$17,940,397	$18,905,269	$21,144,376	21,945,256
ND	$107,243	$124,390	$145,189	$175,060	$183,474	$287,207	$288,717	$292,543	$292,543	306,199
OH	$4,668,106	$7,316,497	$8,953,866	$11,834,654	$12,862,596	$13,812,449	$14,653,307	$15,732,171	$16,762,266	16,794,093
OK	$1,656,387	$2,282,191	$2,890,518	$3,902,893	$4,285,048	$5,081,993	$5,890,896	$5,923,857	$5,923,857	5,928,122
OR	$1,684,631	$2,749,308	$3,438,455	$4,333,257	$4,722,939	$4,836,281	$5,266,094	$5,719,559	$5,902,627	5,943,054
PA	$7,991,467	$12,944,947	$1,693,781	$23,632,455	$26,896,745	$29,471,755	$32,266,464	$37,124,991	$38,316,474	39,891,047
RI	$1,083,242	$1,548,831	$1,843,025	$2,354,312	$2,574,101	$2,814,801	$2,981,815	$3,104,681	$3,189,276	3,189,276
SC	$4,516,376	$6,622,883	$8,161,966	$10,934,388	$13,250,895	$16,641,780	$18,086,947	$18,549,396	$19,323,103	20,521,015
SD	$112,536	$138,843	$161,507	$205,084	$233,352	$338,771	$372,293	$391,032	$705,706	727,255
TN	$3,757,915	$5,736,623	$7,230,546	$9,818,153	$11,468,392	$14,706,935	$16,464,366	$21,178,234	$21,178,234	21,178,234
TX	$16,132,517	$25,697,515	$35,149,403	$50,244,224	$56,932,045	$66,476,848	$70,384,189	$68,629,133	$70,065,527	73,889,574
UT	$810,043	$1,251,524	$1,542,931	$2,083,114	$2,426,761	$2,788,914	$3,111,672	$3,235,191	$3,235,191	3,235,191
VT	$279,529	$342,140	$404,394	$488,047	$510,156	$787,721	$838,895	$883,059	$883,059	883,059
VA	$5,365,718	$8,116,678	$10,452,242	$13,099,292	$14,845,195	$18,847,843	$20,770,666	$20,375,565	$20,817,878	21,086,328
WA	$3,154,250	$4,898,005	$6,404,980	$8,333,780	$9,019,810	$9,311,929	$10,243,929	$10,986,852	$11,121,586	11,198,763
WV	$446,290	$740,356	$937,140	$1,422,541	$1,462,626	$1,705,633	$1,856,487	$1,943,767	$2,021,847	2,095,875
WI	$1,840,433	$2,579,528	$3,054,537	$3,812,983	$4,242,502	$4,918,809	$5,290,698	$5,183,308	$5,214,471	5,227,607

TABLE 9.16

Ryan White CARE (Comprehensive AIDS Resources Emergency) Act Title II Grant Awards, 1996–2005 [CONTINUED]

State	Fiscal year 1996	Fiscal year 1997	Fiscal year 1998	Fiscal year 1999	Fiscal year 2000	Fiscal year 2001	Fiscal year 2002	Fiscal year 2003	Fiscal year 2004	Fiscal year 2005
WY	$113,650	$137,940	$169,038	$196,506	$205,536	$329,954	$340,041	$350,383	360,347	369,918
GU	$4,970	$11,608	$11,052	$19,652	$38,809	$116,169	$118,503	$132,268	135,839	142,852
PR	$9,376,181	$12,920,475	$16,793,353	$23,401,013	$25,647,632	$26,646,201	$28,814,408	$30,748,881	31,098,002	31,098,002
VI	$197,360	$191,525	$222,610	$624,935	$667,110	$833,928	$772,935	$976,601	976,601	976,602
AS						$50,000	$50,000	$52,314	52,314	52,360
MI						$50,000	$51,323	$52,314	52,314	52,360
North Mar						$50,000	$51,323	$54,627	54,627	54,720
RP						$50,000	$50,000	$50,000	50,000	50,000
FSM						$50,000	$50,000	$50,000	50,000	50,000
Totals	$250,414,164	$397,895,000	$504,830,061	$709,904,300	$794,314,000	$874,624,471	$942,189,986	$999,308,000	$1,030,309,284	$1,059,874,618

Notes: GU is Guam, PR is Puerto Rico, VI is Virgin Islands, AS is American Samoa, MI is Marshall Islands, North Mar is Northern Marianas, RP is Republic of Palau, FSM is Federated States of Micronesia.

SOURCE: Adapted from "Ryan White CARE Act Title II Grant Awards," and "Ryan White CARE Act Title II Fiscal Year 2004 Grant Awards," in "HHS Awards More than $1 Billion to States to Help Provide Care, Services and Prescription Drugs for People with HIV/AIDS," News Release, "Ryan White CARE Act: FY 2005 Title II Awards," in "HHS Awards Almost $ 1.7 Billion for HIV/AIDS Care," HHS News, March 2, 2005, Health Resources and Services Administration, HIV/AIDS Bureau, http://www.hhs.gov/news/press/2005pres/20050302.html (accessed November 7, 2005)

CHAPTER 10

OLDER ADULTS

THE LONGEVITY REVOLUTION

As of the early twenty-first century, the United States was on the threshold of a "longevity revolution." Dr. Robert N. Butler, the first director of the National Institute of Aging and chairman of the International Longevity Center, observed that during the twentieth century, life expectancy rose further and faster than during the entire period from ancient Rome (275 BCE, when life expectancy was about twenty-six years) through the year 1900.

The combination of better sanitation (safe drinking water, food, and disposal of waste), improved medical care, and reduced mortality rates for infants, children, and young adults accounted for this tremendous increase. Life expectancy in the United States in 1900 was 47.3 years; by 1970 it had increased to 70.8 years. By 2002 the National Center for Health Statistics projected that life expectancy for those born in that year was 77.3 years. (See Table 10.1.)

THE AGING OF AMERICA

According to the U.S. Census Bureau, 12.4% of the population (approximately thirty-five million people) were sixty-five years of age or older in 2000. From just 4% of the total population in 1900, those age sixty-five and older are projected to account for 20.7% of the population, or 86.8 million people, in the year 2050. (See Table 10.2.)

Baby Boomers

The first children born during the post–World War II "baby boom" (1946–64) will be turning sixty-five in the year 2011. Baby boomers, the largest single generation in the history of the United States, will help swell the age sixty-five and older population to approximately 54.6 million in 2020. (See Table 10.2.)

The Oldest Demographic

Americans age eighty-five and older account for the most rapidly growing age group in the population. Predictions vary as to how fast this "oldest old" segment of the population is increasing. The Census Bureau's prediction is that there will be approximately 20.9 million people age eighty-five and older by the year 2050. (See Table 10.2.) Other demographers forecast more than twice the Census Bureau's estimates for this portion of the general population. Some predict that by mid-century as many as 48.7 million Americans will be over age eighty-five.

LEADING CAUSES OF DEATH AMONG THE ELDERLY

More than six out of every ten people age sixty-five and over who died in 2002 were the victims of diseases of the heart, cancer (malignant neoplasms), or stroke (cerebrovascular diseases). (See Table 10.3.)

Coronary Heart Disease

Coronary heart disease (CHD) is the leading cause of death in the United States and remains the leading cause of death among older Americans. Approximately four out of five people who died of CHD in 2002 were age sixty-five years or older. In 2002, 576,301 people age sixty-five and older died of heart disease. (See Table 10.3.)

The risk of dying from heart disease increases as we age. The death rate from CHD in 2002 for those age seventy-five to eighty-four (1,677.2 deaths per one hundred thousand population) was almost three times the rate for those age sixty-five to seventy-four (615.9 per one hundred thousand). For those age eighty-five and older, the death rate rose sharply to 5,446.8 deaths per one hundred thousand population— nearly nine times the rate for those age sixty-five to

TABLE 10.1

Life expectancy at birth, at 65 years of age, and at 75 years of age, by race and sex, selected years 1900–2002

[Data are based on death certificates]

Specified age and year	All races			White			Black or African American[a]		
	Both sexes	Male	Female	Both sexes	Male	Female	Both sexes	Male	Female
At birth			Remaining life expectancy in years						
1900[b, c]	47.3	46.3	48.3	47.6	46.6	48.7	33.0	32.5	33.5
1950[c]	68.2	65.6	71.1	69.1	66.5	72.2	60.8	59.1	62.9
1960[c]	69.7	66.6	73.1	70.6	67.4	74.1	63.6	61.1	66.3
1970	70.8	67.1	74.7	71.7	68.0	75.6	64.1	60.0	68.3
1980	73.7	70.0	77.4	74.4	70.7	78.1	68.1	63.8	72.5
1985	74.7	71.1	78.2	75.3	71.8	78.7	69.3	65.0	73.4
1990	75.4	71.8	78.8	76.1	72.7	79.4	69.1	64.5	73.6
1991	75.5	72.0	78.9	76.3	72.9	79.6	69.3	64.6	73.8
1992	75.8	72.3	79.1	76.5	73.2	79.8	69.6	65.0	73.9
1993	75.5	72.2	78.8	76.3	73.1	79.5	69.2	64.6	73.7
1994	75.7	72.4	79.0	76.5	73.3	79.6	69.5	64.9	73.9
1995	75.8	72.5	78.9	76.5	73.4	79.6	69.6	65.2	73.9
1996	76.1	73.1	79.1	76.8	73.9	79.7	70.2	66.1	74.2
1997	76.5	73.6	79.4	77.1	74.3	79.9	71.1	67.2	74.7
1998	76.7	73.8	79.5	77.3	74.5	80.0	71.3	67.6	74.8
1999	76.7	73.9	79.4	77.3	74.6	79.9	71.4	67.8	74.7
2000[d]	77.0	74.3	79.7	77.6	74.9	80.1	71.9	68.3	75.2
2001	77.2	74.4	79.8	77.7	75.0	80.2	72.2	68.6	75.5
2002	77.3	74.5	79.9	77.7	75.1	80.3	72.3	68.8	75.6
At 65 years									
1950[c]	13.9	12.8	15.0—		12.8	15.1	13.9	12.9	14.9
1960[c]	14.3	12.8	15.8	14.4	12.9	15.9	13.9	12.7	15.1
1970	15.2	13.1	17.0	15.2	13.1	17.1	14.2	12.5	15.7
1980	16.4	14.1	18.3	16.5	14.2	18.4	15.1	13.0	16.8
1985	16.7	14.5	18.5	16.8	14.5	18.7	15.2	13.0	16.9
1990	17.2	15.1	18.9	17.3	15.2	19.1	15.4	13.2	17.2
1991	17.4	15.3	19.1	17.5	15.4	19.2	15.5	13.4	17.2
1992	17.5	15.4	19.2	17.6	15.5	19.3	15.7	13.5	17.4
1993	17.3	15.3	18.9	17.4	15.4	19.0	15.5	13.4	17.1
1994	17.4	15.5	19.0	17.5	15.6	19.1	15.7	13.6	17.2
1995	17.4	15.6	18.9	17.6	15.7	19.1	15.6	13.6	17.1
1996	17.5	15.7	19.0	17.6	15.8	19.1	15.8	13.9	17.2
1997	17.7	15.9	19.2	17.8	16.0	19.3	16.1	14.2	17.6
1998	17.8	16.0	19.2	17.8	16.1	19.3	16.1	14.3	17.4
1999	17.7	16.1	19.1	17.8	16.1	19.2	16.0	14.3	17.3
2000[d]	18.0	16.2	19.3	18.0	16.3	19.4	16.2	14.2	17.7
2001	18.1	16.4	19.4	18.2	16.5	19.5	16.4	14.4	17.9
2002	18.2	16.6	19.5	18.2	16.6	19.5	16.6	14.6	18.0
At 75 years									
1980	10.4	8.8	11.5	10.4	8.8	11.5	9.7	8.3	10.7
1985	10.6	9.0	11.7	10.6	9.0	11.7	10.1	8.7	11.1
1990	10.9	9.4	12.0	11.0	9.4	12.0	10.2	8.6	11.2
1991	11.1	9.5	12.1	11.1	9.5	12.1	10.2	8.7	11.2
1992	11.2	9.6	12.2	11.2	9.6	12.2	10.4	8.9	11.4
1993	10.9	9.5	11.9	11.0	9.5	12.0	10.2	8.7	11.1
1994	11.0	9.6	12.0	11.1	9.6	12.0	10.3	8.9	11.2

seventy-four. In 2002 women had a lower incidence of death from heart disease than did men at all ages. However, at age eighty-five and over, the death rate for women from heart disease approaches that of men. (See Table 10.4.)

Since the 1950s, deaths from heart disease have consistently declined. (See Table 10.4.) Several factors account for this decrease, including better control of hypertension (high blood pressure) and cholesterol levels in the blood, although the relationship between high cholesterol and heart disease lessens with age and in older age reverses its relation to mortality (B. A. Golomb, "Implications of Statin Adverse Effects in the Elderly," *Expert Opinion on Drug Safety*, vol 4, no. 3, May 2005). Changes in lifestyle, such as the inclusion of physical exercise and a healthy diet, help decrease the incidence of heart disease. The expanding use of trained mobile emergency personnel (paramedics) in most urban areas has also contributed to the decrease, and widespread use of cardiopulmonary resuscitation (CPR) and new drugs have increased the likelihood of surviving an initial heart attack.

TABLE 10.1

Life expectancy at birth, at 65 years of age, and at 75 years of age, by race and sex, selected years 1900–2002 [CONTINUED]

[Data are based on death certificates]

Specified age and year	All races			White			Black or African American[a]		
	Both sexes	Male	Female	Both sexes	Male	Female	Both sexes	Male	Female
1995	11.0	9.7	11.9	11.1	9.7	12.0	10.2	8.8	11.1
1996	11.1	9.8	12.0	11.1	9.8	12.0	10.3	9.0	11.2
1997	11.2	9.9	12.1	11.2	9.9	12.1	10.7	9.3	11.5
1998	11.3	10.0	12.2	11.3	10.0	12.2	10.5	9.2	11.3
1999	11.2	10.0	12.1	11.2	10.0	12.1	10.4	9.2	11.1
2000[d]	11.4	10.1	12.3	11.4	10.1	12.3	10.7	9.2	11.6
2001	11.5	10.2	12.4	11.5	10.2	12.3	10.8	9.3	11.7
2002	11.5	10.3	12.4	11.5	10.3	12.3	10.9	9.5	11.7

[a]Data shown for 1900–60 are for the nonwhite population.
[b]Death registration area only. The death registration area increased from 10 states and the District of Columbia in 1900 to the coterminous United States in 1933.
[c]Includes deaths of persons who were not residents of the 50 states and the District of Columbia.
[d]Life expectancies (LEs) for 2000 were revised and may differ from those shown previously. LEs for 2000 were computed using population counts from census 2000 and replace LEs for 2000 using 1990-based postcensal estimates.
Notes: "—"=Data not available. Populations for computing life expectancy for 1991–99 are 1990-based postcensal estimates of U.S. resident population. In 1997 life table methodology was revised to construct complete life tables by single years of age that extend to age 100. Previously abridged life tables were constructed for 5-year age groups ending with 85 years and over. Life table values for 2000 and later years were computed using a slight modification of the new life table method due to a change in the age detail of populations received from the U.S. Census Bureau.

SOURCE: "Table 27. Life Expectancy at Birth, at 65 Years of Age, and at 75 Years of Age, according to Race and Sex: United States, Selected Years 1900–2002," in *Health, United States, 2005*, Centers for Disease Control and Prevention, National Center for Health Statistics, November 2005, http://www.cdc.gov/nchs/data/hus/hus05.pdf (accessed February 27, 2006)

Until the 1990s almost all research on heart disease focused on white, middle-aged males. Researchers, physicians, and public health officials agree that more research as well as prevention efforts should be directed toward women, racial and ethnic minorities, and older adults. According to the American Heart Association (AHA), 38% of women who have heart attacks die within the first year after the incident, compared with only 25% of men. The AHA also notes that in recent years physicians and researchers have discovered that the symptoms of heart attack can be significantly different for women than for men, suggesting the need for further research and public education efforts.

Cancer

Cancer (malignant neoplasms) is the second-leading cause of death among older adults. In 2002, 391,001 people sixty-five and older died of cancer. (See Table 10.3.) The risk of developing many cancers increases with age and varies by race and ethnicity. (See Table 10.5 and Table 10.6.)

For example, the older a man gets, the more likely he is to develop prostate cancer. The chance of a fatality from prostate cancer also rises with age. The American Cancer Society (*Cancer Facts & Figures 2006*, Atlanta, GA, 2006) reports that each year more than 65% of men newly diagnosed with prostate cancer are older than sixty-five. The probability of developing prostate cancer is one in 10,149 for men who are younger than forty; one in thirty-eight for forty- to fifty-nine-year-olds; and one in fourteen for men ages sixty to sixty-nine. (See Table 10.5.)

Stroke

Stroke (cerebrovascular disease) is the third-leading cause of death and the principal cause of serious disability among older adults, and its incidence increases markedly with age. In 2002, 143,293 people age sixty-five and older died of a stroke. (See Table 10.3.) In 2002 the death rate from stroke for those age sixty-five to seventy-four was 120.3 deaths per one hundred thousand. This rate more than triples for each successive decade of age after that, to 431 deaths from stroke per one hundred thousand for ages seventy-five to eighty-four, and 1,445.9 deaths per one hundred thousand population for those eighty-five and older. (See Table 10.7.)

Stroke is also responsible for late-life dementia, which, together with Alzheimer's disease, accounts for 90% of all dementia (the other 10% are reversible dementias caused by conditions such as head injury, alcoholism, and pernicious anemia). Death rates from stroke have declined since the 1950s. (See Table 10.7.) Stroke, however, leaves approximately one-third of the survivors with severe disabilities, and they require continued care.

DEMENTIA

Older people with mental problems were once labeled "senile." However, researchers have found that physical disorders can cause progressive deterioration of mental and neurological functions. These disorders produce symptoms that are collectively known as dementia. Symptoms of dementia include loss of language functions, inability to think abstractly, inability to care for

TABLE 10.2

Projected population by age and sex, selected years 2000–50

[In thousands except as indicated. As of July 1. Resident population.]

Population or percent, sex, and age	2000	2010	2020	2030	2040	2050
Population						
Total						
Total	282,125	308,936	335,805	363,584	391,946	419,854
0–4	19,218	21,426	22,932	24,272	26,299	28,080
5–19	61,331	61,810	65,955	70,832	75,326	81,067
20–44	104,075	104,444	108,632	114,747	121,659	130,897
45–64	62,440	81,012	83,653	82,280	88,611	93,104
65–84	30,794	34,120	47,363	61,850	64,640	65,844
85+	4,267	6,123	7,269	9,603	15,409	20,861
Male						
Total	138,411	151,815	165,093	178,563	192,405	206,477
0–4	9,831	10,947	11,716	12,399	13,437	14,348
5–19	31,454	31,622	33,704	36,199	38,496	41,435
20–44	52,294	52,732	54,966	58,000	61,450	66,152
45–64	30,381	39,502	40,966	40,622	43,961	46,214
65–84	13,212	15,069	21,337	28,003	29,488	30,579
85+	1,240	1,942	2,403	3,340	5,573	7,749
Female						
Total	143,713	157,121	170,711	185,022	199,540	213,377
0–4	9,387	10,479	11,216	11,873	12,863	13,732
5–19	29,877	30,187	32,251	34,633	36,831	39,632
20–44	51,781	51,711	53,666	56,747	60,209	64,745
45–64	32,059	41,510	42,687	41,658	44,650	46,891
65–84	17,582	19,051	26,026	33,848	35,152	35,265
85+	3,028	4,182	4,866	6,263	9,836	13,112
Percent of total						
Total						
Total	100.0	100.0	100.0	100.0	100.0	100.0
0–4	6.8	6.9	6.8	6.7	6.7	6.7
5–19	21.7	20.0	19.6	19.5	19.2	19.3
20–44	36.9	33.8	32.3	31.6	31.0	31.2
45–64	22.1	26.2	24.9	22.6	22.6	22.2
65–84	10.9	11.0	14.1	17.0	16.5	15.7
85+	1.5	2.0	2.2	2.6	3.9	5.0
Male						
Total	100.0	100.0	100.0	100.0	100.0	100.0
0–4	7.1	7.2	7.1	6.9	7.0	6.9
5–19	22.7	20.8	20.4	20.3	20.0	20.1
20–44	37.8	34.7	33.3	32.5	31.9	32.0
45–64	21.9	26.0	24.8	22.7	22.8	22.4
65–84	9.5	9.9	12.9	15.7	15.3	14.8
85+	0.9	1.3	1.5	1.9	2.9	3.8
Female						
Total	100.0	100.0	100.0	100.0	100.0	100.0
0–4	6.5	6.7	6.6	6.4	6.4	6.4
5–19	20.8	19.2	18.9	18.7	18.5	18.6
20–44	36.0	32.9	31.4	30.7	30.2	30.3
45–64	22.3	26.4	25.0	22.5	22.4	22.0
65–84	12.2	12.1	15.2	18.3	17.6	16.5
85+	2.1	2.7	2.9	3.4	4.9	6.1

SOURCE: "Table 2a. Projected Population of the United States, by Age and Sex: 2000 to 2050," in *U.S. Interim Projections by Age, Sex, Race, and Hispanic Origin*, U.S. Census Bureau, March 18, 2004, http://www.census.gov/ipc/www/usinterimproj/natprojtab02a.pdf (accessed November 8, 2005)

oneself, personality change, emotional instability, and loss of a sense of time or place.

Dementia has become a serious health problem in developed countries, including the United States, because older adults are living even longer. In 2000 the Federal Interagency Forum on Aging-Related Statistics estimated that approximately 10% of those older than age sixty-five, 20% of those older than age seventy-five, and nearly 36% of those over age eighty-five suffer from dementia.

Alzheimer's Disease

Alzheimer's disease (AD) is the single most common cause of dementia. It is a progressive, degenerative disease that attacks the brain and results in severely impaired memory, thinking, and behavior. First described in 1906 by the German neuropathologist Alois Alzheimer, the disorder may strike people in their forties and fifties, but most victims are over age sixty-five.

TABLE 10.3

Leading causes of death and numbers of deaths, by age, 1980 and 2002

[Data are based on death certificates]

Age and rank order	1980		2002	
	Cause of death	Deaths	Cause of death	Deaths
Under 1 year				
...	All causes	45,526	All causes	28,034
1	Congenital anomalies	9,220	Congenital malformations, deformations and chromosomal abnormalities	5,623
2	Sudden infant death syndrome	5,510	Disorders related to short gestation and low birth weight, not elsewhere classified	4,637
3	Respiratory distress syndrome	4,989	Sudden infant death syndrome	2,295
4	Disorders relating to short gestation and unspecified low birthweight	3,648	Newborn affected by maternal complications of pregnancy	1,708
5	Newborn affected by maternal complications of pregnancy	1,572	Newborn affected by complications of placenta, cord and membranes	1,028
6	Intrauterine hypoxia and birth asphyxia	1,497	Unintentional injuries	946
7	Unintentional injuries	1,166	Respiratory distress of newborn	943
8	Birth trauma	1,058	Bacterial sepsis of newborn	749
9	Pneumonia and influenza	1,012	Diseases of circulatory system	667
10	Newborn affected by complications of placenta, cord, and membranes	985	Intrauterine hypoxia and birth asphyxia	583
1–4 years				
...	All causes	8,187	All causes	4,858
1	Unintentional injuries	3,313	Unintentional injuries	1,641
2	Congenital anomalies	1,026	Congenital malformations, deformations and chromosomal abnormalities	530
3	Malignant neoplasms	573	Homicide	423
4	Diseases of heart	338	Malignant neoplasms	402
5	Homicide	319	Diseases of heart	165
6	Pneumonia and influenza	267	Influenza and pneumonia	110
7	Meningitis	223	Septicemia	79
8	Meningococcal infection	110	Chronic lower respiratory diseases	65
8	...	...	Certain conditions originating in the perinatal period	65
9	Certain conditions originating in the perinatal period	84	...	...
10	Septicemia	71	In situ neoplasms, benign neoplasms and neoplasms of uncertain or unknown behavior	60
5–14 years				
...	All causes	10,689	All causes	7,150
1	Unintentional injuries	5,224	Unintentional injuries	2,718
2	Malignant neoplasms	1,497	Malignant neoplasms	1,072
3	Congenital anomalies	561	Congenital malformations, deformations and chromosomal abnormalities	417
4	Homicide	415	Homicide	356
5	Diseases of heart	330	Suicide	264
6	Pneumonia and influenza	194	Diseases of heart	255
7	Suicide	142	Chronic lower respiratory diseases	136
8	Benign neoplasms	104	Septicemia	95
9	Cerebrovascular diseases	95	Cerebrovascular diseases	91
9	...	...	Influenza and pneumonia	91
10	Chronic obstructive pulmonary diseases	85	...	...

Dr. Alzheimer's autopsy of a severely demented fifty-five-year-old woman revealed deposits of "neuritic plaques" and "neurofibrillary tangles." The latter characteristic, the presence of twisted and tangled fibers in the brain cells, is the anatomical hallmark of the disease.

SYMPTOMS. AD has been described as "a dementia of gradual onset and progressive decline." Mild or early AD is not easily distinguishable from the characteristics of normal aging—mild episodes of forgetfulness and disorientation. Gradually, the AD patient may experience confusion; language problems, such as trouble finding words; impaired judgment; disorientation in place and time; and changes in mood, behavior, and personality. The speed with which these changes occur varies, but eventually the disease leaves patients unable to care for themselves.

In the terminal stages of AD, patients require care twenty-four hours a day. They no longer recognize family members or themselves and need help with simple daily activities, such as eating, dressing, bathing, and using the

TABLE 10.3

Leading causes of death and numbers of deaths, by age, 1980 and 2002 [CONTINUED]

[Data are based on death certificates]

Age and rank order	1980 Cause of death	Deaths	2002 Cause of death	Deaths
15–24 years				
. . .	All causes	49,027	All causes	33,046
1	Unintentional injuries	26,206	Unintentional injuries	15,412
2	Homicide	6,537	Homicide	5,219
3	Suicide	5,239	Suicide	4,010
4	Malignant neoplasms	2,683	Malignant neoplasms	1,730
5	Diseases of heart	1,223	Diseases of heart	1,022
6	Congenital anomalies	600	Congenital malformations, deformations and chromosomal abnormalities	492
7	Cerebrovascular diseases	418	Chronic lower respiratory diseases	192
8	Pneumonia and influenza	348	Human immunodeficiency virus (HIV) disease	178
9	Chronic obstructive pulmonary diseases	141	Diabetes mellitus	171
9	. . .	. . .	Cerebrovascular diseases	171
10	Anemias	133	. . .	. . .
25–44 years				
. . .	All causes	108,658	All causes	132,495
1	Unintentional injuries	26,722	Unintentional injuries	29,279
2	Malignant neoplasms	17,551	Malignant neoplasms	19,957
3	Diseases of heart	14,513	Diseases of heart	16,853
4	Homicide	10,983	Suicide	11,897
5	Suicide	9,855	Homicide	7,728
6	Chronic liver disease and cirrhosis	4,782	Human immunodeficiency virus (HIV) disease	7,546
7	Cerebrovascular diseases	3,154	Chronic liver disease and cirrhosis	3,528
8	Diabetes mellitus	1,472	Cerebrovascular diseases	2,992
9	Pneumonia and influenza	1,467	Diabetes mellitus	2,806
10	Congenital anomalies	817	Influenza and pneumonia	1,316
45–64 years				
. . .	All causes	425,338	All causes	425,727
1	Diseases of heart	148,322	Malignant neoplasms	143,028
2	Malignant neoplasms	135,675	Diseases of heart	101,804
3	Cerebrovascular diseases	19,909	Unintentional injuries	23,020
4	Unintentional injuries	18,140	Cerebrovascular diseases	15,952
5	Chronic liver disease and cirrhosis	16,089	Diabetes mellitus	15,518
6	Chronic obstructive pulmonary diseases	11,514	Chronic lower respiratory diseases	14,755
7	Diabetes mellitus	7,977	Chronic liver disease and cirrhosis	13,313
8	Suicide	7,079	Suicide	9,926
9	Pneumonia and influenza	5,804	Human immunodeficiency virus (HIV) disease	5,821
10	Homicide	4,019	Septicemia	5,434
65 years and over				
. . .	All causes	1,341,848	All causes	1,811,720
1	Diseases of heart	595,406	Diseases of heart	576,301
2	Malignant neoplasms	258,389	Malignant neoplasms	391,001
3	Cerebrovascular diseases	146,417	Cerebrovascular diseases	143,293
4	Pneumonia and influenza	45,512	Chronic lower respiratory diseases	108,313
5	Chronic obstructive pulmonary diseases	43,587	Influenza and pneumonia	58,826
6	Atherosclerosis	28,081	Alzheimer's disease	58,289
7	Diabetes mellitus	25,216	Diabetes mellitus	54,715
8	Unintentional injuries	24,844	Nephritis, nephrotic syndrome and nephrosis	34,316
9	Nephritis, nephrotic syndrome, and nephrosis	12,968	Unintentional injuries	33,641
10	Chronic liver disease and cirrhosis	9,519	Septicemia	26,670

Note: ". . ."=Category not applicable.

SOURCE: "Table 32. Leading Causes of Death and Numbers of Deaths, according to Age: United States, 1980 and 2002," in *Health, United States, 2005*, Centers for Disease Control and Prevention, National Center for Health Statistics, November 2005, http://www.cdc.gov/nchs/data/hus/hus05.pdf (accessed February 27, 2006)

TABLE 10.4

Death rates for diseases of the heart, by sex, race, Hispanic origin, and age, selected years 1950–2002

[Data are based on death certificates]

Sex, race, Hispanic origin, and age	1950[a]	1960[a]	1970	1980	1990	2000	2001	2002
All persons				Deaths per 100,000 resident population				
All ages, age adjusted[b]	586.8	559.0	492.7	412.1	321.8	257.6	247.8	240.8
All ages, crude	355.5	369.0	362.0	336.0	289.5	252.6	245.8	241.7
Under 1 year	3.5	6.6	13.1	22.8	20.1	13.0	11.9	12.4
1–4 years	1.3	1.3	1.7	2.6	1.9	1.2	1.5	1.1
5–14 years	2.1	1.3	0.8	0.9	0.9	0.7	0.7	0.6
15–24 years	6.8	4.0	3.0	2.9	2.5	2.6	2.5	2.5
25–34 years	19.4	15.6	11.4	8.3	7.6	7.4	8.0	7.9
35–44 years	86.4	74.6	66.7	44.6	31.4	29.2	29.6	30.5
45–54 years	308.6	271.8	238.4	180.2	120.5	94.2	92.9	93.7
55–64 years	808.1	737.9	652.3	494.1	367.3	261.2	246.9	241.5
65–74 years	1,839.8	1,740.5	1,558.2	1,218.6	894.3	665.6	635.1	615.9
75–84 years	4,310.1	4,089.4	3,683.8	2,993.1	2,295.7	1,780.3	1,725.7	1,677.2
85 years and over	9,150.6	9,317.8	7,891.3	7,777.1	6,739.9	5,926.1	5,664.2	5,446.8
Male								
All ages, age adjusted[b]	697.0	687.6	634.0	538.9	412.4	320.0	305.4	297.4
All ages, crude	423.4	439.5	422.5	368.6	297.6	249.8	242.5	240.7
Under 1 year	4.0	7.8	15.1	25.5	21.9	13.3	11.8	12.9
1–4 years	1.4	1.4	1.9	2.8	1.9	1.4	1.5	1.1
5–14 years	2.0	1.4	0.9	1.0	0.9	0.8	0.7	0.7
15–24 years	6.8	4.2	3.7	3.7	3.1	3.2	3.2	3.3
25–34 years	22.9	20.1	15.2	11.4	10.3	9.6	10.3	10.5
35–44 years	118.4	112.7	103.2	68.7	48.1	41.4	41.7	43.1
45–54 years	440.5	420.4	376.4	282.6	183.0	140.2	136.6	138.4
55–64 years	1,104.5	1,066.9	987.2	746.8	537.3	371.7	349.8	343.4
65–74 years	2,292.3	2,291.3	2,170.3	1,728.0	1,250.0	898.3	851.3	827.1
75–84 years	4,825.0	4,742.4	4,534.8	3,834.3	2,968.2	2,248.1	2,177.3	2,110.1
85 years and over	9,659.8	9,788.9	8,426.2	8,752.7	7,418.4	6,430.0	6,040.5	5,823.5
Female								
All ages, age adjusted[b]	484.7	447.0	381.6	320.8	257.0	210.9	203.9	197.2
All ages, crude	288.4	300.6	304.5	305.1	281.8	255.3	249.0	242.7
Under 1 year	2.9	5.4	10.9	20.0	18.3	12.5	12.0	11.8
1–4 years	1.2	1.1	1.6	2.5	1.9	1.0	1.4	1.0
5–14 years	2.2	1.2	0.8	0.9	0.8	0.5	0.7	0.6
15–24 years	6.7	3.7	2.3	2.1	1.8	2.1	1.8	1.7
25–34 years	16.2	11.3	7.7	5.3	5.0	5.2	5.6	5.2
35–44 years	55.1	38.2	32.2	21.4	15.1	17.2	17.6	18.0
45–54 years	177.2	127.5	109.9	84.5	61.0	49.8	50.7	50.6
55–64 years	510.0	429.4	351.6	272.1	215.7	159.3	151.8	147.2
65–74 years	1,419.3	1,261.3	1,082.7	828.6	616.8	474.0	455.9	440.1
75–84 years	3,872.0	3,582.7	3,120.8	2,497.0	1,893.8	1,475.1	1,428.9	1,389.7
85 years and over	8,796.1	9,016.8	7,591.8	7,350.5	6,478.1	5,720.9	5,506.8	5,283.3
White male[c]								
All ages, age adjusted[b]	700.2	694.5	640.2	539.6	409.2	316.7	301.8	294.1
All ages, crude	433.0	454.6	438.3	384.0	312.7	265.8	257.8	256.0
45–54 years	423.6	413.2	365.7	269.8	170.6	130.7	127.0	128.6
55–64 years	1,081.7	1,056.0	979.3	730.6	516.7	351.8	330.8	324.0
65–74 years	2,308.3	2,297.9	2,177.2	1,729.7	1,230.5	877.8	829.1	807.8
75–84 years	4,907.3	4,839.9	4,617.6	3,883.2	2,983.4	2,247.0	2,175.8	2,112.0
85 years and over	9,950.5	10,135.8	8,818.0	8,958.0	7,558.7	6,560.8	6,157.2	5,939.8
Black or African American male[c]								
All ages, age adjusted[b]	639.4	615.2	607.3	561.4	485.4	392.5	384.5	371.0
All ages, crude	346.2	330.6	330.3	301.0	256.8	211.1	209.0	206.3
45–54 years	622.5	514.0	512.8	433.4	328.9	247.2	242.6	246.0
55–64 years	1,433.1	1,236.8	1,135.4	987.2	824.0	631.2	602.2	605.3
65–74 years	2,139.1	2,281.4	2,237.8	1,847.2	1,632.9	1,268.8	1,245.8	1,192.7
75–84 years[d]	4,106.1	3,533.6	3,783.4	3,578.8	3,107.1	2,597.6	2,569.3	2,449.6
85 years and over	—	6,037.9	5,367.6	6,819.5	6,479.6	5,633.5	5,459.9	5,125.7

toilet. Eventually, they may become incontinent, blind, and unable to communicate. The course of the disease varies widely—some patients die within a few years of diagnosis, while others have lived as long as twenty-five years.

PREVALENCE. In 2002, 58,289 deaths from AD were reported for those age sixty-five and older. (See Table 10.3.) Liesi E. Hebert et al reported in "Alzheimer Disease in the U.S. Population: Prevalence Estimates Using the 2000 Census" (*Archives of Neurology*, vol. 60,

TABLE 10.4

Death rates for diseases of the heart, by sex, race, Hispanic origin, and age, selected years 1950–2002 [CONTINUED]

[Data are based on death certificates]

Sex, race, Hispanic origin, and age	1950[a]	1960[a]	1970	1980	1990	2000	2001	2002
American Indian or Alaska Native male[c]				Deaths per 100,000 resident population				
All ages, age adjusted[b]	—	—	—	320.5	264.1	222.2	200.7	201.2
All ages, crude	—	—	—	130.6	108.0	90.1	89.1	92.0
45–54 years	—	—	—	238.1	173.8	108.5	109.1	104.2
55–64 years	—	—	—	496.3	411.0	285.0	301.1	273.2
65–74 years	—	—	—	1,009.4	839.1	748.2	682.1	638.4
75–84 years	—	—	—	2,062.2	1,788.8	1,655.7	1,384.5	1,422.7
85 years and over	—	—	—	4,413.7	3,860.3	3,318.3	2,895.7	3,162.4
Asian or Pacific Islander male[c]								
All ages, age adjusted[b]	—	—	—	286.9	220.7	185.5	169.8	169.8
All ages, crude	—	—	—	119.8	88.7	90.6	87.3	89.4
45–54 years	—	—	—	112.0	70.4	61.1	60.1	60.6
55–64 years	—	—	—	306.7	226.1	182.6	162.0	154.2
65–74 years	—	—	—	852.4	623.5	482.5	439.1	422.4
75–84 years	—	—	—	2,010.9	1,642.2	1,354.7	1,273.8	1,252.4
85 years and over	—	—	—	5,923.0	4,617.8	4,154.2	3,688.1	3,841.3
Hispanic or Latino male[c, e]								
All ages, age adjusted[b]	—	—	—	—	270.0	238.2	232.6	219.8
All ages, crude	—	—	—	—	91.0	74.7	74.6	74.0
45–54 years	—	—	—	—	116.4	84.3	82.9	80.5
55–64 years	—	—	—	—	363.0	264.8	242.2	256.0
65–74 years	—	—	—	—	829.9	684.8	683.7	657.7
75–84 years	—	—	—	—	1,971.3	1,733.2	1,702.7	1,599.5
85 years and over	—	—	—	—	4,711.9	4,897.5	4,784.3	4,301.8
White, not Hispanic or Latino male[e]								
All ages, age adjusted[b]	—	—	—	—	413.6	319.9	304.8	297.7
All ages, crude	—	—	—	—	336.5	297.5	289.5	289.2
45–54 years	—	—	—	—	172.8	134.3	130.7	133.1
55–64 years	—	—	—	—	521.3	356.3	335.8	327.6
65–74 years	—	—	—	—	1,243.4	885.1	834.7	813.5
75–84 years	—	—	—	—	3,007.7	2,261.9	2,190.4	2,129.9
85 years and over	—	—	—	—	7,663.4	6,606.6	6,195.4	5,994.1
White female[c]								
All ages, age adjusted[b]	478.0	441.7	376.7	315.9	250.9	205.6	198.7	192.1
All ages, crude	289.4	306.5	313.8	319.2	298.4	274.5	267.7	261.0
45–54 years	141.9	103.4	91.4	71.2	50.2	40.9	41.5	41.7
55–64 years	460.2	383.0	317.7	248.1	192.4	141.3	134.3	130.6
65–74 years	1,400.9	1,229.8	1,044.0	796.7	583.6	445.2	429.0	414.7
75–84 years	3,925.2	3,629.7	3,143.5	2,493.6	1,874.3	1,452.4	1,407.9	1,368.2
85 years and over	9,084.7	9,280.8	7,839.9	7,501.6	6,563.4	5,801.4	5,582.5	5,350.6
Black or African American female[c]								
All ages, age adjusted[b]	536.9	488.9	435.6	378.6	327.5	277.6	269.8	263.2
All ages, crude	287.6	268.5	261.0	249.7	237.0	212.6	208.6	205.0
45–54 years	525.3	360.7	290.9	202.4	155.3	125.0	125.9	124.9
55–64 years	1,210.2	952.3	710.5	530.1	442.0	332.8	323.1	312.3
65–74 years	1,659.4	1,680.5	1,553.2	1,210.3	1,017.5	815.2	768.0	734.0
75–84 years[d]	3,499.3	2,926.9	2,964.1	2,707.2	2,250.9	1,913.1	1,849.6	1,821.9
85 years and over	—	5,650.0	5,003.8	5,796.5	5,766.1	5,298.7	5,207.3	5,111.2

no. 8, August 2003) that the prevalence of Alzheimer's disease and the proportion of severe disease increased dramatically with age after age sixty-five. (See Figure 10.1.) While AD can strike as early as the third, fourth, or fifth decade of life, 90% of victims are older than age sixty-five when it becomes apparent.

Hebert and colleagues also noted that the number of people with AD in the U.S. population and their age distribution will change substantially by the mid-twenty-first century. In 2000, 4.5 million people age sixty-five and older were living with AD. By the year 2050 between 11.3 and 16 million people of this age group are expected to be affected with the disease. (See Table 10.8.)

Hebert and colleagues have also determined the percentage change in numbers of people affected by AD expected between 2000 and 2025 in each state (L. E. Hebert et al, "State-Specific Projections through 2025 of Alzheimer Disease Prevalence," *Neurology*, vol. 62, no. 9, May 2004). The ten states predicted to have the highest numbers of people with AD in 2025—California, Florida, Texas, New York, Pennsylvania, Ohio, Illinois, North Carolina, Michigan, and New

TABLE 10.4

Death rates for diseases of the heart, by sex, race, Hispanic origin, and age, selected years 1950–2002 [CONTINUED]

[Data are based on death certificates]

Sex, race, Hispanic origin, and age	1950[a]	1960[a]	1970	1980	1990	2000	2001	2002
American Indian or Alaska Native female[c]				Deaths per 100,000 resident population				
All ages, age adjusted[b]	—	—	—	175.4	153.1	143.6	127.0	123.6
All ages, crude	—	—	—	80.3	77.5	71.9	68.2	68.5
45–54 years	—	—	—	65.2	62.0	40.2	42.7	29.7
55–64 years	—	—	—	193.5	197.0	149.4	126.5	124.3
65–74 years	—	—	—	577.2	492.8	391.8	384.2	365.8
75–84 years	—	—	—	1,364.3	1,050.3	1,044.1	934.3	1,002.5
85 years and over	—	—	—	2,893.3	2,868.7	3,146.3	2,510.3	2,372.5
Asian or Pacific Islander female[c]								
All ages, age adjusted[b]	—	—	—	132.3	149.2	115.7	112.9	108.1
All ages, crude	—	—	—	57.0	62.0	65.0	67.9	67.4
45–54 years	—	—	—	28.6	17.5	15.9	18.4	16.4
55–64 years	—	—	—	92.9	99.0	68.8	62.8	61.8
65–74 years	—	—	—	313.3	323.9	229.6	241.7	239.9
75–84 years	—	—	—	1,053.2	1,130.9	866.2	848.7	796.9
85 years and over	—	—	—	3,211.0	4,161.2	3,367.2	3,186.3	3,067.4
Hispanic or Latino female[c, e]								
All ages, age adjusted[b]	—	—	—	—	177.2	163.7	161.0	149.7
All ages, crude	—	—	—	—	79.4	71.5	71.8	69.7
45–54 years	—	—	—	—	43.5	28.2	27.9	30.2
55–64 years	—	—	—	—	153.2	111.2	107.2	105.7
65–74 years	—	—	—	—	460.4	366.3	363.1	346.4
75–84 years	—	—	—	—	1,259.7	1,169.4	1,155.7	1,090.8
85 years and over	—	—	—	—	4,440.3	4,605.8	4,521.1	4,032.8
White, not Hispanic or Latino female[e]								
All ages, age adjusted[b]	—	—	—	—	252.6	206.8	200.0	193.7
All ages, crude	—	—	—	—	320.0	304.9	298.4	292.3
45–54 years	—	—	—	—	50.2	41.9	42.7	42.6
55–64 years	—	—	—	—	193.6	142.9	136.0	132.0
65–74 years	—	—	—	—	584.7	448.5	431.8	417.4
75–84 years	—	—	—	—	1,890.2	1,458.9	1,414.7	1,377.2
85 years and over	—	—	—	—	6,615.2	5,822.7	5,601.6	5,384.5

[a]Includes deaths of persons who were not residents of the 50 states and the District of Columbia.
[b]Age-adjusted rates are calculated using the year 2000 standard population.
[c]The race groups, white, black, Asian or Pacific Islander, and American Indian or Alaska Native, include persons of Hispanic and non-Hispanic origin. Persons of Hispanic origin may be of any race. Death rates for the American Indian or Alaska Native and Asian or Pacific Islander populations are known to be underestimated.
[d]In 1950 rate is for the age group 75 years and over.
[e]Prior to 1997, excludes data from states lacking an Hispanic-origin item on the death certificate.
Notes: "—"=Data not available. Starting with 2003, rates for 1991–99 were revised using intercensal population estimates based on census 2000. Rates for 2000 were revised based on census 2000 counts. Rates for 2001 and 2002 were computed using 2000-based postcensal estimates. Age groups were selected to minimize the presentation of unstable age-specific death rates based on small numbers of deaths and for consistency among comparison groups.

SOURCE: "Table 36. Death Rates for Diseases of Heart, according to Sex, Race, Hispanic Origin, and Age: United States, Selected Years 1950–2002," in *Health, United States, 2005*, Centers for Disease Control and Prevention, National Center for Health Statistics, November 2005, http://www.cdc.gov/nchs/data/hus/hus05.pdf (accessed February 27, 2006)

Jersey—are the same ten that had the largest numbers in 2000.

DEPRESSION

According to the American Association of Geriatric Psychiatry, more than six million of the more than forty million Americans over the age of sixty-five suffer from depression. Family members and health care professionals often fail to recognize depression among the elderly. Because older people usually suffer from comorbidity (the presence of more than one chronic illness at one time), depression may be masked by the symptoms of other disorders.

The older adult suffering from depression may mistakenly think that depression is simply a reaction to an illness, loss, or a consequence of aging. Many sufferers fail to divulge their depression because of the stigma associated with mental illness.

Suicide

According to Dr. Barry D. Lebowitz, chief of the Adult and Geriatric Treatment and Preventive

TABLE 10.5

Probability of developing invasive cancers over selected age intervals, by sex, 2000–02

	Birth to 39 (percent)	40 to 59 (percent)	60 to 69 (percent)	70 & older (percent)	Birth to death (percent)
All sites[a]					
Male	1.43 (1 in 70)	8.57 (1 in 12)	16.46 (1 in 6)	39.61 (1 in 3)	45.67 (1 in 2)
Female	1.99 (1 in 50)	9.06 (1 in 11)	10.54 (1 in 9)	26.72 (1 in 4)	38.09 (1 in 3)
Urinary bladder[b]					
Male	.02 (1 in 4,375)	.40 (1 in 250)	.93 (1 in 108)	3.35 (1 in 30)	3.58 (1 in 28)
Female	.01 (1 in 9,513)	.12 (1 in 816)	.25 (1 in 402)	.96 (1 in 104)	1.14 (1 in 88)
Breast					
Female	.48 (1 in 209)	4.11 (1 in 24)	3.82 (1 in 26)	7.13 (1 in 14)	13.22 (1 in 8)
Colon & rectum					
Male	.07 (1 in 1,399)	.90 (1 in 111)	1.66 (1 in 60)	4.94 (1 in 20)	5.84 (1 in 17)
Female	.06 (1 in 1,567)	.70 (1 in 143)	1.16 (1 in 86)	4.61 (1 in 22)	5.51 (1 in 18)
Leukemia					
Male	.15 (1 in 650)	.22 (1 in 459)	.35 (1 in 284)	1.17 (1 in 85)	1.50 (1 in 67)
Female	.13 (1 in 788)	.14 (1 in 721)	.19 (1 in 513)	.78 (1 in 129)	1.07 (1 in 93)
Lung & bronchus					
Male	.03 (1 in 3,244)	1.00 (1 in 100)	2.45 (1 in 41)	6.33 (1 in 16)	7.58 (1 in 13)
Female	.03 (1 in 3,103)	.80 (1 in 125)	1.68 (1 in 60)	4.17 (1 in 24)	5.72 (1 in 17)
Melanoma of skin					
Male	.13 (1 in 800)	.51 (1 in 195)	.51 (1 in 195)	1.25 (1 in 80)	1.94 (1 in 52)
Female	.21 (1 in 470)	.40 (1 in 248)	.26 (1 in 381)	.56 (1 in 178)	1.30 (1 in 77)
Non-Hodgkin lymphoma					
Male	.14 (1 in 722)	.47 (1 in 215)	.56 (1 in 178)	1.57 (1 in 64)	2.18 (1 in 46)
Female	.09 (1 in 1,158)	.31 (1 in 320)	.42 (1 in 237)	1.29 (1 in 77)	1.82 (1 in 55)
Prostate					
Male	.01 (1 in 10,149)	2.66 (1 in 38)	7.19 (1 in 14)	14.51 (1 in 7)	17.93 (1 in 6)
Uterine cervix					
Female	.15 (1 in 657)	.28 (1 in 353)	.15 (1 in 671)	.22 (1 in 464)	.74 (1 in 135)
Uterine corpus					
Female	.06 (1 in 1,641)	.72 (1 in 139)	.83 (1 in 120)	1.36 (1 in 74)	2.61 (1 in 38)

Note: Data are for those free of cancer at beginning of age interval. Based on cancer cases diagnosed during 2000 to 2002.
[a]All sites exclude basal and squamous cell skin cancers and in situ cancers except urinary bladder.
[b]Indudes invasive and in situ cancer cases.

SOURCE: "Probability of Developing Invasive Cancers over Selected Age Intervals by Sex, US, 2000 to 2002," in *Cancer Facts and Figures 2006*, American Cancer Society, January 2006, http://www.cancer.org/downloads/stt/CAFF06Prob.pdf (accessed February 27, 2006). Copyright 2006 American Cancer Society Inc. Reprinted with permission.

Intervention Research Branch of the National Institute of Mental Health, almost all older people who commit suicide suffer from depression. Most suicidal older adults visit their primary care physician during the month before ending their lives, and approximately 40% visit the doctor in the week before committing suicide, though frequently for chronic health problems rather than depression. However, their depression apparently had not been accurately diagnosed or effectively treated.

Depression is especially common in nursing homes. Richard N. Jones and his colleagues determined that at least 20% of nursing home residents suffer from clinical depression ("Prevalence and Correlates of Recognized Depression in U.S. Nursing Homes," *Journal of the American Geriatric Society*, vol. 51, no. 10, October 2003). The researchers believe that this may be an underrepresentation of the magnitude of the problem. They note that depression in long-term care settings such as nursing homes is often unrecognized. In addition, when depression is recognized it is often undertreated, treated inadequately, or treated inappropriately.

Feeling lonely, abandoned, or suffering financial woes, many depressed nursing home residents end their lives by nonviolent means such as starving themselves, failing to take prescribed medication, or ingesting large amounts of drugs. This type of suicide, as a result of depression, is different from that committed by the terminally ill who, not wishing to prolong the dying process, refuse life-sustaining medical treatment.

TABLE 10.6

Cancer incidence and mortality rates by site, race, and ethnicity, 1998–2002

Incidence	White	African American	Asian American and Pacific Islander	American Indian and Alaska Native	Hispanic/Latino*
All sites					
Males	556.4	682.6	383.5	255.4	420.7
Females	429.3	398.5	303.6	220.5	310.9
Breast (female)	141.1	119.4	96.6	54.8	89.9
Colon & rectum					
Males	61.7	72.5	56.0	36.7	48.3
Females	45.3	56.0	39.7	32.2	32.3
Lung & bronchus					
Males	76.7	113.9	59.4	42.6	44.6
Females	51.1	55.2	28.3	23.6	23.3
Prostate	169.0	272.0	101.4	50.3	141.9
Stomach					
Males	10.7	17.7	21.0	15.9	17.2
Females	5.0	9.6	12.0	9.1	10.1
Liver & bile duct					
Males	7.4	12.1	21.4	8.7	14.1
Females	2.9	3.7	7.9	5.2	6.1
Uterine cervix	8.7	11.1	8.9	4.9	15.8
Mortality					
All sites					
Males	242.5	339.4	148.0	159.7	171.4
Females	164.5	194.3	99.4	113.8	111.0
Breast (female)	25.9	34.7	12.7	13.8	16.7
Colon & rectum					
Males	24.3	34.0	15.8	16.2	17.7
Females	16.8	24.1	10.6	11.8	11.6
Lung & bronchus					
Males	75.2	101.3	39.4	47.0	38.7
Females	41.8	39.9	18.8	27.1	14.8
Prostate	27.7	68.1	12.1	18.3	23.0
Stomach					
Males	5.6	12.8	11.2	7.3	9.5
Females	2.8	6.3	6.8	4.1	5.3
Liver & bile duct					
Males	6.2	9.5	15.4	7.9	10.7
Females	2.7	3.8	6.5	4.3	5.1
Uterine cervix	2.5	5.3	2.7	2.6	3.5

Note: Data are per 100,000, age-adjusted to the 2000 US standard population.

*Hispanic/Latinos are not mutually exclusive from whites, African Americans, Asian Americans and Pacific Islanders, and American Indians and Alaska Natives.

SOURCE: "Incidence and Mortality Rates by Site, Race, and Ethnicity, US, 1998–2002," in *Cancer Facts and Figures 2006*, American Cancer Society, January 2006, http://www.cancer.org/downloads/stt/CAFF06IrMr.pdf (accessed February 27, 2006). Copyright 2006 American Cancer Society, Inc. Reprinted with permission.

In the United States the suicide rate generally increases with age. In 2002 the "oldest old" (eighty-five years and older) accounted for the highest rate—eighteen suicides per one hundred thousand people. Men age sixty-five and older had a higher rate (31.8 suicides per one hundred thousand), with the oldest old men (age eighty-five and older) most likely to commit suicide (50.7 per one hundred thousand). In contrast, the rate among women age sixty-five and older was 4.1 suicides per one hundred thousand people, and that among women age eighty-five and over was 3.8 suicides per one hundred thousand. (See Table 6.1 in Chapter 6.)

By race, white men over the age of seventy-five had the highest suicide rate—40.6 suicides per one hundred thousand people for those ages seventy-five to eighty-four, and 53.9 per one hundred thousand for those age eighty-five and older. (See Table 6.1 in Chapter 6.) One generally held theory about the very high rates of suicide among white men age seventy-five and over is that they have traditionally been in positions of power and thus have great difficulty adjusting to a life they may consider useless or diminished.

TABLE 10.7

Death rates for cerebrovascular diseases, by sex, race, Hispanic origin, and age, selected years 1950–2002

[Data are based on death certificates]

Sex, race, Hispanic origin, and age	1950[a]	1960[a]	1970	1980	1990	2000	2001	2002
All persons				Deaths per 100,000 resident population				
All ages, age adjusted[b]	180.7	177.9	147.7	96.2	65.3	60.9	57.9	56.2
All ages, crude	104.0	108.0	101.9	75.0	57.8	59.6	57.4	56.4
Under 1 year	5.1	4.1	5.0	4.4	3.8	3.3	2.7	2.9
1–4 years	0.9	0.8	1.0	0.5	0.3	0.3	0.4	0.3
5–14 years	0.5	0.7	0.7	0.3	0.2	0.2	0.2	0.2
15–24 years	1.6	1.8	1.6	1.0	0.6	0.5	0.5	0.4
25–34 years	4.2	4.7	4.5	2.6	2.2	1.5	1.5	1.4
35–44 years	18.7	14.7	15.6	8.5	6.4	5.8	5.5	5.4
45–54 years	70.4	49.2	41.6	25.2	18.7	16.0	15.1	15.1
55–64 years	194.2	147.3	115.8	65.1	47.9	41.0	38.0	37.2
65–74 years	554.7	469.2	384.1	219.0	144.2	128.6	123.4	120.3
75–84 years	1,499.6	1,491.3	1,254.2	786.9	498.0	461.3	443.9	431.0
85 years and over	2,990.1	3,680.5	3,014.3	2,283.7	1,628.9	1,589.2	1,500.2	1,445.9
Male								
All ages, age adjusted[b]	186.4	186.1	157.4	102.2	68.5	62.4	59.0	56.5
All ages, crude	102.5	104.5	94.5	63.4	46.7	46.9	45.2	44.2
Under 1 year	6.4	5.0	5.8	5.0	4.4	3.8	3.1	3.2
1–4 years	1.1	0.9	1.2	0.4	0.3	*	0.3	0.4
5–14 years	0.5	0.7	0.8	0.3	0.2	0.2	0.2	0.2
15–24 years	1.8	1.9	1.8	1.1	0.7	0.5	0.5	0.5
25–34 years	4.2	4.5	4.4	2.6	2.1	1.5	1.6	1.4
35–44 years	17.5	14.6	15.7	8.7	6.8	5.8	5.7	5.3
45–54 years	67.9	52.2	44.4	27.2	20.5	17.5	16.7	16.7
55–64 years	205.2	163.8	138.7	74.6	54.3	47.2	43.4	42.7
65–74 years	589.6	530.7	449.5	258.6	166.6	145.0	140.4	135.0
75–84 years	1,543.6	1,555.9	1,361.6	866.3	551.1	490.8	467.3	445.9
85 years and over	3,048.6	3,643.1	2,895.2	2,193.6	1,528.5	1,484.3	1,380.2	1,317.9
Female								
All ages, age adjusted[b]	175.8	170.7	140.0	91.7	62.6	59.1	56.4	55.2
All ages, crude	105.6	111.4	109.0	85.9	68.4	71.8	69.2	68.2
Under 1 year	3.7	3.2	4.0	3.8	3.1	2.7	2.3	2.5
1–4 years	0.7	0.7	0.7	0.5	0.3	0.4	0.4	0.3
5–14 years	0.4	0.6	0.6	0.3	0.2	0.2	0.2	0.2
15–24 years	1.5	1.6	1.4	0.8	0.6	0.5	0.5	0.3
25–34 years	4.3	4.9	4.7	2.6	2.2	1.5	1.5	1.4
35–44 years	19.9	14.8	15.6	8.4	6.1	5.7	5.4	5.5
45–54 years	72.9	46.3	39.0	23.3	17.0	14.5	13.6	13.6
55–64 years	183.1	131.8	95.3	56.8	42.2	35.3	32.9	32.1
65–74 years	522.1	415.7	333.3	188.7	126.7	115.1	109.3	108.1
75–84 years	1,462.2	1,441.1	1,183.1	740.1	466.2	442.1	428.6	421.2
85 years and over	2,949.4	3,704.4	3,081.0	2,323.1	1,667.6	1,632.0	1,550.4	1,501.5
White male[c]								
All ages, age adjusted[b]	182.1	181.6	153.7	98.7	65.5	59.8	56.5	54.2
All ages, crude	100.5	102.7	93.5	63.1	46.9	48.4	46.6	45.7
45–54 years	53.7	40.9	35.6	21.7	15.4	13.6	12.7	12.9
55–64 years	182.2	139.0	119.9	64.0	45.7	39.7	36.1	35.6
65–74 years	569.7	501.0	420.0	239.8	152.9	133.8	128.5	123.8
75–84 years	1,556.3	1,564.8	1,361.6	852.7	539.2	480.0	458.8	437.5
85 years and over	3,127.1	3,734.8	3,018.1	2,230.8	1,545.4	1,490.7	1,386.2	1,327.4
Black or African American male[c]								
All ages, age adjusted[b]	228.8	238.5	206.4	142.0	102.2	89.6	85.4	81.7
All ages, crude	122.0	122.9	108.8	73.0	53.0	46.1	44.6	43.5
45–54 years	211.9	166.1	136.1	82.1	68.4	49.5	48.8	46.5
55–64 years	522.8	439.9	343.4	189.7	141.7	115.4	111.9	110.3
65–74 years	783.6	899.2	780.1	472.3	326.9	268.5	269.2	262.9
75–84 years[d]	1,504.9	1,475.2	1,445.7	1,066.3	721.5	659.2	613.9	587.8
85 years and over	—	2,700.0	1,963.1	1,873.2	1,421.5	1,458.8	1,349.1	1,252.2

OLDER WOMEN

Women Live Longer Than Do Men

In the United States the life expectancy in 2002 for females born in that year was 5.4 years more than for males born the same year—79.9 years and 74.5 years, respectively. (See Table 10.1.) In 2000 there were eighty-five men ages sixty-five to sixty-nine for every one hundred women in the same age span. As both sexes age, the gap widens. For those age eighty and over, there were only fifty-two men for every one hundred women.

TABLE 10.7

Death rates for cerebrovascular diseases, by sex, race, Hispanic origin, and age, selected years 1950–2002 [CONTINUED]

[Data are based on death certificates]

Sex, race, Hispanic origin, and age	1950[a]	1960[a]	1970	1980	1990	2000	2001	2002
American Indian or Alaska Native male[c]								
All ages, age adjusted[b]	—	—	—	66.4	44.3	46.1	37.5	37.1
All ages, crude	—	—	—	23.1	16.0	16.8	14.2	15.4
45–54 years	—	—	—	*	*	13.3	12.6	15.4
55–64 years	—	—	—	72.0	39.8	48.6	24.1	34.5
65–74 years	—	—	—	170.5	120.3	144.7	131.5	96.6
75–84 years	—	—	—	523.9	325.9	373.3	247.8	276.4
85 years and over	—	—	—	1,384.7	949.8	834.9	833.0	768.3
Asian or Pacific Islander male[c]								
All ages, age adjusted[b]	—	—	—	71.4	59.1	58.0	55.3	50.8
All ages, crude	—	—	—	28.7	23.3	27.2	27.5	25.9
45–54 years	—	—	—	17.0	15.6	15.0	15.9	14.9
55–64 years	—	—	—	59.9	51.8	49.3	46.2	40.4
65–74 years	—	—	—	197.9	167.9	135.6	134.7	112.9
75–84 years	—	—	—	619.5	483.9	438.7	409.8	390.3
85 years and over	—	—	—	1,399.0	1,196.6	1,415.6	1,327.7	1,233.6
Hispanic or Latino male[c, e]								
All ages, age adjusted[b]	—	—	—	—	46.5	50.5	48.9	44.3
All ages, crude	—	—	—	—	15.6	15.8	15.7	15.0
45–54 years	—	—	—	—	20.0	18.1	18.7	18.6
55–64 years	—	—	—	—	49.2	48.8	43.5	45.0
65–74 years	—	—	—	—	126.4	136.1	127.2	124.6
75–84 years	—	—	—	—	356.6	392.9	386.3	338.5
85 years and over	—	—	—	—	866.3	1,029.9	1,005.6	856.7
White, not Hispanic or Latino male[e]								
All ages, age adjusted[b]	—	—	—	—	66.3	59.9	56.5	54.4
All ages, crude	—	—	—	—	50.6	53.9	52.0	51.3
45–54 years	—	—	—	—	14.9	13.0	11.9	12.1
55–64 years	—	—	—	—	45.1	38.7	35.1	34.5
65–74 years	—	—	—	—	154.5	133.1	128.0	123.2
75–84 years	—	—	—	—	547.3	482.3	460.5	441.1
85 years and over	—	—	—	—	1,578.7	1,505.9	1,399.0	1,345.9
White female[c]								
All ages, age adjusted[b]	169.7	165.0	135.5	89.0	60.3	57.3	54.5	53.4
All ages, crude	103.3	110.1	109.8	88.6	71.6	76.9	74.0	73.0
45–54 years	55.0	33.8	30.5	18.6	13.5	11.2	10.2	10.4
55–64 years	156.9	103.0	78.1	48.6	35.8	30.2	27.6	27.4
65–74 years	498.1	383.3	303.2	172.5	116.1	107.3	99.9	99.5
75–84 years	1,471.3	1,444.7	1,176.8	728.8	456.5	434.2	421.6	414.1
85 years and over	3,017.9	3,795.7	3,167.6	2,362.7	1,685.9	1,646.7	1,563.5	1,516.9
Black or African American female[c]								
All ages, age adjusted[b]	238.4	232.5	189.3	119.6	84.0	76.2	73.7	71.8
All ages, crude	128.3	127.7	112.2	77.8	60.7	58.3	56.9	55.8
45–54 years	248.9	166.2	119.4	61.8	44.1	38.1	37.3	35.7
55–64 years	567.7	452.0	272.4	138.4	96.9	76.4	74.4	70.1
65–74 years	754.4	830.5	673.5	361.7	236.7	190.9	189.5	181.2
75–84 years[d]	1,496.7	1,413.1	1,338.3	917.5	595.0	549.2	530.3	532.2
85 years and over	—	2,578.9	2,210.5	1,891.6	1,495.2	1,556.5	1,491.2	1,434.3
American Indian or Alaska Native female[c]								
All ages, age adjusted[b]	—	—	—	51.2	38.4	43.7	44.0	38.0
All ages, crude	—	—	—	22.0	19.3	21.5	23.3	21.5
45–54 years	—	—	—	*	*	14.4	15.1	13.5
55–64 years	—	—	—	*	40.7	37.9	30.4	33.1
65–74 years	—	—	—	128.3	100.5	79.5	133.3	112.4
75–84 years	—	—	—	404.2	282.0	391.1	359.9	304.8
85 years and over	—	—	—	1,095.5	776.2	931.5	830.5	689.9

TABLE 10.7

Death rates for cerebrovascular diseases, by sex, race, Hispanic origin, and age, selected years 1950–2002 [CONTINUED]

[Data are based on death certificates]

Sex, race, Hispanic origin, and age	1950[a]	1960[a]	1970	1980	1990	2000	2001	2002
Asian or Pacific Islander female[c]								
All ages, age adjusted[b]	—	—	—	60.8	54.9	49.1	48.2	45.4
All ages, crude	—	—	—	26.4	24.3	28.7	29.8	29.2
45–54 years	—	—	—	20.3	19.7	13.3	11.3	12.6
55–64 years	—	—	—	43.7	42.1	33.3	35.2	32.1
65–74 years	—	—	—	136.1	124.0	102.8	113.2	112.5
75–84 years	—	—	—	446.6	396.6	386.0	359.6	331.7
85 years and over	—	—	—	1,545.2	1,395.0	1,246.6	1,236.8	1,149.8
Hispanic or Latino female[c, e]								
All ages, age adjusted[b]	—	—	—	—	43.7	43.0	41.6	38.6
All ages, crude	—	—	—	—	20.1	19.4	19.1	18.4
45–54 years	—	—	—	—	15.2	12.4	13.1	12.0
55–64 years	—	—	—	—	38.5	31.9	28.2	27.6
65–74 years	—	—	—	—	102.6	95.2	89.6	85.6
75–84 years	—	—	—	—	308.5	311.3	310.7	307.2
85 years and over	—	—	—	—	1,055.3	1,108.9	1,061.2	918.5
White, not Hispanic or Latino female[e]								
All ages, age adjusted[b]	—	—	—	—	61.0	57.6	54.8	53.9
All ages, crude	—	—	—	—	77.2	85.5	82.6	82.1
45–54 years	—	—	—	—	13.2	10.9	9.8	10.1
55–64 years	—	—	—	—	35.7	29.9	27.4	27.2
65–74 years	—	—	—	—	116.9	107.6	100.3	100.2
75–84 years	—	—	—	—	461.9	438.3	425.6	418.4
85 years and over	—	—	—	—	1,714.7	1,661.6	1,577.4	1,536.7

*Rates based on fewer than 20 deaths are considered unreliable and are not shown.
[a]Includes deaths of persons who were not residents of the 50 states and the District of Columbia.
[b]Age-adjusted rates are calculated using the year 2000 standard population.
[c]The race groups, white, black, Asian or Pacific Islander, and American Indian or Alaska Native, include persons of Hispanic and non-Hispanic origin. Persons of Hispanic origin may be of any race. Death rates for the American Indian or Alaska Native and Asian or Pacific Islander populations are known to be underestimated.
[d]In 1950 rate is for the age group 75 years and over.
[e]Prior to 1997, excludes data from states lacking an Hispanic-origin item on the death certificate.
Notes: "—"=Data not available. Starting with 2003, rates for 1991–99 were revised using intercensal population estimates based on census 2000. Rates for 2000 were revised based on census 2000 counts. Rates for 2001 and 2002 were computed using 2000-based postcensal estimates. Age groups were selected to minimize the presentation of unstable age-specific death rates based on small numbers of deaths and for consistency among comparison groups.

SOURCE: "Table 37. Death Rates for Cerebrovascular Diseases, according to Sex, Race, Hispanic Origin, and Age: United States, Selected Years 1950–2002," in *Health, United States, 2005*, Centers for Disease Control and Prevention, National Center for Health Statistics, November 2005, http://www.cdc.gov/nchs/data/hus/hus05.pdf (accessed February 27, 2006)

(See Table 10.9.) The U.S. Census Bureau found that in 2000 more than two-thirds of all people older than eighty-five were women—approximately three million women, compared with 1.2 million men.

Elderly Women Have More Chronic Diseases Than Do Elderly Men

Older women are more likely than men of the same age to suffer from chronic conditions, such as arthritis, osteoporosis and related bone fractures, AD, and incontinence. Women are also more likely to have more than one chronic disorder at a time (comorbidity). Arnold Mitnitski and colleagues note in "Relative Fitness and Frailty of Elderly Men and Women in Developed Countries and Their Relationship with Mortality" (*Journal of the American Geriatric Society*, vol. 53, no. 12, December 2005) that women, at any given age, were frailer than men although they had a lower mortality rate.

GERIATRICS

Geriatrics is the medical subspecialty concerned with the prevention and treatment of diseases in the elderly. In 1909 Dr. Ignatz L. Nascher coined the term geriatrics from the Greek "geras" (old age) and "iatrikos" (physician). Geriatricians are physicians trained in internal medicine or family practice who obtain additional training and certification in the diagnosis and treatment of older adults. Geriatricians rely on the findings of researchers and gerontologists (nonphysician professionals who conduct scientific studies of aging and older adults) to help older adults "maintain the highest possible degree of function and independence and avoid unnecessary and costly institutionalization."

Gerontology was unheard of before the nineteenth century, when most people died at an early age. Those who reached old age accepted their deteriorating health

FIGURE 10.1

Prevalence of severe, moderate, and mild Alzheimer's disease, in each of three age groups

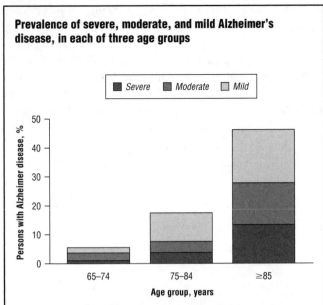

SOURCE: Liesi E. Hebert, et al., "Figure 1. Prevalence of Severe (Mini-Mental State Examination Score, <9), Moderate (Mini-Mental State Examination Score, 10–17), and Mild (Mini-Mental State Examination Score, >18) Alzheimer Disease, in Each of 3 Age Groups, in the Community Population Providing Data for These Estimates," in "Alzheimer Disease in the U.S. Population: Prevalence Estimates Using the 2000 Census," *Archives of Neurology*, vol. 60, no. 8, August 2003

TABLE 10.8

Persons with Alzheimer's disease, by age subgroups, 2000 and projected, 2010–50

[In millions]

Year and series	Age group, years 65–74	75–84	≥85	Total
2000	0.3	2.4	1.8	**4.5**
2010				
Low	0.3	2.4	2.4	**5.1**
Middle	0.3	2.4	2.4	**5.1**
High	0.3	2.5	2.5	**5.3**
2020				
Low	0.3	2.5	2.7	**5.5**
Middle	0.3	2.6	2.8	**5.7**
High	0.4	2.7	3.1	**6.2**
2030				
Low	0.4	3.6	3.2	**7.2**
Middle	0.5	3.8	3.5	**7.7***
High	0.5	4.1	4.0	**8.6**
2040				
Low	0.4	4.6	5.0	**10.0**
Middle	0.4	5.0	5.6	**11.0**
High	0.5	5.6	6.7	**12.8**
2050				
Low	0.4	4.2	6.7	**11.3**
Middle	0.4	4.8	8.0	**13.2**
High	0.5	5.6	9.9	**16.0**

*Value does not total precisely because of rounding.

SOURCE: Liesi E. Hebert, et al., "Current and Projected Number of Persons with Alzheimer Disease (in Millions) Older than 65 Years in the U.S. Population by 3 Age Subgroups," in "Alzheimer Disease in the U.S. Population: Prevalence Estimates Using the 2000 Census," *Archives of Neurology*, vol. 60, no. 8, August 2003

TABLE 10.9

Sex ratio for population 25 years and over by age, 2000 and 2030

[Men per 100 women]

Country	2000 25 to 54 years	55 to 64 years	65 to 69 years	70 to 74 years	75 to 79 years	80 years and over	2030 25 to 54 years	55 to 64 years	65 to 69 years	70 to 74 years	75 to 79 years	80 years and over
United States	98	91	85	79	72	52	98	92	89	86	81	64

SOURCE: Adapted from Kevin Kinsella and Victoria A. Velkoff, "Table 6. Sex Ratio for Population 25 Years and Over by Age: 2000 and 2030," in *An Aging World: 2001*, series P95/01-1, U.S. Census Bureau, November 2001, http://www.census.gov/prod/2001pubs/p95-01-1.pdf (accessed December 12, 2005)

as a part of aging. In the early twentieth century gerontology was born when scientists began to investigate the pathological changes that accompany the aging process.

While many developed countries have recognized the need for more geriatrics education, the United States continues to lag in offering geriatrics courses in its medical schools. As of 2003 only 30% of the ninety-one non-pediatric accredited medical specialties offered in U.S. medical schools had specific geriatrics training requirements. Among those with specific requirements, curriculum expectations were considered modest by the Association of Directors of Geriatric

Academic Programs' (ADGAP) team at the University of Cincinnati School of Medicine's Institute for Health Policy and Health Services Research (Elizabeth J. Bragg and Gregg A. Warshaw, "ACGME Requirements for Geriatrics Medicine Curricula in Medical Specialties: Progress Made and Progress Needed," *Academic Medicine*, vol. 80, no. 3, March 2005).

Decline in Numbers of Geriatricians in the United States

The Alliance for Aging Research has reported that a tremendous shortage of physicians specializing in geriatrics exists, including those in the field of psychiatry known as geropsychiatrists. The Institute for Health Policy and Health Services Research at the University of Cincinnati and ADGAP estimated that there were only 6,776 active certified geriatricians practicing in the United States in 2004.

In its May 2003 *Training and Practice Update*, the ADGAP notes that Medicare, the primary payer for most clinical services provided by geriatricians, reduced the average reimbursement to physicians by 5.4% in 2002. ADGAP suggested that "the growing gap between Medicare reimbursement and the actual costs of delivering medical care may affect the willingness of physicians to continue focusing their careers in geriatric medicine and geriatric psychiatry." The Geriatric Care Act was introduced in 2003, which would help improve payment for geriatricians. As of mid-2006, the bill had not been passed.

CHAPTER 11
PUBLIC OPINION ABOUT LIFE AND DEATH

LIFE AFTER DEATH

Since the dawn of history, many people have believed that human beings do not simply cease to exist upon their death. Numerous religions and cultures teach that the physical body may die and decompose but that some element of the person goes on to what many call the "afterlife."

Between 1972 and 1982, when the Roper Center for Public Opinion Research asked the American public, "Do you believe there is life after death?" 70% said they believed in an afterlife, and 20% said they did not. In 1996, when the Roper Center asked the same question, 73% of respondents said yes, and 16% said no. A 2002 poll conducted by the National Opinion Research Center at the University of Chicago, as part of its General Social Survey, revealed similar results. Seventy-two percent of those polled said they believed that there is a life after death, 17% did not, and 11% were undecided. Clearly, the proportion of the U.S. population believing in an afterlife appears to have remained relatively consistent over three decades.

An October 2005 CBS News poll researched what the most religiously observant Americans said on the subject of afterlife (http://www.cbsnews.com/stories/2005/10/29/opinion/polls/main994766.shtml). About nine in ten of those who attend religious services weekly or almost every week believe that humans transition to an afterlife after the physical body dies.

When asked in polls conducted by the Gallup Organization about an afterlife and what that "eternal destination" might be, many Americans expressed a belief in heaven, where people who led good lives are eternally rewarded after death, and hell, where unrepentant people who led bad lives are eternally punished. From 1997 to 2004 a majority of Gallup Poll respondents—72% in 1997 and 81% in 2004—acknowledged a belief in heaven. (See Figure 11.1.) In the 2004

survey 10% were unsure whether they believed in heaven, and 8% did not believe in it. In addition, a majority of respondents—56% in 1997 and 70% in 2004—acknowledged a belief that hell exists in the afterlife. (See Figure 11.2.) In the 2004 survey 12% were unsure whether they believed in hell and 17% did not believe in it.

CONCERNS ABOUT DEATH

Most Americans say they are not afraid of death. A September 2000 *Los Angeles Times* poll called "Aging in America" reported by Susan Pinkus, Jill Richardson, and Elizabeth Armet found that people over age sixty-five think about and fear death the least, while those ages eighteen to twenty-nine think about and fear it the most. Only 7% of those age sixty-five and older say they are afraid to die, while 20% of eighteen- to twenty-nine-year-olds express fear of dying.

Although a greater proportion of young people appear to think about and fear death than older persons, most are not preoccupied with or fearful of it. In a 2004 Gallup Youth Survey, 1,302 teens ages thirteen to seventeen years were queried about death. The largest proportion of respondents (35%) thinks "hardly at all" about their own deaths. An additional 25% never think about their own deaths, while 30% only sometimes think about dying. Only 2% of teens "almost always" think about their own deaths. (See Figure 11.3.)

In addition, American teens appear to have a realistic attitude about the possibility of their dying at an early age. In a 2003 Gallup Youth Survey, 48% of teens ages thirteen to seventeen responded that they were somewhat likely to die from a car accident before they reached adulthood. (See Figure 11.4.) This belief parallels National Center for Health Statistics data, which show that motor vehicle accidents are the

FIGURE 11.1

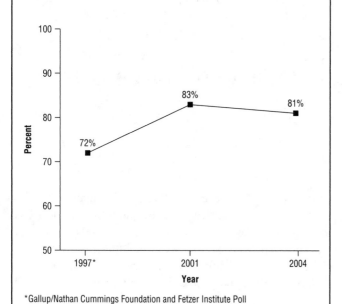

Public opinion on existence of heaven, selected years 1997–2004

FOR EACH OF THE FOLLOWING ITEMS I AM GOING TO READ YOU, PLEASE TELL ME WHETHER IT IS SOMETHING YOU BELIEVE IN, SOMETHING YOU'RE NOT SURE ABOUT, OR SOMETHING YOU DON'T BELIEVE IN…HEAVEN.

*Gallup/Nathan Cummings Foundation and Fetzer Institute Poll

SOURCE: Albert L. Winseman, "Belief in Heaven," in "Eternal Destination: Americans Believe in Heaven, Hell," *The Gallup Poll*, May 25, 2004. Copyright © 2004 by The Gallup Organization. Reproduced by permission of The Gallup Organization.

FIGURE 11.2

Public opinion on existence of hell, selected years 1997–2004

FOR EACH OF THE FOLLOWING ITEMS I AM GOING TO READ YOU, PLEASE TELL ME WHETHER IT IS SOMETHING YOU BELIEVE IN, SOMETHING YOU'RE NOT SURE ABOUT, OR SOMETHING YOU DON'T BELIEVE IN…HELL.

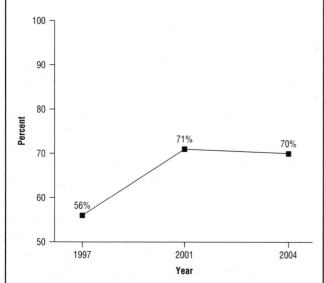

SOURCE: Albert L. Winseman, "Belief in Hell," in "Eternal Destination: Americans Believe in Heaven, Hell," *The Gallup Poll*, May 25, 2004. Copyright © 2004 by The Gallup Organization. Reproduced by permission of The Gallup Organization.

FIGURE 11.3

How often teens think about death, 2004

ABOUT HOW MUCH OF THE TIME DO YOU THINK ABOUT YOUR OWN DEATH?

[Asked of teens aged 13–17]

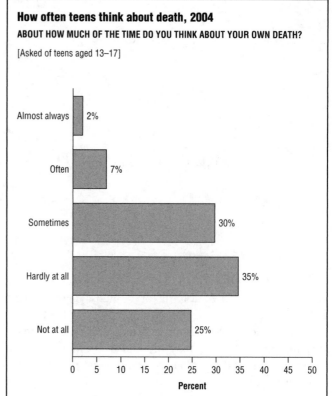

SOURCE: Linda Lyons, "About How Much of the Time Do You Think about Your Own Death?" in "One in 10 Teens Thinks Often about Own Death," *The Gallup Poll*, June 29, 2004. Copyright © 2004 by The Gallup Organization. Reproduced by permission of The Gallup Organization.

leading cause of teen death. In contrast, only 24% of teens thought they were somewhat likely to die at a young age from violent crime, 21% from disease, and 18% from terrorism.

Fearful Aspects of Dying

Although they may not fear death or spend much time thinking about their own deaths, Americans are fearful about some aspects of dying. In a survey published in 2001 and conducted by Yankelovich Partners, *Time* magazine, and CNN, two-thirds of respondents expressed much or some concern about dying in pain. Another two-thirds said they were "very fearful" or "somewhat fearful" of leaving loved ones behind, and 43% of respondents were "very fearful" or "somewhat fearful" about dying alone.

The Yankelovich Partners/*Time*/CNN survey found that the majority of people (73%) would prefer to die at home rather than in a hospital, hospice, or nursing home. Despite these expressed wishes to die at home, less than half (43%) believed they were likely to die at home—28% thought they were likely to die in a hospital, nursing home, or hospice.

FIGURE 11.4

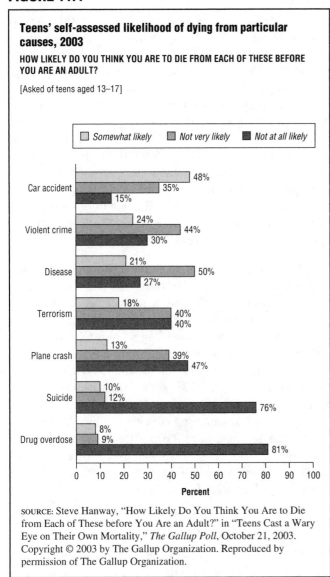

Teens' self-assessed likelihood of dying from particular causes, 2003

HOW LIKELY DO YOU THINK YOU ARE TO DIE FROM EACH OF THESE BEFORE YOU ARE AN ADULT?

[Asked of teens aged 13–17]

SOURCE: Steve Hanway, "How Likely Do You Think You Are to Die from Each of These before You Are an Adult?" in "Teens Cast a Wary Eye on Their Own Mortality," *The Gallup Poll*, October 21, 2003. Copyright © 2003 by The Gallup Organization. Reproduced by permission of The Gallup Organization.

The Seriously Ill Have Different Concerns

When patients with advanced chronic illnesses were asked, in a 1999 survey conducted by Karen E. Steinhauser for the Program on the Medical Encounter and Palliative Care, whether they agreed or strongly agreed about the importance of a variety of end-of-life issues, their concerns were quite different from those of the general population. While dying at home appears to be a priority for many Americans, only 35% of the seriously ill named dying at home as a priority, making it last on their list of concerns. Their top priorities were being kept clean (99%), having a nurse with whom they felt comfortable (97%), knowing what to expect about their physical conditions (96%), trusting their physician (94%), and being free of pain (93%).

In this same survey seriously ill patients also revealed that they felt it was very meaningful to have someone who would listen to them (95%), and more than

nine out of ten said it was important to them to maintain both their dignity (95%) and sense of humor (93%). Almost all believed it was vital to name someone to make decisions for them if they became unable to make them (98%) and to have their financial affairs in order (94%). They did not wish to be a burden to their families (89%) or to society (81%). While only half of seriously ill respondents felt it was important to be able to discuss their spiritual beliefs with their physicians (50%), more than two-thirds (69%) wished to meet with a clergy member, and 85% valued prayer. The highest spiritual priority for seriously ill patients was coming to peace with God (89%).

GETTING OLDER

Living to Age One Hundred

National surveys of the adult population by the Alliance for Aging Research (AAR) have found that Americans would generally like to live longer. In 2001 six in ten Americans (63%) said they would like to live to be one hundred years old. Men (68%) and those ages eighteen to thirty-six (69%) were more likely to want to live to be one hundred years old. These findings are similar to AAR studies from 1991 and 1996.

A more recent poll yielded different results. The October 2005 ABC News/*USA Today* poll "Most Wish for a Long Life—Despite Broad Aging Concerns" revealed that only 20% of a random national sample of one thousand adults wanted to live to be one hundred years or older. Twenty-three percent stated that they would like to live into their nineties, and 29% into their eighties.

Although a majority of Americans polled by the AAR said they would like to live to be one hundred years old, not all expect to get their wish. Nonetheless, 90% of people completing an online survey, and 60% of those who responded by telephone to a 2001 survey by the AAR, expected to live to be at least eighty years old. More than half (62%) of those surveyed online said they expected to live to be at least ninety years old. Earlier AAR surveys, conducted in 1991, 1992, and 1996, also showed that more than half of the respondents (56%, 58%, and 51%, respectively) thought they would live to be at least eighty years old.

Those surveyed by the ABC News/*USA Today* poll were asked how likely they thought it was that they would live to be one hundred years old and still have a good quality of life. Thirty-five percent thought it very or somewhat likely, while 64% thought it somewhat or very unlikely. One percent had no opinion.

Concerns about Aging

The aging of the baby boomers (the generation born between 1946 and 1964) and the growing number of people living longer have focused much attention on concerns that come with aging. The 2001 AAR survey mentioned in the previous section found that while Americans want to live longer, more than half of respondents to the online survey were concerned about losing their health (61%) and living in a nursing home (51%) in old age. Becoming a financial burden to their children (45%) and remaining attractive (46%) concerned less than half of those surveyed online. The 2005 ABC News/*USA Today* poll mentioned in the previous section asked similar questions and found that respondents were most concerned about losing their health (73%). More than half were also worried about losing their mental abilities (69%) and losing their ability to care for themselves (70%). The respondents were also worried about being a burden to their families (54%) and living in a nursing home (52%).

Nursing Homes Get Mixed Reviews

During 2001 the *NewsHour with Jim Lehrer*, the Harvard School of Public Health, and the Henry J. Kaiser Family Foundation conducted a national survey about nursing homes. Among other questions, participants were asked about their willingness to move into a nursing home.

Of the 1,309 adults surveyed, slightly less than half (47%) said they would not like, but would accept, moving into a nursing home if they could not care for themselves at home, while 43% felt that moving into a nursing home would be totally unacceptable. Only 10% of the survey respondents felt they would accept it as the best thing for themselves. A majority felt that nursing homes are understaffed, have staff that are often neglectful or abusive of residents, and are lonely. Almost half (45%) felt that nursing homes make most people who move into them worse off than prior to the move. Further, 86% of respondents believed that "most people who stay in a nursing home never go home."

In June 2005 the Henry J. Kaiser Family Foundation conducted another national survey that included questions about nursing homes (May/June 2005 Health Poll Report Survey). When asked if they thought "that the quality of nursing homes in this country has gotten better, gotten worse, or stayed about the same," only 15% thought they had gotten better. Twenty-four percent thought nursing homes had gotten worse, while 45% felt that they had stayed about the same. Sixteen percent did not answer. Respondents still felt that nursing homes are understaffed (74%), but 68% believed that nursing homes "have staff who are concerned about the well-being of their patients." On the other hand, 60% thought that "the staff at nursing homes are often poorly trained."

SUICIDE

The *General Social Survey 2002* and the *General Social Survey 2004*, both conducted by the National Opinion Research Center at the University of Chicago, found that 58% of respondents in each survey approved of suicide if a person had an incurable disease, but only a small minority approved of it if the person had gone bankrupt (8% [2002], 11% [2004]), had dishonored his or her family (9% [2002], 11% [2004]), or was simply tired of living (15% [2002], 16% [2004]). In comparison, the same poll from 1977 found that a much lower percentage of people (38%) thought suicide was acceptable if one had an incurable illness. Suicide in other situations was also found less acceptable in the 1977 survey than in the 2002 and 2004 surveys.

According to the Centers for Disease Control and Prevention, suicide is the thirteenth-leading cause of death globally, the eleventh-leading cause of death in the United States, and the third-leading cause of death among U.S. young people ages ten to twenty-four (*Morbidity and Mortality Weekly Report*, vol. 53, no. 22, June 11, 2004). Results of a 2004 Gallup Youth survey revealed that 22% of the American teens questioned (ages thirteen to seventeen) had "ever talked or thought about committing suicide." Girls were more likely (28%) than boys (16%) to have had suicidal thoughts. (See Figure 11.5.) When asked if they had ever tried to commit suicide, however, only 4% of girls and 9% of boys had. (See Figure 11.6.)

PHYSICIAN-ASSISTED SUICIDE

Many advocates of physician-assisted suicide believe that people who are suffering from uncontrollable pain should be allowed to end their lives with a lethal dose of medication prescribed by their physician. Dr. Marcia Angell, for example, former executive editor of *The New England Journal of Medicine*, claims that "those with cancer, AIDS, and other neurologic disorders may die by inches and in great anguish, despite every effort of their doctors and nurses." She believes that if all possible palliative efforts have failed to provide pain relief, then physician-assisted suicide should be permitted.

In the United States public opinion changed only slightly with regard to physician-assisted suicide between 2001 and 2004, hovering between 62% and 68% of respondents to Gallup Values and Beliefs polls (see Figure 11.7) supporting physician-assisted suicide. In 2005 the percentage dropped to 58%. Results of the same polls show that, in general, a greater percentage of Americans support euthanasia—allowing a doctor to end the life of a patient who is suffering from an incurable disease and wants to die, without requiring the patient to administer the drugs to him- or herself.

FIGURE 11.5

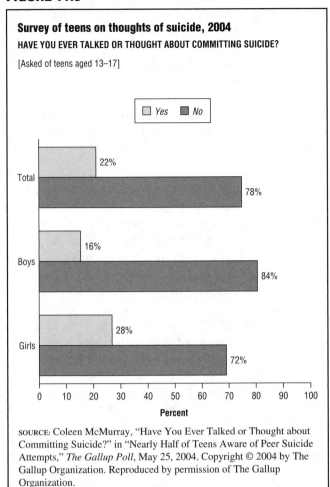

Survey of teens on thoughts of suicide, 2004

HAVE YOU EVER TALKED OR THOUGHT ABOUT COMMITTING SUICIDE?

SOURCE: Coleen McMurray, "Have You Ever Talked or Thought about Committing Suicide?" in "Nearly Half of Teens Aware of Peer Suicide Attempts," *The Gallup Poll*, May 25, 2004. Copyright © 2004 by The Gallup Organization. Reproduced by permission of The Gallup Organization.

FIGURE 11.6

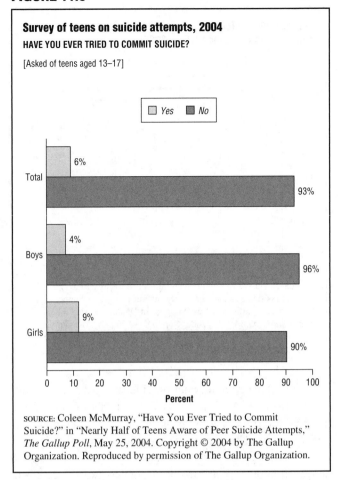

Survey of teens on suicide attempts, 2004

HAVE YOU EVER TRIED TO COMMIT SUICIDE?

SOURCE: Coleen McMurray, "Have You Ever Tried to Commit Suicide?" in "Nearly Half of Teens Aware of Peer Suicide Attempts," *The Gallup Poll*, May 25, 2004. Copyright © 2004 by The Gallup Organization. Reproduced by permission of The Gallup Organization.

Figure 11.7 shows that support for euthanasia has increased considerably since the 1940s.

When the results of the May 2005 Gallup Values and Beliefs poll are analyzed by gender, more men than women support euthanasia (84% vs. 66%, respectively) and doctor-assisted suicide (64% vs. 53%, respectively). In addition, Protestants and Catholics are more supportive of both procedures than are Evangelical Christians, and Democrats are more supportive of them than are Republicans.

Oregon Physician-Assisted Suicide Law

In 1994 Oregon became the first jurisdiction in the world to legalize physician-assisted suicide when that state passed its Death with Dignity Act. Under the act, Oregon law permits physician-assisted suicide for patients with less than six months to live. Patients must request physician assistance three times, receive a second opinion from another doctor, and wait fifteen days to allow time to reconsider.

Before the Death with Dignity Act could take effect, opponents of the law succeeded in obtaining an injunction against it. Three years later, in November 1997,

Oregon's legislature let the voters decide whether to repeal or retain the law. Voters reaffirmed the Death with Dignity Act. In August 1997, prior to voters' reaffirmation of the law, about seven in ten people (69%) surveyed by the Harris Poll indicated they would approve of a similar law allowing physician-assisted suicide in their state. Asked again in 2001 whether they would favor or oppose such a law in their own state, 61% of respondents indicated they favored such legislation.

Using Federally Controlled Drugs for Assisted Suicide

After the Death with Dignity Act took effect in November 1997, Thomas Constantine of the Drug Enforcement Administration (DEA) announced that "delivering, dispensing, or prescribing a controlled substance with the intent of assisting a suicide" would be a violation of the federal Controlled Substances Act (PL 91–513). Then Attorney General Janet Reno overruled Constantine.

In November 2001 U.S. Attorney General John Ashcroft overturned Reno's ruling in an attempt to again allow the DEA to act against physicians who prescribe lethal doses of controlled substances under Oregon's physician-assisted suicide law. In December 2001 the

FIGURE 11.7

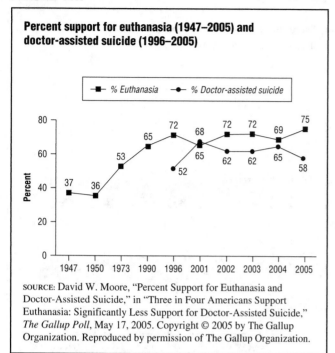

Percent support for euthanasia (1947–2005) and doctor-assisted suicide (1996–2005)

SOURCE: David W. Moore, "Percent Support for Euthanasia and Doctor-Assisted Suicide," in "Three in Four Americans Support Euthanasia: Significantly Less Support for Doctor-Assisted Suicide," *The Gallup Poll*, May 17, 2005. Copyright © 2005 by The Gallup Organization. Reproduced by permission of The Gallup Organization.

Harris Poll asked adults nationwide whether they considered Attorney General Ashcroft's effort to overrule the proposition right or wrong. More than half of respondents (58%) believed his action was wrong. On April 17, 2002, U.S. District Judge Robert E. Jones agreed, noting that "to allow an attorney general—an appointed executive...—to determine the legitimacy of a particular medical practice... would be unprecedented and extraordinary." Jones's ruling reaffirmed the Death with Dignity Act. The Justice Department appealed the ruling to the Ninth Circuit Court of Appeals. On May 26, 2004, the court upheld Jones's ruling against Ashcroft.

In February 2005 the U.S. Supreme Court agreed to hear the Bush administration's challenge to Oregon's physician-assisted suicide law. The debate of this issue began in October 2005 in the High Court.

WITHHOLDING NUTRITION AND HYDRATION: THE TERRI SCHIAVO CASE

The death of Terri Schiavo on April 1, 2005, and the events leading up to her death resulted in an intense debate among Americans over end-of-life decisions and brought new attention to the question of whom should make the decision to stop life support, most specifically nutrition and hydration. Terri Schiavo died on April 1, 2005, after her feeding tube was withdrawn days earlier. Schiavo had been in a persistent vegetative state (PVS) since 1990. Her husband, Michael Schiavo, believing that she would never recover and saying that his wife did not want to be kept alive by artificial means, petitioned a Florida court to remove her feeding tube. Her parents, however, believed that she could feel, understand, and respond. They opposed the idea of removing the feeding tube. After years of legal disputes, the feeding tube was removed permanently and Shiavo died. (See Chapter 8.)

Two primary questions emerged as the nation watched the Schiavo case unfold: (1) If you were in a PVS would you want to be kept alive by artificial means?, and (2) Who should have the final say in the matter if you had not left an advance directive (living will)? A March 29, 2005, Gallup Poll, "Americans Choose Death over Vegetative State" notes that 53% of respondents worry "a great deal" about "the possibility of being vegetable-like for some period of time." In exploring this issue more deeply, the March 13, 2005, ABC News/*Washington Post* poll "Terri Schiavo" asked a random national sample of 1,001 adults: "If you were in this condition [that of Terri Schiavo] would you want to be kept alive or not?" Only 8% said "yes," while 87% said "no." When asked who should have the final say, 65% felt that the spouse should have the final say, while 25% believed it should be the parents.

It may be hard to determine the effect of the Terri Schiavo case on the American public, but in an attempt to do so, a FOX News/Opinion Dynamics poll of March 30, 2005, asked the question: "Prior to the recent coverage of the Terri Schiavo case, had you ever discussed end-of-life medical decisions with your spouse, family, or friends?" A huge majority—78%—reported that they had. Only 20% had not. Thus, a majority of the American public had dealt with this question prior to it being highlighted in the media. Nonetheless, the case appeared to generate strong interest in living wills as suggested by a March 25, 2005, poll by *Time* magazine/SRBI (a company that conducts opinion surveys). Results of the survey revealed that 93% of respondents had heard of a living will, but only 37% had executed such a document. When those who had no living will were asked, "Has the Schiavo case made you think about drafting a living will or discussing with your family your wishes for medical treatment should you be unable to communicate them yourself?" 69% responded "yes."

IMPORTANT NAMES AND ADDRESSES

AARP (formerly the American Association of Retired Persons)
601 E St. NW
Washington, DC 20049
1-888-687-2277
URL: http://www.aarp.org

Aging with Dignity
PO Box 1661
Tallahassee, FL 32302-1661
1-888-594-7437
FAX: (850) 681-2481
E-mail: fivewishes@agingwithdignity.org
URL: http://www.agingwithdignity.org

Alzheimer's Association
225 N. Michigan Ave., 17th Fl.
Chicago, IL 60601-7633
(312) 335-8700
1-800-272-3900
FAX: (312) 335-1110
E-mail: info@alz.org
URL: http://www.alz.org

American Association of Suicidology
5221 Wisconsin Ave. NW
Washington, DC 20015
(202) 237-2280
FAX: (202) 237-2282
URL: http://www.suicidology.org

American Cancer Society
1599 Clifton Rd. NE
Atlanta, GA 30329
(404) 320-33331-800-227-2345
URL: http://www.cancer.org

American Foundation for Suicide Prevention
120 Wall St., 22nd Fl.
New York, NY 10005
(212) 363-3500
1-888-333-2377
FAX: (212) 363-6237
E-mail: inquiry@afsp.org
URL: http://www.afsp.org

Centers for Disease Control and Prevention
1600 Clifton Rd.
Atlanta, GA 30333
(404) 639-3534
1-800-232-4636
E-mail: cdcinfo@cdc.gov
URL: http://www.cdc.gov

Children's Hospice International
1101 King St., Ste. 360
Alexandria, VA 22314
(703) 684-0330
1-800-242-4453
FAX: (703) 684-0226
URL: http://www.chionline.org

Health Resources and Services Administration U.S. Department of Health and Human Services
5600 Fishers Ln.
Rockville, MD 20857
URL: http://www.hrsa.gov

Compassion & Choices (formerly Compassion in Dying and End-of-Life Choices)
PO Box 101810
Denver, CO 80250-1810
1-800-247-7421
FAX: (303) 639-1224
E-mail: info@compassionandchoices.org
URL: http://www.compassionandchoices.org

The Hastings Center
21 Malcolm Gordon Rd.
Garrison, NY 10524-4125
(845) 424-4040
FAX: (845) 424-4545
E-mail: mail@thehastingscenter.org
URL: http://www.thehastingscenter.org

International Task Force on Euthanasia and Assisted Suicide
PO Box 760
Steubenville, OH 43952

(740) 282-3810
URL: http://www.internationaltaskforce.org

March of Dimes
1275 Mamaroneck Ave.
White Plains, NY 10605
(914) 997-4488
1-888-663-4637
URL: http://www.marchofdimes.com

National Association for Home Care and Hospice
228 Seventh St. SE
Washington, DC 20003
(202) 547-7424
FAX: (202) 547-3540
URL: http://www.nahc.org

The National Council on Aging
300 D St. SW, Ste. 801
Washington, DC 20024
(202) 479-1200
1-800-373-4906
FAX: (202) 479-0735
E-mail: info@ncoa.org
URL: http://www.ncoa.org

The National Hospice and Palliative Care Organization
1700 Diagonal Rd., Ste. 625
Alexandria, VA 22314
(703) 837-1500
1-800-658-8898 (Help Line)
1-800-646-6460 (Service Center)
FAX: (703) 837-1233
E-mail: nhpco_info@nhpco.org
URL: http://www.nhpco.org

National Institute on Aging
31 Center Dr., MSC 2292
Building 31, Room 5C27
Bethesda, MD 20892
(301) 496-1752
1-800-222-2225
FAX: (301) 496-1072
URL: http://www.nia.nih.gov

National Right to Life Committee
512 Tenth St. NW
Washington, DC 20004
(202) 626-8800
E-mail: NRLC@nrlc.org
URL: http://www.nrlc.org

Older Women's League (OWL)
3300 N. Fairfax Dr., Ste. 218
Arlington, VA 22201
(703) 812-7900

1-800-825-3695
FAX: (703) 812-0687
E-mail: owlinfo@owl-national.org
URL: http://www.owl-national.org

United Network for Organ Sharing
700 N. Fourth St.
PO Box 2484
Richmond, VA 23218
(804) 782-4800
1-888-894-6361

FAX: (804) 782-4817
URL: http://www.unos.org

Visiting Nurse Associations of America
99 Summer St., Ste. 1700
Boston, MA 02110
(617) 737-3200
FAX: (617) 737-1144
E-mail: vnaa@vnaa.org
URL: http://www.vnaa.org

RESOURCES

The National Center for Health Statistics (NCHS) of the Centers for Disease Control and Prevention (CDC), in its annual publication *Health, United States*, provides a statistical overview of the nation's health. The NCHS periodicals *National Vital Statistics Reports* supply detailed U.S. birth and death data. The CDC reports on nationwide health trends in its *Advance Data* reports, *Morbidity and Mortality Weekly Report*, *HIV/AIDS Surveillance Report*, *Trends in Health and Aging*, and *Longitudinal Studies of Aging*. The Centers for Medicare and Medicaid Services report on the nation's spending for health care.

The U.S. Census Bureau publishes a wide variety of demographic information on American life. *U.S. Interim Projections by Age, Sex, Race, and Hispanic Origin* incorporate the results of the 2000 census, and *An Aging World: 2001* (2001) provides information on aging.

The Alliance for Aging Research promotes scientific research on human aging and conducts educational programs to increase communication and understanding among professionals who serve the elderly.

In 2004 Partnership for Caring and Last Acts merged to create Last Acts Partnership. This organization provided education, service, and counseling about end-of-life care. In 2005 Last Acts Partnership ceased its activities, and all rights and copyrights to material produced by Partnership for Caring, Last Acts, and Last Acts Partnership were obtained by the National Hospice and Palliative Care Organization (NHPCO). NHPCO's mission is "improving end-of-life care and expanding access to hospice care with the goal of profoundly enhancing quality of life for people dying in America and their loved ones." NHPCO and the Hospice Association of America both collect data about hospice care.

The United Network for Organ Sharing (UNOS) manages the national transplant waiting list, maintains data on organ transplants, and distributes organ donor cards. The primary purposes of the U.S. Organ Procurement and Transplantation Network (OPTN) "are to operate and monitor an equitable system for allocating organs donated for transplantation; maintain a waiting list of potential recipients; match potential recipients with organ donors according to established medical criteria for allocation of organs and, to the extent feasible, for listing and delisting transplant patients; facilitate the efficient, effective placement of organs for transplantation; and increase organ donation." The Scientific Registry of Transplant Recipients (SRTR) evaluates the scientific and clinical status of organ transplantation in the United States. Valuable information on these topics is available in the *2005 OPTN/SRTR Annual Report*.

The National Right to Life Committee can provide a copy of *The Will to Live*, an alternative living will, while Compassion and Choices (formed in 2005 from Compassion in Dying and End-of-Life Choices) provides news and bulletins on Oregon's Death with Dignity Act and other end-of-life legislation. The American Bar Association Commission on Law and Aging publishes information related to advance directives.

For cancer statistics, a premier source is the American Cancer Society's annual *Cancer Facts and Figures*.

Journals that frequently publish studies dealing with life-sustaining treatment, medical ethics, and medical costs include *Annals of Internal Medicine*, *Journal of the American Geriatrics Society*, *Journal of the American Medical Association*, the *Lancet*, and the *New England Journal of Medicine*.

The Gallup Organization, Harris Interactive, Polling Report, and Roper Center for Public Opinion Research have all conducted opinion polls on topics related to death and dying.

The Henry J. Kaiser Family Foundation provides a wealth of information on Medicare, Medicaid, health insurance, prescription drugs, HIV/AIDS, and nursing homes.

INDEX

Page references in italics refer to photo-graphs. References with the letter t *fol-lowing them indicate the presence of a table. The letter* f *indicates a figure. If more than one table or figure appears on a particular page, the exact item number for the table or figure being referenced is provided.*

A

"A Definition of Irreversible Coma," *Journal of the American Medical Association*, 7
   See also Harvard Criteria
Abe Perlmutter, Michael J. Satz, State Attorney for Broward County, Florida v., 100
ACP (American College of Physicians)
   end-of-life care guidelines, 18
   on euthanasia and assisted suicide, 72
Acquired immunodeficiency syndrome (AIDS)
   end-of-life care, 19
   grants, 129*t*–130*t*, 131*t*–132*t*
   health care costs, 122–123
   mortality rates, 23, 28*t*
Active euthanasia. *See* Euthanasia and assisted suicide
Ad Hoc Committee of the Harvard Medical School, 7–8, 97
ADA (American Dietetic Association), 31
Adkins, Janet, 71
Adolescents. *See* Children and youth
Advance directives
   artificial nutrition and hydration, 82, 93
   clarity in, 96
   combined laws, 95–96
   cultural differences, 19
   do-not-resuscitate orders, 29–30
   durable powers of attorney for health care as, 79–82
   forms, 80*t*–82*t*
   history, 77

legislation, 83*t*–92*t*, 93*f*
living wills as, 77–79
pain management, 93–94
Patient Self-Determination Act, 96
   See also Durable power of attorney for health care; Health care agents; Living wills
Afterlife
   ancient view, 1
   public opinion, 149
   spiritualism, 3
Age and aging
   Alzheimer's disease, 147*f*, 147*t*
   infant mortality, 44*t*
   leading causes of death, 137*t*, 138*t*
   mortality rates, 25*t*, 26*t*, 27*t*
   mortality rates for heart disease, 139*t*, 140*t*, 141*t*
   mortality rates for strokes, 144*t*, 145*t*, 146*t*
   mortality rates for suicide, 59*t*, 60*t*, 61*t*, 62*f*
   nursing home residents, 125*t*
   population projections, 136*t*
   population ratio, 147(10.9*t*)
   public opinion, 151–152
   See also Older adults
Agents, health care. *See* Health care agents
AIDS. *See* Acquired immunodeficiency syndrome (AIDS)
"Apparent death," 2, 3*f*
Alzheimer's disease
   health care costs, 125
   older adults, 136–137, 139–141, 147*f*, 147*t*
   See also Dementia
AMA (American Medical Association), 17–18, 72
American Academy of Pediatrics, 50
American College of Physicians (ACP)
   end-of-life care guidelines, 18
   on euthanasia and assisted suicide, 72
American Dietetic Association (ADA), 31

American Medical Association (AMA), 17–18, 72
American Nurses Association (ANA), 72
ANA (American Nurses Association), 72
Ancient civilizations, 1
Anencephaly, 43–44, 47*t*
ANH (Artificial nutrition and hydration). *See* Artificial nutrition and hydration (ANH)
Artificial nutrition and hydration (ANH)
   legal tests for ending, 31
   as life support, 31
   state laws, 94*f*, 95*f*
   withdrawing, 82, 93, 104–105, 104–108, 154
Asch, David A., 70–71
Ashcroft, John, 73–74, 110, 153–154
Assisted suicide. *See* Euthanasia and assisted suicide
Assisted Suicide Funding Restriction Act of 1997, 69
Autonomy, patient. *See* Patient autonomy

B

Baby boomers, 133
Baby Doe, 48–49, 50
Balanced Budget Act of 1997, 115–116, 119
Barber v. Superior Court of the State of California, 101
Barendregt, Marie, 75
Belgian Act on Euthanasia, 76
Belgium, 76
Beverly Requena, In the Matter of, 102
Bioethics
   anencephaly, 44
   brain death, 7
   in death and dying, 13–22
   euthanasia and assisted suicide, 71–72
   life support, 98
   medical practice, 16–18
   spinal bifida, 44